Costs & Funding following the Civil Justice Reforms: Questions & Answers

Costs & Funding following the Civil Justice Reforms: Questions & Answers

2nd Edition

SWEET & MAXWELL

Practical Law

First Edition 2015 by Peter Hurst, Simon Middleton and Roger Mallalieu
Second Edition 2016 by Peter Hurst, Simon Middleton and Roger Mallalieu

Published in 2016
by Thomson Reuters (Professional) UK Limited,
trading as Sweet & Maxwell, Friars House, 160 Blackfriars Road, London, SE1 8EZ
(Registered in England & Wales, Company No.1679046. Registered Office and address for service: 2nd floor, 1 Mark Square, Leonard Street, London, EC2A 4EG).

For further information on our products and services, visit
www.sweetandmaxwell.co.uk
Printed in Great Britain by CPI Grp Ltd, Croydon
Typeset by Servis Filmsetting, Stockport, SK2 5AJ

No natural forests were destroyed to make this product; only farmed timber was used and re-planted.

A CIP catalogue record for this book is available from the British Library.

ISBN 978-0-41405-652-7

Contributors

Peter Hurst LLB MPhil FCIArb, General Editor. Peter was the Senior Costs Judge of England & Wales, at the Royal Courts of Justice, from 1992 to 2014. During a judicial career which has spanned thirty years, he was also Judicial Taxing Officer of the House of Lords from 2002 to 2009 and of the United Kingdom Supreme Court from 2009 to 2014 and also of the Judicial Committee of the Privy Council from 2002 to 2014. He sat not only as a costs judge in the SCCO but also as a recorder in civil and criminal matters, including costs appeals from District Judges. He sat as an assessor with High Court Judges dealing with numerous costs appeals. He was invited to sit with the Court of Appeal as an assessor when that Court was dealing with difficult or complex costs appeals. He joined 39 Essex Chambers as a door tenant in December 2014.

He is the author of *Civil Costs* (Sweet & Maxwell Litigation Library), now in its fifth edition, and *Criminal Costs* (OUP). He was, until retirement, a member of the Senior Editorial Board of *Civil Procedure* (the *White Book*, Sweet & Maxwell) as well as being an editor contributing the commentary on all the costs rules and practice directions. He is now an advisory editor of the *White Book*.

Simon Middleton was appointed a District Judge in 2004 and a Regional Costs Judge at the inception of the scheme in 2005. He has sat in both the Midlands and the Western regions. Before his appointment he was a solicitor with Higher Court (Civil Advocacy) qualification.

Simon was a member of the Judicial College tutor team for six years. In that capacity he was a member of the team charged with delivering education on the April 2013 reforms. He is currently one of the Course Directors appointed for civil education. In that role he is responsible for, amongst other things, the current training on case and costs management.

Simon has written and lectured extensively on the subject of costs and case and costs management.

Roger Mallalieu is a barrister at 4 New Square specialising in matters relating to costs, litigation funding and civil procedure. He routinely ranks as one of the leading juniors in the field of costs law of all types and has appeared in a considerable number of the leading cases in the area. He is regularly instructed on important test issues and appears regularly in the Court of Appeal and other higher courts on such matters.

Publisher's Note

Costs & Funding following the Civil Justice Reforms: Questions & Answers is a unique book. Produced in conjunction with **Practical Law™**, it tackles common practitioner questions on the effects of the 2013 Jackson reforms on costs and funding. The authors answer questions on topics ranging from funding of litigation, case and costs management and proportionality to settlement offers, QOCS and summary assessment. The second edition updates the questions, answers and commentary in light of new and ongoing case law and legislation in the fast-evolving costs and funding landscape post-Jackson.

Subscribers to the *White Book Service* 2016 will receive this book gratis as part of their subscription. It is up-to-date to 26 February, 2016, but makes reference to changes made by the Civil Procedure (Amendment) Rules 2016 (SI 2016/234) and the 83rd CPR Update, which come into force generally on 1 April and 6 April 2016.

This book would not have been possible without the time, help and expertise of Peter Hurst, Simon Middleton and Roger Mallalieu. The publisher wishes to thank them for the impressive speed with which they wrote, updated and edited the book. This project was the result of collaboration between the Dispute Resolution team at Practical Law and the author team; it would not have got off the ground without either of them.

We welcome any feedback—please email *whitebook@sweetandmaxwell.co.uk*

Contents

		Page
Chapter 1	**Introduction** *Peter Hurst*	1
Chapter 2	**Funding Litigation** *Roger Mallalieu*	7
Chapter 3	**Proportionality** *Simon Middleton*	39
Chapter 4	**Case and Costs Management** *Simon Middleton*	55
Chapter 5	**Part 36 and Other Settlement Offers including ADR and Costs Consequences** *Peter Hurst*	125
Chapter 6	**Qualified One-Way Costs Shifting** *Roger Mallalieu*	183
Chapter 7	**Fixed Costs; Indemnity Costs; Litigants in Person** *Peter Hurst*	201
Chapter 8	**Assessments of Costs and Payment on Account of Costs** *Simon Middleton*	225
Chapter 9	**The Effect of the Jackson Civil Justice Reforms on Solicitor-Client Costs** *Roger Mallalieu*	257

List of Questions

Page

Chapter 1 **Introduction**

Chapter 2 **Funding Litigation**

Q1. Is it possible to assign pre LASPO Conditional Fee Agreement and to retain between the parties recoverability of success fees? 24

Q2. What is the effect on recoverability of the success fee of assigning a pre-April 2013 CFA post-April 2013? 25

Q3. Is it possible to vary a pre-April 2013 CFA and still recover the success fee? 25

Q4. My client instructed me prior to April 1, 2013, but I was not able to offer a CFA until later. Is it possible to backdate the CFA to the date of first instruction? 26

Q5. My client entered into a CFA prior to April 1, 2013, but has now died. I wish to offer the personal representatives a CFA to continue the claim. Will I be able to recover the success fee? 26

Q6. Is a pre-April 2013 ATE policy premium still recoverable if the policy holder changes solicitors post-April 2013? Should the policy be 'assigned' to the new firm? 27

Q7. If a staged premium ATE policy was incepted prior to April 1, 2013, but the further staged premiums are only incurred after that date, will the further premiums be recoverable? 27

Q8. Is there a long stop date whereby a party who has entered into a pre-April 2013 funding arrangement in relation to a claim must issue proceedings? 28

Q9. Is a notice of funding required for a Damages Based Agreement? 28

Q10. How should the success fee be calculated in a post-April 2013 CFA? 28

Q11. If the solicitor has entered into a pre-April 2013 CFA, but counsel's CFA with the solicitor postdates April 2013, is counsel's success fee recoverable between the parties? 29

Q12. I wish to enter into a CFA with my client whereby in addition to the success fee being capped as required by s.58 of the Courts & Legal Services Act 1990 and the CFA Order 2013, the total costs payable under the agreement will also be capped as a percentage of the damage. I have been told that this means my agreement is a contingency fee agreement, or DBA, and must comply with the DBA Regulations 2013. Is this correct? 29

Q13. What is the effect on the success fee where a CFA relating to a group claim was entered into before April 1, 2013, but some of the claimants were added after that date? 30

Q14. I currently have an insolvency case on a CFA with a success fee and have ATE insurance in place. I have not yet issued. If the Government removes the exemption from LASPO for insolvency related cases, presumably the success fee and premium will still be recoverable from the other side if the claim is successful even if I haven't issued before the exemption is removed? 30

Q15. What exactly is a hybrid DBA, and what is the difference between a concurrent hybrid DBA and a sequential hybrid DBA? 31

Q16. Where a CFA in one of the excepted cases (where the success fee is still recoverable) is entered into and the proceedings are issued on the same day but only served four months later and we realise that we haven't served a Notice of Funding some weeks after service, what advice would you give? For example, should a formal application seeking relief be made? 31

Q17. Is a claimant entitled to recover the success fee under his "pre 1 April, 2013" CFA from the defendant, where the claim was only commenced and the funding was only notified after 1 April 2013? Please explain why the amendment to s.58A(6) does not apply to CFAs entered into prior to 1 April, 2013, in circumstances where the funding is notified after 1 April, 2013? 32

Q18. In the excepted cases, where a success fee is still recoverable: 32

Q19. In a clinical negligence case, where a claimant obtains a breach and causation report and the defendant then admits liability, could the claimant recover the cost of the premium if it then obtained ATE insurance in relation to obtaining a quantum report? 33

Q20. Our client entered into a CFA and ATE insurance policy before April 2013 in relation to insolvency proceedings. Since then, another party has been added as a party to the CFA and ATE insurance policy. Are we required to notify the defendants of this variation to the CFA and ATE insurance? If so, how do we notify them and do we need to file the notice? 33

Q21. We act for two claimants, one of whom is insolvent. We have entered into an ATE policy and are planning to rely on the insolvency exemption to LASPO 2012 if we are successful, so that we can recover the ATE premium from the defendant. Will the fact that only one of the claimants is insolvent prevent us from relying on the insolvency exemption to LASPO 2012? If we are allowed to recover the ATE premium from the defendant, will it be reduced to 50 per cent to reflect the fact that only one of the claimants is insolvent? 34

Q22. If a claimant with a pre-1 April, 2013 ATE insurance policy is successful at first instance, an appeal is granted and a top-up of the

ATE premium (after 1 April, 2013) is required to cover the appeal, is the post-1 April, 2013 ATE top-up premium recoverable from the other side if the appeal is successful? 34

Q23. Do you think the exceptional circumstances which applied in *Jenkins v Young Brothers Transport* to allow the assignment of a CFA might apply in the following circumstances: One part of an LLP was trading under the name of SS until the LLP demerged, at which point the SS business and trading name was transferred to SL Ltd. The LLP continued to trade as a separate entity, but the SRA has treated SL Ltd as a successor practice rather than a new practice. Can we or should we:

- Enter into new CFAs with all our clients (in which case how will costs incurred prior to the transfer be dealt with and, in particular, what will happen to any recoverable success fees under pre-April 2013 CFAs)?
- Novate or assign the existing CFAs?
- Rely on having told our clients of the change of legal entity? 35

Q24. I note that insolvency proceedings are excluded from ss.44 and 46 of LASPO 2012 where proceedings in England and Wales brought by:

- A person acting in the capacity of a liquidator of a company in creditors' voluntary liquidation (CVL) or compulsory liquidation; a trustee in bankruptcy; or an administrator.
- A company that is in: CVL; compulsory liquidation; or administration.

What is the situation if you act for an insolvency practitioner outside the jurisdiction (the insolvent company also being outside the jurisdiction) who is bringing a claim in England and Wales against a company based in England and Wales for monies owed. If you enter into a CFA with the client in these circumstances, will the success fee be recoverable from the other side if your client is successful? 35

Q25. What are the rules on recoverability of success fees in a defamation matter and, assuming that recoverability is allowed, does the success fee have to be capped in any way? 36

Q26. Given that success fees in CFAs entered into from 1 April, 2013 are not recoverable in English civil litigation (apart from in the excepted cases), are they recoverable in arbitrations? Nothing in the Arbitration Act or LCIA Rules appears to preclude an arbitrator awarding a success fee under a CFA. 36

Q27. What is the authority or rule which specifies that if a DBA in a non-employment matter does not comply with the Damages-Based Agreements Regulations 2013, it will not be enforceable? 37

Q28. Under the DBA Regulations 2013, a party can recover costs from the other side based on normal costs recovery principles, but subject to the indemnity principle. Given then that the lawyer may not be entitled to any costs until actual recoveries are made at the end of a case, does this not cause a problem with seeking costs from the other side at interim hearings as the case progresses? Appropriate drafting of the DBA might seek to get around this but it would seem that such drafting would be a highly complex task with various pitfalls. For example, if the DBA provided that sums would immediately become due to the solicitor as and when costs are recovered from the other side, are those costs considered part of the ultimate recovery from the client and to be deducted and as a kind of payment on account, or would the solicitor be entitled to those costs plus the agreed success percentage? Wouldn't that breach the DBA Regulations? 37

Chapter 3 **Proportionality**

Q1. Is there any distinction between proportionality and reasonableness in reality? 43

Q2. Is there not a risk that similar claims will have different outcomes because of the determination by separate case managing judges of what is proportionate in a particular case? 44

Q3. Is proportionality a 'fixed sum' throughout the life of a claim? 44

Q4. If there is no 'good reason' to depart from the budget on assessment how does the court apply the proportionality 'cross check' under CPR 44.3(2) at the end of the assessment? 46

Q5. How do the transitional provisions relate to proportionality at assessment? 46

Q6. Does the court look at the sums reasonably claimed or the sums recovered when determining 'the sums in issue in the proceedings' under CPR 44.3(5)(a)? 47

Q7. Why is only the conduct of the paying party included in the definition? 48

Q8. If the effect of CPR 44.3(2) is that the sum to be allowed on an assessment is that which is proportionate, why does the court trouble first with undertaking an assessment of what is reasonably ncurred and reasonable in amount? 49

Q9. Is proportionality to be applied in all cases, or, as some wish to suggest, is it really for the small to medium value claims, where disproportionate costs are more likely? 50

Q10. What relevance, if any, does proportionality have in cases where an order for costs is made on the indemnity basis? 51

Q11. Is the effect of proportionality that in a case about money, the costs cannot exceed the sums in dispute? 52

Q12. How useful are the comments in cases such as *CIP Properties (AIPT) Limited v Galliford Try Infrastructure Limited* , *GSK Project Management Limited v QPR Holdings Limited* and *Stocker v Stocker* [2015] EWHC 1634 (QB) in setting benchmarks for proportionality? 54

Q13. In the case of *Stocker v Stocker* Mr Justice Warby observed: "I readily acknowledge the importance of ensuring that the costs budgeting process does not result in a party being unable to recover the costs necessary to assert their rights." Does this mean that proportionate costs can never be less than those that are necessary? 54

Chapter 4 **Case and Costs Management**

Q1. How prescriptive is the wording of CPR 3.12(1) and (1A)? In particular can the court costs manage cases that fall within the definition of those outside the scheme and when may the court exclude cases from the regime under CPR 3.12(1)(e)? 76

Q2. Can parties agree to dispense with costs management? 78

Q3. Does costs management apply to the disposal stage of a claim after the entry of a default judgment for damages to be decided by the court? 78

Q4. Do the provisions apply to a claim brought under CPR 8, where the court has expressly listed a case management conference? 79

Q5. What should parties do when the notice of provisional allocation under CPR 26.3 is to the multi track, but one or more parties believe that the appropriate allocation is to the fast track? 79

Q6. Does the fact that a party has a contractual right to indemnity costs against the other party mean costs management is not applicable or pointless because the claimant has a contractual right to claim costs under *Gomba Holdings (UK) Ltd v Minories Finance Ltd (No.2)?* 80

Q7. In respect of those cases where the value of the claim is less than £50,000 and a party fails to file and exchange Precedent H by the date set out in the CPR 26.3(1) notice, but does file and exchange it by the extended date given in the further notice under CPR 26.3(7A), does CPR 3.14 apply? Is CPR 3.8(4) of any relevance in this situation? 81

Q8. What effect, if any, does the Practice Note released in the Chancery Division in July 2015 have on the time for filing and exchanging Precedents H? If there is any effect, does this apply outside the Chancery Division? 82

Q9. The Shorter Trial Pilot Scheme available for certain claims issued after 1 October 2015 under CPR 51 PD N disapplies CPR 3.12 and the costs management regime unless the parties agree otherwise (CPR 51 PD N 2.58). Why might parties wish to opt in? 83

Q10. Should a party file its Precedent H on the basis of the way in which it thinks the claim should progress, e.g. if it thinks a split trial is appropriate should the budget be completed on that basis? 84

Q11. Is it better for a party to over-estimate costs in the budget filed and exchanged, on the basis that it is then likely to see a higher budget set and less likely to need to go back to the court asking for the budget to be varied under CPR 3 PD E 7.6? Conversely, if a party recognises that it is likely to be the paying party is underestimation better, trying to persuade the court to reduce the budgets of all parties to that level to limit the potential liability for costs or limit the work that can be undertaken, making the outcome of the claim less certain as a result? 85

Q12. If one party puts in an absurdly low budget is it advisable for the other party to agree it or will this suggest an acceptance that any costs above that level are not reasonable and proportionate and so prejudice its own budget which is significantly higher? 85

Q13. If a defendant brings an additional claim against a party other than the claimant, does the defendant need to produce two budgets—one for the defence of the claim and one for the pursuit of the additional claim—or will one total budget suffice? 85

Q14. Does the budget have to be on Precedent H or can parties produce their own forms provided that they recognisably contain the same information? 86

Q15. How detailed should be the assumptions upon which the budget is based? 86

Q16. The guidance for completion of Precedent H is brief and it is not always clear where certain items of work should be included. Is there any sanction for inserting items in what the court may regard as the wrong phase of the budget? 87

Q17. The Precedent H guidance notes have been amended to include a specific reference to CPR 44.3 (5) and 44.4(3) and state that when deciding the reasonable and proportionate costs the court will include in its consideration *'where and the circumstances in which the work was done as opposed to where the case is heard'*. What is the significance of these amendments? 87

Q18. Should the costs of surveillance evidence be included in a budget? If not, if surveillance evidence is subsequently obtained, should applications be made under CPR 3 PD E 7.6 to amend the budgets? 88

Q19. Will the introduction of 'J--Codes' lead to Precedent H being completed to include all costs—including those of a solicitor/client nature? 90

Q20. Do the costs allocated to contingencies count when determining whether or not a budget exceeds £25,000 and, in consequence, in determining whether only page 1 of the Precedent H needs to be completed? 90

Q21. Does the introduction of costs management mean that the court is rarely likely to dispense with a case/costs management conference and deal with directions and budgets as a paper exercise? 90

Q22. A number of courts are issuing detailed directions when listing a CCMC. Are these necessary and should they be standardised? 91

Q23. Does CPR 3.14 apply to any failure to file a costs budget? 92
Q24. Should the discussions that the parties have when attempting to agree the costs budgets be without prejudice? 93
Q25. Does the court give the directions first and subsequently costs manage? 93
Q26. Should costs lawyers attend CCMCs? 93
Q27. The court has suggested that costs already incurred at the time of the costs management order can be the subject of a costs management order. Is this correct? 94
Q28. The court seems to have adopted a number of approaches to dealing with incurred costs. Is it possible to discern clear guidance on the treatment of these costs in the budgeting exercise? 94
Q29. Are incurred costs relevant to the overall costs at the budgeting stage or only relevant on a phase by phase basis? 96
Q30. What happens if the total incurred costs means that even with the most proportionate case management possible it is not possible to budget costs 'to be incurred' at a level that when added to those 'incurred costs', comes within the court's overall assessment of proportionality? 97
Q31. If there has been a significant front loading of the costs so that by the time of the costs management hearing the costs already spent exceed what the court regards as the proportionate expenditure on the claim, can the court set a budget going forward of nil? 99
Q32. What can be done to avoid the potential injustice of the court setting a phase budget by basing this on an overall view of the proportionate sum for that phase, deducting the incurred costs and budgeting the difference, only for the assessing judge then to reduce the incurred costs undermining the basis upon which the budget was set? 99
Q33. Should the court set hourly rates as part of the budgeting exercise? 100
Q34. If the court does not set the budget by reference to hourly rates and time, then why does Precedent H require this information and, linked to this, what does '*the underlying detail in the budget for each phase used by the party to calculate the totals claimed is provided for reference purposes only to assist the court in fixing a budget*' in CPR 3 PD E 7.10 mean? 101
Q35. How can the court set the budget without assessing prospectively the work that is required and the appropriate hourly rate(s) at which that work should be done? 101
Q36. If the court is budgeting only be reference to a global sum and not taking account of the respective hourly rates, surely this means that a party who has agreed a lower hourly rate retainer will be able to do more work than one with a higher hourly rate? If so this appears unfair. 102

Q37. If the court does set the hourly rate in the budget what happens if, at assessment, the assessing court sets a different hourly rate for the non budgeted work? 103
Q38. Upon taking over instructions for a client from another firm it is clear that the 'incurred costs' for the pre-action phase in the Precedent H filed and exchanged by that firm are considerably lower than the amount of costs that the client paid that firm for work done during that period. Whilst estimating future costs may be somewhat speculative, is there any explanation for why the incurred costs in Precedent H differ from 'actual costs' incurred? 103
Q39. Is the budget 'without prejudice' to any subsequent assessment? 103
Q40. What, if anything, can the court do when the parties agree budgets or phases of the budgets in sums that the court thinks are disproportionate? Is there a potential tension between CPR 3.15(3) and CPR 3 PD E 7.6? 104
Q41. How important is the breakdown between disbursements and solicitors' fees in an approved/agreed budget? 105
Q42. To which sum do the percentages in CPR 3 PD E 7.2 apply—the total sum in the Precedent H after the budget has been set or just those parts of the Precedent H that the court has budgeted? 105
Q43. Should parties re-file budgets after the CCMC when a costs management order has been made under CPR 3.15? 107
Q44. Can the parties agree to vary their budgets from that recorded by the court in a costs management order, where there has been no 'significant development' in the litigation, but both are unhappy with the amount budgeted by the court? 107
Q45. Once a budget has been set, should solicitors be monitoring the budgets? 107
Q46. What if a client still wants the legal representatives to incur costs that the court has not allowed within the budget? 108
Q47. What effect will a 'costs sanction' for unreasonable conduct, as suggested by the Court of Appeal in Denton v T H White, have on a costs budget? 108
Q48. Can you explain how an award of costs on the standard basis differs from an award of costs on the indemnity basis in circumstances where a costs budget is in place? 109
Q49. If an award of indemnity costs is made and CPR 3.18 does not apply, does the budget still form the starting point for the assessment of costs? 110
Q50. What guidance is there on what may constitute 'good reason' under CPR 3.18 to enable a departure from a budget at assessment? 110
Q51. Does CPR 3.18(b) prescribe an automatic sanction where the receiving party has failed to amend its budget prospectively and can show no 'good reason' for this failure or, as is suggested in *Simpson v MGN Ltd & anor* (see above), is it for the court,

applying the overriding objective, to determine what the just and proportionate sanction should be? 111
Q52. Does the statement of truth on the budget prevent a solicitor recovering more than the budget from the client? 111
Q53. Can a trial judge ordering a detailed assessment of the costs of a party subject to a costs management order, give guidance to the assessing judge on what may be 'good reason' to depart from the budget set.? 112
Q54. Can the budgeted sum exceed the sum due from that party to the solicitor under the contractual retainer, and, if so, is this a permitted breach of the indemnity principle? 112
Q55. What is the position if a Part 7 claim commences as a fast track claim, but subsequently it becomes apparent that the claim is undervalued and needs to be re-tracked to the multi track, but it is not within one of the costs management exceptions in CPR 3.12(1)? 113
Q56. Is a party who was acting in person at the costs management conference (and so has no budget), but who subsequently instructs solicitors, required to exchange and file a Precedent H? 114
Q57. Is a further Precedent H required with a pre-trial checklist ("PTCL") as CPR 29 imposes no such requirement and yet the wording of the Precedent H guidance still suggests this is work included at the PTR stage? 115
Q58. Can a party make repeated agreed variations or, in default of agreement, applications to the court to vary a budget? 115
Q59. It seems that some parties are not applying to vary budgets, but instead prefer to wait to argue 'good reason' to depart from the budget at any subsequent assessment. Is this because it is easier to depart from a budget retrospectively when the work may be easier to justify than to vary prospectively when the work may be seen to be speculative? 116
Q60. If a costs management order has been made in a case but not long afterwards a party makes a potentially determinative application for summary judgment ("SJ"), should the parties apply promptly for the budgets to be revised? Suppose that they do, but the hearing for SJ is likely to come on before the application to revise costs budgets can be heard what should they do? Could the potential respondent to the SJ application not justifiably seek, in such circumstances, an order that the costs thrown away by this change of tack by the applicant be paid by it in any event? 117
Q61. What sort of applications fall within the provisions of CPR 3 PD E 7.9? How does this link with the provision for contingencies in the budget? 118
Q62. Can the court costs manage detailed assessment proceedings? 118
Q63. If an appeal is launched against a decision on an interim application that falls within a discrete phase (e.g. against an order

in respect of permission for expert evidence) does CPR 3 PD E 7.6 apply and should budgets be revised with a view to agreement or an application to vary? 119

Q64. Does the decision of the Court of Appeal in *Denton v T H White* mean that relief from sanction will be granted provided that there is no prejudice to any other party that cannot be compensated by a costs order and that a trial date can still be met? 120

Q65. What is the purpose of the reference in CPR 36.23 to CPR 36.17(4)(b)? 121

Q66. Does the emphasis on proportionality impact on the situation where a claim falls within fast track financial limits, but the number of witnesses is such that the time needed for trial exceeds one day? 122

Q67. Do the case management rules apply as much to litigants in person as to represented parties? 123

Q68. Will cost capping be ordered more rarely? 123

Chapter 5 **Part 36 and Other Settlement Offers including ADR and Costs Consequences**

Q1. Is there anything in CPR Part 36 or the Privy Council Rules which prevents a Part 36 offer being made in costs proceedings before the Privy Council? (Rule 2.1). 157

Q2. My firm needs to serve an expert's report out of time. The Defendants are Objecting to relief from sanctions. How does this affect potential Part 36 Offers? (Rule 3.9). 157

Q3. Can a valid Part 36 offer include settlement terms which (if accepted), impose conditions; require a defendant to do something other than pay money; or provide for interest to run after the end of the relevant period? Rule 2.1; Rule 36.2(2), (Rule 36.5(4)). 158

Q4. If a defendant makes a Part 36 Offer which does not take into account its counterclaim and the offer is then accepted, what happens to the counterclaim? (Rule 36.5). 158

Q5. When considering whether a claimant has failed to obtain a judgment more advantageous than a defendant's Part 36 offer how do you deal with any interest element that the judge awards the claimant at trial? Assuming that the defendant's offer was inclusive of interest until the expiry of the relevant period do you compare that figure with the principal sum that the judge awards at trial plus any interest awarded too up to the date of judgment? Or can you argue that for the purposes of working out whether the judgment is more advantageous you should only take into account the principal sum awarded and interest up to the date of expiry of the Part 36 offer? 159

Q6. What is the position when a Part 36 offer is made pre-action and accepted after the issue of proceedings, but before the proceedings have been served on the defendant, where service has been reserved for up to four months? Rule 36.7. 159

Q7. If an offeree serves a notice of acceptance during the relevant period, when does that acceptance take effect, given that the offeror may apply for permission to withdraw or vary its offer within seven days of the notice of acceptance (or, if earlier, before the first day of trial)? If the offeror's application is unsuccessful, it is not clear when the notice of acceptance will be treated as having been accepted. (Rule 36.9; 36.10). 160

Q8. What is the position where a Part 36 Offer is withdrawn at the same time as the claimant purports to accept it? (Rule 36.9, 36.10). 160

Q9. Where there has been a split trial or a trial of preliminary issues, what is the position with regard to Part 36 Offers which may have been made? (Rule 36.12). 161

Q10. I act for a proposed claimant in a dispute where legal proceedings have yet to be issued. The proposed defendant has served a Part 36 offer by form N242A which states that the defendant will be liable for the claimant's costs in accordance with Part 36.13. Part 36.13 states the claimant will be entitled to the Costs of proceedings including their recoverable pre-action costs. Does this mean my client can only recover pre action costs as part of the costs of any proceedings? If this is so, can I agree that the pre-action costs are recoverable and if so, if the amount cannot be agreed can I issue costs only proceedings pursuant to Part 8A to have the court adjudicate upon costs? (Rule 36.13). 163

Q11. If a defendant accepts a claimant's Part 36 offer after proceedings have been issued, is a consent order to dispose of the proceedings necessary? (Rule 36.13(1). 164

Q12. Where there is a Part 36 offer, what is the position where the offeree seeks clarification of the offer? 164

Q13. If a defendant makes a Part 36 offer in relation to its counterclaim, which is accepted within the relevant period, does that mean that the defendant is automatically "entitled to the costs of the proceedings" (that is, the costs relating to both the original claim and the counterclaim) under CPR 36.13(1)? What about the situation where the defendant makes a Part 36 offer in relation to its counterclaim and the original claim too? Again, if it is accepted within the RP, does that mean that the defendant is automatically entitled to the costs of the proceedings under CPR 36.13(1)? Or can the court look at the reality of the situation and, in particular, at whether the offer leads to a net payment being made to the defendant/counterclaimant. (Rule 36.13(7)). 166

Q14. Are costs recoverable if a claimant's Part 36 Offer is accepted in circumstances where the claimant's costs budget has not been filed on time? (Rule 36.13). 168

Q15. In a claim by a claimant (C) against two separate defendants (D1 and D2), where separate allegations are advanced against each defendant, if C makes a Part 36 offer to settle the whole of his claim which is addressed to both D1 and D2 as "the offeree", and only D1 accepts the offer, is the claim against D2 stayed, even though D2 did not accept the offer? (Rule 36.14). 169

Q16. Can you explain how an award of costs on the standard basis (e.g. under CPR 36.17(3)(a)) differs from an award of costs on the indemnity basis (e.g. under CPR 36.17(4)(b)) in circumstances where a costs budget is in place? The definition of 'standard basis' and 'indemnity basis' appear to be hard to reconcile with the concept of costs budgets, because there should be no doubts about reasonableness to resolve in anyone's favour if the costs are within the court-approved costs budget. (Rule 36.17(4). 169

Q17. Is it appropriate to award a lower additional amount under CPR 37.17(4)(d) than the prescribed amount because the proceedings were determined early, for example, as a result of summary judgment being given, rather than going to full trial? 169

Q18. Is the following case still good law—*Hammersmatch Properties (Welwyn) Ltd v Saint Gobain Ceramics and Plastics Ltd* ? Is Eder J's costs decision in *Sugar Hut etc. v AJ Insurance* reintroducing *Carver* by the back door? (Rule 36.17). 170

Q19. Do you agree that it may be difficult to decide who has obtained the more advantageous result in a detailed assessment? Also, does r.36.17(4)) about enhancing claimants' recovery by 10 per cent apply in detailed assessments? (Rule 36.17). 170

Q20. How does the cap on damages in the IPEC apply where there is also a claim for costs? (Rule 36.17(4). 171

Q21. We represent a client in a case where we feel that the client is bound to succeed. We are considering making a claimant Part 36 offer to settle at 100 per cent liability plus costs. This would save the Defendant the time and cost of preparing for trial and the trial itself. Will this succeed? (Rule 36.17). 171

Q22. If I make a successful Part 36 Offer am I sure to recover all my costs? (Rule 44.2). 172

Q23. When the question of costs is being decided is it possible for a party to refer to without prejudice correspondence in order to establish that the other party did not respond to Part 36 Offers? (Rule 44.2). 172

Q24. Where a Part 36 offer is accepted in a small claim that has not yet been allocated to the small claims track, is it the case that the fixed costs regime will generally apply? (Rule 46.13). 173

Q25. What is the requirement for open offers in detailed assessment proceedings meant to achieve and how they will co-exist with Part 36 Offers? (PD47 para 8.3). 173

Q26. How are Calderbank offers treated in relation to costs? (Rule 44.2(4)). 174
Q27. Does anyone/any kind of company (for example) have to use ADR because the law says so? If so I would be grateful if you would direct me to that law or illuminate what kind of people MUST use ADR. 175
Q28. When we suggest mediation on behalf of clients we are often met with a variety of reasons why there should be no mediation. Have you any suggestions? 177
Q29. There must be drawbacks to Mediation – What are they? 179
Q30. Can you please advise on the available options where the parties to an on-going case have essentially agreed on every issue other than costs. It is at an early stage (just post CCMC). Both sides are saying that the other should pay their costs. Both parties are alleging that the other's conduct has been in breach of the pre-action protocol. Because of the circumstances it is uncertain which party (if any) will be deemed to have "won" the case. What are the options available to the parties? It doesn't seem correct that the main case should proceed as everything other than costs is essentially agreed. I see from the practice note that costs only proceedings are not available where it is not decided as to who is paying who's costs. So, for example, could the parties make an application to end the current proceedings and just deal with costs, or go straight to assessment? 179
Q31. I have a matter in which my client has successfully sued for professional negligence. The opponent made a Part 36 offer which was accepted and the damages settled. The issue remaining is our costs. The Part 36 offer included an offer to pay reasonable expenses. Having assessed our costs schedule the opponent has made a Part 36 offer significantly less than our costs. How does one challenge the offer made by the opponent for costs? This is a matter in which we do not want this to go to court for a detailed assessment but would certainly want a better offer than is currently being made. 179
Q32. Are you aware of any cases where a refusal to mediate a small claims track claim has resulted in the court making an adverse costs award against the refusing party? It is settled that refusal to accept an offer which is not beaten at trial is not "unreasonable behaviour" for the purposes of CPR Part 27 and will not lead to adverse costs consequences, but it is unclear what effect, if any, refusal to mediate might have on the usual "no costs" rule. 180
Q33. What is the proper approach to assessing costs in an Arbitration? 180

Chapter 6 **Qualified One-Way Costs Shifting**
Q1. How will QOCS apply where a claim compromises both a personal injury and a non personal injury element? 193

Q2. Will QOCS be extended to other areas in due course? 194
Q3. Do parties still have to costs budget where QOCS applies and, if so, is the agreeing of budgets in such cases likely to be more difficult? 194
Q4. Is QOCS excluded where the claimant has Before the Event Insurance? 195
Q5. Does QOCS apply to costs incurred prior to 1 April, 2013? 195
Q6. Is QOCS excluded where the claimant has entered into a Precommencement funding arrangement, even if the claimant then is advised to not pursue the claim by the initially instructed solicitor but later does so under a post April 2013 funding arrangement with a different firm? 195
Q7. The claimant has incurred costs unnecessarily in an unmeritous claim. They have now served a notice of discontinuance and, as QOCS applies, they are not liable for the defendant's costs (unless an exception applies). In the above circumstances, is it possible for the defendant to apply for a wasted costs order even though a notice of discontinuance has been filed by the claimant? 196
Q8. I need to discontinue proceedings against a number of defendants in an action. Obviously, when I file a notice of discontinuance, there will be a deemed order for costs against the claimant. According to your maintained guidance "Discontinuance: an overview" the court may vary such an order only in some circumstances. However, my understandings of QOCS (from CPR 44.14, 44.15 and 44.16) is that an order for costs may only be enforced if the claim has been struck out (no court permission needed) or if it is fundamentally dishonest (court permission needed). We do not have sufficient time to obtain written consent from each and every defendant in a consent order but in any event consider that we would be QOCS protected even by serving a Notice of Discontinuance. 197
Q9. Can a personal injury claimant who had a pre-action CFA (entered into before 1 April 2013) with a 100 per cent success fee, and who wishes to proceed with the claim with the benefits of QOCS protection, terminate the existing CFA, on the basis that the law firm will waive its success fee, and enter into a new post-Jackson CFA? Would the claimant then be able to benefit from QOCS, even though the pre-action base costs are covered under a CFA entered into before 1 April 2013? Alternatively, could the client and or the solicitor agree to end the existing CFA, but enter into a new, post LASPO CFA, with any success fee payable by the client only, but with the CFA expressly covering all work done since first instruction and thereby benefit from QOCS? 198
Q10. Will qualified one way costs shifting apply where a personal injury claimant entered into a CFA pre Jackson reforms but did

not enter into an after the event insurance policy until after the introduction of QOCS? 199

Q11. Does QOCS apply to just personal injury? We have a commercial litigation matter for breach of contract so nothing to do with personal injury. 199

Q12. Does QOCS apply to claims for damages for clinical negligence? 199

Q13. Where a claimant is currently subject to an 'old style' CFA (pre-April 2013 whereby QOCS would not apply) but the client seeks the protection of QOCS, would the previous presence of the old style CFA prevent the claimant ever obtaining the benefit of QOCS under the workings of CPR 44.17 If the claimant was to continue as a litigant in person would she then obtain the benefit of QOCS? 199

Chapter 7 **Fixed Costs; Indemnity Costs; Litigants in Person**

Q1. What indications are there about fixed costs for the future? Are there any arguments for fixed fees? 212

Q2. What guidance can be given about retainer arrangements to emphasise the importance of the advice to a client about these and ensuring that retainer arrangements are still clear and enforceable where a legal representative is asked to represent a client in litigation which will inevitably involve the application of fixed costs? 213

Q3. In proceedings in the Intellectual Property Enterprise Court where costs are awarded against a party for unreasonable behaviour does the stage costs cap in Part 45 apply? 214

Q4. Following the decision in *Chaplair v Kumari*, it is clear that a landlord can recover costs of proceedings under a leasehold indemnity in its favour irrespective of whether the claim would fall within the fixed costs regimes of the small and fast tracks. What is the position in relation to residential possession claims under CPR Part 55, to which the fixed costs regime under CPR Part 45 applies? 214

Q5. Is the indemnity basis applicable in cases where there is an abuse of process or where a party has been guilty of unreasonable conduct? 215

Q6. What is the position of litigation funders in relation to orders for costs, particularly orders for costs on the indemnity basis? 216

Q7. The rules suggest that costs management does not affect indemnity costs. However there is now a confusion about this since Coulson J's decision in *Elvanite Full Circle Ltd v Amec Earth and Environmental UK Ltd* suggests otherwise. 216

Q8. In a County Court decision by a district judge, the Court ordered a claimant who had exaggerated his claim to pay costs on the indemnity basis. The Court found that the claim would have been resolved by the end of June 2012 had the claimant not exaggerated his claim. 217

Q9. What is the position of a solicitor or barrister acting on his or her own behalf? 217
Q10. If a litigant in person instructs a barrister under the Direct Access scheme can the litigant recover any costs? 219
Q11. Is it possible for the Court to make an order for costs on the indemnity basis against a litigant in person? 219
Q12. Is it possible for a firm of solicitors which is an LLP to be regarded as a litigant in person for the purpose of a costs assessment? 220
Q13. To what extent will the Court grant some leeway to a litigant in person who fails to comply with a rule practice direction or Court order? 220
Q14. Is it possible for a company to be represented by a McKenzie friend? 223
Q15. Will the Court order interim payments to enable litigants in person to obtain legal representation? 223

Chapter 8 **Assessments of Costs and Payments on Account of Costs**

Q1. What is the position when form N260 is either served/filed late or not at all? 233
Q2. Does the introduction of the breakdown of time spent on documents on the Form N260 mean that the court will deal with challenges to this on an item by item basis or will the court make one overall assessment of time spent on documents? 235
Q3. How does the proportionality cross check at CPR 44.3(2) work in the summary assessment process that is already one undertaken with a broad brush? 235
Q4. How can the court use the costs budgets at assessment of the costs of the claim when neither the N260 nor the bill is divided into the same phases as the Form H to enable easy comparison? 236
Q5. Albeit in a family context, does not the case of *SB v MB* (Costs) suggest that summary assessment is confined to fast track trials and other hearings lasting a day or less? 238
Q6. Does the decision in *Transformers and Rectifiers Limited v Needs Limited* mean that summary assessments of the costs a) of applications, whether disposed of either at a hearing or on the papers and, b) after trials, may be conducted by a judge other than the one who dealt with the application/trial? 238
Q7. In the light of the voluntary 'new bill' pilot introduced in the SCCO what, if anything, should practitioners be doing in anticipation of the new bill format becoming compulsory? 239
Q8. Who is responsible for the costs of providing the breakdown required in a model form like Precedent Q? 239
Q9. Does qualified one-way costs shifting ("QOCS") apply to the detailed assessment procedure? 240

Q10. Is there any sanction if a paying party fails to make an open offer under CPR 47 PD 8.3? 241
Q11. Does the £75,000 limit for provisional assessment include or exclude VAT? 241
Q12. Does the £75,000 limit for provisional assessment include 'additional liabilities' (where the transitional provisions still permit recovery of these between the parties)? 242
Q13. There seems to be a feeling that a paying party who does not serve Replies to the Points of Dispute is at a disadvantage at a provisional assessment. Should receiving parties serve Replies in this situation as a matter of course? 242
Q14. Does the costs cap include or exclude success fees (where the transitional provisions still permit recovery of success fees between the parties)? 242
Q15. Can the court make an award of indemnity costs under CPR 36.17(4)(b) in provisional assessment proceedings and, if so, what, if any effect does this have on the costs cap of £1,500. 242
Q16. Does the costs cap include the additional amount under CPR 36.17(4)(d) as applied by CPR 47.20? 243
Q17. How does the £1,500 cap operate in respect of cases that are dealt with under the provisional assessment provisions, but where there are interim applications, e.g. to set aside a default costs certificate, for an interim costs certificate or for relief from sanction? 244
Q18. Is the amount of the bill or the sum in which it is assessed in a provisional assessment likely to inform how much of the capped fee is awarded, e.g. does a bill of £70,000 justify an award of a higher proportion of the £1,500 than a bill of £20,000? 244
Q19. Can the court make more than one award of costs for the provisional assessment and, if so, is the total amount apportioned between the parties limited to £1,500 or may there be separate awards to each party, each with a cap of £1,500? 245
Q20. Does the £1,500 cap on costs under CPR 47.14 include costs incurred in 'Costs Only Proceedings' under CPR 46.14? 245
Q21. How does the court deal with the proportionality cross check after a provisional assessment where the assessed bill is returned to the parties to do the arithmetic? 246
Q22. Is there a sanction if the receiving party fails to file the required documents with the request for provisional assessment and can this be rectified? If so how? 248
Q23. What happens in respect of the costs where at an oral hearing a party does not achieve an adjustment in its favour of 20 per cent or more, but the adjustment made does make a CPR 47.20 offer relevant? 250

Q24. Under CPR 36.17(4)(d) can a party recover the additional sum on a detailed assessment by operation of CPR 47.20 if it has already received an additional amount in respect of the substantive award in the claim? 251
Q25. Is the determination of disbursements under the procedure set out at CPR 47 PD 5.7 a provisional assessment? 252
Q26. Is there any rule of thumb as to what proportion of the costs claimed the court will order as a reasonable sum by way of payment on account? 253
Q27. Must a party have filed a Form N260 (or equivalent statement of costs) if it wishes to seek a payment on account of costs? 255
Q28. When may a departure from the general rule at CPR 44.2(8) be justified? 255

Chapter 9 **The Effect of the Jackson Civil Justice Reforms on Solicitor–Client Costs**
Q1. Have the 'Jackson' reforms changed the basis on which I, as a solicitor, can charge my client? 273
Q2. Can you advise the client of the full range of funding options but then say but we as a firm do not offer X, or Y or only offer X or Y on this basis? 273
Q3. My case is subject to costs management. Am I required to seek my client's approval to the budget and does the budget, if agreed or approved, limit the costs I can charge my client? 274
Q4. Do the revised rules on Part 36 apply in a solicitor–client assessment? 274
Q5. Can I charge/recover for preparing the solicitor–client estimate? 275
Q6. It is still not clear how solicitors should go about doing estimates of costs for their clients and the extent to which Precedent H is sufficient/useful for this purpose. Can you express a view? 276

Table of Cases

A&M v Royal Mail Group unreported 27 August 2015 and 1 October 2015 CC (Birmingham) 9–19
AB v CD [2011] EWHC 602 (Ch) 5–57
ABCI (formerly Arab Business Consortium International Finance & Investment Co) v Banque Franco-Tunisienne (Costs) [2002] EWHC 567 (Comm) 7–16
AF v BG [2009] EWCA Civ 757; [2010] 2 Costs L.R. 164 .... 5–06, 5–40, 5–49
Agassi v Robinson (Inspector of Taxes) [2005] EWCA Civ 1507; [2006] 1 W.L.R. 2126; [2006] 1 All E.R. 900; [2006] S.T.C. 580, CA; [2006] 2 Costs L.R. 283; [2006] B.T.C. 3; [2005] S.T.I. 1994; (2005) 155 N.L.J. 1885; (2006) 150 S.J.L.B. 28; [2005] N.P.C. 140 7–21
Ahmud & Co Solicitors v MacPherson [2015] EWHC 2240 (QB) 9–06, 9–23
Akhtar v Bhopal Productions (UK) Ltd [2015] EWHC 154 (IPEC); [2015] F.S.R. 30 7–14
Akhtar & Khan v Ball unreported 10 July 2015 6–21
Allen v Colman Coyle LLP [2007] EWHC 90075 (Costs) 9–23
Altomart v Salford Estates (No.2) Ltd [2014] EWCA Civ 1408; [2015] C.P. Rep. 8; [2014] 6 Costs L.R. 1013 ....5–61, 8–26
Amber Construction Services Ltd v London Interspace HG Ltd [2007] EWHC 3042 (TCC); [2008] B.L.R. 74; [2008] 5 Costs L.R. 715; [2008] 1 E.G.L.R. 1; [2008] 9 E.G. 202; [2008] Bus. L.R. D46 7–01
Americhem Europe Ltd v Rakem Ltd [2014] EWHC 1881 (TCC); 155 Con. L.R. 80; [2014] 4 Costs L.R. 682 ....4–16, 4–39
AMH v Scout Association unreported Case No. HQ 13X05225 SCCO 9–01
Angel Airlines v Dean & Dean [2008] EWHC 1513 (QB); [2009] 2 Costs L.R. 159 9–08
Art & Antiques Ltd v Magwell Solicitors [2015] EWHC 2143 (Ch) 5–38
Astonleigh Residential Care Home Ltd v Goldfarb [2014] EWHC 4100 (Ch) 8–51
Axelrod v University Hospitals of Leicester NHS Trust unreported CC (Liverpool) 2–11
Bailes v Bloom unreported 23 November 2015 QBD 5–48
Bank of Ireland v Philip Pank Partnership [2014] EWHC 284 (TCC); [2014] 2 Costs L.R. 301 ....4–16, 4–39
Bank St Petersburg PJSC v Arkhangelsky [2015] EWHC 2997 (Ch) 7–25, 7–26
Bataillon v Shone [2015] EWHC 3177 (QB) 5–16, 5–53
Beasley v Alexander [2012] EWHC 2715 (QB); [2013] 1 W.L.R. 762; [2012] 6 Costs L.R. 1137; [2013] R.T.R. 7 5–14
Benaim (UK) Ltd v Davies Middleton & Davies Ltd (No.1) [2004] EWHC 737 (TCC); (2004) 154 N.L.J. 617 2–44
Bent v Highways and Utilities Construction & Allianz Insurance [2011] EWCA Civ 1539; [2012] 2 Costs L.O. 127 5–18
Birmingham City Council v Forde; sub nom. Forde v Birmingham City Council [2009] EWHC 12 (QB); [2009] 1 W.L.R. 2732; [2010] 1 All E.R. 802; [2009] 2 Costs L.R. 206; [2009] N.P.C. 7 2–19
Blackmore v Cummins [2009] EWCA Civ 1276; [2012] 2 Costs L.O. 127 8–13
Blankley v Central Manchester and Manchester Children's University Hospitals NHS Trust [2015] EWCA Civ 18; [2015] 1 W.L.R. 4307; [2015] 1 Costs L.R. 119 2–09
BP v Cardiff & Vale University Local Health Board [2015] EWHC B13 (Costs) 3–10
Brahilika v Allianz Insurance Plc unreported 30 July 2015 CC (Romford) 6–09
Brand v Berki [2015] EWHC 3373 (QB) 7–24
Brighton & Hove Bus v Brooks [2011] EWHC 2504 6–10

Bristol and West Building Society v Evans Bullock & Co unreported 5 February 1996 CA 5–07
Broadhurst v Tan [2016] EWCA Civ 94 ....8–31A
Buckland v Watts [1970] 1 Q.B. 27; [1969] 3 W.L.R. 92; [1969] 2 All E.R. 985; (1969) 113 S.J. 384 ....7–08, 7–09
Budana v Leeds Teaching Hospitals NHS Trust unreported CC (Hull)....................2–19
Butt v Nizami [2006] EWHC 159 (QB); [2006] 1 W.L.R. 3307; [2006] 2 All E.R. 140; [2006] 3 Costs L.R. 483; [2006] R.T.R. 25; (2006) 103(9) L.S.G. 30; (2006) 156 N.L.J. 272....................9–16
C v D [2011] EWCA Civ 646; [2012] 1 W.L.R. 1962; [2012] 1 All E.R. 302; [2011] C.P. Rep. 38; 136 Con. L.R. 109; [2011] 5 Costs L.R. 773; [2011] 2 E.G.L.R. 95; [2011] 23 E.G. 86 (C.S.); (2011) 161 N.L.J. 780....................5–07, 5–25
Caliendo v Mischon De Reya LLP [2015] EWCA Civ 1029; [2016] C.P. Rep. 3; [2015] 5 Costs L.R. 849 2–07
Capital For Enterprise Fund A LP v Bibby Financial Services Ltd [2015] 6 Costs L.R. 1059....................4–76
Carillion J M Ltd v PHI Group Ltd [2012] EWCA Civ 588; [2012] C.P. Rep. 37; [2012] B.L.R. 329; [2012] T.C.L.R. 5; 142 Con. L.R. 96; [2012] 4 Costs L.O. 523; [2012] C.I.L.L. 3180 ....5–07, 5–18
Carleton (Earl of Malmesbury) v Strutt & Parker (A Partnership) [2008] EWHC 424 (QB); 118 Con. L.R. 68; [2008] 5 Costs L.R. 736; (2008) 105(15) L.S.G. 24; (2008) 158 N.L.J. 480; (2008) 152(14) S.J.L.B. 29....................5–31
Carver v BAA Plc [2008] EWCA Civ 412; [2009] 1 W.L.R. 113; [2008] 3 All E.R. 911; [2008] C.P. Rep. 30; [2008] 5 Costs L.R. 779; [2008] P.I.Q.R. P15; [2008] LS Law Medical 351; (2008) 152(17) S.J.L.B. 28....................5–17, 5–53, 5–54
Cashman v Mid Essex Hospital Services NHS Trust [2015] EWHC 1312 (QB); [2015] 3 Costs L.O. 411 5–55
Casseldine v Diocese of Llandaff Board for Social Responsibility unreported 3 July 2015 CC (Cardiff)....................2–08, 6–06, 6–20, 6–23, 6–27
Chantrey Vellacott v The Convergence Group plc [2007] EWHC 1774 (Ch)....................5–19
Chaplair Ltd v Kumari [2015] EWCA Civ 798; [2015] C.P. Rep. 46; [2015] H.L.R. 39....................7–14, 7–15
CIP Properties (AIPT) Ltd v Galliford Try Infrastructure Ltd [2014] EWHC 3546 (TCC); [2015] 1 All E.R. (Comm) 765; 156 Con. L.R. 202; [2014] 6 Costs L.R. 1026....................3–04, 4–23, 4–36
CIP Properties (AIPT) Ltd v Galliford Try Infrastructure Ltd [2015] EWHC 481 (TCC); [2015] B.L.R. 285; 158 Con. L.R. 229; [2015] 2 Costs L.R. 363; [2015] C.I.L.L. 3641 ....3–18, 3–19, 4–18, 4–40, 4–51, 4–52, 4–53
Commissioners of Customs and Excise v Ross [1990] 2 All E.R. 65; [1990] S.T.C. 353....7–09
Conlon v Royal Sun Alliance Insurance Plc [2015] EWCA Civ 92; [2015] C.P. Rep. 23; [2015] 2 Costs L.O. 319 5–60
Courtwell Properties Ltd v Greencore PF (UK) Ltd [2014] EWHC 184 (TCC); [2014] 2 Costs L.O. 289; [2014] C.I.L.L. 3481 ....3–17, 4–21
Coventry v Lawrence; sub nom. Lawrence v Fen Tigers Ltd [2015] UKSC 50; [2015] 1 W.L.R. 3485; [2015] 4 Costs L.O. 507; [2015] H.R.L.R. 16....................2–03, 2–12
Coward v Phaestos Ltd [2014] EWCA Civ 1256; [2015] C.P. Rep. 2; [2014] 6 Costs L.O. 843 ....5–16, 5–62
Crosbie v Munroe [2003] EWCA Civ 350; [2003] 1 W.L.R. 2033; [2003] 2 All E.R. 856; [2003] C.P. Rep. 43; [2003] 3 Costs L.R. 377; [2003] R.T.R. 33; (2003) 100(20) L.S.G. 27; (2003) 147 S.J.L.B. 356....................4–85, 8–36, 8–37
Crouch v Kings Healthcare NHS Trust [2004] EWCA Civ 1332; [2005] 1 W.L.R. 2015; [2005] 1 All E.R. 207; [2005] C.P. Rep. 10; [2005] 2 Costs L.R. 200; [2005] P.I.Q.R. Q4; [2005] Lloyd's Rep. Med. 50; (2005) 83 B.M.L.R. 47; (2004) 101(44) L.S.G. 29; (2004) 154 N.L.J. 1616; (2004) 148 S.J.L.B. 1245 5–01

Cumper v Pothecary [1941] 2 KB 58; [1941] 2 All E.R. 516 5–44
D Pride & Partners v Institute for Animal Health [2009] EWHC 1617 (QB); [2009] 5 Costs LR 803 5–18
Daniels v Commissioner of Police of the Metropolis [2005] EWCA Civ 1312; [2006] CP Rep.9; (2005) 102(44) L.S.G. 30 5–31
David Truex (A Firm) v Kitchin [2007] EWCA Civ 618; [2007] 4 Costs L.R. 587; [2007] 2 F.L.R. 1203; [2007] P.N.L.R. 33; [2007] Fam. Law 903; (2007) 157 N.L.J. 1011; (2007) 151 S.J.L.B. 926; [2007] N.P.C. 87 9–19
Davies v Jones [2009] EWCA Civ 1164; [2010] 2 All E.R. (Comm) 755; [2010] 1 P. & C.R. 22; [2010] 1 E.G.L.R. 67; [2010] 5 E.G. 114; [2009] 46 E.G. 142 (C.S.); [2009] N.P.C. 126 2–09
Day v Day (Costs) [2006] EWCA Civ 415; [2006] CP Rep 35; (2006) 103(13) L.S.G. 235–28
Denton v TH White Ltd; Utilise TDS Ltd v Cranstoun Davies; Decadent Vapours Ltd v Bevan [2014] EWCA Civ 906; [2014] 1 W.L.R. 3926; [2015] 1 All E.R. 880; [2014] C.P. Rep. 40; [2014] B.L.R. 547; 154 Con. L.R. 1; [2014] 4 Costs L.R. 752; [2014] C.I.L.L. 3568; (2014) 164(7614) N.L.J. 17 ....1–04, 1–05; 2–07, 3–13, 3–17, 4–04, 4–05, 4–20, 4–21, 4–70, 4–87, 5–36, 5–50, 7–18, 7–24, 8–16, 8–43
Dilip v Paynes Dairies Ltd unreported 15 October 2015 CC (Leicester) 5–60
Dorchester Group Ltd (t/a Dorchester Collection) v Kier Construction Ltd [2015] EWHC 3051 (TCC); [2016] C.I.L.L. 3753 5–35
Drew v Whitbread [2010] EWCA Civ 53; [2010] 1 W.L.R. 1725; [2010] C.P. Rep. 22; [2010] 2 Costs L.R. 213; [2010] P.I.Q.R. P11; (2010) 107(8) L.S.G. 23; (2010) 160 N.L.J. 270 ....3–11, 4–76
Dufoo v Tolaini; sub nom. Quiet Moments Ltd, Re [2014] EWCA Civ 1536; [2014] 6 Costs L.R. 1106 5–17
East West Corp v DKBS 1912 (Costs); Utaniko Ltd v P&O Nedlloyd BV (Costs); sub nom. East West Corp v Dampskibsselskabet AF 1912 A/S (Costs); P&O Nedlloyd BV v Utaniko Ltd (Costs); Dampskibsselskabet AF 1912 A/S v East West Corp (Costs) [2002] EWHC 253 (Comm); [2002] 2 Lloyd's Rep. 222; [2002] All E.R. (D) 361 5–57
El-Demellawy v European Bank for Reconstruction and Development [2015] EWHC 3291 (QB) 7–24
Elsevier Ltd v Munro [2014] EWHC 2728 (QB); [2014] 5 Costs L.O. 797 5–53
Elvanite Full Circle Ltd v AMEC Earth & Environment [2013] EWHC 1643 (TCC); [2013] 4 All E.R. 765; [2013] B.L.R. 473; [2013] T.C.L.R. 7; [2013] 4 Costs L.R. 612; [2013] C.I.L.L. 3385 ....3–17, 4–20, 7–17, 7–18, 8–50
Evans v Royal Wolverhampton Hospitals NHS Foundation Trust [2014] EWHC 3185 (QB); [2014] 6 Costs L.O. 899 5–44
Excalibur Ventures LLC v Texas Keystone Inc [2015] EWHC 566 (Comm) 8–50
Excalibur Ventures LLC v Texas Keystone Inc (Defendants and Costs Claimants) and Psari Holdings Ltd (Costs Defendants) [2014] EWHC 3436 (Comm); [2014] 6 Costs L.O. 975 7–17
Excelsior Commercial & Industrial Holdings Ltd v Salisbury Hammer Aspden & Johnson [2002] EWCA Civ 879; [2002] C.P. Rep. 67; [2002] C.P.L.R. 693 ....7–07, 7–16
Experience Hendrix LLC v Times Newspapers Ltd [2008] EWHC 458 (Ch) 5–14
Feltham v Bouskell (Costs) [2013] EWHC 3086 (Ch); [2014] 1 Costs L.O. 29 ....5–16, 5–53
Fitzpatrick Contractors Ltd v Tyco Fire & Integrated Solutions (UK) Ltd [2009] EWHC 274 (TCC); [2009] B.L.R. 144; 123 Con. L.R. 69; [2010] 2 Costs L.R. 115; [2009] C.I.L.L. 2700 5–45
Flex Associates Ltd, Re [2009] EWHC 3690 (Ch) 7–16
Fox v Foundation Piling Ltd [2011] EWCA Civ 790; [2011] C.P. Rep. 41; [2011] 6 Costs L.R. 961 ....4–13, 5–16
Franks v Sinclair (Costs) [2006] EWHC 3656 (Ch); [2007] W.T.L.R. 785 7–07

Fred Perry (Holdings) Ltd v Brands Plaza Trading Ltd (t/a Brands Plaza) [2012] EWCA Civ 224; [2012] 6 Costs L.R. 1007; [2012] F.S.R. 28 4–03
Garritt-Critchley v Ronnan [2014] EWHC 1774 5–31
Gomba Holdings (UK) Ltd v Minories Finance Ltd (No.2) [1993] Ch. 171; [1992] 3 W.L.R. 723; [1992] 4 All E.R. 588; [1992] B.C.C. 877; (1992) 136 S.J.L.B. 54; [1992] N.P.C. 12 4–29
Gosling v Hailo unreported 29 April 2014 CC (Cambridge) 6–11
Gresport Finance Ltd v Battaglia [2015] EWHC 2709 (Ch) 5–31
Group M UK Ltd v Cabinet Office [2014] EWHC 3863 (TCC); [2014] 6 Costs L.R. 1090 8–16
GSK Project Management Ltd (In Liquidation) v QPR Holdings Ltd [2015] EWHC 2274 (TCC); [2015] B.L.R. 715; [2015] T.C.L.R. 9; [2015] 4 Costs L.R. 729; [2015] C.I.L.L. 3724 .... 3–18, 3–19, 4–51, 4–53
Gulati v MGN Ltd [2015] EWHC 1805 (Ch); [2015] 4 Costs L.R. 659 5–07
H v Dent (Costs) [2015] EWHC 2228 (Fam); [2015] Fam. Law 1323 7–22
Hahn v NHS England unreported 3 August 2015 CC (Liverpool) 2–11
Halborg v EMW Law LLP [2015] EWHC 2005 (Ch); [2015] 4 Costs L.O. 427 7–23
Hall & Barker, Re (1878) 9 Ch. D. 538 9–06
Hallam Estates Ltd v Baker [2014] EWCA Civ 661; [2014] C.P. Rep. 38; [2014] 4 Costs L.R. 660; (2014) 164(7608) N.L.J. 19 ....4–24, 4–33
Halsey v Milton Keynes General NHS Trust [2004] EWCA Civ 576; [2004] 1 W.L.R. 3002; [2004] 4 All E.R. 920; [2004] C.P. Rep. 34; [2004] 3 Costs L.R. 393; (2005) 81 B.M.L.R. 108; (2004) 101(22) L.S.G. 31; (2004) 154 N.L.J. 769; (2004) 148 S.J.L.B. 629 .... 5–26, 5–31, 5–64
Hammersmatch Properties (Welwyn) Ltd v Saint-Cobain Ceramics & Plastics Ltd [2013] EWHC 2227 (TCC); [2013] B.L.R. 554; 149 Con. L.R. 147; [2013] 5 Costs L.R. 758; [2013] 3 E.G.L.R. 123; (2013) 163(7571) N.L.J. 20......... 5–17, 5–18, 5–53, 5–54
Hartmann Capital Ltd (In Special Administration), Re [2015] EWHC 1514 (Ch); [2015] Bus. L.R. 983 2–03
Hatton v Connew [2013] EWCA Civ 1560 4–12
Hatton v Kendrick [2002] EWCA Civ 1783; [2003] C.P. Rep. 32 7–20
Hawksford Trustees Jersey Ltd v Stella Global UK Ltd [2012] EWCA Civ 987; [2012] 1 W.L.R. 3581; [2012] C.P. Rep. 41; [2012] 5 Costs L.R. 886; [2013] Lloyd's Rep. I.R. 337 ....2–40, 6–06
Hayward v Zurich Insurance Co Plc [2015] EWCA Civ 327; [2015] C.P. Rep. 30; [2015] Lloyd's Rep. I.R. 585 6–11
Hegglin v Person(s) Unknown [2014] EWHC 3793 (QB); [2015] 1 Costs L.O. 65 ....4–78, 4–91
Henry v News Group Newspapers Ltd [2013] EWCA Civ 19; [2013] 2 All E.R. 840; [2013] C.P. Rep. 20; [2013] 2 Costs L.R. 334; (2013) 163 N.L.J. 140; (2013) 157(5) S.J.L.B. 31 4–73
Hertel v Saunders [2015] EWHC 2848 (Ch); [2015] 5 Costs L.R. 825 5–18
Hobbs v Guy's & St Thomas' NHS Foundation Trust [2015] EWHC B20 (Costs) 9–14
Howell v Lees-Millais [2011] EWCA Civ 786; [2011] 4 Costs L.O. 456; [2011] W.T.L.R. 1795 5–25
Hyde v Milton Keynes NHS Trust [2015] EWHC B17 (Costs) 9–01
Igloo Regeneration (General Partner) Ltd v Powell Williams Partnership (Costs) [2013] EWHC 1859 (TCC); [2013] 5 Costs L.O. 746; (2013) 157(28) S.J.L.B. 31 7–07
Jenkins v Young Brothers Transport Ltd [2006] EWHC 151 (QB); [2006] 1 W.L.R. 3189; [2006] 2 All E.R. 798; [2006] 3 Costs L.R. 495.................... 2–09, 2–19, 2–40, 2–41
JJ Food Service Ltd v Zulhayir [2013] EWCA Civ 1304; [2014] C.P. Rep. 15 7–09
Jolly v Harsco Infrastructure Services Ltd [2012] EWHC 3086 (QB); [2013] 1 Costs L.R. 115 5–15
Jones v Spire Healthcare Ltd unreported 11 September 2015 CC (Liverpool) 2–09

Joseph v Boyd & Hutchinson [2003] EWHC 413 (Ch); [2003] 3 Costs L.R. 358; (2003) 100(19) L.S.G. 29 7–20
Joyce v West Bus Coach Services Ltd [2012] EWHC 404 (QB); [2012] 3 Costs L.R. 540 5–09
Kazakhstan Kagazy Plc v Zhunus [2015] EWHC 404 (Comm); 158 Con. L.R. 253 ....3–04, 8–13
Kellar v Williams [2004] UKPC 30; [2005] 4 Costs L.R. 559; (2004) 148 S.J.L.B. 821 2–19
Kellie v Wheatley & Lloyd Architects Ltd [2014] EWHC 2886 (TCC); [2014] B.L.R. 644; [2014] 5 Costs L.R. 854 4–20
Kelly v Black Horse Ltd [2013] EWHC B17 (Costs) 2–11
Kilby v Gawith [2008] EWCA Civ 812; [2009] 1 W.L.R. 853; [2008] C.P. Rep. 33; [2008] 6 Costs L.R. 959; [2009] R.T.R. 2; (2008) 105(22) L.S.G. 25; (2008) 152(21) S.J.L.B. 28 9–16
Kingsley v Orban [2014] EWHC 2991 (Ch); [2014] B.P.I.R. 1468 8–15
Kishenin v Von Kalkstein-Bleach; sub nom. Kishenin v Von Kalsten Bleach [2015] EWCA Civ 1184 7–24
Kite v Phoenix Pub Group unreported 6–21
KL Communications Ltd v Fu [2015] EWHC 2026 (IPEC) 7–24
Kuddus v Chief Constable of Leicestershire [2001] UKHL 29; [2002] 2 A.C. 122; [2001] 2 W.L.R. 1789; [2001] 3 All E.R. 193; (2001) 3 L.G.L.R. 45; [2001] Po. L.R. 181; (2001) 98(28) L.S.G. 43; (2001) 151 N.L.J. 936; (2001) 145 S.J.L.B. 166 6–21
Kunaka v Barclays Bank Plc [2010] EWCA Civ 1035; [2011] 2 Costs L.R. 179 5–45
Landau v Big Bus Company unreported 31 October 2014 6–06
Laporte v Commissioner of Police of the Metropolis [2015] EWHC 371 (QB); [2015] 3 Costs L.R. 471 ....5–26, 5–64
LG Blower Specialist Bricklayer Ltd v Reeves; sub nom. Gibbon v Manchester City Council [2010] EWCA Civ 726; [2010] 1 W.L.R. 2081; [2011] 2 All E.R. 258; [2010] C.P. Rep. 40; [2010] 5 Costs L.R. 828; [2010] P.I.Q.R. P16; [2010] 3 E.G.L.R. 85; [2010] 36 E.G. 120; [2010] 27 E.G. 84 (C.S.) 5–07, 5–16
Libyan Investment Authority v Goldman Sachs International [2014] EWHC 3364 (Ch) 7–16
London Scottish Benefits Society v Chorley [1884] 13 Q.B.D. 872 7–20
Long v Value Properties Ltd; sub nom. 1,3 and 5 Argall Avenue, Re [2014] EWHC 2981 (Ch); [2015] 3 All E.R. 419; [2014] 5 Costs L.R. 915 2–07
Lotus Cars Ltd v Mechanica Solutions Inc [2014] EWHC 76 (QB) 4–36
Lownds v Home Office [2002] EWCA Civ 365; [2002] 1 W.L.R. 2450; [2002] 4 All E.R. 775; [2002] C.P. Rep. 43; [2002] C.P.L.R. 328; [2002] 2 Costs L.R. 279; (2002) 99(19) L.S.G. 28; (2002) 146 S.J.L.B. 86 .... 3–02, 3–03, 3–10, 9–14
MacDonald v Taree Holdings Ltd [2001] C.P.L.R. 439; [2001] 1 Costs L.R. 147; (2001) 98(6) L.S.G. 45 ....8–14, 8–15
MacLennan v Morgan Sindall (Infrastructure) Plc [2013] EWHC 4044 (QB); [2014] 1 W.L.R. 2462; (2014) 158(2) S.J.L.B. 37 4–10
Malloch v Aberdeen Corp [1973] 1 W.L.R. 71; [1973] 1 All E.R. 304; 1973 S.L.T. (Notes) 5; (1972) 117 S.J. 72 7–09
Mars UK Ltd v Teknowledge Ltd (Costs) [1999] 2 Costs L.R. 44; [2000] F.S.R. 138; (1999) 22(10) I.P.D. 22097 8–50
McDaniel & Co v Clarke [2014] EWHC 3826 (QB); [2014] 6 Costs L.R. 963 ....9–01, 9–19
Mehmi v Pincher unreported hearing 20 July 2015 CC (Liverpool) 8–41, 8–43
Merck KGAA v Merck Sharp & Dohme Corp [2014] EWHC 3920 (Ch) 5–45
MGN Ltd v United Kingdom (39401/04); sub nom. Mirror Group Newspapers Ltd v United Kingdom (39401/04) [2011] 1 Costs L.O. 84; [2011] E.M.L.R. 20; (2011) 53 E.H.R.R. 5 ECHR 2–12
Mid-East Sales Ltd v United Engineering and Trading Co (PVT) Ltd [2014] EWHC 1457 (Comm); [2014] 2 All E.R. (Comm) 623; [2014] 4 Costs L.O. 605 8–43

Minotaur Data Systems Ltd, Re; sub nom. Official Receiver v Brunt [1999] 1 W.L.R. 1129; [1999] 3 All E.R. 122; [1999] B.C.C. 571; [1999] 2 B.C.L.C. 766; [1999] 2 Costs L.R. 97; [1999] B.P.I.R. 560; (1999) 96(12) L.S.G. 33; (1999) 149 N.L.J. 415; (1999) 143 S.J.L.B. 98; [1999] N.P.C. 27 7–09
Mitchell v News Group Newspapers Ltd [2013] EWCA Civ 1537; [2014] 1 W.L.R. 795; [2014] 2 All E.R. 430; [2014] B.L.R. 89; [2013] 6 Costs L.R. 1008; [2014] E.M.L.R. 13; [2014] C.I.L.L. 3452; (2013) 163(7587) N.L.J. 20 .... 1–04, 1–05, 2–07, 4–04, 4–05, 4–19, 4–87, 5–36, 5–50
Mole v Hunter [2014] EWHC 658 (QB) 7–09
Montgomery v Lanarkshire Health Board; sub nom. NM v Lanarkshire Health Board [2015] UKSC 11; [2015] A.C. 1430; [2015] 2 W.L.R. 768; [2015] 2 All E.R. 1031; 2015 S.C. (U.K.S.C.) 63; 2015 S.L.T. 189; 2015 S.C.L.R. 315; [2015] P.I.Q.R. P13; [2015] Med. L.R. 149; (2015) 143 B.M.L.R. 47; 2015 G.W.D. 10-179 9–01
Morgan v Spirit Group Ltd [2011] EWCA Civ 68; [2011] C.P. Rep. 22; [2011] 3 Costs L.R. 449; [2011] P.I.Q.R. P9 8–18
Motto v Trafigura Ltd [2011] EWCA Civ 1150; [2012] 1 W.L.R. 657; [2012] 2 All E.R. 181; [2011] 6 Costs L.R. 1028 9–13
Multiplex Construction (UK) Ltd v Cleveland Bridge UK Ltd [2010] EWCA Civ 449; [2010] C.I.L.L. 2863 5–17
Murray v Bernard [2015] EWHC 2395 (Ch); [2015] 5 Costs L.O. 567 5–31
N J Rickard Ltd v Holloway unreported 3 November 2015 CA (Civ Div) 5–49
Nader (t/a Try Us) v Customs and Excise Commissioners [1993] S.T.C. 806 CA 7–09
Nokes v Heart of England NHS Foundation Trust [2015] EWHC B6 2–11
Northrop Grumman Mission Systems Europe Ltd v BAE Systems (AL Diriyah C41) Ltd [2014] EWHC 3148 (TCC); [2014] TCLR 8; 156 Con. L.R. 141; [2014] 6 Costs L.O. 879; [2014] C.I.L.L. 3572 5–31
Northstar Systems Ltd v Fielding (Costs); Ultraframe (UK) Ltd v Fielding (Costs); sub nom. Ultraframe (UK) Ltd v Fielding (No.2) [2006] EWCA Civ 1660; [2007] 2 All E.R. 983; [2007] C.P. Rep. 12; [2007] 2 Costs L.R. 264 4–76
O'Beirne v Hudson [2010] EWCA Civ 52; [2010] 1 W.L.R. 1717; [2010] C.P. Rep. 23; [2010] 2 Costs L.R. 204; [2010] P.I.Q.R. P10 5–60
O'Brien v Shorrock; sub nom. Motor Insurers Bureau v O'Brien [2015] EWHC 1630 (QB); [2015] 4 Costs L.O. 439 2–22
Onay v Brown [2009] EWCA Civ 775; [2010] 1 Costs LR 29 CA 5–04
Ontulmus v Collett [2014] EWHC 4117 (QB) 5–20
OOO Abbott v Design & Display Ltd [2014] EWHC 3234 (IPEC) 5–56, 8–32
Owners and/or Bareboat Charterers of the Ship Samco Europe v Owners of the Ship MSC Prestige; sub nom. Samco Europe, The (Costs); MSC Prestige, The (Costs) [2011] EWHC 1656 (Admlty); [2011] 2 C.L.C. 679; [2012] B.L.R. 267; (2011) 161 N.L.J. 988 5–07
Pamplin v Express Newspapers Ltd (Costs) [1985] 1 W.L.R. 689; [1985] 2 All E.R. 185 QBD 8–40
Pentecost v John [2015] EWHC 1970 (QB); [2015] 4 Costs L.O. 497 2–22
PGF II SA v OMFS Co 1 Ltd [2013] EWCA Civ 1288; [2014] 1 W.L.R. 1386; [2014] 1 All E.R. 970; [2014] C.P. Rep. 6; [2014] B.L.R. 1; 152 Con. L.R. 72; [2013] 6 Costs L.R. 973; [2013] 3 E.G.L.R. 16; [2013] 44 E.G. 98 (C.S.); (2013) 157(42) S.J.L.B. 37 .... 5–26, 5–49
Prince Abdulaziz v Apex Global Management Ltd; sub nom. Apex Global Management Ltd v Fi Call Ltd [2014] UKSC 64; [2014] 1 W.L.R. 4495; [2015] 2 All E.R. 206; [2015] 1 All E.R. (Comm) 1183; [2015] 1 Costs L.O. 79 4–05
Proctor v Raleys Solicitors (A Firm) [2015] EWCA Civ 300 9–01
Purser v Hibbs [2015] EWHC 1792 (QB) 4–41, 5–13
Qader v Esure Services Ltd [2015] EWHC B18 (TCC) 7–04

R. (Bar Standards Board) v Disciplinary Tribunal of the Council of the Inns of Court and Sivanandan (Interested Party) [2014] EWHC 1570 (Admin); [2014] 4 All E.R. 759 7–20
R. (Burkett) v London Borough of Hammersmith & Fulham [2004] EWCA Civ 1342; [2005] C.P. Rep. 11; [2005] 1 Costs L.R. 104; [2005] J.P.L. 525; [2005] A.C.D. 73; (2004) 101(42) L.S.G. 30; (2004) 148 S.J.L.B. 1245 6–09
R. (CJ) v Cardiff City Council [2011] EWCA Civ 1590; [2012] 2 All E.R. 836; [2012] P.T.S.R. 1235; [2012] C.P. Rep. 15; [2012] 1 F.C.R. 461; [2012] H.L.R. 20; [2012] B.L.G.R. 157; [2012] A.C.D. 44 5–57
R. (Idira) v Secretary of State for the Home Department [2015] EWCA Civ 1187 ....4–05, 4–87
R. (MVN) v Greenwich LBC (Costs) [2015] EWHC 2663 (Admin) 5–57
R. (Whitston) v Secretary of State for Justice [2014] EWHC 3044 (Admin); [2015] A.C.D. 5 2–03
R. (Wulfsohn) v Legal Services Commission; sub nom. R. (on the application of Wulfsohn) v Legal Service Commission [2002] EWCA Civ 250; [2002] C.P. Rep. 34; [2002] 3 Costs L.R. 341 7–08
Rallison v North West London Hospitals NHS Trust [2015] EWHC 3255 (QB); [2015] 6 Costs L.O. 771 8–50
Ralph Hume Garry (A Firm) v Gwillim [2002] EWCA Civ 1500; [2003] 1 W.L.R. 510; [2003] 1 All E.R. 1038; [2003] C.P. Rep. 16; [2003] 1 Costs L.R. 77; (2002) 99(45) L.S.G. 35; (2002) 152 N.L.J. 1653; (2002) 146 S.J.L.B. 237 9–05
Rawlinson & Hunter Trustees SA v ITG Ltd [2015] EWHC 1924 (Ch) 8–52
Redwing Construction Ltd v Wishart [2011] EWHC 19 (TCC); [2011] B.L.R. 186; [2011] T.C.L.R. 5; [2011] 2 Costs L.O. 212; [2011] Lloyd's Rep. I.R. 331; [2011] 1 E.G.L.R. 13; [2011] 15 E.G. 94; [2011] C.I.L.L. 2997; (2011) 161 N.L.J. 137 2–11
Rees v Gateley Wareing (a firm) [2014] EWCA Civ 1351; [2014] 6 Costs L.O. 953 9–04
Reid v Buckinghamshire Healthcare NHS Trust [2015] EWHC B21 5–31
Revenue and Customs Commissioners v GKN Group; sub nom. GKN Group v Revenue and Customs Commissioners; Test Claimants in the FII Group Litigation v Revenue and Customs Commissioners [2012] EWCA Civ 57; [2012] 1 W.L.R. 2375; [2012] 3 All E.R. 111; [2012] S.T.C. 953; [2012] C.P. Rep. 20; [2012] B.T.C. 35; [2012] S.T.I. 217 7–26
Rogers v Merthyr Tydfil CBC [2006] EWCA Civ 1134; [2007] 1 W.L.R. 808; [2007] 1 All E.R. 354; [2007] 1 Costs L.R. 77; [2006] Lloyd's Rep. I.R. 759; (2006) 150 S.J.L.B. 1053 2–25
Rolf v De Guerin [2011] EWCA Civ 78; [2011] C.P. Rep. 24; [2011] B.L.R. 221; [2011] 5 Costs L.R. 892; [2011] 7 E.G. 97 (C.S.); (2011) 108(8) L.S.G. 20; [2011] N.P.C. 17 5–31
Romer & Haslam, Re [1893] 2 Q.B. 286 9–06
Rowles-Davies v Call 24–7 Ltd [2010] EWHC 1695 (Ch); (2010) 160 N.L.J. 1043 5–18
RTS Flexible Systems Ltd v Molkerei Alois Muller GmbH & Co AG [2010] UKSC 14; [2010] 1 W.L.R. 753; [2010] Bus. L.R. 776; [2010] 3 All E.R. 1; [2010] 2 All E.R. (Comm) 97; [2010] 1 C.L.C. 388; [2010] B.L.R. 337; 129 Con. L.R. 1; [2010] C.I.L.L. 2868; (2010) 107(12) L.S.G. 20; (2010) 160 N.L.J. 421; (2010) 154(11) S.J.L.B. 28 5–05
RXDX v Northampton BC [2015] EWHC 2938 (QB); [2015] 5 Costs L.R. 897 5–16
Sargeant v UK Insurance Ltd [2015] EWHC 3304 (QB) 7–24
Sarpd Oil International Ltd v Addax Energy SA [2015] EWHC 2426 (Comm); [2015] 4 Costs L.R. 751 ....4–50, 8–50
Sarwar v Alam; sub nom. Sawar v Alam [2001] EWCA Civ 1401; [2002] 1 W.L.R. 125; [2001] 4 All E.R. 541; [2002] 1 Costs L.R. 37; [2002] R.T.R. 12; [2002] Lloyd's Rep. I.R. 126; [2002] P.I.Q.R. P15; (2001) 151 N.L.J. 1492 ....2–08, 9–01
Savoye v Spicers Ltd [2015] EWHC 33 (TCC); [2015] 1 Costs L.R. 99; [2015] C.I.L.L. 3629 3–04

SB v MB (Costs) [2014] EWHC 3721 (Fam) 8–20, 8–21
Seals v Williams [2015] EWHC 1829 (Ch); [2015] 4 Costs L.O. 423; [2015] W.T.L.R. 1265 5–33
SG (a child) v Hewitt (Costs) [2012] EWCA Civ 1053; [2013] 1 All E.R. 1118; [2012] 5 Costs L.R. 937 ....5–19, 5–45
Sharland v Sharland; sub nom. S v S [2015] UKSC 60; [2015] 3 W.L.R. 1070; [2015] 2 F.L.R. 1367; [2015] 3 F.C.R. 481; [2015] Fam. Law 1461 5–29
Sharp v Blank [2015] EWHC 2685 (Ch) 4–24
Sibthorpe v Southwark LBC; sub nom. Morris v Southwark LBC [2011] EWCA Civ 25; [2011] 1 W.L.R. 2111; [2011] 2 All E.R. 240; [2011] C.P. Rep. 21; [2011] 3 Costs L.R. 427; [2011] H.L.R. 19; (2011) 108(6) L.S.G. 18; (2011) 161 N.L.J. 173; [2011] N.P.C. 11 9–04
Siegel v Pummell [2015] EWHC 195 (QB); [2015] 3 Costs L.O. 357 7–07
Simmons v Castle [2012] EWCA Civ 1288; [2013] 1 W.L.R. 1239; [2013] 1 All E.R. 334; [2013] C.P. Rep. 3; [2012] 6 Costs L.R. 1150; [2013] E.M.L.R. 4; [2013] P.I.Q.R. P2; [2013] Med. L.R. 4; (2012) 162 N.L.J. 1324; (2012) 156(39) S.J.L.B. 31 6–02
Simpkin Marshall Ltd, Re [1959] Ch 229; [1958] 3 W.L.R. 693; [1958] 3 All E.R. 611; (1958) 102 S.J. 878..9–03
Simpson v MGN Ltd [2015] EWHC 126 (QB); [2015] 1 Costs L.R. 139 ....3–08, 4–20, 4–73, 4–74
Sinclair v Dorsey & Whitney (Europe) LLP [2015] EWHC 3888 (Comm) 4–05, 4–87
Slick Seating Systems v Adams [2013] EWHC 1642 (QB); [2013] 4 Costs LR 576 ....4–20, 8–20
Smith v Trafford Housing Trust (Costs) [2012] EWHC 3320 (Ch); (2012) 156(46) S.J.L.B. 31 5–19
Solomon v Cromwell Group Plc [2011] EWCA Civ 1584; [2012] 1 W.L.R. 1048; [2012] 2 All E.R. 825; [2012] C.P. Rep. 14; [2012] 2 Costs L.R. 314; [2012] R.T.R. 24; [2012] P.I.Q.R. P9..5–46, 8–45
Stocker v Stocker [2015] EWHC 1634 (QB); [2015] 4 Costs L.R. 651; [2015] E.M.L.R. 24 ....3–18, 3–19
Sugar Hut Group Ltd v A J Insurance [2014] EWHC 3775 (Comm); [2015] 2 Costs L.R. 179 ....5–18, 5–53, 5–54
Summit Navigation Ltd v Generali Romania Asigurare Reasigurare SA [2014] EWHC 398 (Comm); [2014] 1 W.L.R. 3472; [2015] 1 All E.R. (Comm) 360; [2014] 2 Costs L.R. 367 4–16
Surrey v Barnet & Chase Farm Hospitals NHS Trust [2015] EWHC B16 (Costs)...........2–08, 2–11, 9–01
Sutherland v Turnball [2010] EWHC 2699 (QB) 5–45
Symphony Group PLC v Hodgson [1994] Q.B. 179; [1993] 3 W.L.R. 830; [1993] 4 All E.R. 143; [1997] Costs L.R. (Core Vol.) 319; (1993) 143 N.L.J. 725; (1993) 137 S.J.L.B. 134..6–21
Tasleem v Beverley; sub nom. Bartkauskaute v Bartkauskiene [2013] EWCA Civ 1805; [2014] 1 W.L.R. 3567; [2014] C.P. Rep. 25; [2014] 4 Costs L.O. 551.......8–36, 8–37
Tchenguiz v Serious Fraud Office [2014] EWCA Civ 1471 7–07
Ted Baker Plc v Axa Insurance UK Plc [2012] EWHC 1779 (Comm); [2012] 6 Costs L.R. 1023..5–14, 5–45
Tel-Ka Talk Ltd v Revenue & Customs Commissioners [2010] EWHC 90175 (Costs); [2011] S.T.C. 497; [2011] S.T.I. 267..2–02, 9–03
TGA Chapman v Christopher [1998] 1 W.L.R. 12; [1998] 2 All E.R. 873; [1997] C.L.C. 1306; [1998] Lloyd's Rep. I.R. 1..6–13
Thai Airways International Public Co Ltd v KI Holdings Co Ltd (formerly Koito Industries Ltd) [2015] EWHC 1476 (Comm); [2015] 3 Costs L.R. 545 5–16

Thevarajah v Riordan [2015] UKSC 78; [2016] 1 W.L.R. 76; [2015] 6 Costs L.R. 1119 4–05
Thewlis v Groupama Insurance Co Ltd [2012] EWHC 3 (TCC); [2012] BLR 259; [2012] T.C.L.R. 3; 142 Con. L.R. 85; [2012] 5 Costs L.O. 560 5–04
Thomas Pink Ltd v Victoria's Secret UK Ltd [2014] EWHC 3258 (Ch); [2015] 3 Costs L.R. 463 8–50
Thompson v Bruce [2011] EWHC 2228 (QB) 5–45
Tibbles v SIG Plc (t/a Asphaltic Roofing Supplies) [2012] EWCA Civ 518; [2012] 1 W.L.R. 2591; [2012] 4 All E.R. 259; [2012] C.P. Rep. 32; [2013] 1 Costs L.O. 41 4–05
Transformers and Rectifiers Ltd v Needs Ltd [2015] EWHC 1687 (TCC); [2015] 3 Costs L.R. 611; [2015] C.I.L.L. 3702 .... 8–02, 8–21, 8–22
Troy Foods v Manton [2013] EWCA Civ 615; [2013] 4 Costs L.R. 546 3–08
Trustees of Stokes Pension Fund v Western Power Distribution (South West) Plc [2005] EWCA Civ 854; [2005] 1 W.L.R. 3595; [2005] 3 All E.R. 775; [2005] C.P. Rep. 40; [2005] B.L.R. 497; [2006] 2 Costs L.R. 226; (2005) 102(30) L.S.G. 28 5–01
Turner & Co v O Palomo SA [2000] 1 W.L.R. 37; [1999] 4 All E.R. 353; [1999] 2 Costs L.R. 184; [1999] N.P.C. 114 9–06
United Building and Plumbing Contractors v Kajla [2002] EWCA Civ 628; [2002] C.P. Rep. 53 7–09
Van Oord UK Ltd v Allseas UK Ltd [2015] EWHC 3385 (TCC) 5–06, 5–49
Vava v Anglo American South Africa Ltd [2013] EWHC 2326 (QB); [2013] 5 Costs LR 805 6–09
Venn v Secretary of State for Communities & Local Government [2014] EWCA Civ 1539 7–05
Vestergaard Frandsen A/S v Bestnet Europe Ltd [2014] EWHC 4047 (Ch) 5–59
Viridor Waste Management Ltd v Veolia ES Ltd [2015] EWHC 2321 (Comm) 4–05
Wagenaar v Weekend Travel Ltd (t/a Ski Weekend) [2014] EWCA Civ 1105; [2014] C.P. Rep. 46; [2014] 5 Costs L.O. 803; [2014] P.I.Q.R. P23 .... 6–04, 6–19, 8–25
Watchorn v Jupiter Industries Ltd; sub nom. Husky Group Ltd, Re [2014] EWHC 3003 (Ch); [2015] 3 Costs L.O. 337; [2015] B.P.I.R. 184 5–16
Webb v Liverpool Women's NHS Foundation Trust [2015] EWHC 449 (QB); [2015] 3 Costs L.O. 367 5–58
Webb Resolutions Ltd v E-Serv Ltd [2014] EWHC 49 (QB); [2014] 1 Costs L.R. 182 .... 8–15, 8–43
Wheeler v Chief Constable of Gloucestershire [2013] EWCA Civ 1791 8–15
Williams v Jervis [2009] EWHC 1838 (QB) 5–19
Willis v MRJ Rundell & Associates Ltd [2013] EWHC 2923 (TCC); [2013] 6 Costs L.R. 924; [2013] 3 E.G.L.R. 13; [2013] C.I.L.L. 3428 4–53
Wilsons Solicitors LLP v Bentine; Stone Rowe Brewer LLP v Just Costs Ltd [2015] EWCA Civ 1168; [2015] 6 Costs L.O. 779 .... 9–08, 9–23
Worthington v 03918424 Ltd unreported 16 June 2015 (Manchester) 7–19
Yampolskaya v AB Bankas Snoras (In Bankruptcy); sub nom. Akcine Bendore Bankas Snoras (In Bankruptcy) v Antonov [2015] EWHC 2136 (QB) 7–24
Yentob v MGN Ltd [2015] EWCA Civ 1292; [2015] 6 Costs L.R. 1103 5–15
Yeo v Times Newspapers Ltd [2015] EWHC 209 (QB); [2015] 1 W.L.R. 3031; [2015] 2 Costs L.O. 243; [2015] E.M.L.R. 18 .... 4–18, 4–19, 4–51, 4–53

Table of Statutes

1934 Law Reform (Miscellaneous Provisions) Act (c.41) 5–10, 6–04
1974 Solicitors Act (c.47) 9–04, 9–05, 9–08
Pt III 7–13
ss.56—75 9–01
s.57 ....2–02, 2–13, 9–03
(2) 9–03
s.59 ....9–03, 9–04
s.64 9–06
s.69 9–05
s.70 ....9–06, 9–07, 9–23
(1) 9–06, 9–23
(2) 9–06
(3) 9–06
(5) 9–08
(9) 9–06, 9–08, 9–23
s.74(3) 4–75
s.87 9–03
1975 Litigants in Person (Costs and Expenses) Act (c.47) ...7–08, 7–09
s.1 7–08
(1) 7–08
1976 Fatal Accidents Act (c.30) 5–10, 6–04, 6–08
1978 Civil Liability (Contribution) Act (c.47) 5–07, 6–04
1981 Senior Courts Act (c.54) ....
s.51 ....2–31, 5–19, 7–22, 9–02
1986 Insolvency Act (c.45) 2–03
1990 Town & Country Planning Act (c.8)
s.288 7–05
1990 Courts & Legal Services Act (c.41) 7–25
s.57 ....9–03, 9–04
s.58 ....2–02, 2–04, 2–06, 2–17, 2–29, 2–30, 2–44, 9–04, 9–16
(1) 2–02
(2) 9–16
(4) 2–19
(c) 2–04, 2–43
(4A) 2–02
(b) 2–02
(4B) 2–02, 2–04, 2–06
(b) 2–04
(5) 2–02, 9–04
(6) 2–44
s.58A 2–04, 9–04
(4) 2–44
(6) 2–02, 2–34, 2–35, 2–38
s.58AA 2–02, 2–13, 2–17, 2–30, 9–04
(2) 2–45
(4) 2–13, 2–45
(b) 2–45
(9) 9–04
s.58C 2–10, 2–11, 2–25
s.61 9–04
1996 Arbitration Act (c.23) 2–44, 5–36, 5–69
s.1 5–36
s.4 5–36
s.7 5–36
s.9 5–36
s.61 ....5–36, 5–69
s.63 5–36
(5) 5–69
1996 Housing Grants, Construction and Regeneration Act (c.53) 5–35
1999 Access to Justice Act (c.22)
s.11 6–02
s.20 2–40
s.29 2–10
s.30 2–10
2007 Legal Services Act (c.29)
Sch.3 7–25
2009 Local Democracy, Economic Development and Construction Act (c.20)
Pt 8 5–35
2012 Legal Aid, Sentencing & Punishment of Offenders Act (c.10) 1–07, 2–01, 2–08, 2–31, 2–38, 9–01
s.26 6–02
Pt 2 1–07
s.44 .2–02, 2–03, 2–04, 2–31, 2–41
(6) 2–03, 2–08, 2–09, 2–19, 2–22, 2–29, 2–31, 2–35, 2–38

ss.44—46 1–06
s.45 2–13
s.46 .... 2–10, 2–41, 6–01
(3) 2–40
s.47 2–10
s.48 .... 1–07, 2–03
2015 Criminal Justice and Courts Act (c.2)
s.57 .... 6–08, 6–10, 6–11
(3) 6–11

Table of Statutory Instruments

1965 Rules of the Supreme Court (SI 1965/1776) 5–69
Ord.62 r.3(3) 5–69
r.12 5–69
r.18 7–20
(6) 7–20
Appendix 2 5–69
para.1 5–69
1980 Litigants in Person (Costs and Expenses) Order (SI 1980/1159) 7–08
1998 Civil Procedure Rules (SI 1998/3132) 3–01, 3–06, 3–18, 4–01, 4–03, 4–05, 4–23, 4–30, 4–37, 4–65, 4–80, 4–82, 5–07, 5–49, 5–64, 7–05, 7–20, 8–02, 8–26, 8–51, 9–01, 9–16, 9–20, 9–23
Pt 1 4–25
r.1.1 .... 3–02, 4–02, 4–07, 4–41, 4–82
(1) 3–03
(2)(e) 4–89
(f) 4–02, 4–03
r.1.2(f) 8–03
Pt 2 8–48
r.2.1 .... 5–37, 5–38
r.2.3 6–04
(1) 6–26
r.2.11 4–30
Pt 3 .... 3–08, 6–21
Pt 3 II 9–12
r.3.1(2)(ll) 4–80
(m) 4–02, 5–33
(7) 4–05
r.3.1A 4–90, 7–09, 7–24
(1) 4–90
r.3.4(2)(a) 6–09, 7–01
(b) 6–09
r.3.8 4–05
(3) 4–30
(4) 4–05, 4–30
r.3.9 .... 2–07, 3–03, 4–02, 4–03, 4–04, 4–05, 4–73, 4–87, 5–37, 5–61, 7–24, 8–26, 8–41
(1) 4–03
r.3.12 ...... 3–04, 3–16, 4–16, 4–18, 4–23, 4–26, 4–32, 4–46, 4–50, 4–51, 4–56, 6–17
(1) 4–23, 4–27, 4–78
(a) 4–15
(b) 4–15
(c) 4–78, 4–83
(e) . 4–15, 4–23, 4–24, 4–91
(1A) 4–15, 4–23, 4–27, 4–85, 4–86, 4–91
(2) 4–01, 4–63
rr.3.12—3.18 .... 4–02, 4–14, 4–65, 4–80
r.3.13 ...... 4–23, 4–24, 4–26, 4–28, 4–30, 4–33, 4–44, 4–46, 4–47, 4–80, 4–88, 9–13
(1)(a) 4–26
(b) 4–18, 4–26
(2) 4–16, 4–30, 4–31, 4–44
r.3.14 ...... 4–13, 4–16, 4–24, 4–25, 4–28, 4–30, 4–33, 4–46, 4–88, 5–50
r.3.15 ...... 1–03, 1–05, 4–15, 4–16, 4–18, 4–22, 4–46, 4–51, 4–56, 4–63, 4–66, 4–78
(1) 4–50, 8–50
(2) 4–24, 4–25, 4–50, 4–65
(3) 4–19, 4–41, 4–63, 4–67, 4–82
r.3.16 4–79
r.3.17 ...... 3–03, 3–16, 4–01, 4–22, 4–24, 4–25, 4–41, 4–63, 4–78, 4–82
r.3.18 ...... 3–08, 3–09, 3–17, 4–20, 4–21, 4–41, 4–50, 4–52, 4–55, 4–62, 4–65, 4–70, 4–71, 4–72, 4–73, 4–76, 4–77, 4–82, 4–88, 6–17, 8–19, 8–50, 9–22
(a) 4–20
(b) 4–20, 4–74
r.3.19(5)(b) 4–91
rr.3.19—3.21 1–10
r.3.20 .... 4–80, 4–91
PD 3E 1–03, 3–08, 4–02, 4–14, 4–16, 4–20, 4–37, 4–56, 4–65, 4–80, 4–91

para.2 .... 1–03, 4–23, 4–27
(b) 4–15
paras 2—5 4–15
para.5 4–23
(a)—(f) 4–15
para.6 .... 4–33, 4–37
para.6.2 4–38
para.6A 4–16
para.7.2 .... 4–65, 9–24
para.7.3 ...... 3–03, 3–06, 4–18, 4–52, 4–54, 4–56, 4–57, 4–64, 4–71, 4–72, 4–91, 8–19
para.7.4 ...... 3–13, 4–18, 4–39, 4–50, 4–51, 4–52, 4–54, 9–22
para.7.6 ...... 3–08, 3–13, 4–11, 4–17, 4–19, 4–34, 4–41, 4–63, 4–73, 4–79, 4–80, 4–81, 4–82, 4–84, 4–86
para.7.7 .... 4–16, 4–66
para.7.8 .... 4–15, 4–90
para.7.9 ...... 3–13, 4–17, 4–19, 4–42, 4–83, 4–84
para.7.10 ..... 4–18, 4–56, 4–57
PD 3F 4–80, 4–91
para.2 4–91
para.4.1 4–91
Pt 7 .... 1–03, 4–15, 4–24, 4–26, 4–31, 4–78, 5–46, 8–36, 8–51
r.7.2(1) 5–42
Pt 8 .... 4–27, 5–04, 5–22, 5–46, 7–04, 8–36, 8–37, 9–07
PD 8A 5–45
para.6.4 4–27
PD 8B 5–04, 5–22
r.12.4(1) 7–01
r.13.3(2) 8–43
r.14.1 5–35
r.14.4(3) 7–01
r.14.5(6) 7–01
r.16.3 4–24
(2)(b) 4–24
(7) 4–78
r.20.2 5–04
r.20.3 .... 5–04, 5–40
Pt 21 .... 4–15, 9–19
r.21.1(2) 7–03
r.21.10 7–05
r.21.12 9–19
(7) 9–19
PD 21 9–19
PD 22 para.2.2A 3–17, 3–19, 4–34, 4-61, 4–75
para.5 4–34
Pt 23 5–08
r.23.8 8–22
PD 23A para.6.2(c) 4–44
Pt 24 .... 4–83, 7–01
r.25.13(2)(c) 5–31
r.26.3 .... 4–02, 4–06, 4–26, 4–28, 4–30
(1) 4–16, 4–30, 4–31
(6A) 4–30, 4–31
(7A) 4–30
(b) 4–30
r.26.6(3) 4–02, 4–07
r.26.7(3) 4–02, 4–07
r.26.8(2) 7–01
PD 26 para.12.3(2) 4–26
para.12.4 4–26
Pt 27 .... 5–67, 7–15
r.27.2 7–15
r.27.14 .... 2–36, 7–15
(5) 4–02, 4–07
(6) 4–02, 4–07
Pt 29 4–80
r.29.1(2) ... 4–02, 4–08, 4–09, 4–90
r.29.4 4–44
r.29.5 4–30
(1)(a) 4–30
PD 29 para.2.6A 4–40
para.8.1(1) 4–80
para.10.5 .... 8–02, 8–21
r.31.5 .... 4–09, 9–15
(1) 4–09
(2) 4–09
(3)—(8) 4–02, 4–09
(7) 4–09, 4–17, 4–22
(b) 4–17
r.31.6 4–09
r.31.22 7–07
r.32.1 4–10
r.32.2 9–15
(3) 4–02, 4–10, 4–22, 4–89
r.32.14 4–34
r.35.4 .... 4–02, 4–11, 9–15
(2) 4–11
PD 35 para.11 .... 4–02, 4–12
Pt 36 .... 2–01, 3–17, 4–13, 4–21, 4–41, 4–88, 5–01, 5–02, 5–03, 5–04, 5–06, 5–07, 5–16, 5–17, 5–18, 5–20, 5–25, 5–26, 5–28, 5–37, 5–42, 5–45, 5–46, 5–49, 5–61, 5–62, 8–06, 8–08, 8–25, 8–35, 8–44, 8–45, 8–46, 8–47, 9–06, 9–22, 9–23
s.I 5–04, 5–06, 5–42, 5–49

r.36.1 5–04
r.36.2 .... 5–04, 5–48, 5–49
(2) 5–38, 5–39, 5–49
(c) 5–49
(d)..............................5–18
(3) 5–04, 5–40, 5–49
(5) 5–04
r.36.3 .... 5–03, 5–04, 5–12, 5–45
(e).........................5–12, 5–45
(g).........................4–21, 5–06
r.36.4(1)................................5–05
(2) 5–05
r.36.5 ...... 5–04, 5–18, 5–39, 5–42, 5–48, 5–49
(1) 5–06, 5–40, 5–49
(c) 5–49
(d)..............................5–18
(2) 5–06
(4) 5–38, 5–41
r.36.7 .... 5–06, 5–40, 5–41, 5–42
r.36.9 .... 5–42, 5–43, 5–44
(1) 5–07, 5–43
(2) 5–07
(3) 5–07
(4) 5–07
(b)..............................5–07
(5) 5–07
r.36.10 .... 5–07, 5–08, 5–15, 5–42, 5–43, 5–44, 9–23
(1) 5–04, 5–25
(3) 5–44
(4) 5–25, 5–48
(5) 5–13, 5–25, 7–19
r.36.11 ....5–03, 5–15
(1) 5–09
(2) 5–09
(3) 5–10
(4) 5–10
r.36.12 ..... 5–03, 5–12, 5–44, 5–45
r.36.13 .... 5–04, 5–06, 5–10, 5–15, 5–45, 5–49
(1) 5–13, 5–25, 5–46, 5–47, 5–48, 5–49, 5–50
(2) 5–13, 5–47
(4) 4–41, 5–13, 5–25, 5–48, 5–50
(5) 4–41, 5–13, 5–25, 5–45, 7–19
(b)....................4–88, 5–21
(5)—(7).................5–13, 5–45
(7) 5–48, 5–49
r.36.14 .... 5–15, 5–16, 5–17, 5–19, 5–45, 5–50, 5–51, 5–56, 9–23
(1) 5–47
(1A) 5–17
(2) 5–45
(3) 5–16, 5–40, 5–51
(a) 5–16
(b)..............................5–18
(c) 5–18
(d)..............................5–16
(4) 5–19
r.36.15 5–51
(1)—(4)...........................5–11
r.36.16 ....5–03, 5–45
(1)—(4)...........................5–14
r.36.17 .... 5–15, 5–16, 5–17, 5–19, 5–45, 5–53, 5–54, 5–56, 8–32, 8–45, 8–48
(1) 4–88
(1)—(3)...........................5–15
(2) 5–17, 5–62
(3) 5–15, 5–45, 8–46
(a) 4–88, 5–21, 5–51
(4) 5–15, 5–16, 5–49, 5–51, 5–54, 5–55, 5–56, 5–57, 8–31, 8–47
(b).......... 4–21, 4–88, 5–18, 5–21, 5–51, 8–30, 8–31
(c) 5–18
(d).......... 4–02, 4–13, 5–16, 5–23, 5–52, 5–53, 5–55, 8–31, 8–32, 8–47, 8–48
(5) 5–13, 5–16, 5–19, 5–45
(e) 5–57
(6) 5–16
(7) 5–07, 5–15
(8) 5–15
r.36.20 ....5–06, 5–49
r.36.21 5–15
r.36.23 .... 4–88, 5–21, 5–50
s.II 5–04, 5–22
r.36.24 5–22
r.36.25 5–22
r.36.26 ....5–22, 5–23
r.36.27 5–22
r.36.28 5–22
r.36.29 5–23
(1)—(4)...........................5–23
r.36.30 5–24
PD 36A....................................5–01
para.1.2...........................5–06
para.2.............................5–08
para.3.1...........................5–47
r.38.4 6–21

r.38.6 .... 6–21, 6–22
(1) 6–21
r.39.4 4–89
r.39.6 7–25
r.41.3A 5–10
r.43.2(1)(a) 8–28
PD 43 para.11.7 2–28
para.11.8 2–28
Pts 43—48 2–07
Pt 44 .... 2–27, 5–16, 5–62
r.44.1 ...... 8–02, 8–22, 8–25, 8–27, 8–32, 8–37
r.44.2 ...... 4–76, 5–17, 5–26, 5–42, 5–49, 5–57, 5–58, 6–07
(2)(a) 4–82
(4) 5–17, 5–28, 5–54, 5–61
(a) 3–14, 5–17, 5–54
(b) 3–11, 5–17
(c) 5–17, 5–54, 9–23
(6) 3–11, 8–35
(7) 8–35
(8) 7–04, 8–13, 8–51
r.44.3 .... 2–16, 4–52, 4–71
(1) 4–52
(1)—(3) 7–06
(2) 3–03, 3–05, 3–09, 3–15, 8–17
(a) 3–04, 3–06, 3–08, 3–10, 3–14, 3–16, 3–18, 3–20, 4–20, 4–21, 4–32, 4–48, 4–52, 4–53, 8–10, 8–38, 8–39
(4) 7–06
(5) 3–03, 3–05, 3–06, 3–10, 3–18, 3–19, 3–20, 4–07, 4–19, 4–32, 4–40, 4–41, 4–58, 4–82, 4–89, 8–18, 8–34, 8–38, 8–39, 9–14
(a) 3–10, 3–11
(c) 4–41
(d) 8–39
(e) 4–41
(6)(g) 5–19
(7) 3–10, 8–02, 8–06
r.44.3B 2–07
(1)(d) 2–07
r.44.4 .... 3–11, 4–76
(1)(a) 3–15
(b) 3–17
(2) 8–18, 9–07
(3) 3–10, 3–14, 3–17, 4–40, 8–34, 9–07
(g) 4–40
r.44.5 .... 7–15, 9–02
(3) 3–02, 3–10
r.44.6 8–02
(a) 2–31
(b) 7–04
r.44.9(1)(b) 5–46, 5–47
Pt 44 Pt II 6–03, 6–07
r.44.11 4–70
(1)(b) 4–70
(2)(a) 4–70
r.44.13 ..... 6–04, 6–19, 6–22, 8–25
(1) 6–01, 6–04, 6–25, 8–25
(3) 6–15
r.44.14 .... 6–08, 6–09, 6–15, 6–18, 6–21
(1) 6–08
(2) 6–07, 8–25
r.44.15 .... 2–07, 6–08, 6–09, 6–21, 6–22
(1) 6–08
r.44.16 .... 6–08, 6–10, 6–12, 6–15, 6–21
(1) 6–08, 6–11
(2) 6–11, 6–12, 6–13
(a) 6–12
(b) 6–12
(3) 6–13
r.44.17 .... 6–05, 6–06, 6–20, 6–23, 6–24, 6–26, 6–27
Pt III 6–16
r.44.18 2–16
(2)(b) 2–16
PD 44 6–15
para.3 4–25, 4–53, 4–80, 4–91
para.3.1 4–91
para.3.6 3–16
para.3.7 3–16
paras 4.1—4.2 5–28
para.4.2 5–20
para.9 8–02
para.9.1 8–21
para.9.2 8–21
(a) 8–21
(b) 8–21
para.9.5 8–15
(3) 4–37, 8–03
(4) 8–04, 8–15
para.9.6 8–14
para.9.7 8–22
para.12 6–11
para.12.1 6–03
para.12.2 6–12
para.12.4(a) 6–11

(b) 6–11
(c) 6–11, 6–21
para.12.5 6–13
para.19 2–07
(3) 2–27
Pts 44—48 2–07
Pt 45 1–09, 7–01, 7–05, 7–13, 7–14
s.I 7–01
r.45.1 7–15
(1) 7–01
(2)(a) 7–01
(b) 7–01
r.45.2 7–01
r.45.3 .... 7–01, 8–04
r.45.4 7–01
r.45.5 7–15
r.45.6 7–15
s.II 5–46, 7–01
r.45.9(2) 7–01
(4) 7–01
s.III 7–01
r.45.18 .... 5–22, 7–03
r.45.20 5–23
r.45.24 7–04
r.45.26 5–23
s.IIIA 5–06, 5–15, 5–49, 7–01, 7–04
r.45.29A 7–04
r.45.29J 7–04
s.IV 7–01, 7–04
r.45.30(1) 7–04
(2) 7–04
(3) 7–04
s.V 7–01, 7–04
r.45.33 7–04
(3)—(6) 7–04
r.45.34 7–04
r.45.35 7–04
r.45.36 7–04
s.VI 7–01, 7–05
r.45.37(1) 7–05
(2) 7–05
s.VII 7–01, 7–05
r.45.41 7–05
(2) 7–05
r.45.42 7–05
r.45.43 7–05
r.45.44 7–05
PD 45 paras 1.1—1.3 7–01
paras 4.1—4.3 7–05
para.5.1 7–05
para.5.2 7–05
r.46.2 6–13
r.46.4 9–18
r.46.5 .... 7–08, 7–09
(3)(c) 7–09
(4)(a) 7–20
(6) 7–20, 7–23
(a) 7–23
(b) 7–23
r.46.9 .... 9–10, 9–12, 9–17, 9–20
(3) 9–12
(a) 9–12
(b) 9–12
(c) 4–69, 4–75, 9–10
(4) 9–17
r.46.10 9–10
r.46.13 5–59
(2) 5–60
(3) 5–60
r.46.14 .... 5–46, 8–35, 8–36, 8–37
(5) 5–46
(6) 5–46
PD 46 para.3 7–20
para.3.2 7–20
para.8.2 5–60
Pt 47 .... 5–47, 7–04, 8–06, 8–08, 8–33, 8–37
r.47.1 .... 4–85, 8–48
r.47.6 4–85
(1) 8–36
r.47.11 8–33
r.47.13 8–29
r.47.14 .... 4–85, 8–35, 8–36
(1) 8–33
(7) 8–06
r.47.15 .... 8–07, 8–27, 8–37, 8–45, 8–49
(4) 8–09
(5) 8–10, 8–33, 8–35, 8–49
(6) 8–07
(10) 8–45, 8–46
(b) 8–47
r.47.16(1) 8–33
r.47.20 .... 8–06, 8–10, 8–31, 8–32, 8–35, 8–43, 8–45, 8–46, 8–47
(1)(a) 8–35
(b) 8–35
(3) 4–19, 8–35
(a) 5–61, 8–26
(4) 5–25, 8–35
(e) 8–44
(7) 8–25, 8–48
PD 47 8–27
para.1.1 8–48
para.5.1A 8–06

para.5.2(f) 8–06, 8–23
para.5.7 .... 8–06, 8–48, 8–49
para.5.8 3–10
para.8.2 .... 8–06, 8–29
para.8.3 ...... 5–60, 5–61, 8–06, 8–25, 8–26, 8–40
para.12 8–29
para.12.1 8–06
para.13.2 .... 8–08, 8–40, 8–42, 8–43
(i) 8–41, 8–42, 8–43
(m) 8–06
para.13.4 8–09
para.13.6 8–09
para.13.9 8–12
para.13.11 8–08
para.13.13 .... 8–40, 8–41, 8–42, 8–43
para.14 .... 8–07, 8–49
para.14.2 ..... 8–29, 8–31, 8–33
(2) 8–12, 8–40
para.14.3 8–40
(b)—(e) 8–08
para.14.4(1) 8–33
(2) 8–10, 8–38
para.14.5 .... 8–11, 8–45
para.19 5–25
para.32 .... 2–07, 2–27
para.32.5 2–38
Sch. 8–06
r.48.1 .... 2–07, 2–27, 2–38
(1) 2–34
r.48.2 ...... 2–09, 2–19, 2–29, 6–02, 6–05, 6–19, 6–20, 6–24
(1)(i)(aa) 6–06
r.48.6(6) 7–20
r.48.8 .... 9–07, 9–08, 9–10
(2) 9–07
r.48.9 9–08
(5) 9–19
r.48.10 .... 9–08, 9–10
PD 48 2–34
para.54.1 9–08
PD 51G 3–08, 3–17
para.1.3 3–08
para.4.2 3–08
para.6 9–12
PD 51L 8–06, 8–19
PD 51N 4–32
para.2.58 4–32
para.2.59 .... 4–32, 8–05
para.2.60 4–32
Pt 52 4–81
r.52.3(5) 8–43
r.52.9A 7–09
(4) 7–09
Pt 55 .... 7–14, 7–15
s.II 7–15
r.61.4(10)—(12) 5–07
r.63.26 .... 7–04, 7–14
2000 Conditional Fee Agreements Regulations (SI 2000/692) 2–14
2000 Conditional Fee Agreements Order (SI 2000/823)
art.4 2–43
2001 Litigants in Person (Costs and Expenses) (Magistrates' Courts) Order (SI 2001/3438) 7–08, 7–09
2006 Civil Procedure (Amendment No.3) Rules (SI 2006/3435) 5–01
2009 Judicial Committee (Appellate Jurisdiction) Rules Order (SI 2009/224) 5–37
r.43(1) 5–37
2013 Legal Aid, Sentencing and Punishment of Offenders Act 2012 (Commencement No. 5 and Saving Provision) Order (SI 2013/77) 2–03
art.4 2–39
(b) 2–43
2013 Recovery of Costs Insurance Premiums in Clinical Negligence Proceedings Regulations (SI 2013/92) 6–05
2013 Civil Procedure (Amendment) Rules (SI 2013/262)
r.16 2–07
2013 Damages-Based Agreements Regulations (SI 2013/609) 2–13, 2–17, 2–29, 2–33, 2–45, 2–46, 9–19
reg.1 .... 2–14, 2–17
reg.4 .... 2–14, 2–17, 2–33, 2–46
(1)(b) 2–14
(2) 2–15
(3) 2–14
reg.5 2–14

2013 Conditional Fee Agreements Order (SI 2013/689) 2–04, 2–06, 2–19, 2–29
art.2 2–02
art.4 2–04
art.5 ....2–04, 2–06
(1)(b) 2–05
(2) 2–04
art.6 2–04
2013 Recovery of Costs Insurance Premiums in Clinical Negligence Proceedings (No.2) Regulations (SI 2013/739) 2–11, 2–37
2014 Civil Procedure (Amendment No. 8) Rules (SI 2014/3299) 5–01
r.18(1) 5–03
(2) 5–03
Sch.1 5–01
2015 Alternative Dispute Resolution for Consumer Disputes (Competent Authorities and Information) Regulations (SI 2015/542) 5–63
Pts 1—3 5–63
reg.3 5–63
Pt.4 5–63
reg.19 5–63
reg.19A 5–63
Pt.5 5–63
Sch.1 5–63
2015 Alternative Dispute Resolution for Consumer Disputes (Amendment) Regulations (SI 2015/1392) 5–63
reg.2(3) 5–63
2016 Civil Procedure (Amendment) Rules 2016 (SI /2016) 5–63

CHAPTER 1

Introduction

In 2014 the publishers of Civil Procedure (the White Book) decided in conjunction with Practical Law to publish "Costs and Funding Following the Civil Justice Reforms: Questions and Answers". This book was published alongside the White Book 2015. It was described by the publishers as a *"unique book"* which tackled common practitioner questions on the effects of the 2013 Jackson Reforms on Costs and Funding. The book covered Litigation Funding, Proportionality, Case and Costs Management, Part 36 Settlement Offers, QOCS, the Assessment of Costs and the Effect of the Reforms on Solicitor Client Costs. The book was well received and the publishers have accordingly asked the authors to produce this second edition. **1–01**

On 13 May 2015[1], both Lord Justice Jackson and Lord Dyson, the Master of the Rolls, spoke. Lord Justice Jackson stated that the interconnection of his proposals is of overarching importance. He was insistent that the Government should not cherry pick those recommendations which appealed to it and ignore the rest. He had spent a great deal of time working on the interlocking of all the proposals. Most of the reforms had been accepted but, he said, they would take time to bed in. This was a useful time to take stock of the reforms and how they were working.

In his paper "Confronting Costs Management"[2], Sir Rupert lists seven benefits of costs budgeting; four objections and suggested solutions; and eight problems. Among his suggestions for dealing with these problems are: **1–02**

- There is presently a problem of judicial inconsistency. The solution to this problem lies in better judicial training. The costs management training provided to all civil judges in early 2013 was necessarily brief, because there were many other aspects of the 2013 civil justice reforms to be covered. Now, however, there is a full day module on costs management available on judicial refresher courses. This module has been developed in the light of experience and is now, by all accounts excellent. Unfortunately it is elective, not compulsory. Sir Rupert recommended that (a) this course should be compulsory for all civil judges; and, (b) all civil judges should be encouraged to read the comprehensive chapter on costs management in this publication.
- A standard form of costs management order. Again to address inconsistency throughout the jurisdiction.

[1] At a function organised by Harbour Litigation Funding Limited.
[2] The speech is available together with that of Lord Dyson MR at: *www.judiciary.gov.uk/announcements/speeches/*.

- Costs budgets should be filed 14 days before the CCMC to avoid early filed budgets being overtaken by events.
- A revised precedent H to deal with various perceived problems.
- The introduction of a summary of a bill of costs in a form matching precedent H to help detailed assessment after costs management.

1–03 Sir Rupert's main concern was with the delay that was occurring in certain courts, particularly in London, in clinical negligence cases. In relation to this he suggested that:

> *"Such delays do not promote access to justice at proportionate costs. On the contrary, they inhibit access to justice and tend to drive up costs.*
> *The solution: I propose that the recent amendments to Rule 3.15 and PD3E . . . be repealed . . .*
> *(i) In most contested Part 7 and in most cases of the type identified in PD3E paragraph 2, costs management by a competent judge or master promotes financial certainty and reduces the costs expended on the litigation to proportionate levels.*
> *(ii) However, the court should not manage cases in any case if it lacks the resources to do so without causing significant delay and disruption to that or other cases. Possibly the directions questionnaire should include an additional question to assist the courts in exercising its discretion."*[3]

1–04 Returning to his theme that his recommendations formed an interlocking whole, Sir Rupert pointed out that others introduced reforms which drive up costs without any reference to him or the recommendations in his final report. In this respect, he cited the virtual abolition of legal aid, which has led to a great increase in the number of litigants in person; and the increase in court fees. In addition to this, the Civil Procedure Rule Committee's drafting of some of the suggested rule amendments has not always achieved what Sir Rupert intended. The result of this can be seen in the decisions in *Mitchell* and *Denton*[4]. The Court of Appeal decision in *Mitchell* caused widespread unintended consequences.

1–05 In the Court's decision in *Denton* it was suggested that *Mitchell* had been misinterpreted and a different interpretation was provided in *Denton*. Even then, Lord Justice Jackson gave a powerful dissenting judgment in respect of the third stage of the procedure for relief from sanctions. It has to be said that had Sir Rupert been a member of the Court of the Appeal in *Mitchell*, it seems most unlikely that the judgment would have been handed down in the form which caused so much difficulty. Even now we have the anomalous situation that the author of the Jackson Reforms finds himself in a minority in the

[3] Following this costs management in clinical negligence cases in the Queen's Bench Division in London has been suspended, at least until January 2016. It is understood that a number of County Courts around the country have also ceased to undertake costs management in clinical negligence cases, citing lack of resources.

[4] *Mitchell v. News Group Newspapers Limited* [2013] EWCA Civ.1537, *Denton v. TH White Limited and Others* [2014] EWCA Civ. 906.

Court of Appeal when it comes to interpreting how those reforms should be interpreted and applied.

The Master of the Rolls then spoke and was very supportive of costs management which he felt to be in the public interest. Having said that, he accepted that the current system is not perfect. A sub-committee of the CPRC had been set up under the chairmanship of Coulson J who would report in due course[5]. The indications are that the number of non-clinical negligence and non-PI cases, where budgets are agreed, is rising. Lord Dyson agreed the need for more judicial training and for standard forms of costs management orders. Whilst he was rather less supportive of the proposed amendment to r.3.15, he agreed that it should be given serious consideration.

Lord Justice Jackson delivered the 2015 Mustill Lecture[6] in Leeds on **1–06**
16 October 2015. In that Lecture he examined the Civil Justice Reforms and whether insolvency litigation should be exempt from the abolition of recoverability of success fees and after the event insurance premiums. Sir Rupert pointed out that, by written ministerial statement on 24 March 2012, the Government announced that the implementation of ss.44 to 46 of the Legal Aid Sentencing and Punishment of Offenders Act 2012 would be delayed until April 2015. The purpose of this was to allow time for insolvency practitioners to adjust to the changes and to make alternative arrangements for litigation funding. The thrust of Sir Rupert's Lecture was that the exemption should not continue but should come to an end, exactly as the Government had proposed in May 2012. In his view the Profession had had more than enough time to prepare for the changes. He set out four reasons why the exemption was not justified. These included that insolvency practitioners had managed perfectly satisfactorily throughout the 20th century before the introduction of recoverable success fees in 2000. Sir Rupert concluded by querying whether the continuation of the exemption was actually lawful as being contrary to ECHR. He does not answer that question since he is still a serving judge. He does however suggest that the Government should do what it said it would do.

R3, the Association of Business Recovery Professionals, the leading organi- **1–07**
sation for insolvency, restructuring and turnaround specialists in the UK, has issued a robust statement suggesting that abolishing the exemption from LASPO for insolvency cases would create a "windfall" for third-party funders.

In November 2015 both the Bar Council and the ABI supported the call for a permanent exemption for insolvency cases in a letter to the Lord Chancellor. Notwithstanding these representations, on 17 December 2015 Lord Faulks, Minister of State for Justice, made the following announcement:

"The government has made a priority of addressing the high costs of civil litigation in England and Wales. To that end, part 2 of the Legal Aid, Sentencing and

[5] The sub-committee has reported back to the CPRC. A final decision on any amendments to the system is still awaited.
[6] Available at: *www.judiciary.gov.uk/announcements/speeches/.*

Punishment of Offenders (LASPO) Act 2012 reforms the operation of 'no win, no fee' conditional fee agreements. Those reforms came into effect generally in April 2013 but were delayed in respect of insolvency proceedings.

After further consideration, the government has decided that the 'no win, no fee' reforms should now be applied to insolvency proceedings. The provisions will come into force for these cases in April 2016.

It has already been announced that there will be a post-implementation review of the LASPO Act part 2 reforms between April 2016 and April 2018. The review will take place towards the end of that period. The review under section 48 of the Act in relation to mesothelioma cases will also take place as part of the post-implementation review."

1–08 According to Lord Faulks, on an earlier occasion, the Government is keen to do more to reform "*enormous*" legal costs. He said: "I don't think we have got a grip on the overall amount that lawyers charge". He cited the German example: "The Germans . . . have very much more in the way of fixed costs. Once you decide to go [down] the court route you know what is coming at the end of the road".

1–09 The German model was used by Lord Justice Jackson and his assessors when considering the fixed and predictable costs regimes under Part 45. Sir Rupert recommended (and still recommends) that there should be a fixed costs regime for the whole of the fast-track and at the lower end of the multi-track. The system of costs used in Germany cannot simply be transferred into the English system since the civil procedure in each jurisdiction is entirely different. In Germany the judge takes a far more inquisitorial and proactive role. This is reflected in the fact that in Germany there are some 6,000 judges as against approximately 1,000 in this jurisdiction.

1–10 Mr Justice Flaux, the judge in charge of the Commercial Court, expressed the view, at a recent Law Society Commercial Litigation Conference, that a tariff of recoverable costs would be introduced into the commercial arena by the Government. Flaux J made it clear that he was not "advocating" fixed costs and had "not the faintest idea" what the tariff should be based on. He said: "How do you assess how complex a case is? Certainly not by how much money is at stake". He went on to point out that Commercial Court cases do not fit into any type of mould, making it hard to make fixed fees work. He was in favour of the greater use of costs capping orders to control excessive costs. The Civil Procedure Rule Committee had considered recommending that CPR 3.19 to 3.21 dealing with costs capping be revoked. It now appears, however, that the decision has been taken to retain these rules.

On 28 January 2016 Lord Justice Jackson delivered a speech about extending fixed costs to the whole of the Fast Track and the lower end of the Multi Track up to claims for £250,000.[7]

[7] https://www.judiciary.gov.uk/wp-content/uploads/2016/01/fixedcostslecture-1.pdf

He suggests that his ideas should include clinical negligence actions. He sets out a grid with four different value bands and ten stages based on the stages in Precedent H. His scheme is essentially a variation of the ABC/123 scheme in use in New Zealand. It remains to be seen how quickly the Government will react to his proposals.

Against this background, another of Sir Rupert's recommendations has come to the fore with the publication of the new format bill of costs and the J-Codes. In his final report, Sir Rupert Jackson recommended:

> "*106. A new format of bills of costs should be devised, which will be more informative and capable of yielding information at different levels of generality.*
> *107. Software should be developed which will (a) be used for time recording and capturing relevant information and (b) automatically generate schedules for summary assessment of bills for detailed assessment as and when required. The long term aim must be to harmonise the procedures and systems which will be used for costs budgeting, costs management, summary assessment and detailed assessment*".

The job of implementing these recommendations was given to the Jackson Review EW-UTBMS[8] Development Steering Committee, originally under the chairmanship of Jeremy Morgan QC and latterly under that of Alex Hutton QC. The members of the Committee have worked extremely hard to produce a new format Bill of Costs which is compatible with Precedent H in that the work is recorded by phase and task. This is achieved by use of the J-Codes. **1–11**

The Hutton Committee published a guidance document to the new format Bill of Costs on 31 July 2015. The Committee also published an example of a completed Bill of Costs in Excel as well as a print version and a blank template.

The J-Codes themselves are set out in the Civil Litigation J-Code Set Overview and Guidelines published by the Jackson Review Drafting Group on 27 July 2014. **1–12**

The new regime is being piloted on a non-mandatory basis at the Senior Courts Costs Office from 1 October 2015 with the objective of introducing the system on a compulsory basis at some point.

Members of the Civil Procedure Rules Committee received the "Interim Consultation Response of the Hutton Committee", dated 30 November 2015, and a letter dated 3 December 2015 from the Chair of the Law Society's Civil Justice Committee to Lord Justice Richards. There was a general discussion of the issue in the light of that material and with input from the Senior Costs Judge and Alexander Hutton QC, it was acknowledged that the proposal went beyond a pilot and had major implications for the profession. It was agreed that the matter needed to be given careful further consideration by the MoJ and by the Committee and that it was too soon for any decision to be taken.

The documents already referred to contain a formidable amount of detail

[8] Uniform Task-Based Management System.

which will require solicitors and costs lawyers alike to familiarise themselves with this information and ultimately to become adept in its use.

Sir Rupert's objective was that the new Bill should provide more transparent explanation than was currently provided about what work was done in the various time periods and why. The Bill, in his view, should provide a user-friendly synopsis of the work done, how long it took and why. He also suggested that the Bill should be "inexpensive to prepare" and be capable of presenting the Bill at different levels of generality. Finally, he suggested that the Court would have to have IT systems capable of receiving bills in electronic format[9].

1–13 The CPRC has been considering draft rule amendments to the costs management regime following a report from the chair of the subcommittee, Coulson J. It is expected that the amended rules will come into force in April 2016. **Chapter 4** sets out the latest information about the expected changes.

Further developments were announced in the Chancellor's Autumn Statement: namely the abolition of general damages for soft tissue injuries from 2017 and the increase in the small claims limit for personal injuries to £5,000. Both these measures are bound to have a significant impact on low value personal injury claims, particularly road traffic whiplash claims.

1–14 The Courts have continued to hand down judgments on various aspects of the Jackson Reforms. This book sets out to bring the reader up to date and also to answer questions which have been troubling practitioners. Readers will find not only many of the questions which appeared in the first edition, with their answers brought up to date, but also a host of new questions with their answers based on the latest decisions of the Courts.

[9] Final Report Chapter 45, paragraph 5.3ff.

CHAPTER 2

Funding Litigation

Introduction

The Legal Aid, Sentencing & Punishment of Offenders Act 2012 and associated secondary legislation has had a significant impact on the funding of litigation. Some aspects, in particular the greater restrictions on availability of public funding, are beyond the scope of this section. 2–01

This section will instead focus on the changes to funding arrangements available to litigants, in particular Conditional Fee Agreements (CFAs), Damages Based Agreements (DBAs) and After the Event Insurance (ATE).

Lord Justice Jackson's Final Report contained detailed and inter-related proposals for the means of Funding Litigation. These included:

- emphasising the benefits of public funding and stressing the 'vital necessity' to avoid any further cutbacks in its availability or eligibility[1];
- recommendations for the encouragement of take up of Before the Event Insurance in certain circumstances[2]; and
- perhaps most notably, a recommendation for the abolition of between the parties recovery of ATE premiums,[3] allied to the introduction of qualified one way costs shifting for certain litigants and the abolition of the between the parties recoverability of success fees in CFAs,[4] in turn allied to a 10 per cent increase in awards for general damages, the enhancement of Part 36 benefits for claimants and the capping of success fees chargeable by solicitors in personal injury claims.

Whilst broadly Jackson LJ's package of reforms in relation to CFAs, ATE, and QOCS were adopted, his call for public funding not to be further restricted was not, and the reforms of funding introduced did not always follow his precise recommendations.

This can be seen in particular in relation to QOCS, where Jackson LJ's proposal for a means-tested model based on that applicable to public funding costs protection was not adopted,[5] but also in relation to DBAs, where the reforms introduced have not had the desired effect in practice of making a new form of funding widely available to litigants.

The transitional provisions in relation to the abolition of between the parties' recovery of success fees and ATE premiums have given rise to problems of their

1 Final Report, p.70.
2 Final Report, p.79.
3 Final Report, p.89.
4 Final Report, p.112.
5 For further details, see Ch.6 on QOCS.

own. These have become particularly apparent in circumstances where, for one reason or another, there is some need to vary or change the funding arrangement after 1 April, 2013 in circumstances where that arrangement was first entered into prior to that date. These issues will be considered further below.

Conditional Fee Agreements

2–02 Section 44 of LASPO amended s.58A(6) of the Courts & Legal Services Act 1990 to provide that a costs order may no longer include provision requiring another party to pay part of the successful party's success fee. This was a simple reversal of the position prior to 1 April 2013.

Whilst certain changes were made to s.58 in relation to the specific requirements for a CFA in personal injury claims[6], the basic circumstances in which a CFA could be entered into, its basic requirements and the type of cases where such an agreement was lawful were not amended.

Accordingly, the effect of the amendment to s.58A(6) was simple—where success fees had formerly been recoverable in principle between the parties, they are now no longer recoverable and, where a CFA with a success fee is entered into, such success fees will have to be paid by the client, with no prospect of any between the parties' recovery.

It is important to note that the fundamental principle in s.58(1) of the Act, that a CFA which does not satisfy all of the conditions applicable to it by virtue of s.58 shall be unenforceable, remains unchanged.

Equally, Lord Justice Jackson's clear recommendation that the indemnity principle should be abrogated, at least in part to limit the scope for satellite litigation in relation to issues of enforceability of retainers, was rejected. The call was repeated in early 2015,[7] and in September 2015 the Civil Justice Council Working Group on DBA Reform made a reasoned recommendation for its abolition, at least in the context of DBAs, but recognised that this was closely tied to the question of the abolition of the principle more generally, which was 'a thorny policy issue' and one where the Government has shown a marked disinclination to intervene[8]. At present there is no particular reason to anticipate that any of these calls will be heeded.

Accordingly, a failure to comply with the requirements of s.58, including the new requirements imposed by s.58(4A) and (4B) in relation to personal injury CFAs, will leave the litigant, and their solicitor, exposed to the well-rehearsed arguments that the agreement is unenforceable and that accordingly no costs under the CFA may be recovered between the parties. Whether the removal of the between the parties recovery of success fees will result directly or indirectly in a reduction in the appetite or ability of paying parties to take such points remains to be seen.

[6] These are the 'specified claims' under s.58(4A)(b) by virtue of art.2 of the Conditional Fee Agreements Order 2013 (SI 2013 No.689).

[7] *http://www.judiciary.gov.uk/wp-content/uploads/2014/10/litigation-post-jackson-world.pdf* [Accessed 29 January, 2015].

[8] Civil Justice Council, The Damages-Based Agreements Reform Project – 'Drafting and Policy Issues', 2 September 2015, Chapter 23.

The final point to note in relation to issues of general application is that s.58(5) of the 1990 Act remains untrammelled. This is the section that provides that where the CFA is a non-contentious business agreement under s.57 of the Solicitors Act 1974, s.58(1) does not render it unenforceable. The scope of this was considered in detail by then Senior Costs Judge in 2010 in an authoritative judgment[9] and the ability to use CFAs (and now DBAs) which are not subject to the restrictions of ss.58 and 58AA for what might be termed non-contentious business is an option which is potentially a valuable one, particularly in the commercial sphere, though one which needs to be approached carefully.

Transitional provisions

The transitional provision provided for by s.44(6) states that: **2–03**

> *"The amendment made by [the subsection] does not prevent a costs order including provision in relation to a success fee payable by a person ("P") under a conditional fee agreement entered into before [1 April 2013] if—*
> *(a) the agreement was entered into specifically for the purposes of the provision to P of advocacy or litigation services in connection with the matter that is the subject of the proceedings in which the costs order is made, or*
> *(b) advocacy or litigation services were provided to P under the agreement in connection with that matter before the commencement day."*

This ensured that the court retains its discretion to allow a between the parties success fee where the CFA was entered into before 1 April 2013. The one proviso is that the CFA relates to a specific matter which is the subject of the proceedings before the court **or** advocacy or litigation services were in fact provided under the CFA before 1 April, 2013.[10]

In addition, s.48 of the Act contained saving provisions allowing for the continued between the parties recovery of success fees in diffuse mesothelioma claims. On 4 December, 2013 the Government announced that this exception was to be removed and success fees would cease to be recoverable between the parties in such claims. However, in October 2014 the High Court[11] ruled that the consultation process leading to that decision had been flawed and that the decision had to be quashed, leading to the Government announcing that there would be a further review of whether or not to remove the exception. Accordingly, if and when the mesothelioma exception will be lifted remains to be seen.

---

[9] *Tel-Ka Talk Ltd v Revenue & Customs Commissioners* [2010] EWHC 90175 (Costs).

[10] The latter part of this provision appears primarily directed to the position in relation to Collective Conditional Fee Agreements (CCFAs). Such an agreement may have been entered into prior to 1 April, 2013, but may cover all claims of a particular type a solicitor is undertaking for a particular client or funder. The agreement may therefore cover claims in respect of matters which had not even arisen prior to 1 April, 2013. If the transitional provision simply focused on the date of the funding arrangement, the CCFA could be used to ensure the ongoing recovery of additional liabilities even in respect of post-April 2013 instructions. Accordingly, in such circumstances, it is not the date of the CCFA which is relevant (because the CCFA did not relate to a specific matter which is the subject of proceedings) but rather whether the legal representative had started to provide services in respect of that specific matter before 1 April, 2013.

[11] *R (Ex parte Whitston) v Secretary of State for Justice* [2014] EWHC 3044 (Admin).

Implementation of s.44 was also 'suspended' in relation to publication and privacy proceedings and insolvency proceedings. In respect of publication and privacy proceedings, this was intended to be only until further, related, reforms, including the possible extension of QOCS to such claims, initially anticipated in October 2013 and then April 2014, were introduced. However, the position remains under review by the Government and no further date has been set for implementation.

In respect of insolvency proceedings, the implementation was originally intended to be postponed until April 2015 only. However, in a written ministerial statement on the 26 February 2015, the Government announced that the implementation in respect of insolvency proceedings was to be further suspended pending further consideration of the 'appropriate way forward'.

Lord Justice Jackson's speech at the 2015 Mustill Lecture[12] set out a detailed analysis of the position, including noting the possible argument that the continuation of the exemption could be unlawful notwithstanding the decision of the Supreme Court in *Coventry v Lawrence*[13].

Whether as a result of that analysis or otherwise, on 17 December, 2015 the Government announced that the insolvency exemption would end with effect from 1 April, 2016 – and presumably with effect on funding arrangements entered into on or after that date.

It should in any event be noted that the insolvency exception is a narrow one and only applies to office holders or companies in administration bringing proceedings under the Insolvency Act 1986—see the Legal Aid, Sentencing & Punishment of Offenders Act 2012 (Commencement No.5 & Saving Provisions) Order 2013. Other cases, which might fall within a general description of 'insolvency' claims do not benefit from the exception and are subject to the general removal of between the parties recoverability of additional liabilities—see *Re Hartmann Capital* [2015] EWHC 1514 (Ch).

Such specific types of cases aside, therefore, the key point remains that where the CFA was entered into before 1 April, 2013 the success fee continues to be recoverable in principle. If entered into on or after 1 April, 2013 the success fee is irrecoverable from the paying party.

Personal injury claims—additional requirements

2–04 Section 44 of LASPO amended s.58 and s.58A of the Courts & Legal Services Act 1990 to impose additional conditions on CFAs, including the requirement that in certain classes of case, primarily personal injury claims (but for the time being excluding mesothelioma claims), the success fee does not exceed a maximum limit expressed as a percentage of certain types of damages.[14]

There is a strange circularity in the 2013 Order in that the types of cases

[12] "The Civil Justice Reforms And Whether Insolvency Litigation Should Be Exempt" *https://www.judiciary.gov.uk/wp-content/uploads/2015/10/mustill-jackson-lj.pdf*

[13] [2015] UKSC 50.

[14] As set out in the Conditional Fee Agreements Order 2013.

in respect of which the cap on the success fee imposed by s.58(4)(c) applies (personal injury claims—see art.4) are expressly specified in the Order. However, art.6 provides that, for the time being, art.4[15] does not apply to publication, privacy and insolvency proceedings. Given that they are not specified in art.4, art.4 could not apply to them in any event, so this part of art.6 serves no purpose. It is assumed that art.6 was phrased in this way in anticipation of the success fee cap possibly being extended to cover such proceedings if and when success fees in such claims are no longer recoverable between the parties, though why those parts of art.6 would be needed at that point is a moot question.

The key restriction in relation to a post-April 2013 CFA for a claim involving personal injury is contained in Article 5 of the Order, which must be read in conjunction with s.58(4B) of the 1990 Act.

The success fee in any such agreement must be limited to a maximum of 25 per cent of specified classes of damages awarded in the proceedings, in respect of proceedings at first instance. Note, the express reference in s.58(4B)(b) is to 'awarded' and not to damages actually recovered.

The specified classes of damages are general damages for pain, suffering and loss of amenity and damages for pecuniary loss, other than future pecuniary loss, in both cases net of any sums recoverable as CRU (Compensation Recovery) (art.5(2)).

Accordingly, under such a CFA, the success fee, which cannot be recovered between the parties, cannot exceed 25 per cent of the damages for general damages and past pecuniary loss (net of CRU).

It is important not to confuse the cap on the quantum of the success fee 2–05
with the percentage of the success fee itself. The maximum percentage success fee, that is to say the maximum percentage by which the solicitors' base fees may be multiplied, remains at 100 per cent, in all claims where a CFA is permissible. The 25 per cent cap operates as a financial limit on how much of the success fee the client may be charged.

If the amount of damages for general damages and past loss awarded is sufficiently high, or the amount of base fees to which the success fee is to be applied, or the percentage success fee itself is sufficiently low, then the full success fee may be payable, because it is less than the cap. Where, however, the success fee calculated at the applicable percentage on the base fees payable under the agreement exceeds 25 per cent of the prescribed damages, then the amount of the success fee is limited accordingly.

The interaction of the maximum limit on the percentage success fee (100 per cent) with the newly introduced cap on the maximum fee chargeable caused some confusion initially in some quarters and some errors of drafting, particularly in relation to CFAs which covered appeal proceedings.

This is because, under art.5(1)(b) of the 2013 Order, the cap on the maximum success fee is lifted from 25 per cent to 100 per cent in relation to proceedings

[15] And art.5, which sets the maximum percentage success fee in cases covered by art.5.

other than at first instance. It is important to note that this is still a cap. It is merely that the effect of the cap in this situation is that the maximum success fee is limited to the full amount of the net damages for general damages and past loss, rather than only 25 per cent of that sum. This 100 per cent cap is separate and distinct from the 100 per cent limit on the success fee itself.

2–06 As a matter of practice, it would appear that many practitioners have chosen to ignore the ability to include a higher cap on the success fee where the CFA covers matters other than first instance proceedings. This is no doubt because of the concerns about ensuring that the agreement is fully compliant with both caps where it covers both first instance and appellate proceedings and because of the danger of a simple error leading to the entire CFA being deemed unenforceable. Undoubtedly, the simpler and safer, if potentially less remunerative, course is to apply the 25 per cent cap alone.

The cap is intended to be inclusive of VAT—that is to say that the maximum success fee chargeable, including VAT, should not exceed the 25 per cent limit. Peculiarly, this is not specified within art.5, but rather is explained in the Explanatory Note to the Order which, as it states, is not part of the Order itself.

It is generally accepted that the cap should include any success fee payable to counsel (including VAT) under any CFA in relation to the same matter between the solicitor and counsel. However, it is fair to note that neither the 2013 Order nor s.58 of the 1990 Act, as amended, specify this. As a result, it is open to argument that reference to 'the success fee' specified under s.58(4B) of the 1990 Act, which must be subject to a maximum limit, is to the success fee (that is to say the solicitor's success fee) chargeable under the CFA, and that any success fee chargeable under any separate CFA (for example with counsel) is subject to a separate, but identical maximum limit. That does not appear to have been the intention, but appears to be an argument left open by the drafting.

Notification and advice requirements

2–07 Prior to April 2013, the between the parties notification requirements in relation to additional liabilities were contained in CPR 44.15, CPR 44 PD 19 and CPR 47 PD 32. These were replaced by substitution as part of the general substitution of CPR 44–48[16] and have no effect in relation to retainers entered into on or after 1 April, 2013, save in relation to insolvency, publication and privacy and mesothelioma claims where they continue for as long as such claims are exempt from the general prohibition on recovery of additional liabilities[17]. However, they have continued effect in relation to pre-commencement funding arrangements[18] (as do the former provisions of CPR

[16] Effected by r.16 of the Civil Procedure (Amendment Rules) 2013 (SI 2013/262).

[17] See CPR 48.2(i)(b). The insolvency exception will end with effect from the 1 April. 2016.

[18] As defined in CPR 48.2, which broadly means a CFA or ATE policy entered into prior to 1 April, 2013 (or a CCFA where, in the individual case in which costs are being considered, work was begun in relation to that case under the CCFA prior to 1 April, 2013).

43–48 generally, for example in relation to the between the parties assessment of success fees) by virtue of CPR 48.1.

Accordingly, care must be taken in the unlikely event, for example, of a claimant who entered into a pre-April 2013 CFA where a letter before claim has not yet been sent, or, perhaps more likely, where proceedings have not yet been issued, to ensure that the proper notification is given as required by the 'old' rules. Similarly, in the more common situation of assessment of costs where the funding arrangement is a pre-April 2013 CFA (or there is a pre-April 2013 ATE premium) the requirements of old CPR 47 PD 32 must be observed if the between the parties recoverability of the additional liabilities is not to be jeopardised.

The confusion which surrounded the correct interpretation of the 'new' CPR 3.9 following the Court of Appeal's decision in *Mitchell*[19] pending clarification in *Denton*[20] led to a much stricter approach being taken towards any breaches of these notification requirements and the application of old CPR 44.3B.

That strict approach has now been moderated in light of *Denton*, as seen, for example, in *Caliendo*[21]. The existence of the strict approach did result in some clarification of the scope of the sanctions under CPR 44.3B being provided in *Long v Value Properties Ltd*,[22] which may be material in cases of such breaches in relation to pre-April 2013 funding arrangements.[23]

Implementation issues

There have only been a limited number of reported cases in relation to the implementation of the changes to the structure of CFAs, though that may largely be because it will take some time for any post LASPO CFA cases involving any substantial amounts of costs to come before the court. 2–08

However, there are a number of latent issues. Key amongst those are issues relating to changes of funding around the time of the introduction of LASPO and in relation to the transfer and assignment of CFAs.

In relation to the former, the core issue relates to the reasonableness of claimants incurring additional liabilities—and seeking to recover the same from an unsuccessful opponent—where those claimants had available to them an alternative form of funding which would not have involved any additional liability.

Anecdotally, there were a substantial number of claims, particularly clinical negligence claims, where there was a change of funding—commonly from public funding to a CFA/ATE arrangement—shortly prior to 1 April, 2013.

---

[19] *Mitchell v News Group Newspapers Ltd* [2013] EWCA Civ 1537; [2014] 1 WLR 795.

[20] *Denton v T H White Ltd* [2014] EWCA Civ 906; [2014] 1 WLR 3926.

[21] *Caliendo v Mischon De Reya LLP* [2014] EWHC 3414.

[22] *Long v Value Properties Ltd* [2014] EWHC 2981.

[23] In that case, it was made clear that the sanction of disallowance of the success fee under CPR 44.3B(1)(d) for late service of the relevant information in relation to the CFA in detailed assessment proceedings was limited to the loss of the success fee for the period of the default, rather than there being a disallowance of the entire success fee for the whole case, as had previously generally been thought to be the case.

In principle, such cases should not involve any new issue of principle. The issue of the choice of funding is one of reasonableness and the broad principles have been relatively well established since *Sarwar*[24]. However, LASPO and the number of cases involving a change of funding in early 2013 appear to have thrown the issue into sharp focus and it may be that appellate cases will shed new light on precisely how the test of reasonableness should be approached in these cases and, in particular, whether the issue is one to be viewed purely objectively, or whether there is a subjective element. One of the first reported cases on these issues is *Surrey*[25] in which Master Rowley concluded that the claimant's change of funding was unreasonable, primarily because of an apparent failure by the claimant's solicitors to provide sufficient advice to the claimant—in particular as to the availability of the 10 per cent enhancement on general damages—to allow the claimant to provide an 'informed' consent to the switch. it is understood an appeal will be heard sometime in 2016.

In relation to the transfer and assignment of CFAs, the common scenario where this occurs is where a personal injury claimant has entered into a pre-commencement funding arrangement, as defined in s.44(6) of LASPO, but wishes to change firms after that date. By virtue of the strict wording of the transitional provision, the claimant will not be entitled to QOCS protection if he enters into a new, post-LASPO agreement with the new firm of solicitors. Equally, if he enters into such a new agreement, the success fee under the new agreement will be irrecoverable and the claimant may be exposed to a deduction from any damages in respect of that success fee.

The decision of a regional costs judge in the case of *Casseldine*[26] suggests that there may be some scope for a more purposive interpretation, whereby, provided the court can be satisfied that, despite having entered into a pre-commencement funding arrangement, there were no circumstances whereby the claimant, if successful, would have been able to seek recovery of an additional liability from the opponent, the court will allow the claimant the benefit of QOCS protection despite the earlier CFA. However, the correctness of the reasoning in *Casseldine* is open to some doubt until such matters are the subject of higher judicial consideration. Moreover, the ratio in *Casseldine* itself appears to be limited to the relatively unusual situation where the first firm of solicitors 'walked away' from the case, rather than some of the more common scenarios where clients change firms.

An equally common scenario, capable of causing difficulties with the transitional provisions, is where a firm of solicitors is changing status (for example from a partnership to LLP or ABS), or wishes to transfer a number of clients to another firm.

Perhaps the most common questions in this scenario are whether the CFAs

[24] *Sarwar v Alam* [2002] 1 WLR 125.
[25] *Surrey v Barnet & Chase Farm Hospitals NHS Trust* [2015] EWHC B16 (Costs).
[26] *Casseldine v Diocese of Llandaff Board for Social Responsibility* (unreported, Cardiff County Court, 3 July, 2015).

(or indeed other retainers) may lawfully be assigned and, if so, whether they should be.

It is beyond the scope of this chapter to describe in detail the fundamental legal principles relating to assignment and novation. It suffices to note that the key argument revolves around the differences between novation and assignment. Novation results in the original agreement coming to an end, as a matter of law, and a new contract on the same terms and relating to the same subject matters, coming into being between one of the original parties and the new party, with the other original contracting party being released from the contract. Whereas assignment merely transfers the existing rights under a contract from one party (the assignor) to another (the assignee). **2–09**

Accordingly, it is contended that if a CFA is capable of assignment, then the effect of that assignment is that the CFA continues. It would follow, therefore, that the assignment of a pre-April 2013 CFA from, say, one solicitor to another post-April 2013 would result in the CFA still being regarded as a 'pre-commencement funding arrangement' for the purposes of s.44(6) of LASPO, CPR 48.2 and all other related provisions. Accordingly, the recoverability of the success fee would be preserved.

The correctness of that argument is likely to be the subject to detailed challenge and, ultimately, higher appellate authority. At the time of writing, there is some authority, principally Rafferty J's decision in *Jenkins*[27], which supports the principle that a CFA is capable of assignment and does not offend the usual principle that only the benefit (in general under a CFA, the solicitor's right to payment) and not the burden (in general under a CFA, the solicitor's obligation to perform) can be assigned.

However, the weight of that authority is open to question, particularly since Rafferty J expressly stated that she was not laying down any issue of general principle, but was merely deciding the case on its particular facts. In addition, it is open to argument whether the principle of conditional benefit and burden was properly analysed in that case (particularly in light of the Court of Appeal's comments in *Davies v Jones*[28]) and whether all issues in relation to the law of assignment were fully raised or argued.

It is still relatively early stages in respect of these arguments. In *Jones v Spire Healthcare Ltd*[29], a Regional Costs Judge concluded that he was not bound by Jenkins, because the case before him concerned a different factual scenario and reason for change of solicitor than in Jenkins. He went on to hold that assignment of the benefit and burden under a CFA was not possible. That decision is under appeal, though at present only to Circuit Judge level. A number of other similar cases are understood to be in progress or awaiting decisions and resolution of the issue is likely to require a decision at the Court of Appeal level or above, which hopefully will occur before too long.

[27] *Jenkins v Young Brothers Transport Ltd* [2006] EWHC 151 (QB).
[28] *Davies v Jones* [2009] EWCA Civ 1164.
[29] Liverpool County Court, 11 September 2015, unreported.

Similar difficulties may arise in the context of the need to appoint a Litigation Friend in cases where the claimant has entered into a pre-April 2013 CFA but has subsequently been found to lack capacity, or where the claimant was a child when a pre-April 2013 CFA was entered into with a Litigation Friend, but the claimant has subsequently attained the age of 18.

It was hoped that some general guidance on these latter issues might be forthcoming in the Court of Appeal's decision in *Blankley*, but in the end it focused on the narrow issue of whether the claimant's supervening incapacity had caused the CFA in question to be terminated by reason of frustration because the claimant could not give instructions to the solicitor.[30]

Among the issues to be looked at by the Civil Justice Council working group on the impact of the Jackson reforms is the question of problems arising out of changes in the client's or the lawyer's status or basis of instruction in cases which straddle April 2013. No recommendations in this regard have yet been made and considerable uncertainty remains in this area.

After the Event Insurance

2–10 Section 46 of LASPO introduced s.58C of the Courts & Legal Services Act 1990 with the effect of repealing s.29 of the Access to Justice Act 1999 (and s.47 LASPO repealed the similar s.30 of the 1999 Act in relation to the 'notional' premiums charged by bodies such as trade unions). These legislative changes had the effect of preventing the between the parties recovery of ATE premiums where such policies were taken out on or after 1 April, 2013.

Again, this ties in (in personal injury claims) with the introduction of QOCS, in that the existence of a pre-LASPO ATE policy prevents the claimant being eligible for QOCS protection.

As with success fees, an exception exists allowing for continued between the parties recoverability in mesothelioma, publication and privacy and insolvency proceedings, such exceptions being subject to the same process of review and possible revocation in due course (with the insolvency exception now being confirmed as ending with effect from the 1 April, 2016).

The wording of the general transitional provision, however, is different from that in relation to CFAs, in that pursuant to s.58C of the 1990 Act, the amendments (i.e. the revocation of between the parties recoverability) do not apply "in relation to a costs order made in favour of a party who took out a costs insurance policy in relation to the proceedings before [1 April, 2013]".

Accordingly, the test is whether 'a' costs insurance policy was taken out in relation to the proceedings prior to 1 April, 2013. The apparent effect is that the amendments (that is to say, the revocation of recoverability) do not apply at all where this is the case. It seems open to argument, therefore, that provided the claimant has taken out a single pre-April 2013 ATE policy, the claimant is entitled to seek to recover between the parties any (reasonably incurred) ATE premiums for any subsequent policies. This was probably not

[30] *Blankley v Central Manchester Children's University Hospital NHS Trust* [2015] EWHC 18.

the intention and places too great a stress on the reference to 'a' costs insurance policy.

However, the precise limits of the section and whether, for example, it is possible to recover the costs of post-April 2013 'top up' or further staged premiums in respect of a pre-April 2013 policy—or indeed of an entirely discrete further policy provided 'a' policy of some type was taken out prior to April 2013—will no doubt be considered in detail in forthcoming cases.

A saving provision relating to the continued between the parties recoverability of ATE premiums in very limited circumstances in Clinical Negligence claims was provided by s.58C of the 1990 Act and the Recovery of Costs Insurance Premiums in Clinical Negligence Proceedings (No.2) Regulations 2013 (finally laid before Parliament four days before the implementation date after a flawed earlier provision). **2–11**

These allow for the continued recovery between the parties of ATE premiums in clinical negligence claims in certain circumstances, namely where:

- the claim has a value in excess of £1,000; and
- the insured risk relates to liability for the cost of an expert's report on issues of liability or causation.

The recoverable premium is limited to the cost of such a limited policy or, if the policy is wider, to the part of the premium that can be identified as relating to that part of the risk identified above.

The process of implementation of the clinical negligence exception was not a smooth one, with the original statutory instrument being found to be unhelpfully drafted, and possibly ultra vires. The second version does not appear to have addressed all of these problems and, in particular, there appears to be a tension between the authority delegated to the Lord Chancellor to make provision for continued recoverability, under s.58C of the 1990 Act, and the precise provision he has made under the 2013 Regulations. Some of these issues were addressed by the court in *Nokes*[31] and have been further addressed in an appeal in a County Court appellate case named *Axelrod*[32], heard in December 2015, in respect of which judgment is awaited at the time of writing. Further cases seeking to resolve some of the ambiguities created by the implementation provisions are likely.

More generally, the changes in relation to between the parties recoverability of ATE premiums were on a more limited basis and, unlike the CFA and DBA provisions, related only to the removal of the between the parties recoverability issue and not to a fundamental change to the nature and terms of such arrangements.

General implementation issues are most likely to relate to matters such as whether a further premium paid after 1 April, 2013 to 'top up' an existing

31 *Nokes v Heart of England Foundation NHS Trust* [2015] EWHC B6.
32 *Axelrod v University Hospitals of Leicester NHS Trust* (Liverpool County Court).

policy should be regarded as part of the same pre-commencement funding arrangement (thereby being recoverable) or whether it should be regarded as a new policy.

In addition there will be issues arising out of what was, anecdotally, a rush to incept a substantial number of policies at the very end of March 2013. These might include issues such as the adequacy of funding advice given to claimants in such hurried circumstances, the suitability of the premium, and the provision of proper notification of funding, etc[33].

Such matters probably do not raise any new issues of principle and are likely to fall to be decided on established, pre-April 2013 principles. That said, it could be argued that the revocation of the between the parties recovery of additional liabilities and the recognition that the previous scheme was flawed may, as time goes on, lead to a more robust judicial approach when it comes to questioning the reasonableness of ATE premiums in particular (and it might be said that such an approach has already started to become evident even prior to April 2013). Cases such as *Redwing*[34], *Black Horse*[35] and *Hahn*[36] offer some limited support for this theory.

Coventry v Lawrence[37]

2–12 The pending hearing and decision in this case was a cause of much uncertainty at the time of the previous edition. Judgment was handed down on 22 July, 2015 and in light of the majority, 5:2, decision that the pre-April 2013 funding arrangements did not breach Article 6 of the European Convention on Human Rights, the judgment may now be relegated to a footnote in the history of the pre-April 2013 regime. However, as Lord Justice Jackson noted in the Mustill lecture, supra, there may be issues, in particular in relation to those instances where between the parties recoverability has been preserved post April 2013, where arguments in this regard remain. Moreover, whether the European Court of Human Rights would agree with the Supreme Court's analysis, particularly given its decision in the *Naomi Campbell* case[38], if given the opportunity, means that there is some residual uncertainty.

Damages-Based Agreements (DBAs)

2–13 The introduction of DBAs was long awaited. They had, of course, been in existence for some time in relation to employment tribunal matters and the use of a contingency fee arrangement was permissible under s.57 of the Solicitors Act 1974 in relation to non-contentious business matters. The proposed introduction of a regulated form of arrangement whereby the solicitor's payment

[33] See, for example, *Surrey v Barnet & Chase Farm Hospitals NHS Trust* [2015] EWHC B16 – under appeal at the time of writing – and a number of similar cases dealing with issues of funding which are presently awaiting judgment or appeal.
[34] *Redwing Construction Ltd v Wishart* [2011] EWHC 19 (TCC).
[35] *Kelly v Black Horse Ltd* [2013] EWHC B17 (Costs).
[36] *Hahn v NHS England* (unreported, Liverpool County Court, 3 August 2015.)
[37] *Coventry v Lawrence* [2015] UKSC 50.
[38] *MGN Ltd v United Kingdom* (2011) 53 EHRR 195.

would be directly proportionate to the client's recovery, in general litigation, was seen by many, if not all, as a positive step in widening the available forms of funding.

Unfortunately, the precise method of their introduction has been widely criticised as being too narrow and restrictive, with the result that to date there appears to have been very limited use of DBAs in circumstances where they were prohibited prior to April 2013.

The widening of the permissibility of DBAs in contentious business was achieved by virtue of s.45 of LASPO, amending the existing s.58AA of the 1990 Act, with effect from 1 April, 2013. By virtue of s.58AA(4), a DBA is now permissible in all matters save those which cannot presently be subject of an enforceable CFA (primarily criminal and family matters).

As with CFAs, a DBA must comply with the conditions imposed by the permitting statute. If it fails to do so, it is unenforceable. Again, as with CFAs, an exception exists for agreements which fall under s.57 of the Solicitors Act 1974, that is to say Non Contentious Business Agreements.

Beyond the basic requirements of the agreement being in writing and not relating to prohibited classes of proceedings, the amended s.58AA provides that for such an agreement to be enforceable it must comply with the requirements of the DBA Regulations 2013. It is therein that the problems are said to lie.

Jackson LJ had proposed that in order for a DBA to be 'valid', there **2–14**
should be a requirement for a client to receive specific and independent advice before it was signed.[39] The recommendation was not implemented—primarily it would appear out of concerns that it might lead to a return to the sort of between the parties arguments over enforceability and adequacy of advice which had been a feature of the Conditional Fee Agreement Regulations 2000. However, there are certain requirements for the provision of information in relation to DBAs in employment matters (set out in reg.5 of the DBA Regulations 2013). Presumably, such advice is thought to be more desirable and, perhaps more importantly, less likely to lead to indemnity principle arguments of the type which were notoriously prevalent in relation to CFAs generally as a result, in particular, of the specific advice requirements under the (now revoked) CFA Regulations 2000, given the limited scope for between the parties costs recovery before the Employment Tribunal.

The basic provisions in relation to DBAs in employment matters have not changed and the remainder of this section will focus on the requirements in non-employment matters.

The effect of the 2013 Regulations is that a solicitor is entitled to agree with his client that he shall be paid by way of a percentage of the damages ultimately recovered by the client. Such 'payment', as defined by reg.1 of the 2013 Regulations, must be net of any between the parties costs recovered

[39] Final Report, p.133.

or recoverable by way of profit costs or counsel's fees (reg.4)—the so called 'Ontario' model. In other words, the solicitor cannot enjoy the benefit of both the 'payment' from the client and the between the parties costs recovery, but must allow such between the parties costs recovery to reduce the client's liability to pay the 'payment'.

In addition, the agreement can allow for the solicitor to charge disbursements to the client (other than counsel's fees) on top of the percentage fee (with credit being given against that charge for any between the parties costs recovered or recoverable in respect of such disbursements) (reg.4(1)(b)).

The 2013 Regulations include a requirement for any DBA (other than one in relation to employment proceedings) to contain a cap on the amount of the client's recovered damages which may be used to pay the solicitor's fee under the DBA. In proceedings generally the sum is 50 per cent (inclusive of VAT) (reg.4(3)—and unlike the CFA Order, the Regulation does expressly mention VAT).

2–15 In personal injury claims there is a stricter limit, with the cap being restricted to 25 per cent of the same classes of damages as apply in relation to the cap on a success fee under a CFA, namely general damages and damages for pecuniary loss other than future pecuniary loss (reg.4(2)).

This latter restriction immediately illustrates a potential, though not necessarily insuperable, obstacle to the use of a DBA in personal injury litigation. With a post-April 2013 CFA, the success fee is capped at 25 per cent of the prescribed classes of damages. However, there is no cap on base fees (other than their reasonableness) and counsel's fee can be charged in addition to the base fees and success fee (though counsel's success fee is probably included in the cap).

With a DBA, however, the total fee, including counsel's fee, is capped at 25 per cent of the same classes of damages. Whilst there will be cases where the figures are such that a DBA is still attractive, the most valuable heads of loss in a large personal injury case are usually future losses (care, loss of earnings, etc.) and not past losses or general damages and the limitation of the total fee under a DBA to a fraction of those heads of loss will limit their attractiveness and suitability in all but a small minority of cases.

This is before any more general obstacles to the use of a DBA are considered, as to which see below.

Between the parties costs recovery

2–16 CPR 44.18 provides that the fact of a DBA will not affect between the parties costs recovery and that between the parties costs shall be assessed in accordance with CPR 44.3. The rule itself is somewhat vague in this regard, and the limited use of DBAs to date means that its scope has yet to be properly tested.

However, it is generally understood that it is intended to result in between the parties costs being assessed on a 'conventional' basis, that is to say on the basis of an hourly rate and time spent basis.

What is clear is that the between the parties costs will not be assessed by reference to the 'payment' the client is liable to pay the solicitor under the DBA save that, as noted below, such payment may act as an indemnity principle 'cap' on the opponent's total liability. Accordingly, clients entering into a DBA must be made expressly aware that there is likely to be a fundamental difference (and often a shortfall) between the payment due under the DBA and the equivalent sum in profit costs an opponent is likely to be ordered to pay if the claim succeeds.

The between the parties assessment will involve the court identifying a 'notional' hourly rate where none has been contractually agreed, much as occurs in between the parties assessments in publicly funded cases.

It also means that a solicitor who believed that acting on a DBA would allow the firm to avoid having to conduct detailed time recording would be wrong. Not only would a lack of detailed time recording hamper any between the parties costs recovery, it could be very unfortunate were the DBA to be challenged on a solicitor–client basis.

As noted previously, the indemnity principle has not been disapplied, despite Jackson LJ's recommendation. This is expressly reflected in CPR 44.18(2)(b) which recites that a party may not recover more by way of costs than the total amount payable under the DBA.

Accordingly, if the 'notional/conventional' between the parties costs in a case exceed the sum payable under a DBA, then the between the parties costs recovery will be limited to the DBA sum. However, if the 'notional/conventional' between the parties costs are less than the DBA sum, then because the assessment is conducted on that 'notional' basis, the between the parties costs recovery will be limited to that conventional sum.

Problems with DBAs

Some issues have already been highlighted above. Specific problems include: 2–17

- The wording of para.4 of the DBA Regulations 2013, and in particular the definition of 'payment' appears to prevent the use of hybrid DBAs. That is to say, it appears to prevent the agreement allowing the legal representative to be paid anything by way of profit costs other than the percentage share of damages if the case is won or nothing if the case is lost. Hybrid or discounted DBAs would allow for the solicitor to charge a low hourly rate win or lose, with a percentage share of damages on success. Discounted CFAs have been popular in commercial litigation, where a client is able and prepared to pay something win or lose, but wishes to share the risk with the solicitor. Hybrid DBAs would potentially be popular for offering the same opportunity whilst tying the reward directly to the amount of recovery. The present drafting appears to prevent such agreements and the wording of the regulations appears to mean that such agreements would be unenforceable. It is a moot point whether this is a deliberate decision, but it would appear to be so. That impression was emphasised by the fact that when asking the Civil Justice Council to consider some technical revisions to the DBA Regulations in November 2014 the Ministry of Justice appeared to rule out revising them to permit (or to make clear that they already permitted) hybrid DBAs. The Master of the Rolls referred to the Government having decided to 'not permit hybrid DBAs'.[40] Lord Justice Jackson called for the Government to rethink its position in this regard and gave cogent reasons why the position should be reconsidered.[41]

- This also appears to create a problem with using a DBA in a form similar to a CFA 'lite'. That is to say a DBA which includes a provision allowing for the solicitor to retain between the parties costs in full in the event that the between the parties costs payable on the hypothetical hourly rate/time spent basis (the 'Ontario model') exceed the sum which would otherwise be payable under the agreement on a simple percentage of damages basis. There seems no particular reason why such an agreement should not be permissible if CFA lites are to remain permissible. It would not require an opponent to pay more than a reasonable and proportionate sum. At the same time, the prospect of enhanced between the parties recovery would facilitate the greater use of DBAs on a solicitor–client basis. However, such agreements do not presently appear to be permissible under the 2013 Regulations.
- The Regulations appear to require the legal representative's fee to be calculated only by reference to damages 'ultimately recovered' by the client (reg.1), whilst at the same time requiring the solicitor to give credit for any between the parties costs (profit costs or counsel's fees) which are 'paid or payable' to the client (reg.4). In other words, the legal representative bears the risk of the opponent's solvency, having to give credit for between the parties costs payable, even if not received, whilst only being able to charge the client his percentage fee where damages are actually received. The same applies to disbursements.
- The Regulations do not contain any provisions for payment on termination of the agreement. There appears to be nothing preventing the agreement providing that, if the client instructs another firm and subsequently wins the claim, the 'payment' under the agreement will be payable in full. However, the restriction on permitting any other form of 'payment' appears to prevent the rendering of a partial charge, on an hourly rate basis or otherwise, if the client simply 'walks away' or if the firm feels obliged to cease acting.

The limiting effect of these matters is enhanced by the continuing treatment of DBAs and CFAs in litigation as islands of legality whereby, if

[40] *http://www.judiciary.gov.uk/related-offices-and-bodies/advisory-bodies/cjc/working-parties/civil-justice-council-cjc-to-look-at-damages-based-agreements-revisions/* [Accessed 29 January, 2015].
[41] *http://www.litigationfutures.com/news/jackson-outlines-two-pronged-strategy-promote-dbas* [Accessed 29 January, 2015].

the requirements of s.58AA and s.58 respectively are not fully complied with, the agreement is unenforceable. In conjunction with the continued application of the indemnity principle this exposes the solicitor to a risk that if the DBA departs in any material fashion from the strictures of the Regulations, the agreement will be unenforceable and no payment at all will be permitted.

It is not clear to what extent these restrictions were intended (though it now seems clear that the continued non permissibility of hybrid DBAs, at least, is intentional). However, the combined effect of all of these factors has resulted in very limited use of DBAs.

Future Amendment

As mentioned above, the Civil Justice Council Working Group has been asked to look at a number of technical issues. These are: **2–18**

- dividing into two sets the existing regulations with employment tribunal regulations (as per the 2010 regime) separated from regulations for civil litigation proceedings;
- changing the regulations so that defendants will be able to use DBAs, by widening the application of the regulations where the party receives a specified financial benefit (rather than restricting them to receiving a payment);
- reviewing whether the regulations should contain provisions on terminating the DBA;
- clarifying that different forms of litigation funding cannot be used during a case when a DBA is being used to fund litigation; and
- clarifying that the lawyer's payment can only come from damages, and the payment should be a percentage of the sum ultimately received (not awarded or agreed).

The CJC's report was published in September 2015[42] and focused primarily on the issue of hybrid DBAs.

The report contains 45 recommendations, which are not repeated here. It noted that the inability to enter into what it describes as 'concurrent hybrid DBAs'— that is to say a hybrid DBA as described above, as opposed to the ability to have separate, consecutive retainers (perhaps first a conventional retainer and then a DBA) has had an 'incredibly chilling effect' on the take up of DBAs, but ultimately concluded that the introduction of such arrangements, whether generally or only in relation to certain practice areas, remained a policy decision for the Government.

Other recommendations included changes to make DBAs more available for use by Defendants, an increase in the 25 per cent DBA cap for personal

[42] The Damages-Based Agreements Reform Project Drafting And Policy Issues—*https://www.judiciary.gov.uk/wp-content/uploads/2015/09/dba-reform-project-cjc-aug-2015.pdf.*

injury claims to 50 per cent for Defendants, and greater freedom as to the 'trigger points' for payment of the DBA fee and for the effect of early termination of DBAs. The CJC's call for further modifications to try and improve the use of DBAs has been supported by the Master of the Rolls. Whether the call and recommendations will be heeded remains to be seen and no timetable has yet been set for any revision. Absent such revision DBAs are likely to remain little used.

Questions and answers

Q1. Is it possible to assign a pre LASPO Conditional Fee Agreement and to retain between the parties recoverability of success fees?

2–19 This is a complex question and the answer is uncertain. The case of *Jenkins*[43] offers some support for the argument that a CFA is capable of assignment, but is High Court appellate authority only, was decided on its own peculiar facts and may not be followed or might be capable of being distinguished in future cases. If *Jenkins* is correct, then the assignment of a CFA is at least possible in principle.

If an assignment of a CFA can validly take place then following the principle of the effect of an assignment, the existing agreement continues and accordingly there would appear to be a good argument that the assigned agreement should be regarded as being the same CFA and therefore the same 'pre-commencement funding arrangement' for the purposes of CPR 48.2 and/or s.44(6) of LASPO. However, even if the assignment is valid, there are public policy arguments which might lead a court to conclude that the agreement should not be so regarded.

These are complex issues and there will be no certainty unless and until they are resolved in an authoritative judgment.

Care needs to be taken when considering such assignments. In particular, with personal injury CFAs, if a pre-LASPO CFA 'assignment' was held not to be valid, there would be an argument that there were two CFAs, a pre-LASPO CFA and a post-LASPO CFA, on the same terms—namely the terms of the original agreement. However, standard pre-LASPO CFA terms for a personal injury CFA would not comply with the requirements for the capping of a success fee under s.58(4) of the 1990 Act and the CFA Order 2013 and it might be argued that the 'new' CFA on the 'old' terms was therefore unenforceable. This could result in all costs (and not just the success fee) under the new CFA being irrecoverable both against the client and, by virtue of the indemnity principle, between the parties.

In *Jones*, supra, the court held that it was not bound by Jenkins, because in that particular case the transfer of retainer had occurred as a result of the first firm entering administration and its cases being 'bought' by a second firm, rather than as a result of any particular desire of the individual claimant to follow a particular solicitor from firm to firm. The assignment was held not to

[43] *Jenkins v Young Brothers Transport Ltd* [2006] EWHC 151 (QB).

be valid. It was held that there was, in fact and law, a 'new', novated CFA at the date of the purported assignment. The claim was a personal injury claim and, as a result of the new CFA not containing the 'LASPO cap', the new CFA was unenforceable (see above). An appeal in *Jones* is due to be heard in December 2015. Judgment is awaited in a further case (*Budana v Leeds Teaching Hospitals NHS Trust (Hull County Court)*) and there will no doubt be others and further appeals. Given the concerns in relation to *Jenkins*, the possibility of factual and legal distinctions being drawn and the ability of judges at High Court level upwards to reach a different decision in any event, it is likely to require a decision at Court of Appeal level or higher before any degree of certainty can be introduced.

One final point to note is that there may be steps which can be taken to mitigate the risks of the sort of outcome in *Jones*, such as the use of 'fallback' retainers which only operate, for example, in the event of an assignment failing or a CFA being declared unenforceable as a result. There does not appear to have been such an arrangement in *Jones*. Such arrangements are not, themselves, entirely beyond the scope of argument, though they have been used in other areas and the use of them was supported by Sir Christopher Clarke in the High Court decision of *Forde*[44]. Such arrangements would probably need to be entered into before the case concluded[45].

Q2. What is the effect on recoverability of the success fee of assigning a pre-April 2013 CFA post-April 2013?

The general question of assignment is addressed in the previous question. 2–20
Subject to that answer, if the assignment is effective there would appear to be a strong argument that the CFA remains a pre-commencement funding arrangement and the success fee remains recoverable in principle between the parties, subject to assessment of reasonableness of the percentage in the usual way.

Q3. Is it possible to vary a pre-April 2013 CFA and still recover the success fee?

In principle, this seems possible. A variation does not change the date of the 2–21
original agreement. However, in practice it may depend on the variation. If the variation was seen in some way to offend the broad principle against the inter partes recoverability of additional liabilities incurred after 1 April, 2013 then there would be a substantial risk of it being disallowed. To take an extreme example, if the pre-April CFA had provided for a five per cent success fee, but was varied after the 1 April, 2013 to include a 100 per cent success fee on a retrospective basis, the court might well disallow the success fee, though it could probably do so (subject to the facts) on the simple basis that even if the success fee was recoverable in principle, the increase was unreasonable on a between the parties basis.

44 *Birmingham City Council v Forde* [2009] EWHC 12 (QB).
45 See *Kellar Carib West Ltd v Williams* [2004] UKPC 30.

Variation is sometimes confused with issues of construction or rectification of CFAs. Where there is some doubt as to the precise meaning of terms in a CFA, these may be resolved by reference to standard principles of construction and this simply involves identifying the true terms of the original agreement. This would have no effect on the recoverability of any success fee under the CFA. Similarly, where it can be established that the written terms do not properly record the true intention of the parties, it may be possible for the CFA to be rectified. Again, rectification is not variation—it is simply ensuring that the written document properly records the true agreed terms, and would probably not affect the recoverability of any success fee. Variation may not always be the only solution to perceived problems with a pre-April 2013 CFA.

Q4. My client instructed me prior to 1 April, 2013, but I was not able to offer a CFA until later. Is it possible to backdate the CFA to the date of first instruction?

2–22 The first point is that the use of the term 'backdating' is dangerous and has been the subject of judicial criticism. It suggests some form of deception and that the date on the written document does not reflect the date on which it was entered into. This should never happen. If an agreement is intended to have retrospective effect, it should expressly state the date on which it was entered into and expressly state the earlier date from which it is said to apply. Note also the High Court's comments in this regard in the decision of *O'Brien*[46].

As to applying a CFA retrospectively so that it can benefit from pre-LASPO principles of recoverability, this would not seem possible. Section 44(6) of LASPO provides that the amendments do not apply if the relevant CFA was 'entered into' prior to 1 April 2013. Here, the agreement would be entered into after that date, but with retrospective effect. There seems no contractual reason why the agreement would not have retrospective effect, but it would not turn the CFA into a pre-LASPO CFA and the success fee would be irrecoverable.

Q5. My client entered into a CFA prior to 1 April, 2013, but has now died. I wish to offer the personal representatives a CFA to continue the claim. Will I be able to recover the success fee?

2–23 It is a moot point whether the original CFA is automatically assigned to the personal representatives on the death of the client. Certain contracts are so assigned by operation of law on death (unless the contract provides otherwise). However, personal contracts are generally an exception to this and it is arguable whether a CFA falls into this category.

Equally, there is no reason in principle why the CFA should not expressly provide for the consequences on death of the client, including for its continuation. There is nothing preventing the (now) deceased making contractual

[46] *O'Brien v Shorrock & MIB* [2015] EWHC 1630 (QB) and see also the decision in *Pentecost v John* [2015] EWHC 1970 (QB).

provision to bind his personal representatives on his death, though such provision is rare in CFAs.

In addition, it was very common in CFAs, particularly personal injury CFAs, for the CFA to expressly provide that the agreement ended on the death of the client. The Law Society standard model prior to April 2013, expressly so provided. If such a CFA was used, then there is no need to consider whether it is arguable in law that the CFA persists, because the issue has been expressly addressed in the CFA and it does not.

In summary, therefore, there are certain circumstances, depending on the terms of the original CFA and how it is categorised by a court, where there may be arguments that the original CFA may continue in some way, though this could only be determined by reference to the specific terms of the CFA. If the CFA is a standard Law Society model (or one of the many variants based thereon) or if these specific circumstances do not apply, then any new CFA is likely to be seen to be a post-LASPO CFA and accordingly the success fee will be irrecoverable.

Q6. Is a pre-April 2013 ATE policy premium still recoverable if the policy holder changes solicitors post–April 2013? Should the policy be 'assigned' to the new firm?

An ATE policy is a contract between the claimant and the insurer. Provided 2–24
the policy is not voided or terminated by virtue of the change of solicitor (and this is often the case, particularly with policies issues by the solicitor under delegated authority) then in principle the policy remains in place and, as a pre-April 2013, the premium charged for it remains recoverable in principle between the parties.

There should be no question of 'assignment' of the policy to the new firm. Neither the new firm nor the old are likely to be parties to the contract of insurance.

Q7. If a staged premium ATE policy was incepted prior to 1 April, 2013, but the further staged premiums are only incurred after that date, will the further premiums be recoverable?

Probably. Staged premiums were a common feature of litigation and their 2–25
use had been expressly approved by the courts in cases such as *Rogers v Merthyr Tydfil CBC*.[47] Their existence and use was well known at the time of the amendment of the rules and it would have been simple for the rule to provide that only the stages incurred prior to 1 April, 2013 would be recoverable, if that had been the intention. Instead, s.58C of the 1990 Act refers to 'a policy of insurance' having been 'taken out' prior to 1 April, 2013 and the taking out of a staged policy would appear to satisfy that requirement, with the effect that subsequent premiums under the policy remain recoverable in principle.

[47] *Rogers v Merthyr Tydfil CBC* [2006] EWCA Civ 1134; [2007] 1 W.L.R. 808.

The point may be tested, however, if there has been abuse of the system with polices being incepted on a widescale basis for nominal premiums merely to get them 'on the books' prior to 1 April, 2013 and then substantial premiums being later charged when the case is properly evaluated. Whether this has occurred and how the courts will approach claims for premiums in such cases remains to be seen.

Q8. Is there a long stop date whereby a party who has entered into a pre-April 2013 funding arrangement in relation to a claim must issue proceedings?

2–26 No (save, of course, for the general law of limitation in respect of that party's claim). However, the funding arrangement must relate to the 'matter that is the subject matter of the proceedings in which the costs order is made'. Accordingly, if the claim subsequently brought is seen to relate to a different matter, then any additional liabilities will not be recoverable (and indeed there may be an issue as to what retainer in fact covers the proceedings that have been issued, with potential consequences between the parties as a result of the application of the indemnity principle and on a solicitor–client basis).

Q9. Is a notice of funding required for a Damages Based Agreement?

2–27 No. The requirements for notices of funding in (old) CPR 44 were revoked with effect from 1 April, 2013. They continue to apply in relation to pre-April 2013 funding arrangements and in the excepted cases referred to above (as do the requirements relating to provision of information about additional liabilities on detailed assessments in CPR 47 PD 32) and should be complied with fully in respect of such arrangements (see CPR 48.1). This includes the provision under the 'old' CPR 44 PD 19.3 whereby there is a requirement to provide notice of change if the information previously provided is no longer accurate. Accordingly, if there is a change in relation to a pre-April 2013 CFA or ATE which means information provided in respect of those arrangements is no longer accurate, the opposing party should be notified accordingly.

Q10. How should the success fee be calculated in a post-April 2013 CFA?

2–28 The maximum success fee remains at 100 per cent. In setting the success fee, the solicitor is entitled to have regard to those matters set out at the revoked CPR 43 PD 11.7 and 11.8. In addition, the solicitor is entitled to take into account matters such as the delay in payment under a CFA (a matter which could be used to justify the success fee on a solicitor–client basis prior to April 2013 but not on a between the parties basis). The main component of the success fee is likely to remain the risk of losing and not being paid, and in that regard the traditional 'ready reckoner' remains useful.

Ultimately, however, the issue is one of agreeing a reasonable success fee with the client in light of the terms and conditions of the CFA, the risks to which it exposes the solicitor of not being paid their base fees in whole or part, any additional financial burden placed on the solicitor, such as the arrangements for paying disbursements and the likely delay in payment overall, and the application of these matters to the facts of the case.

It is important to explain the success fee clearly and properly to the client and to ensure their informed agreement. It is vital that the client is informed that the success fee is not recoverable between the parties in any circumstances, even if the claim is won, and will remain payable by the client.

Q11. If the solicitor has entered into a pre-April 2013 CFA, but counsel's CFA with the solicitor postdates April 2013, is counsel's success fee recoverable between the parties?

It has been suggested in some quarters that this is the case. The point is proba- 2–29
bly arguable. However, the wording of s.44(6) refers to the between the parties recovery of a success fee under a CFA not being prevented if the agreement was entered into before 1 April, 2013. It would seem to fit with the spirit and intent of the changes and the wording of the statute (and CPR 48.2) that each agreement is looked at individually. The solicitor's success fee would be recoverable in principle, but counsel's would (probably) not be.

Q12. I wish to enter into a CFA with my client whereby in addition to the success fee being capped as required by s.58 of the Courts & Legal Services Act 1990 and the CFA Order 2013, the total costs payable under the agreement will also be capped as a percentage of the damages. I have been told that this means my agreement is a contingency fee agreement, or DBA, and must comply with the DBA Regulations 2013. Is this correct?

No, it would appear not. As a matter of pure terminology, any agreement 2–30
where the payment depends on the outcome of the case is probably a form of contingency fee agreement. However, that loose terminology has been replaced by the specific terminology used in s.58 and s.58AA.

A CFA whereby the fees payable under the CFA are not calculated by reference to the damages awarded, but whereby there is an overall cap on the amount that can be paid by reference to the damages is a CFA. It is not a DBA. The key distinction is that the cap is precisely that. If the fees payable are less than the cap, then the fees payable are those fees, as calculated. The cap merely operates as an overall limit, rather than as the method of calculation of the fees.

A DBA, by contrast, is an agreement where the fee payable is determined as a percentage of the damages recovered. It is not a cap, but rather the primary method of determination of the applicable fee.

Prior to the introduction of recoverable success fees, the Law Society model CFA used to provide for a cap on the success fee payable under the CFA. The new provisions for personal injury CFAs operate on a similar model. The agreements remain CFAs and this principle applies even if the capping effect is extended beyond the success fee to the fees generally.

Q13. What is the effect on the success fee where a CFA relating to a group claim was entered into before 1 April, 2013, but some of the claimants were added after that date?

2–31 The answer to this is unclear. The transitional provisions in relation to the recoverability of success fees in s.44 of LASPO are statutory provisions and do not admit of a discretion (indeed, their express effect is to remove any discretion to allow a success fee in respect of cases covered by s.44).

Accordingly, and despite the possible temptation to do so, a court managing a GLO probably cannot simply exercise a discretion to decide how to treat such a situation (for example by reference to s.51 Senior Courts Act 1981) but is limited to considering the particular CFA and how it interacts with the provisions of s.44(6).

Section 44(6) appears to require the court to look not merely at the date of the CFA but at whether the CFA was entered into for the purposes of providing services to a specific person in relation to the subject matter of the claim or, if not entered into for a specific person (for example, a CCFA), whether services were provided, before 1 April, 2013, to the specific person in whose favour the costs order has been made.

The CCFA analogy appears the most apt here and there must be a substantial likelihood that the later joining claimants will be held not to be able to recover the success fee in respect of their claims. This may involve some question of a pro rata division of any success fee payable on common costs. The quid pro quo would be that the later joining claimants would benefit from QOCS (if it is a personal injury claim).

However, alternative approaches are possible and it is conceivable, given that the potential claimants in a GLO could be seen as being a limited and identifiable class of persons, that a court might conclude that the test under CPR 44.6(a) was satisfied in respect of all claimants when the CFA was first entered into and accordingly a success fee is recoverable in respect of all claimants.

The precise outcome will be heavily affected by the terms of the CFA, the precise circumstances of the case, the terms of any related documentation, such as costs sharing agreements, and the court's approach to the interpretation of s.44(6), which at present is uncertain.

Q.14. I currently have an insolvency case on a CFA with a success fee and have ATE insurance in place. I have not yet issued. If the Government removes the exemption from LASPO for insolvency related cases, presumably the success fee and premium will still be recoverable from the other side if the claim is successful even if I haven't issued before the exemption is removed?

2–32 The answer to this is largely covered by **Q.8**. The key date is the date on which the funding arrangement was entered into, provided it properly relates to the claim that was issued. It has now been confirmed that the insolvency exception will end with effect from the 1 April, 2016. Whilst it cannot be ruled out entirely that the Government will implement some different form of transitional provision from that which applies and applied in respect of all other cases in April 2013, there seems no good reason to believe that this will happen. Accordingly, and assuming that the same transitional provisions are adopted, provided the CFA and ATE are incepted before the date fixed for the ending of recoverability (1 April, 2016, therefore on or before 31 March, 2016), the additional liabilities will continue to be recoverable.

As noted in the commentary above, in any insolvency case care should be taken to ensure that the case falls within the narrow scope of the exemption. Not all 'insolvency' cases will.

Q.15. What exactly is a hybrid DBA, and what is the difference between a concurrent hybrid DBA and a sequential hybrid DBA?

There is no statutory definition of a hybrid DBA. It is a term that has developed amongst practitioners. It is broadly understood to refer to a DBA which provides for some element of payment to the solicitor other than the pure, all or nothing, contingent payment anticipated by reg.4 of the DBA Regulations 2013. Perhaps the closest comparator is with a discounted CFA, where the solicitor receives an element of payment, whether or not the case is won or lost, but with a higher payment in the event of success. Whilst the issue is not totally closed to argument, the DBA Regulations appear to prevent a DBA from operating in this way. **2–33**

A sequential hybrid DBA is generally understood to refer to the situation where the solicitor initially agrees some form of non DBA retainer, but then agrees at a later stage to switch to a DBA arrangement. The DBA arrangement might retrospectively cover all work done, or may be limited only to future work. In either case, because the DBA itself does not provide for any payment to the solicitor other than the contingent payment in respect of the work it covers, it is not thought to fall foul of the apparent prohibition on hybrid arrangements under the Regulations.

A concurrent hybrid DBA is the sort of DBA described at the start of this answer – that is to say one that provides for both the contingent DBA payment and some other form of payment under a single agreement. For the reasons given, it is generally understood that such arrangements are not permitted. The inability to enter into such arrangements is colloquially understood to be one of the major reasons for the limited use of DBAs since April 2013.

Q.16. Where a CFA in one of the excepted cases (where the success fee is still recoverable) is entered into and the proceedings are issued on the same day but only served four months later and we realise that we haven't served a Notice of Funding some weeks after service, what advice would you give? For example, should a formal application seeking relief be made?

2–34 The first point to note is that the problem may be greater than indicated. Although the provisions on providing Notices of Funding, as continued in force in such cases by virtue of CPR 48.1(1), relate to the date of issue and service, it is open to argument whether it is still a requirement to provide such notice at an earlier date. The requirement to do so, contained in the previous version of the Practice Direction on Pre-Action Conduct, has not been replicated in the current version of the Practice Direction and CPR 48.1(1) does not continue the application of the old version for these purposes. Accordingly, it is not clear whether the requirement to provide notification of a relevant funding arrangement 'as soon as possible and in any event either within seven days of entering into the funding arrangement concerned or, where a claimant entered into a funding arrangement before sending a letter before claim, in the letter before claim' still applies.

Best practice would be to follow that course in any event. In the event of non-compliance with a relevant provision, best practice would be to remedy the provision as soon as the error is noted. This could be done by inviting the opponent to agree that relief from sanction should be granted in respect of any breach – where appropriate by inviting the opponent to agree that it will not take the point on assessment and that a formal application need not be made. In the event that the opponent does not agree, issue a prompt application for relief, even if it is then agreed that the hearing of the application may be adjourned pending the outcome of the claim or any detailed assessment proceedings. In some cases, where the sums at risk are substantial, it may be appropriate to proceed to determination of the application without delay.

Q.17. Is a claimant entitled to recover the success fee under his "pre 1 April, 2013" CFA from the defendant, where the claim was only commenced and the funding was only notified after 1 April 2013? Please explain why the amendment to s.58A(6) does not apply to CFAs entered into prior to 1 April, 2013, in circumstances where the funding is notified after 1 April, 2013?

2–35 Yes. The amendment to s.58(A)(6) of the Courts & Legal Services Act 1990 does not apply to CFAs entered into prior to the 1 April, 2013 by virtue of the express provision at s.44(6) LASPO – subject to satisfying the precise terms of that section.

Q.18. In the excepted cases, where a success fee is still recoverable:

- **Do you have to provide a notice of funding when issuing proceedings, even if it will be allocated to the small claims track?**
- **What date do you give in the N251 Notice of Funding when the matter is funded by a CCFA. Is it the date of the CCFA with the insurer or the date of the subsequent signed retainer with the insured client?**

The answer to the first question is 'yes' unless you are willing to accept that any additional liabilities potentially claimable from the opponent if the case succeeds are to be surrendered. Whilst, in a case likely to be allocated to the Small Claims Track, this might seem to be an inevitable consequence of the general costs limitations, there is no certainty at the time of issue that a claim will be allocated to or will remain in that track, or that there may not be circumstances under CPR 27.14 where costs might be sought despite such allocation. Accordingly, not serving an N251 may be shutting out a potential claim for additional liabilities. 2–36

In relation to the second question, the N251 requires the date of the agreement. That is the date of the CCFA.

Q.19. In a clinical negligence case, where a claimant obtains a breach and causation report and the defendant then admits liability, could the claimant recover the cost of the premium if it then obtained ATE insurance in relation to obtaining a quantum report?

Yes, in principle. The recoverability of a premium under the Recovery of Costs Insurance Premiums in Clinical Negligence Proceedings (No.2) Regulations 2013 is not contingent on whether or not the Claimant takes out some other ATE in respect of other aspects of the case. The premium for the ATE insurance in respect of the other aspects of the case would not be recoverable. 2–37

Q.20. Our client entered into a CFA and ATE insurance policy before April 2013 in relation to insolvency proceedings. Since then, another party has been added as a party to the CFA and ATE insurance policy. Are we required to notify the defendants of this variation to the CFA and ATE insurance? If so, how do we notify them and do we need to file the notice?

Assuming this case falls within the insolvency exception (which some, but not all, insolvency cases will do) then the April 2013 date is a red herring. 2–38

In relation to the addition of parties to an existing CFA, the notification requirements under the former CPR 47 PD 32.5, as preserved in operation by CPR 48.1, require notification to be given where 'a claimant [or defendant] has entered into a [relevant] funding arrangement'. Accordingly, the matter should be looked at from the perspective of each individual party. The additional party here has now entered into a relevant funding arrangement by joining the existing CFA and notice should be given by way of a fresh N251 in respect of that particular party. It may be appropriate, depending on the facts, to provide additional information to make clear, for example, the date from which the client's liability under that arrangement runs it if is otherwise unclear.

If the case is not within the insolvency exception then the later joining party will (probably) fall foul of s.58A(6) Courts & Legal Services Act 1990 and s.44(6) LASPO and will not be able to recover any additional liabilities, despite the CFA having been entered into earlier by the other party.

Q21. We act for two claimants, one of whom is insolvent. We have entered into an ATE policy and are planning to rely on the insolvency exemption to LASPO 2012 if we are successful, so that we can recover the ATE premium from the defendant. Will the fact that only one of the claimants is insolvent prevent us from relying on the insolvency exemption to LASPO 2012? If we are allowed to recover the ATE premium from the defendant, will it be reduced to 50 per cent to reflect the fact that only one of the claimants is insolvent?

2–39 This point is open to argument. The saving provision in art.4 of the Legal Aid, Sentencing and Punishment of Offenders Act 2012 (Commencement No.5 and Saving Provision) Order 2013 provides that the amendments removing recoverability of additional liabilities 'do not apply to. . .proceedings' of various types. The Order does not provide that the amendments do not apply to particular claimants.

This suggests that, provided the proceedings themselves are within the exception, any of the parties to the proceedings may rely on that exception, regardless of whether they are one of the identified classes of legal persons referred to in the Order.

However, the underlying premise in the exception appears to have been to allow particular office holders and companies being wound up or entering into administration to benefit from the continued availability of funding arrangements with recoverable additional liabilities. Accordingly, a purposive construction of the Order may exclude parties other than those identified within the Order from its operation.

If one party is excluded from the operation of the exemption, it will not necessarily follow that only 50 per cent (or indeed as much as 50 per cent) of the premium will be recoverable. It may be that the remaining party is able to show that the all or the majority of the cost of the premium would have been incurred by it in any event and that it is liable for that premium in full (whether jointly and severally with the other party or otherwise). The precise outcome is likely to be fact dependent.

Q.22. If a claimant with a pre-1 April, 2013 ATE insurance policy is successful at first instance, an appeal is granted and a top-up of the ATE premium (after 1 April, 2013) is required to cover the appeal, is the post-1 April, 2013 ATE top-up premium recoverable from the other side if the appeal is successful?

2–40 This is open to argument. However, in light of the terms of s.46(3) LASPO and the Court of Appeal's decision in *Hawksford Trustees*[48] which held that appeals were to be regarded as separate proceedings for the purposes of s.20 Access to Justice Act 1999, it seems highly likely that the appeal would be regarded as separate proceedings. If that is correct, a post-April 2013 premium in respect of an ATE policy for that appeal would not fall

[48] *Hawksford Trustees Jersey Ltd v Stella Global UK Ltd* [2012] EWCA Civ 987.

within the transitional provisions under s.46(3) and therefore would be irrecoverable.

Q.23. Do you think the exceptional circumstances which applied in *Jenkins v Young Brothers Transport* to allow the assignment of a CFA might apply in the following circumstances: One part of an LLP was trading under the name of SS until the LLP demerged, at which point the SS business and trading name was transferred to SL Ltd. The LLP continued to trade as a separate entity, but the SRA has treated SL Ltd as a successor practice rather than a new practice. Can we or should we:

- **Enter into new CFAs with all our clients (in which case how will costs incurred prior to the transfer be dealt with and, in particular, what will happen to any recoverable success fees under pre-April 2013 CFAs)?**
- **Novate or assign the existing CFAs?**
- **Rely on having told our clients of the change of legal entity?**

The issue of *Jenkins* is covered in some detail in the main text. In the instant case, there would appear to be a transfer of retainers from one legal entity (the old LLP, trading in part as SS) to another (SL Ltd). If the retainers were assigned, then whether such assignment is effective will depend on the outcome of the arguments identified in the main text. Which of the identified courses of action would be best on the facts of the individual case is a matter of detailed advice which is beyond the scope of this text. 2–41

Q.24. I note that insolvency proceedings are excluded from ss.44 and 46 of LASPO 2012 where proceedings in England and Wales brought by:

- **A person acting in the capacity of a liquidator of a company in creditors' voluntary liquidation (CVL) or compulsory liquidation; a trustee in bankruptcy; or an administrator.**
- **A company that is in: CVL; compulsory liquidation; or administration.**

What is the situation if you act for an insolvency practitioner outside the jurisdiction (the insolvent company also being outside the jurisdiction) who is bringing a claim in England and Wales against a company based in England and Wales for monies owed. If you enter into a CFA with the client in these circumstances, will the success fee be recoverable from the other side if your client is successful?

The situation described appears to fall outside the scope of art.4 of the Legal Aid, Sentencing and Punishment of Offenders Act 2012 (Commencement No.5 and Saving Provision) Order 2013. Accordingly, any additional liabilities are unlikely to be recoverable. This will therefore be unaffected by the ending of the insolvency exception with effect from 1 April, 2016. 2–42

Q.25. What are the rules on recoverability of success fees in a defamation matter and, assuming that recoverability is allowed, does the success fee have to be capped in any way?

2–43 By virtue of art.4(b) of the Legal Aid, Sentencing and Punishment of Offenders Act 2012 (Commencement No. 5 and Saving Provision) Order 2013 the commencement of the provisions removing the recoverability of additional liabilities is suspended in respect of publication and privacy proceedings. Accordingly, success fees are recoverable in principle in such cases in the same way as before April 2013.

There is no statutory provision imposing a cap on the success fee other than the 100 per cent maximum percentage set by Lord Chancellor pursuant to s.58(4)(c) and art.4 of the Conditional Fee Agreements Order 2000 (SI 2000/823).

Q.26. Given that success fees in CFAs entered into from 1 April, 2013 are not recoverable in English civil litigation (apart from in the excepted cases), are they recoverable in arbitrations? Nothing in the Arbitration Act or LCIA Rules appears to preclude an arbitrator awarding a success fee under a CFA.

2–44 It is entirely correct that neither the Arbitration Act 1996 nor the rules of any of the main institutions deal directly with the issue of the recoverability of success fees.

The lawfulness of such arrangements will be determined by reference to the law of the country in which the arrangement is entered into, the law of the place of arbitration and the law of the country where any award (including costs) would be enforced.

Assuming the question relates to whether a success fee would be awarded in principle in what might loosely be termed an 'English' arbitration, following *Benaim UK Ltd v Davies Middleton & Davies Ltd* [2004] EWHC 737 (TCC) it was generally accepted that such additional liabilities may be awarded in principle. However, whether such an award would be made in practice and, if so, whether the amount awarded would be at the level sought is very much within the discretion of the tribunal and in practice tends to be far less certain than would be the position in court proceedings.

Following the LASPO changes it is strongly arguable that success fees are no longer recoverable in arbitrations. Section 58A(4) of the Courts & Legal Services Act 1990 makes clear that the reference to proceedings under s.58 is wide enough to include an arbitration. Pursuant to the amended s.58(6) of the Act, 'a costs order made in proceedings [which appears to include an arbitration] may not include provision requiring the payment by one party of all or part of a success fee'. Accordingly, and subject to the transitional provisions, there would appear to be a strong case for contending that success fees are no longer recoverable within arbitrations within the English and Welsh jurisdictions.

Q.27. What is the authority or rule which specifies that if a DBA in a non-employment matter does not comply with the Damages-Based Agreements Regulations 2013, it will not be enforceable?

Section 58AA(2) of the Courts & Legal Services Act, which provides that a DBA relating to any matter (employment or non-employment) and which does not satisfy the conditions specified in subsection (4) shall be unenforceable. The conditions in subsection (4) include 'such other requirements as to [the DBA's] terms and conditions as are prescribed. Amongst the prescribed conditions are the relevant sections of the DBA Regulations 2013. In addition, subsection 4(b) prescribes that, if regulations so provide, the agreement must not provide for a payment about the prescribed amount or for a payment about an amount calculated in a prescribed manner. The DBA Regulations 2013 contains prescriptions of this kind which must therefore be complied with if the agreement is not to be unenforceable by force of clear and unambiguous primary statutory legislation. 2–45

Q.28. Under the DBA Regulations 2013, a party can recover costs from the other side based on normal costs recovery principles, but subject to the indemnity principle. Given then that the lawyer may not be entitled to any costs until actual recoveries are made at the end of a case, does this not cause a problem with seeking costs from the other side at interim hearings as the case progresses? Appropriate drafting of the DBA might seek to get around this but it would seem that such drafting would be a highly complex task with various pitfalls. For example, if the DBA provided that sums would immediately become due to the solicitor as and when costs are recovered from the other side, are those costs considered part of the ultimate recovery from the client and to be deducted and as a kind of payment on account, or would the solicitor be entitled to those costs plus the agreed success percentage? Wouldn't that breach the DBA Regulations?

Yes, this does cause a problem. It is one of the issues addressed by the CJC Working Group's report. For the reasons given in the question, the inclusion within the DBA of some sort of immediate right to payment may well breach the prohibition under Regulation 4 (which does not apply in employment matters) on any payment other than the specified contingency payment under the Regulations and expenses. It is one of the matters that may be addressed in any future amendment to the Regulations. 2–46

CHAPTER 3

Proportionality

Introduction

The terms of reference for the costs review conducted by Jackson LJ[1] were "to make recommendations in order to promote access to justice at proportionate cost". The need for change was acknowledged in the foreword to the final report, which stated: 3–01

> *"In some areas of civil litigation costs are disproportionate and impede access to justice. I therefore propose a coherent package of interlocking reforms, designed to control costs and promote access to justice."*

Inevitably, therefore, proportionality lies at the core of the package of reforms—it permeates into every aspect of the civil litigation process. The overriding objective has been amended to include specific reference to proportionality, costs and case management are determined by it and any assessment of costs is subject to it. Almost three years on from the April 2013 amendments to the Civil Procedure Rules, proportionality still provokes more debate, more controversy and more concern than any other aspect of the reforms. What does it mean, when does it arise, and what impact does it have on litigation?

Proportionality—the concept

Proportionality is not a new concept. Whilst the amended overriding objective[2] refers to "dealing with a case . . . at proportionate cost", the previous version, from introduction in 1999, defined "dealing with a case justly" by reference, amongst other things, to proportionate cost. However, in reality, prior to April 2013, proportionality only had a retrospective role at the conclusion of a case, at the time of the assessment of costs. Where it was suggested that the costs claimed were disproportionate, the Court of Appeal required the assessing judge to determine that issue at the outset of the assessment adopting the *Home Office v Lownds*[3] two-stage approach: 3–02

> *"In other words what is required is a two-stage approach. There has to be a global approach and an item by item approach. The global approach will indicate whether the total sum claimed is or appears to be disproportionate having particular regard to the considerations which Pt. 44.5(3) states are relevant. If the costs as a whole are not disproportionate according to that test then all that is normally required is that each item should have been reasonably incurred and the*

[1] Review of Civil Litigation Costs: Final Report, December 2009.

[2] CPR 1.1: "These Rules are a new procedural code with the overriding objective of enabling the court to deal with cases justly and at proportionate cost".

[3] *Home Office v Lownds* [2002] EWCA Civ 365.

cost for that item should be reasonable. If on the other hand the costs as a whole appear disproportionate then the court will want to be satisfied that the work in relation to each item was necessary and, if necessary, that the cost of the item is reasonable."

Immediately it is apparent that this approach does not genuinely meet the requirement of dealing with a case at proportionate cost. Even if the first stage of *Lownds* resulted in a finding that the costs were disproportionate, the court could not change the way it had dealt with the case procedurally. Instead all it could do was to reduce the amount of costs recoverable between the parties. Even this retrospective ability to reduce the recoverable costs did not lead to proportionality in its purest sense, as there was no certainty that necessarily incurred costs were proportionate—in essence the imposition of the 'necessarily incurred' test seemed more a sanction for incurring disproportionate costs than any genuine attempt to reduce the costs to a level that was proportionate. Indeed, in giving his judgment in *Lownds*, Lord Woolf had hinted at the purists' position on proportionality when commenting:

"If, because of lack of planning or due to other causes, the global costs are disproportionately high, then the requirement that the costs should be proportionate means that no more should be payable than would have been payable if the litigation had been conducted in a proportionate manner."

Something more was needed to ensure that cases are managed so that no more is spent as the case progresses than is proportionate.

Proportionality—what does it mean and when does it arise?

3–03 The 2013 reforms seek to provide that 'something more' by requiring the court to:

- deal with each case "at proportionate cost" (CPR 1.1(1));
- ensure that every case management decision is made taking account of the costs involved in each procedural step (CPR 3.17);
- set costs budgets that are proportionate (CPR 3 PD E 7.3);
- determine whether or not to grant relief from sanction by giving particular weight to the need for litigation to be conducted at proportionate cost (CPR 3.9); and
- undertake assessments of costs on the basis that only proportionate costs will be awarded, even if that means reasonably or necessarily incurred costs are disallowed. CPR 44.3(2)(a) signals the demise of the *Lownds* test at assessment, reversing the timetable for consideration of proportionality. The court will assess those costs that are reasonably incurred and reasonable in amount and, having done so, step back and determine if the resultant figure is proportionate. If it is not, then the court will reduce the costs to the sum it determines is the proportionate figure.

Of course, the court can only fulfil the functions set out above by reference to the proportionate costs for a claim. How does it determine that sum? The simple answer is by reference to CPR 44.3(5), which contains the definition of proportionate costs as follows:

> *"Costs incurred are proportionate if they bear a reasonable relationship to:*
> *(a) the sums in issue in the proceedings;*
> *(b) the value of any non monetary relief in issue in the proceedings;*
> *(c) the complexity of the litigation;*
> *(d) any additional work generated by the conduct of the paying party; and*
> *(e) any wider factors involved in the proceedings, such as reputation or public importance."*

Accordingly, the court must identify which of the factors listed in CPR 44.3(5) are relevant to any case and, having done so, relate that to a costs figure. It is this step that many critics of the new approach see as unsatisfactory. They view the process as an entirely unscientific one—as the factors do not readily equal a sum in pounds and pence. The simple answer from those proponents of the process is that there is no 'absolute' answer, but, as with many exercises of judicial discretion, there is a range of answers and, provided the discretion has been exercised properly, none within that range are wrong. This is nothing new. Indeed, if different judges were asked to assess the same bill of costs at the conclusion of a claim, the likelihood is that there would be as many different figures as there were judges assessing the bill, but, again on the proviso that those judges had properly exercised their discretion, none of the assessments would be 'wrong'.

It is for this reason that in the 15th Implementation Lecture on 29 May, 2012 the Master of the Rolls Lord Neuberger stressed the case-sensitive nature of proportionality and anticipated little case law on the topic: **3–04**

> *"While the change in culture should reduce the scope of costs assessments at the conclusion of proceedings, it will not obviate the need for a robust approach to such assessments. Again the decision as to whether an item was proportionately incurred is case-sensitive, and there may be a period of slight uncertainty as the case law is developed.*
>
> *That is why I have not dealt with what precisely constitutes proportionality and how it is to be assessed. It would be positively dangerous for me to seek to give any sort of specific or detailed guidance in a lecture before the new rule has come into force and been applied. Any question relating to proportionality and any question relating to costs is each very case-sensitive, and when the two questions come together, that is all the more true. The law on proportionate costs will have to be developed on a case by case basis. This may mean a degree of satellite litigation while the courts work out the law, but we should be ready for that, and I hope it will involve relatively few cases."*

It is hard to see what further guidance is either necessary or likely other than in extremely general terms. Unnecessary because the very flexibility of the definition makes it hard to think of any case where relevant features impacting on costs do not fall to be taken into account within one of the five factors. Unlikely because each case is fact sensitive, the ambit of judicial discretion is broad and any decision falling outside the parameters would only define proportionality in a very broad sense in that specific case. Beyond that, any comments will be of a general nature, e.g. in *CIP Properties (AIPT) Ltd v Galliford Try Infrastructure Ltd*[4] where Coulson J commented that:

> *"Costs budgets are generally regarded as a good idea and a useful case management tool. The pilot schemes (including the one here in the TCC) have worked well. They are not automatically required in cases worth over £2 million or £10 million, principally because the higher the value of the claim, the less likely it is that issues of proportionality will be important or even relevant. A claimant's budget of £5 million might well be disproportionate to a claim valued at £9 million, but such a level of costs is probably not disproportionate to a claim worth £50 million."*[5]

and in *Savoye and Savoye Limited v Spicers Limited*[6], a case concerning enforcement of an adjudication, Akenhead J concluded that:

> *"...for the purposes of costs assessment, the Court should have regard when assessing proportionality and the reasonableness of costs, in the context of the current case or type of case to the following:*
>
> *(a) The relationship between the amount of costs claimed for and said to have been incurred and the amount in issue. Thus, for example, if the amount in issue in the claim was £100,000 but the costs claimed for are £1 million, absent other explanations the costs may be said to be disproportionate."*

Whilst the court in *Kazakhstan Kagazy Plc & ors v Zhunus & ors*[7] purported to define what is 'reasonable and proportionate' as "...the lowest amount (of costs) which it (a party) could reasonably have been expected to spend in order to have its case conducted and presented proficiently, having regard to all the circumstances", this appears to overlook the provisions of CPR 44.3(2)(a), which is not considered in the judgment and which could not be clearer that proportionality trumps reasonableness. Accordingly any attempt to define proportionality by equating it to, or by any measurable reference to, reasonableness appears to overlook this procedural provision. In any event this decision was concerned with payments on account of costs and not the assessment of recoverable costs. (See **Q1**. below for more detailed consideration of the link between reasonableness and proportionality).

Those seeking certainty are, in effect, wishing for something akin to a form of fixed fee regime for all cases. Given the variety of claims it is almost

[4] *Properties (AIPT) Ltd v Galliford Try Infrastructure Ltd* [2014] EWHC 3546 (TCC).

[5] The reference to £2 million and £10 million being to the respective versions of CPR 3.12 in place from 1 April, 2013 and 22 April, 2014.

[6] *Savoye and Savoye Limited v Spicers Limited [2015] EWHC 33 (TCC).*

[7] *Kazakhstan Kagazy Plc & ors v Zhunus & ors [2015]EWHC 404 (Comm).*

inevitable that any regime of fixed fees would be set with a very broad brush. Be careful for what you wish.

Proportionality—the effect on litigation

For a more detailed consideration of the effect on litigation see **Chapter 4**— 3–05
Case and Costs Management. In essence, though, proportionality will arise at all stages of a case, as any case management decision engages the overriding objective, which now includes the obligation to deal with a case at proportionate costs, regardless of any additional burdens imposed by specific provisions. This applies to all claims, regardless of track and regardless of value where there is no fixed cost regime in place. The court, and the parties, should have proportionality in mind whether they are dealing with the lowest value small claim or the highest value multi track. It follows that any party seeking any specific case management direction must be prepared to justify it in the context of a consideration of the factors at CPR 44.3(5).

The discretion offered by the flexible definition of proportionality means that it can be adapted to meet the diverse considerations of all claims, which is just as well as, despite Jackson LJ's recommendation, fixed fees have yet to be introduced for non personal injury fast track claims. Indeed Jackson LJ regards this as a serious omission because CPR 44.3(5) was not designed as a mechanism to control costs in the fast track. Both he, and Dyson MR returned to this theme, encouraging the implementation of further fixed fee schemes to all fast track claims and some lower value multi track claims, in their respective *Confronting Costs Management* lectures in May 2015[8]. Without fixed fees and costs management in fast track a significant emphasis in fast track claims remains on proportionality after the costs have been spent under CPR 44.3(2)(a) at assessment.

This discretion means that provided that the court has considered the factors in CPR 44.3(5) when reaching any decision on proportionality it will have made no error of principle and so appealing any decision will be extremely difficult.

Questions and answers

Q1. Is there any distinction between proportionality and reasonableness in reality?

The answer, as an exercise of semantic interpretation of the CPR, is yes, because 3–06
throughout the CPR the two are referred to separately—see for example CPR 3PDE.7.3 which requires the court to approve budgets for phases that are "reasonable and proportionate" and CPR 44.3(2)(a) which clearly draws a distinction between the two. Indeed it is the latter provision that makes it clear that some costs may be reasonable, but not proportionate.

In practice, there will be cases where the court, having assessed the reasonable costs, then applies the CPR 44.3(5) factors to the proportionality

[8] Harbour Lecture '*Confronting Costs Management*' May 2015.

cross check under CPR 44.3(2)(a) and determines that those costs are also proportionate—indeed the court's assessment of proportionality might be at a higher figure than the reasonable costs for a variety of reasons (e.g. because of limits imposed by the contractual retainer). There will also be cases where the same cross-check reveals the reasonable costs are still disproportionate. Perhaps the better answer, therefore, is, not necessarily so.

Q2. Is there not a risk that similar claims will have different outcomes because of the determination by separate case managing judges of what is proportionate in a particular case?

3–07 Yes—there is such a risk. The determination of proportionality will dictate what case management directions are given. Different determinations will lead to different directions, e.g. permission for an expert in one case and not in another. However, that does not mean that the judges are necessarily 'wrong', simply that one has exercised discretion in another way from the other. Of course, that happens, and legitimately so, regardless of proportionality, on a daily basis in all courts—not just on procedural matters, but on factual disputes of a similar nature. Whilst there is judicial discretion there will be instances where there are a number of outcomes—none of which are 'wrong'. This question ought to be linked, however, with consideration of whether the risk is justified as an attempt to curb disproportionate costs and to promote access to justice. It is too early to say whether the drive to introduce proportionality will achieve this aim.

However, it is surely unarguable that a system that provides transparency of the 'recoverable costs' at large at an early stage will focus the attention of the parties and enable them to make decisions and give their legal representatives instructions on a more informed basis as to how they wish a claim pursued or defended, than a system where they find out the exact extent of the other party/parties' costs only when they are ordered to pay them and find out the shortfall between their legal fees and the exact amount of those that they may recover from the other party at assessment, after the costs have been spent.

Q3. Is proportionality a 'fixed sum' throughout the life of a claim?

3–08 This depends entirely on the specific features of any claim, e.g. an assessment of proportionality is made at the costs management stage in a claim where two heads of loss are pursued, each with a considerable value. After disclosure it becomes apparent that one head of loss is unsustainable and the claimant discontinues that part of the claim. At that stage plainly the sum in issue has altered. In those circumstances there has been a significant development for the purposes of CPR 3 PD E 7.6 and we would expect the parties either to agree revised budgets or, in the absence of agreement, to seek the approval of the court to revised budgets on the basis that what was proportionate for the claim as originally presented is not for the claim that then remains (remember that revision where there is a significant development is expressly referred to as '*upwards or downwards*' in CPR 3 PD E 7.6). In other words, the proportionality of a claim may alter throughout its course.

However, this does not mean that as a matter of routine the court will revisit earlier decisions on proportionality. Many saw the decision to grant permission to appeal in *Troy Foods v Manton*[9] as opening the door to revisiting proportionality in costs managed cases at subsequent assessment. This interpretation overlooks some important points as follows:

- This was simply a decision on whether or not to permit an appeal. As such it is not a binding authority.
- The case was under the pilot scheme at what was CPR 51 PD G. At para.4.2 of the practice direction, the objective of costs management was said to be "to control the costs of litigation in accordance with the overriding objective". The overriding objective was in its pre-April 2013 form without specific reference to dealing with a case at proportionate costs. Whilst para.1.3 of the Practice Direction makes a reference to proportionate costs it does so in the context of the relevance of costs already incurred. Nowhere in the Practice Direction does it state that the court is expressly charged with setting the budget by reference to proportionality.
- The costs managing judge appeared to have applied a test of approving the budget "provided it was not so unreasonable as to render it obviously excessive or, as he put it, 'grossly disproportionate'". Accordingly, permission was given on the basis that it was arguable the judge had applied the wrong test and been overgenerous as a result.
- When setting a budget under the costs management provisions of CPR 3 and 3 PD E, the court is required to budget phases by reference to what is 'reasonable and proportionate'. In other words, the court has assessed the proportionality of any phases budgeted already.
- Despite the approach taken by the court in *Simpson v MGN*[10] (which is considered in **Chapter 4**) it seems CPR 3.18 could not be clearer—on a standard basis assessment the court will not depart from the last approved or agreed budget for each phase of the proceedings unless it is satisfied that there is 'good reason' to do so. To do otherwise would be to adopt no more than an inappropriate appellate function.

Accordingly, unless there is 'good reason' to depart from the last budget, the court will not revisit the proportionality determination of any phase of the claim that has been budgeted (see **Chapter 4** for consideration of 'good reason' in this context). Indeed, were the reverse to be correct, then the purpose of costs management would be defeated.

[9] *Troy Foods v Manton* [2013] EWCA Civ 546.
[10] *Simpson v MGN [2015] EWHC 126 (QB)*

Q4. If there is no 'good reason' to depart from the budget on assessment, how does the court apply the proportionality 'cross check' under CPR 44.3(2)(a) at the end of the assessment?

3–09 At the end of the assessment the court will have determined the reasonably incurred and reasonable in amount of non budgeted costs (i.e. those incurred before the costs management order) and these must then be added to the budgeted sum. The proportionality cross check is then applied, but on the basis that this cannot reduce the overall costs to less than the budgeted sum, for, as is set out above, those costs were subject to a determination of proportionality at the time the budget was set and the wording of CPR 3.18 precludes departure from this sum. Accordingly, if the total of the assessed costs is not proportionate, then the court must reduce the costs to a level that is proportionate, but that cannot be less than the budgeted costs. For example, if the total of the budget for the 'to be incurred' part of the phases budgeted, whether by agreement between the parties, approval of the court or a combination of both, is £50,000 (and there is no 'good reason' to depart from this) and the total for the assessed non budgeted costs is £30,000, but the court determines that the combined sum of £80,000 is disproportionate, then the proportionate figure that the court assesses under CPR 44.3(2)(a) is somewhere between £50,000 to £80,000. It cannot be less than £50,000.

Q5. How do the transitional provisions relate to proportionality at assessment?

3–10 Three possible scenarios arise—two of which are straightforward and the other presents some practical difficulties.

CPR 44.3(7) makes it clear that the 'new' proportionality provisions—namely the new definition of proportionality at 44.3(5) and the cross check at 44.3(2)(a) do not apply to:

- at all to a case which was issued before 1 April 1, 2013; and
- to those bits of work done on a case prior to 1 April, 2013, where the case was issued after 31 March, 2013.

This transitional provision leads to three scenarios as follows:

1) In cases issued before 1 April, 2013, *Lownds* still applies and if proportionality is challenged at assessment it must be dealt with at the outset, by reference to what were the 'seven pillars of wisdom' at 44.5(3) and which are now the first seven of eight 'pillars' at 44.4(3). The outcome will be that the costs are either assessed against a necessarily or reasonably incurred test.
2) In cases which are issued after 31 March, 2013 and no work is done on that case prior to that date, then the new provisions apply to all the costs.
3) In cases where the claim is issued after 31 March, 2013 but some work is done before that date, the *Lownds* approach must be adopted in respect

of the work done prior to 1 April, 2013 and the new test to all the work after 31 March, 2013.

It is the last of the three scenarios above that presents challenges. Parties seeking assessment of costs, whether by summary or detailed assessment, will need to ensure that the costs pre and post April 1, 2013 are clearly separated (this is likely to mean two Forms N260 or separate parts in a bill, something which the SCCO called for in *BP v Cardiff & Vale University Local Health Board*[11] and which from 6 April 2016 will become a requirement under CPR 47 PD 5.8(7), which makes mandatory the division of a bill for detailed assessment in to parts matching the relevant proportionality test where the transitional arrangements provide that both the 'old' and 'new' provisions apply under 3) above. Experience to date suggests that this express provisions will be welcomed by the judiciary as to date such a clear division has not routinely been provided. However, this provisions does not apply to summary assessment and the risks that remain if there are not separate N260s for the relevant periods are that:

- It is not proportionate to adjourn off the summary assessment to another date or for written submissions and the court may be forced to do the best it can on the information available. This may result in the court concluding that if a party has not troubled to separate out the two periods, the sanction (and proportionate way forward) is to assess all the costs under the new test.
- The court does adjourn and demands a re-drawn Form N260, but does not permit any recovery of costs for so doing.

If there are separate Forms N260 or separate parts of the bill, (and, as stated above, under CPR 47 PD.5.8(7) the bill will be divided into the relevant 'proportionality test' period), the court's function is invidious. It must do one proportionality determination at the beginning (for the pre–1 April, 2013 costs) and one at the end (for the post 31 March, 2013 costs). However, both exercises are artificial, because the court cannot aggregate the costs of both parts to do the exercise under each discrete test. To do so would be to ignore the clear language of CPR 44.3(7). Instead the court will have to identify the work undertaken in each period and apply the relevant test to determine the proportionality of that work.

Q6. Does the court look at the sums reasonably claimed or the sums recovered when determining 'the sums in issue in the proceedings' under CPR 44.3(5)(a)?

Obviously at the time that proportionality is considered for the purposes of budget setting and case management, the court does not know what sums will ultimately be recovered. At that stage the determination must be based on what is claimed—which emphasises the importance of realistic valuation 3–11

[11] *BP v Cardiff & Vale University Local Health Board [2015] EWHC B13 (Costs).*

(how often does the statement of value on a claim form limit to a particular sum, but the subsequent schedule of loss attached to later served Particulars of Claim reveal that the alleged losses are significantly higher than that sum, but there is no application to increase the statement of value?). If there is an argument, namely that the claim is exaggerated, then all that does is confirm that the sums claimed are in issue (and remember the wording of CPR 44.3(5)(a) is '*the sums in issue in the proceedings*').

At the conclusion of the claim the court will know what sum was recovered. The fact that the sum may be less than was claimed does not, of itself, necessarily alter the determination of proportionality. The fact that one sum was claimed and one was recovered does not mean that the original sum was not in issue. However, this does assume that it was reasonable to pursue the claim as stated.

If, for example, it emerges that the claim was exaggerated, but the claimant still obtains an award of some costs, then in cases costs managed, this may well be a 'good reason' to depart from the budget as that will have been set on a basis that the claimant knew was wrong. In non budgeted cases conduct can be considered when assessing the reasonable costs under CPR 44.4 and the 'real' value is likely to apply on the proportionality 'cross check'.

In contrast, if the claimant recovers a lower sum than that claimed, but it was reasonable to pursue the higher sum, e.g. if there was a complicated causation argument where the defendant's expert evidence was preferred or where the case turned on a factual dispute and the court preferred the evidence of the defendant's witnesses, then it is likely that will not alter 'the sums in issue' for the purpose of proportionality and so will not represent a 'good reason' to depart from the budget in costs managed cases and will not influence proportionality in non budgeted cases.

In practice, in both scenarios the limited recovery is likely to sound in the award of costs itself, with something less than a full costs order being made under CPR 44.2(4)(b) and 44.2(6). The court must be astute to avoid 'double jeopardy', although as is clear from *Drew v Whitbread*[12] conduct may be considered both on the award and the assessment of costs.

Q7. Why is only the conduct of the paying party included in the definition?

3–12 This question really arises at two stages—at case/costs management and at assessment. It is important, though, when considering the question to remember the full wording of this factor. It is not conduct generally, which falls to be considered, but only conduct of the paying party which generates additional work.

At the case/costs management stage

3–13 At the costs management stage the rationale is that the past conduct of the parties (for at this stage it is not clear who will be the receiving and who the paying party) is not relevant. This is because the court can only budget the

[12] *Drew v Whitbread* [2010] EWCA Civ 53.

costs "to be incurred". As such, the court can control conduct going forward by proportionate costs and case management. In other words, the court's directions should preclude the possibility of conduct generating additional work. The court sets and manages the progression of the case. If a party persists in conduct that is likely to generate additional work, then the other party may always apply under CPR 3 PD E 7.6 to vary the budget as a result of that conduct or seek discrete costs sanctions on any applications that arise outside the budget under CPR 3 PD E 7.9, relying on the stark warnings given by the Court of Appeal about non co-operation in *Denton v T H White*,[13] which resonate beyond the specific scenario which was under consideration:

> *"The court will be more ready in the future to penalise opportunism. The duty of care owed by a legal representative to his client takes account of the fact that litigants are required to help the court to further the overriding objective."*[14]

In any event, CPR 3 PD E 7.4 requires the court to take incurred costs into account when considering the reasonableness and proportionality of the costs to be budgeted. So, if unreasonable and/or disproportionate costs have been incurred by a party as a result of its conduct up to costs management, it may find its budget going forward suffers as a result.

At the assessment stage

The reason that the conduct of the receiving party does not form part of 3–14
the definition at assessment seems more complicated. Whilst it is likely that such conduct will already have been taken into account by the court when making the award of costs—see CPR 44.2(4)(a)—that is by no means certain as it may not always be obvious at that stage whether certain conduct has generated additional costs. However, conduct is also taken into account at the assessment—see CPR 44.4(3). Both these provisions, though, relate to the conduct of the parties. So if the argument is that conduct has already been considered, then that ought also to apply to the conduct of the paying party.

The explanation may be that it is difficult to imagine a situation where any additional costs of the receiving party generated by the conduct of that party survive the test of whether they are reasonably incurred or reasonable in amount and, as such, have already been disallowed by the time that the court does the proportionality cross check. In contrast, the receiving party's additional costs caused by the paying party's conduct will survive the test of whether they were reasonably incurred and reasonable. If the court does not remind itself that these reasonably incurred and reasonable in amount costs include those extra costs, there is a danger that the overall sum is deemed disproportionate and the paying party escapes the consequences of its actions.

Q8. If the effect of CPR 44.3(2)(a) is that the sum to be allowed on an assessment is that which is proportionate, why does the court trouble

[13] *Denton v T H White* [2014] EWCA Civ 906.
[14] para.43.

first with undertaking an assessment of what is reasonably incurred and reasonable in amount?

3–15 There are a number of reasons why the court must first assess the reasonable sum. These are:

- Because that is what the combined effect of CPR 44.4(1)(a) and 44.3(2) require of the court.
- The effect of the indemnity principle. The increasing use of fixed fee solicitor and client retainers and pressure on hourly rates means that there may well be cases where the proportionate sum exceeds the reasonable sum. However, to proceed straight to the proportionality assessment would lead to the assessment of a sum that exceeds the permitted recovery under the retainer. Linked to the point above is that it is also not sufficient in such a situation to say that as the costs claimed are less than the proportionate sum, they then should be allowed in full. This is because, as said above, proportionality does not necessarily equal reasonableness. The court must be satisfied under CPR 44.4(1)(a) that the costs are both proportionate and reasonable. There may still be items of costs that were unreasonably incurred or unreasonable in amount even if the overall sum is proportionate. Those items should not be allowed, even if that means the eventual sum assessed is reduced still further from what may be the proportionate sum. In these cases proportionality acts as a cap and not as fixed costs.
- That, as seen under **Q7** above, the question of the conduct of the parties demands an assessment of what is reasonable by looking at items where it is said that this has generated additional costs. It is only the assessment of reasonableness that introduces the conduct of the receiving party and informs the court as to whether the conduct of the paying party sounds in the proportionality determination.

Q9. Is proportionality to be applied in all cases, or, as some wish to suggest, is it really for the small to medium value claims, where disproportionate costs are more likely?

3–16 Whilst costs management is limited to those claims specifically referred to in CPR 3.12, and any other claims where the court orders it, this does not limit the all encompassing relevance of proportionality. It is part of the overriding objective and, as such, all case management decisions must be made against the obligation on the court to deal with cases at proportionate cost whatever the value of a claim. This is reinforced by CPR 3.17, which provides that:

> *"When making any case management decision, the court . . . will take into account the costs in each procedural step."*

Even in those cases where the filing of Precedent H is required and the court chooses not to make a costs management order, the rules on the relevance of that budget at assessment have been strengthened. CPR 44 PD 3.6 and 3.7

reiterate and expand previous provisions. They enable the assessing court, where there is a difference of 20 per cent or more between the costs claimed and those shown in a budget, to:

- Restrict the recoverable costs where reliance has been placed on the budget by the paying party to what is reasonable even if that results in a sum less than that which would otherwise be proportionate and reasonable.
- Regard the difference between the costs claimed and those in the budget as evidence that the costs claimed are unreasonable or disproportionate, even where no reliance on the budget is established.

Expect the court to be more robust in applying these provisions, than it was before 1 April, 2013.

Proportionality also has a role to play in non fixed fee fast track and small claims track cases. Indeed, cases that might previously have been allocated to multi track (e.g. because the time estimate for trial exceeded one day) may now be allocated to fast track with directions targeted to reduce the time estimate to one day and cases that are over the small claim track limit may now be allocated to that track as the consent of the parties to this is no longer required. In both these tracks, directions will be targeted to ensure that the cases are dealt with proportionately (and that includes the amount of court time that they occupy).

So far as assessments of costs are concerned, in respect of these that fall under the new proportionality regime (see **Q5** above), then the court must apply the proportionality cross check under CPR 44.3(2)(a) as the 'court will only allow costs which are proportionate'. It is no longer a case of proportionality only arising if raised by the paying party.

Q10. What relevance, if any, does proportionality have in cases where an order for costs is made on the indemnity basis?

Proportionality is still relevant before the costs order is made, as the court will have case managed on a proportionate basis. Where the order for indemnity costs has significance is on the assessment of the amount of costs. When conducting an assessment on the indemnity basis under CPR 44.4(1)(b), the court must decide whether costs were unreasonably incurred or unreasonable in amount—it is not required to consider proportionality. Albeit that the rule number may have changed (from CPR 44.4(3)) this does not alter the provision in place before April 2013. However, where the change in outcome is marked is in cases where a costs management order has been made. This is because CPR 3.18, which provides that the court will not depart from the last approved or agreed budget at assessment unless there is 'good reason', expressly only applies to cases where the court is assessing costs on the 'standard basis'. 3–17

Whilst Coulson J in *Elvanite Full Circle Ltd v AMEC Earth & Environment*[15]

[15] *Elvanite Full Circle Ltd v AMEC Earth & Environment* [2013] EWHC 1643.

suggested that even where there was an order for indemnity costs, the budget should be the starting point, it must be remembered that he was considering a budget prepared under CPR 51 PD G. The budget form (Form HB) did not require any certification suggesting that the budget was constrained in any way by proportionality—in other words it was probably a fair reflection of all the costs that the client was likely to incur and so represented an approximation of indemnity costs. Now the budget does require a certification linking the sums included to those that are proportionate as is set out in CPR 22 PD 2.2A:

> *"This budget is a fair and accurate statement of incurred and estimated costs which it would be reasonable and proportionate for my client to incur in this litigation."*[16]

As a result the link between the budget sum and indemnity costs relied upon by Coulson J is no more. If there was still any vestige of doubt, that has been dispelled by the Court of Appeal in the judgment of Dyson MR and Vos LJ in *Denton v T H White*.[17] The relevant section of the judgment was considering sanctions in costs for non co-operation between the parties. It dealt with indemnity costs as a possibility and said this:

> *"If the offending party ultimately loses, then its conduct may be a good reason to order it to pay indemnity costs. Such an order would free the winning party from the operation of CPR rule 3.18 in relation to its costs budget."*

It is clear from this that there is a greater benefit to a receiving party of an order for indemnity costs than was the case before the 2013 reforms. However, the test for whether or not an order for indemnity costs is merited has not altered. However, as Akenhead J observed in *Courtwell Properties Limited v Greencore PF (UK) Limited*,[18] where a party entitled to an automatic standard basis costs order under Part 36 sought an order for indemnity costs instead:

> *". . . parties must act in a proportionate way . . . Where the indemnity costs application depends on evidence which is likely to involve material conflicts of evidence, the applicant party needs to think long and hard about whether it is appropriate to pursue the application."*

Q11. Is the effect of proportionality to prescribe that in a case about money, the costs cannot exceed the sums in dispute?

3–18 Before 1 April, 2013, there was an acceptance within the CPR that there were cases where the proportionate cost would exceed the sum in issue. Section 11 of the then Costs Practice Direction expressed it in these terms:

> *"11.1 In applying the test of proportionality the court will have regard to rule 1.1(2)(c). The relationship between the total of the costs incurred and the financial*

[16] para.43.
[17] *Denton v T H White* [2014] EWCA Civ 906.
[18] *Courtwell Properties Limited v Greencore PF (UK) Limited* [2014] EWHC 184 (TCC).

value of the claim may not be a reliable guide. A fixed percentage cannot be applied in all cases to the value of the claim in order to ascertain whether or not the costs are proportionate.
11.2 In any proceedings there will be costs which will inevitably be incurred and which are necessary for the successful conduct of the case. Solicitors are not required to conduct litigation at rates which are uneconomic. Thus in a modest claim the proportion of costs is likely to be higher than in a large claim and may even equal or possibly exceed the amount in dispute."

What is immediately clear is that 11.2 accords precedence to 'necessary' costs. Work that was necessary informed the assessment of proportionality. This is no longer the situation, for CPR 44.3(2)(a) expressly gives primacy to proportionality, even if that means that necessary costs (and by implication necessary work) are not recoverable. This does no more than codify the comments at Ch.3 para.5.10 of Jackson LJ's Final Report[19] under the bold heading 'Costs do not become proportionate because they were necessary'.

Does this mean that costs can never exceed the amount in dispute? The answer must surely be no, but not because a certain amount of work is necessary in any given claim, but, instead, because CPR 44.3(5) does not limit the relationship between proportionality and costs solely to the amount in issue. If there are other relevant factors then those inform the determination of the proportionate sum. This, again, illustrates the flexibility of the definition that enables it to apply to all circumstances. The Final Report concluded, when making the recommendation for the new definition of proportionality, that:

"Proportionality of costs is not simply a matter of comparing the sum in issue with the amount of costs incurred, important though that comparison is. It is also necessary to evaluate any non-monetary remedies sought and any rights which are in issue, in order to compare the overall value of what is at stake in the action with the costs of resolution."[20]

Notwithstanding this, it is likely to be rare indeed for costs to exceed the sums in dispute. As Stuart-Smith J observed in *GSK Project Management Ltd v QPR Holdings Ltd*[21]:

"My starting point is that a case would have to be wholly exceptional to render a costs budget of £824,000 proportionate for the recovery of £805,000 plus interest."

This confirms that where the only relevant factor under CPR 44.3(5) is the sum in issue, it is difficult to envisage a court determining that it is proportionate for the parties to spend more than this sum in determining the dispute.

[19] Review of Civil Litigation Costs: Final Report, December 2009.
[20] Ch.3 para.5.5.
[21] *GSK Project Management Ltd v QPR Holdings Ltd [2015] EWHC 2274 (TCC).*

Q12. How useful are the comments in cases such as *CIP Properties (AIPT) Limited v Galliford Try Infrastructure Limited*[22], *GSK Project Management Limited v QPR Holdings Limited*[23] and *Stocker v Stocker*[24] *[2015] EWHC 1634 (QB)* in setting benchmarks for proportionality?

3–19 As set out at **3–04** above, proportionality, other than in terms of very general (and relatively obvious) observations, is case and fact specific. Accordingly, whilst some general guidance may emerge from authorities—such as those set out in **3–04** and **Q11** above—proportionality in each individual case will depend upon the outcome of the consideration of the CPR 44.3(5) factors in that specific case.

What does emerge, by way of reinforcement, is that when preparing budgets parties should remember the wording of the statement of truth on Precedent H and the requirement at CPR 22 PD 2.2A (see **Q10** above) for the costs set out in the budget to be a statement of the proportionate incurred and estimated costs. Failure to do so is likely to result in unfavourable comment and possible costs sanctions, as occurred in *GSK Project Management Limited* where Stuart-Smith imposed a costs order upon the claimant for producing a '*grossly excessive*' costs budget.

Q13. In the case of *Stocker v Stocker*[25] Mr Justice Warby observed: "I readily acknowledge the importance of ensuring that the costs budgeting process does not result in a party being unable to recover the costs necessary to assert their rights." Does this mean that proportionate costs can never be less than those that are necessary?

3–20 No. CPR 44.3(2)(a) makes this quite clear:

> *"Costs which are disproportionate in amount may be disallowed or reduced even if they were reasonably or necessarily incurred."*

In fact the extract quoted in the question needs to be put in context. It comes at the conclusion of a paragraph considering 'purely financial proportionality'. Of course costs are proportionate if they bear a reasonable relationship to the five factors at CPR 44.3(5) and not simply the sums in issue in the proceedings. However, Warby J did acknowledge the difficulty 'to cut radically, at a stroke, the costs of this class of litigation' (libel claims), suggesting overtly that this would need to be a gradual process. However, that said, he had no hesitation in concluding that "the Defendant's global costs figure is clearly considerably out of proportion to what is at stake and the nature of the issues, and should be substantially reduced for that reason. . ."

[22] *CIP Properties (AIPT) Limited v Galliford Try Infrastructure Limited [2015] EWHC 481 (TCC).*
[23] *GSK Project Management Limited v QPR Holdings Limited [2015] EWHC 2274 (TCC).*
[24] *Stocker v Stocker [2015] EWHC 1634 (QB).*
[25] *Stocker v Stocker [2015] EWHC 1634 (QB).*

CHAPTER 4

Case and Costs Management

Introduction

Although the title of this chapter suggests that case and costs management are two separate exercises, in reality they are two sides of the same coin. As Jackson LJ commented in his Final Report: **4–01**

> *"First, case management and costs management go hand in hand. It does not make sense for the court to manage a case without regard to the costs which it is ordering the parties to incur. The Rubicon was crossed on 26th April 1999, when the court assumed under the CPR wide powers and responsibilities for case management."*[1]

This link is something to which Jackson LJ returned in May 2015[2], when acknowledging that the court was adopting various approaches to case and costs management in practice, and concluding that:

> *"The objective of the 2013 civil justice reforms is to enable the court to manage each case so that it proceeds at proportionate cost"* para. 7.2.

and

> *"In my view the norm shall be for the court to do both case management and costs management at a single hearing"* para. 7.5.

The April 2013 amendments to the CPR inextricably linked both in CPR 3.12(2), when defining the purpose of costs management as being "that the court should manage both the steps to be taken and the costs to be incurred by the parties to any proceedings". CPR 3.17 strengthens the link between the two by requiring the court to have regard to any available budgets and to take account of costs when making any case management decision. In fact, it may be artificial to talk of both case and costs management as, in those cases where costs management orders are standard (see below), the latter is simply part of the former.

In this chapter we shall consider the procedural changes made to the existing case management provisions of the CPR and the costs management rules that were introduced in April 2013 separately, and then illustrate how they combine in a seamless practical application.

In his Final Report Jackson LJ asked if costs management was worth the candle. He answered the question in the affirmative giving two reasons in support of that answer. The first is set out above. The other reason was:

---

[1] Review of Civil Litigation Costs: Final Report, December 2009, Ch.40 para.7.1.

[2] "Confronting costs management" 13.5.2015.

> *"Secondly, I am in full agreement with the Law Society's view that costs management, if done properly, will save substantially more costs than it generates."*[3]

Presented with the same question two years after the introduction of the April 2013 amendments, Jackson LJ remained as emphatic, stating unequivocally[4]:

> *"The first and most important conclusion to be drawn from the experience of the last two years is the same as that which was drawn from the pilots. Costs management works"* para. 2.1.

It is clear that the changes made to case management cannot work in isolation and 'proper' costs management is essential to the success of the reforms.

The changes made to the existing CPR case management provisions

4–02 The principal procedural change that affects and informs all case management decisions (and informs costs management decisions) is the change to the overriding objective at CPR 1.1 to introduce the obligation to deal with a case "at proportionate cost". All the other changes are designed to achieve this objective. These are:

1. Enforcing stricter compliance with court orders, rules and practice directions (both in CPR 1.1(2)(f) and 3.9).
2. Replacing allocation questionnaires with directions questionnaires designed to provide more relevant case information (CPR 26.3).
3. A greater discretion to the court when determining the track to which to allocate claims and an increase to the small claims limit (CPR 26.6(3) and the removal of what was CPR Pts 26.7(3), 27.14(5) and (6)).
4. The encouragement to use standardised directions to ensure consistency and facilitate the production of orders (CPR 29.1(2)).
5. More targeted disclosure provisions (CPR 31.5(3–8)).
6. More prescriptive powers in respect of witness statements (CPR 32.2(3)).
7. The provision of more information about any expert evidence proposed (CPR 35.4).
8. The option to hear the oral evidence of experts concurrently (CPR 35 PD 11).
9. Increasing the incentive for claimants to make realistic settlement proposals (CPR 36.17(4)(d)).
10. The introduction of costs management (CPR 3.12–3.18 and CPR 3 PD E).

From 1 October 2015 the court has also expressly been given the power to hear an Early Neutral Evaluation with the express aim of helping the parties to settle a case (by an extension of the broad jurisdiction under CPR

[3] Review of Civil Litigation Costs: Final Report, December 2009, Ch.40 para.7.1.
[4] "Confronting costs management" 13.5.15.

3.1(2)(m)) — recognising that this may result in earlier and more proportionate resolution.

1. *Enforcing stricter compliance with court orders, rules and practice directions (both in CPR 1.1(2)(f) and 3.9)*

In the Final Report, Jackson LJ identified the change of culture that was required, commenting: **4–03**

> *"First, the courts should set realistic timetables for cases and not impossibly tough timetables in order to give an impression of firmness. Secondly, courts at all levels have become too tolerant of delays and non-compliance with orders. In so doing they have lost sight of the damage which the culture of delay and non-compliance is inflicting upon the civil justice system. The balance therefore needs to be redressed."*[5]

In the pre-April 2013 case of *Fred Perry (Holdings) Ltd v Brands Plaza Trading Ltd,*[6] the Court of Appeal gave an indication of the imminent alteration of emphasis, leaving no doubt that a wind of change was blowing:

> *"The Rule Committee has recently approved a proposal that the present rule 3.9(1) be deleted . . . It is currently anticipated that this revised rule will come into force on 1st April 2013. After that date litigants who substantially disregard court orders or the requirements of the Civil Procedure Rules will receive significantly less indulgence than hitherto."*[7]

Whether the warnings went unheeded or whether some practitioners failed to appreciate quite how much less indulgence was to be afforded by the court is unclear, but from November 2013, and the decision in *Mitchell v News Group Newspapers Ltd,*[8] until July 2014, and the clarification provided in *Denton v T H White*[9] the court reverberated to the sounds of applications for relief from sanctions and the disappointed cries of those whose applications were dismissed. *Denton* has clarified that the court should approach these applications in three stages: **4–04**

- **Stage 1** requires an evaluation of the breach. The Court of Appeal made it clear that this must be looked at in isolation—concentrate solely on the seriousness and significance of this breach. If there have been other failures/misconduct by the defaulting party, those must be ignored at this stage, but may merit consideration at stage 3. The court then moves on to stages 2 and 3. If it has concluded that there is not a serious or significant breach, then stages 2 and 3 may not occupy much court time, but if there has been a serious or significant breach then the final 2 stages take on a greater importance.

---

[5] Review of Civil Litigation Costs: Final Report, December 2009, Ch.39 para.6.5.

[6] *Fred Perry (Holdings) Ltd v Brands Plaza Trading Ltd* [2012] EWCA Civ 224.

[7] Jackson LJ, para.4.

[8] *Mitchell v News Group Newspapers Ltd* [2013] EWCA Civ 1537.

[9] *Denton v T H White* [2014] EWCA Civ 906.

- **Stage 2** involves consideration of whether there was good reason for the breach. The Court of Appeal declined to produce an 'encyclopaedia' of what might constitute 'good reason'. This will be fact specific. However, *Mitchell* at para.41 sets out some examples.
- **Stage 3** At this stage the court considers "all the circumstances of the case", but, remembering that the two factors specifically mentioned in CPR 3.9 carry 'particular weight' (although Jackson LJ dissented, on the basis that the two factors were mentioned to draw attention to them, but that they carried no weight above any others). It is worth noting that the Court of Appeal specifically drew attention to the fact that the importance of complying with rules, practice directions and orders had received insufficient emphasis in the past stating:

"The court must always bear in mind the need for compliance with rules, practice directions and orders, because the old lax culture of non-compliance is no longer tolerated."

4–05 It is clear from the extract above that those who think that the position has reverted to what it was on 31 March, 2013 remain due for an unpleasant shock. For those who pointed to the dissenting judgment of Jackson LJ In *Denton* to counter this, his comments in the Preface to the White Book 2015[10] leave no room for uncertainty. He accepted the majority judgment as the correct construction of CPR 3.9 and added:

> *"It is very important that in the euphoria with which some have greeted Denton, we do not slip back into the 'old culture of non compliance. . ."*

If further evidence of a shift towards compliance was required, it was provided in *HRH Prince Abdulaziz Bin Mishal Bin Abdulaziz Al Saud v Apex Global Management Ltd,*[11] where the Supreme Court, whilst at pains to reiterate that generally case management and CPR was the domain of the Court of Appeal, confirmed that:

> *"The importance of litigants obeying orders of court is self-evident. Once a court order is disobeyed, the imposition of a sanction is almost always inevitable if court orders are to continue to enjoy the respect which they ought to have . . . One of the important aims of the changes embodied in the Civil Procedure Rules and, more recently, following Sir Rupert Jackson's report on costs, was to ensure that procedural orders reflected not only the interests of the litigation concerned, but also the interests of the efficient administration of justice more generally."*[12]

So, whilst the change may not be as dramatic as *Mitchell* suggested, relief will still be granted more sparingly than previously.

Hand in hand in *Denton* with guidance on relief was:

[10] *White Book* 2015 Preface page xvi.
[11] *HRH Prince Abdulaziz Bin Mishal Bin Abdulaziz Al Saud v Apex Global Management Ltd* [2014] UKSC 64.
[12] paras 23–25.

i) an entreaty by the Court of Appeal (coupled with costs threats if ignored) for parties to co- operate and not use court rules as technical trip wires. This links to the amendment made to CPR 3.8 in April 2014 to add a provision at 3.8(4) enabling parties to agree extensions to the period for compliance with orders, rules and practice directions that specify the consequences of a failure to comply, provided that this does not jeopardise any hearing. This costs threat was carried out in *Viridor Waste Management v Veolia Environmental Services [2015] EWHC 2321 (Comm).* The court concluded that the defendant had taken an opportunistic and unreasonable advantage of late service of Particulars of Claim in opposing the application for relief from sanction. As a consequence the defendant was subjected to an indemnity costs order; and

ii) a reminder to members of the judiciary to ensure that "the directions that they give are realistic and achievable". The Court of Appeal acknowledged that it was of no use to set a timescale so tight that it was obvious that it could not be met, stressing that "the court must have regard to the realities of litigation in making orders in the first place". This harks back to the extract from Jackson LJ's Final Report quoted above, in which he stressed that the court should set realistic timetables for cases and not impossibly tough timetables in order to give an impression of firmness (see above and the Final Report Ch.39 para.6.5).

The Master of the Rolls had cause to re-visit his comments in i) above in *R (on the application of Idira v The Secretary of State for the Home Department*[13] and left no doubt in so doing that *Denton* did not represent a return to the pre-*Mitchell* regime, stressing that absence of prejudice did not inevitably lead to relief being granted, saying:

> *"At para.43 in Denton, this court said that parties should not "adopt an unco-operative attitude in unreasonably refusing to agree extensions of time and in unreasonably opposing applications for relief from sanctions". It added: "it is unacceptable for a party to try to take advantage of a minor inadvertent error. . ..". I would emphasise the words "unreasonably" and "minor inadvertent". A party is not required to agree to an extension of time in every case where the extension will not disrupt the time-table for the appeal or will not cause him to suffer prejudice. If the position were otherwise, the court would lose control of the management of the litigation."*

Similarly the fact that refusal to grant relief will cause significant prejudice to the party in default does not mean that relief should be granted. In *Sinclair & anor v Dorsey & Whitney & ors*[14] a professional negligence claim said to be valued at £30 million was struck out for breach of an unless order to provide security for costs. An application for relief was dismissed on application of

[13] *R (on the application of Idira v The Secretary of State for the Home Office [2015] EWCA Civ 1187.*

[14] *Sinclair & anor v Dorsey Whitney & ors unreported QBD 20.11.15.*

the *Denton* 3 stage test. The fact of prejudice was insufficient when considered in all the circumstances and giving particular weight to the two factors in CPR 3.9.

The latest decision in the ill-fated case of *Thevarajah v Riordan & ors*[15] (three visits to the Court of Appeal and this one to the Supreme Court), confirmed, if confirmation was needed, that compliance with the terms of an unless order after the date set for compliance does not amount to a material change in circumstance as required pursuant to *Tibbles v SIG Plc*[16] (one of the factors necessary to support an application under CPR 3.1(7) for the court to vary or revoke an order).

2. *Replacing allocation questionnaires with directions questionnaires designed to provide more relevant case information (CPR 26.3)*

4–06 Directions questionnaires should assist the court with determining proportionate case management decisions. More information is required about proposed expert evidence and, unless there is a valid explanation for being unable to do so, expect the court to police the requirement to provide details of witnesses <u>and</u> the issue(s) to which their evidence will be addressed. Questionnaires that suggest that this information is 'to be advised' are likely to receive short shrift and their authors may find themselves the recipients of orders, including 'unless orders' to provide the information or a satisfactory explanation of why it cannot be provided or face the consequences (e.g. being unable to rely upon any witness evidence).

3. *A greater discretion to the court when determining the track to which to allocate claims and an increase to the small claims limit (CPR 1.1 and 26.6(3) and the removal of what was CPR Parts 26.7(3), 27.14(5) and (6))*

4–07 The court must take account of proportionality when allocating. Accordingly those claims that might previously have been allocated to the multi track simply because of time estimate (e.g. where the value is within fast track limits and none of the other CPR 44.3(5) proportionality factors justifies allocation to the multi track, but there are a number of witnesses) are now likely to be allocated to fast track with a restriction on the evidence that may be adduced to ensure the claim is disposed of within a day. Similarly the omission of CPR Part 26.7(3), which prevented a court allocating a claim to the small claims track if the value exceeded the limit for that track without the agreement of all parties, seems designed to enable the court to allocate more claims to the limited 'fixed fee on issue' regime of that track.

This aim is bolstered by the removal of previous provisions (CPR 27.14(5) and (6)), which enabled parties agreeing to allocation to the small claims track to include an agreement that fast track costs would still apply and that any appeal would carry the costs consequences as if it had been a fast track claim.

---

[15] *Thevarajah v Riordan & ors [2015] UKSC 78.*
[16] *Tibbles v SIG Plc [2012] EWCA Civ 518.*

These provisions are no more and so whether a claim with a fast track value is allocated to the small claims track with or without the consent of the parties, the limited small claims track costs allowances prevail.

At the same time the proportion of claims proceeding in the small claims track has been increased as the financial scope of that track has been doubled to £10,000 (save for personal injury and housing disrepair claims with a claim for specific performance of repairs, where the financial limit remains unaltered at £1,000, but with the personal injury limit to be raised to £5,000[17]).

4. The encouragement to use standardised directions to ensure consistency and facilitate the production of orders (CPR 29.1(2))

The proliferation of different forms of directions up and down the country was identified by Jackson LJ as a source of unnecessary cost. If the same form of order is used in all courts, then the parties can use them as a starting point when discussing proposed directions as they will not be confronted by 'local' variations, there will be consistency of orders produced, less risk that a direction will be overlooked or that a direction will be phrased ambiguously (not to be underestimated given the potential sanction for non compliance) and the final order will be easier for the court to generate. Accordingly he recommended that: 4–08

> *" . . . a menu of standard paragraphs for case management directions should be prepared for each type of case of common occurrence and made available to all district judges both in hard copy and online. These standard directions should then be used by district judges as their starting point in formulating initial case management directions."*[18]

CPR 29.1(2) was introduced to achieve this by linking to a raft of standard orders. However, the uptake appears to have been distinctly lukewarm. The directions are under review, but in the meantime, some courts are insisting that draft directions are filed adopting the standard template orders and others are not. It is hard to see how practitioners can be faulted by the court if they use the standard orders under CPR 29.1(2) as the provision does state that these *'should'* be taken as the starting point.

5. More targeted disclosure provisions (CPR 31.5(3–8))

In the 7th Implementation Lecture,[19] Jackson LJ referred to the costs of the disclosure process in these terms: 4–09

> *"Even in medium sized actions where all the documents are in paper form, disclosure can be a major exercise which generates disproportionate costs."*

The resultant attempt to curb the costs of this phase of litigation can be found

[17] Spending Review and Autumn Statement 2015 (25.11.15).
[18] Ch.39 para.5.3.
[19] 7th Implementation Lecture: Controlling the Costs of Disclosure, 24, November, 2011.

at CPR 31.5. This introduces the 'disclosure report' (Form N263), which is designed to facilitate discussion between the parties as to the appropriate disclosure order prior to the first case management conference and to inform the court, in general terms, of the types of documents involved, by whom and where they are held, how electronic documents are stored, the costs of 'standard disclosure' and what disclosure order is suggested. CPR 31.5(7) then sets out a menu of possible disclosure options. It is no surprise that other than a catch-all provision, 'standard disclosure' is listed as the last of the disclosure options. The pre-amble to the menu stresses that the court will decide which option to order 'having regard to the overriding objective and the need to limit disclosure to that which is necessary to deal with the case justly'. The reference to the overriding objective plainly imposes the requirement for proportionality.

CPR 31.5(1) and (2) combine to exclude personal injury claims from the new provisions. Standard disclosure remains the 'norm' in these claims, but with a residual discretion to the court to order otherwise (which it should exercise where appropriate — e.g. by limiting to the issue of limitation, liability, quantum etc. as appropriate.)

The 7th Implementation Lecture left little doubt as to the importance of the new disclosure provisions:

> *"The order made at the first CMC concerning disclosure will have a profound impact on the future course of the case and also upon the final costs of the litigation. Therefore this issue merits careful thought and analysis when the parties initially and the court ultimately are making their selection from the menu of possible disclosure orders."*

Notwithstanding the exhortation to select from the menu after careful thought and analysis, anecdotal evidence suggests that 'standard disclosure' is the type most generally suggested in the N263, perhaps unsurprisingly, as the requirement to cost this form of disclosure and it being the default disclosure option in the standard orders under CPR 29.1(2), steer parties towards it. Even if standard disclosure is to remain more routinely used than had been envisaged under the reforms, the definition of standard disclosure that appears at CPR 31.6 merits repetition as it is far narrower than many appear to think:

> *"31.6 Standard disclosure requires a party to disclose only —*
> *(a) the documents on which he relies; and*
> *(b) the documents which —*
> *(i) adversely affect his own case;*
> *(ii) adversely affect another party's case; or*
> *(iii) support another party's case; and*
> *(c) the documents which he is required to disclose by a relevant practice direction"*

Tales of trial judges inundated with bundles based on 'standard disclosure' from which they are taken to only a few pages may be apocryphal, but do not be surprised if some judges add to an order for standard disclosure "as defined by CPR 31.6".

6. More prescriptive powers in respect of witness statements (CPR 32.2(3))

The court has always had the power to control evidence under CPR 32.1. However, the specific reference in CPR 32.2(3) to the ability of the court to give directions identifying and limiting the issues upon which factual evidence is to be given, identifying specific witnesses and limiting the length and format of statements, gives the court the ability to case manage factual evidence in a proportionate way. The identity of witnesses and the facts to which their evidence will be directed should be readily available from Section F of the Directions Questionnaire. Notwithstanding this, draft directions and orders still routinely make no attempt to limit evidence whether by number of witnesses or length of statements. Given that proportionate trial time estimates require strict control of evidence it appears inevitable that this case management provision will, and should, be used increasingly. **4–10**

An early illustration of the use of this provision was in *MacLennan v Morgan Sindall (Infrastructure) Plc*.[20] The court was concerned with a significant claim for loss of earnings in a severe brain injury claim. This element of loss raised four broad issues upon which the claimant wished to call 43 witnesses. The defendant sought an order under CPR 32.2(3) limiting the number to eight. In the end the court made an order restricting the number of witnesses to 28 and identifying those issues with which the witnesses would deal.

7. The provision of more information about any expert evidence proposed (CPR 35.4)

It is curious that almost three years after the introduction of CPR 35.4, any party still completes a directions questionnaire and attends a subsequent case management conference, indicating that expert evidence is required without providing details of the expert, the issues that the expert will address and the likely cost of the expert. Curious because: **4–11**

- This information is a pre-requisite to the court giving permission for expert evidence. CPR 35.4(2) makes the provision of this information mandatory (qualified to the extent that the name is required where reasonably practicable) when applying for permission to rely upon expert evidence in any type of claim.
- Notwithstanding the failure to provide this information, some parties still feel able to complete the costs budget providing details of what the reasonable and proportionate expenditure on the expert phase will

[20] *MacLennan v Morgan Sindall (Infrastructure) Plc* [2013] EWHC 4044 (QB) Green J.

be—inserting figures for the expert—at a stage when the expert has not even been identified and the extent of that expert's remit not determined.

There is a real risk that if this information is not available, the court will simply not give permission. This means that in those cases that are costs managed, they will be costs managed without provision for permission for that/those expert(s) whom the party in default seeks to rely upon, with inevitable implications on the expert phase of the budget. If the party in default sees the way the wind is blowing and does not pursue the application for permission at the case management conference, but, instead, seeks to rely on a subsequent free standing application, it is likely to confront difficulties as the rectification of a previous failure is unlikely to be viewed as a 'significant development' for the purpose of budget variation under CPR 3 PD E 7.6. Even if the court were minded to entertain the subsequent application and permit the expert evidence, this would mean consequential recasting of the directions and variations of costs budgets at considerable expense. It is not difficult to envisage what the costs order in respect of that additional expenditure would be!

8. The option to hear the oral evidence of experts concurrently (CPR 35 PD 11)

4–12 CPR 35 PD 11 provides the court with the option of taking expert evidence concurrently and sets out, subject to judicial discretion to alter the process, the procedure to adopt. In reality though, the process is inevitably case and judge specific.

There was a pilot run in the Manchester 'Construction and Technology' and 'Mercantile' Courts. The feedback from that was limited, inevitably due to the small number of cases involved prior to the pilot report. However, there seemed to be a consensus that in the right case utilising this option could save court time and facilitate the evidential process. There has yet to emerge any authority that sheds light on the potentially challenging issue of ensuring that the parties feel they have had a sufficient opportunity to advance the expert evidence that they wish in this format. Albeit in a different scenario (that of experts and site inspections), the case of *Hatton v Connew*[21] is a timely reminder of the need for the court to take expert evidence in an appropriate fashion which is fair to the parties.

9. Increasing the incentive for claimants to make realistic settlement proposals (CPR 36.17(4)(d))

4–13 Giving the lead judgment in *Fox v Foundation Piling Ltd*,[22] Jackson LJ highlighted one of the major reasons that cases that ought to resolve without the expense of a trial failed so to do:

[21] *Hatton v Connew* [2013] EWCA Civ 1560.
[22] *Fox v Foundation Piling Ltd* [2011] EWCA Civ 790.

"A not uncommon scenario is that both parties turn out to have been over-optimistic in their Part 36 offers. The claimant recovers more than the defendant has previously offered to pay, but less than the claimant has previously offered to accept."[23]

Therefore, it was not a surprise that CPR Pt 36 was amended to increase the incentive for the parties to adopt more realistic valuations to encourage earlier settlement. That amendment comes in the form of CPR 36.17(4)(d)). If a claimant makes a relevant Part 36 offer, then in addition to the 'established' consequences (an entitlement to indemnity costs and increased interest on both the substantive award and the costs), there will be an award of an additional amount, unless the court thinks it unjust to make such an award. The additional amount is 10 per cent of the damages awarded up to £500,000 and that sum plus 5 per cent of the damages awarded that are over £500,000, with a cap on the additional amount of £75,000.

The re-written CPR 36 from April 2015 also contains an incentive for an offeree to accept an offer where the offeror has fallen foul of the provisions of CPR 3.14 by failing to file a costs budget — this is to avoid the situation where the 'risk' to the offeree is limited solely to future court fees[24].

Part 36 is considered in more detail in **Chapter 5**.

10. The introduction of costs management (CPR 3.12–3.18 and CPR 3 PD E).

In the Final Report, Jackson LJ described costs management in these terms: **4–14**

"(i) The parties prepare and exchange litigation budgets or (as the case proceeds amended budgets).
(ii) The court states the extent to which those budgets are approved.
(iii) So far as possible, the court manages the case so that it proceeds within the approved budgets.
(iv) At the end of the litigation, the recoverable costs of the winning party are assessed in accordance with the approved budget."[25]

In essence these four characteristics form the basis of the regime introduced at CPR 3.12–3.18 and at CPR 3 PD E. However, the implementation and regulation of costs management has proven, and is proving, more challenging than the simple assertion of the regime's principles. To facilitate the understanding and practical application of the regime, it is simplest to approach it under the following five headings:

A. Which cases are subject to costs management?
B. What procedural requirements are imposed on the parties in respect of costs management?

[23] para.46.
[24] See **Q65**. below for further consideration of this.
[25] Review of Civil Litigation Costs: Final Report, December 2009, Ch.40 para.1.4.

C. How does the court 'costs manage'?
D. Variation of budgets
E. The effect of a costs management order on subsequent assessment

A. Which cases are subject to costs management?

4–15 Although costs management is less than three years old, there has already been substantial revision of the rules regulating which types of cases are covered by the regime. The current provisions relate to those cases issued after 22 April, 2014 but incorporate some further amendments from April 2016 in respect of those who are children, as defined by CPR 21, at the time of the making of the claim and those with a limited life expectancy (five years or less). In summary, the regime applies to:

- All CPR Part 7 where the amount claimed or the limit in the statement of value is less than £10,000,000 (CPR 3.12 (1)(a) and (b)) save i) where the party was a child at the time that the claim was made (note that this exclusion covers those parties who cease to be a child during the proceedings unless the court orders otherwise), ii) where the claimant has a limited or severely impaired life expectancy (CPR 3 PD E 2(b)) iii) where the court orders otherwise (CPR 3 .12(1)(e)) iv) where proceedings are subject to fixed or scale costs.
- Any other proceedings (including applications) where the court so orders (CPR 3.12(1A)). CPR 3 PD E 2–5 'Other cases' sets out both the procedure that will apply where costs management is proposed by either the court of its own motion or the parties in cases not otherwise within the scheme and the types of case that are particularly suitable (the types of case are set out in CPR 3 PD E 5(a)–(f)).

If the initial form of CPR 3.15 was deemed less than prescriptive as to when the court should costs manage, the current version leaves little room for doubt. The court will make a costs management order in cases where a costs budget has been filed and served unless it can be satisfied that the litigation can be conducted justly and at proportionate costs in accordance with the overriding objective without such an order being made. Given that the court cannot make this assessment until it has seen the budgets, it is hard to imagine why the court will not always be making costs management orders, because either the budgets are plainly disproportionate immediately triggering court concern or they are obviously proportionate in which case, to ensure that costs stay that way, and as it will take no time to do, it seems prudent that the court would make a costs management order in the terms of those parts of the Precedent H that it is permitted to budget. Whilst there remains an 'opt out' for the court in CPR 3.12(1)(e), this is surely a provision to be used sparingly, otherwise it risks undermining the regime and may result in both forum shopping (for those keen to avoid budgeting) and the suggestion of 'local practice directions'. To that extent, agreements between the parties to avoid the costs management regime will need to be well reasoned to survive the rigorous consideration that they merit.

This level of prescription saw the one area of potential disagreement between Jackson LJ and Dyson MR in their respective *'Confronting costs management'* lectures in May 2015. Jackson LJ envisaged the possibility of courts not case managing if they lacked the resources to do so other than at the risk of delay and disruption to the particular case before them and other cases generally. Dyson MR perceived a risk that the *'lack of resources'* card might be 'played' in many cases with costs management becoming the exception and not the 'norm'.

Litigants in person are exempted from the obligation to file and exchange costs budgets (CPR 3 P DE 7.8), although they must be served with the budget of any other represented party and clearly are entitled to make representations about the budget at any costs management hearing.

B. What procedural requirements are imposed on the parties in respect of costs management?

In general terms the parties (other than litigants in person) in receipt of a notice of provisional allocation to the multi track (CPR 26.3(1)) where the statement of the value of the claim is less than £50,000 must exchange and file a budget in Precedent H with their Directions Questionnaires. In all other multi track cases Precedent H must be exchanged and filed twenty one days before the first case management conference or, if the case is one not automatically subject to costs management under CPR 3.12, the budget must be exchanged and filed by any date specified by the court. Failure to comply results in the automatic sanction under CPR 3.14, namely that the defaulting party is treated as having filed a budget comprising only applicable court fees. The effect of this for any party subject to a costs management order on this basis is that only future court fees may be budgeted, but costs incurred at the time of the order are still recoverable, subject to assessment, as a costs management order only relates to "the costs to be incurred" (CPR 3.15). **4–16**

As of April 2016 parties who have exchanged costs budgets (so not litigants in person) must file an agreed budget discussion report no later than seven days before the CCMC (CPR 3.13(2)). This must set out the figures agreed for each phase, the figures not agreed for each phase and a brief summary of the grounds of dispute (CPR 3 PD E 6A).

The budget must be in the form of Precedent H attached to CPR 3 PD E. Where the total costs do not exceed £25,000 or where the statement of value in the Claim Form does not exceed £50,000, then only page 1 of the Precedent H should be completed. There have been two cases already that seek to test the prescription of this requirement. In *The Bank of Ireland v Philip Pank Partnership*[26] the claimant failed to include the full wording of the statement of truth, although the budget was signed and dated by the legal representative.

[26] *The Bank of Ireland v Philip Pank Partnership* [2014] EWHC 284 (TCC) Stuart-Smith J.

The court found that this omission did not render the budget a nullity and as such, the claimant had complied with the requirement to file and exchange its budget. Instead the Precedent H was simply subject to an irregularity. In the second case, *Americhem Europe Limited v Rakem Limited,*[27] the same judge found that the failure to have a budget signed by a senior legal representative (it was signed by a costs draftsman) also did not render a budget a nullity, again amounting to no more than an irregularity. The judge, having noted that this was the second occasion when he had to deal with a mere irregularity in budget form, took the opportunity to cite from the judgment of Leggatt J in *Summit Navigation Ltd v Genrali Romania Asigurare*[28]as follows:

> *"But, as the Master of the Rolls emphasised . . . it is not the aim of the reforms to turn rules and compliance into 'trip wires' . . . "*

If the court makes a costs management order, then CPR 3 PD E 7.7 requires a party to re-file and re-serve the budget in the form approved by the court. In fact some courts are budgeting electronically using the first page of the budget in a self calculating form, so that the budget recalculates as the hearing progresses. In those cases, to reduce costs and ensure absolute clarity of the outcome of the costs management exercise, the courts are simply attaching the first page of each budget as costs managed to the directions order and dispensing with the requirement at 3 PD E 7.7, saving the time and resource of re-filing and re-serving.

4–17 The preparation of the Precedent H itself is assisted by a guidance note on what work to insert in which phases within the form. Whilst the guidance was updated in July 2015 and has been updated again in April 2016, it remains brief, some would say too brief. Note that CPR 3 PD E 6(b) now expressly requires the guidance to be followed. However, in general terms, it does identify the allocation of work amongst the phases of Precedent H. All costs incurred, even those pre-action, that are attributable to a phase of the budget should be inserted in the 'incurred' columns in the specific phase and all work to be incurred should be inserted in the 'estimated' columns in the specific phases.

One obvious lacuna in the guidance relates to work that has already commenced, such as on an interim application, which by definition is not contingent, but which does not fit neatly into any of the phases, e.g. applications for interim payments, security for costs, etc. Remembering that the budget should inform the other parties and the court, there is a danger that the exercise becomes one of form over substance. So long as this work is clearly identified, and the budget attributes incurred and estimated expenditure transparently, does it really matter if it is included as a contingency even though it is already a reality?

The guidance also contains the occasional oddity:

[27] *Americhem Europe Limited v Rakem Limited* [2014] EWHC 1881 (TCC) Stuart-Smith J.
[28] *Summit Navigation Ltd v Genrali Romania Asigurare* [2014] EWHC 398 (Comm) Leggatt J.

- Under the Case Management Conference ("CMC") phase the suggestion is that any subsequent CMC should not be included in this phase. This begs two obvious questions—why have an 'estimated' column for this phase and where does any budget for a subsequent CMC ordered by the court fit in the budget? Anecdotally, it seems that some courts are ignoring the guidance and budgeting for the cost of a later CMC in the 'estimated' column of Precedent H for this phase. Certainly this provides ready clarity when the budget comes to be examined against expenditure later. It also avoids the problem of where else to budget a future CMC as the guidance is silent upon this. As it is a certainty (as the court will have ordered it), it cannot be a contingency.
- Why is specific disclosure excluded from the disclosure phase when it is one of the types of disclosure order mentioned in the menu of orders at CPR 31.5(7)? The answer, presumably, is that the original guidance form pre-dated the change to CPR 31.5(7) and this has been overlooked on subsequent revisions. Whatever the reason it is unhelpful when the court is encouraging parties to move away from the default position of standard disclosure. As Jackson LJ saw disclosure as one of the most expensive phases of litigation, it makes no sense that if the guidance is followed when the court makes an order under CPR 31.5(7)(b), it does not budget the costs. If, as with non party disclosure, it is deemed a contingent cost, this too appears illogical. This is because CPR 31.5(7)(b) envisages a request for specific disclosure being made with disclosure of a party's own list. Accordingly, the time between case management order and compliance with the disclosure order is minimal. The notion that at the CMC this might be only a contingency is not credible. However, even if it is a contingency the court must budget it, so uncertainty over the proportionate expenditure cannot be the reason for it being excluded from the phase. As the court has to budget it anyway, why not do it within the phase within which it most naturally arises—namely disclosure? Another option is to regard specific disclosure as so uncertain as to fall within CPR 3 PD E 7.9. However, it is hard to argue that something is uncertain when it is what the court is ordering to take place! The final option is to treat any subsequent request for specific disclosure as a 'significant development in the litigation' justifying a budget variation under CPR 3 PD E 7.6. Again, it is difficult to see the occurrence of something the court has ordered as a 'significant development'. What makes the guidance even more confusing is that it suggests that work considering the scope of disclosure by other parties and undertaking investigations having reviewed that disclosure (which may well involve consideration of whether specific disclosure is required) should be included in this phase.
- Why is mediation (which is a form of ADR) specifically excluded from the ADR/Settlement phase and is to be included as a contingency? One answer may be so that the court can readily identify the costs attributable

for this discrete form of ADR. However, if that is the case, this would sit more happily as a named phase rather than as a contingency.
- The PTR phase refers to "preparation of updated costs budgets and reviewing opponent's budget". However, budgets only need to be updated once set by the court in the event of 'significant developments in the litigation' under CPR 3 PD E 7.6 and not as a matter of routine.

C. How does the court 'costs manage'?

4–18 The only provisions in respect of the form of the budgeting exercise itself are in CPR 3.12, 3.15 and 3 PD E 7.3, 7.4 and 7.10. These provide that:

- The court cannot budget costs already incurred[29]. Having said that the court cannot budget costs already incurred, CPR 3 P DE 7.4 seems to countenance a situation where costs incurred between the date of the budget and the date of the costs management hearing may be budgeted. However, both CPR 3.12 and 3.15 use the words 'costs to be incurred'. As the rule takes precedence over the practice direction, only future costs may be budgeted. The amendment at CPR 3.13(1)(b) means that there is no longer any risk of significant delay between the preparation of the budget and the costs management hearing, save where the claim form statement of value is limited to £50,000 (and the delay there should be shorter, because one would expect the budgets to be lower and therefore the hearing to require a lesser time estimate). However, if there is delay in listing in those cases parties may consider filing and exchanging updated budgets and making an application to be heard at the costs management for permission to rely on the updated budgets at that hearing. However, in this situation the court is likely to expect to see the same figure in the grand total on p.1 as in the earlier budget—for all that has changed is the passage of time means that some costs that were estimated in the future have now been incurred and so the incurred costs have gone up, but by the same amount as the originally 'estimated' costs have reduced, unless during that 'delay period' the assumptions upon which the budget was originally prepared have altered. In all cases the parties must discuss their respective budgets and must file an agreed budget discussion report seven days before the CCMC.
- Whilst the court cannot budget costs already incurred these are still relevant to the costs management process. CPR 3 PDE 7.4 provides that the court may record its comments on incurred costs and, more importantly, will take these into account when considering the reasonableness and proportionality of all subsequent costs. This means that when determining the sum to budget for costs 'to be incurred' for a phase, the court's decision will be informed by the amount already spent e.g. if the court concludes that the reasonable and proportionate sum for the disclosure

[29] See **Q27** for further consideration of this.

phase is £8,000 and £6,000 has already been incurred, the budget for the phase will be £2,000. The treatment of incurred costs has arisen in a number of cases[30], has proved challenging, has resulted in a variety of approaches being adopted by the court and is considered in more detail in the Q&A section of this chapter.[31]

- When undertaking the budgeting exercise, the court is only charged with setting a total sum which is reasonable and proportionate for each phase of the proceedings. The court is expressly not required to do a detailed assessment and, whilst it 'may have regard to the constituent elements of each total figure', it is not compelled to do so. In other words, the court simply sets one figure per phase for the future costs of that phase.
- The parties may agree budgets or discrete phases of the budgets. If they do this, then the court either makes a costs management order in respect of these costs recording the extent of the agreement or elects not to make a costs management order. Some see this as a curious provision. Whilst parties are to be encouraged to co-operate and narrow issues, the apparent inability of the court to interfere with agreement of what it may see as disproportionate costs seems an odd fetter in the pursuit of proportionality. If the court manages the case on a different basis from that upon which the parties have based their agreement of budget, then the court will expect the parties to revisit the budgets (as the basis upon which agreement has been reached has been altered). If, however, the proportionate case management directions are in line with those upon which agreement of budgets was reached, then the court either makes a costs management order on the basis of the agreement or makes no costs management order. Remember that costs (and costs liabilities to another party) are those of the client. Any agreement of all or part of a budget requires client approval, which is why access to the client during, or very specific instructions from the client before, a costs management hearing is essential.

In other words the precise mechanics of costs management are not prescribed. However, it is imperative that the exercise itself does not become disproportionate. The adoption of the broad brush of setting one total sum per phase as required under CPR 3 PD E 7.3 combined with the avoidance of arguments that are of the type routinely raised at the assessment stage, seems to meet this requirement, both in respect of the proportionality of the exercise for the parties and for the court in allocating its resources between cases. That this was the intention was confirmed by Jackson LJ in his *'Confronting costs Management'* lecture in May 2015 when he said this:

---

[30] e.g. in *CIP Properties (AIPT) v Galliford Try Infrastructure Ltd & ors (Costs No.2)[2015] EWHC 481(TCC)* and *Yeo v Times Newspapers Ltd [2015] EWHC 209 (QB)*.

[31] See **Qs 28-30** for further consideration of this.

> *"At the conclusion of the exercise the court should approve a single total figure for each phase of the proceedings. The party is then free to spend that sum as it sees fit. The court should not specify rates or numbers of hours. That adds to the length of CCMCs and is unnecessary micro-management"*[32]

The introduction of CPR 3 PD E 7.10 from April 2016 reinforces this and should toll the death knell for the arguments of those keen that the court should set an hourly rate and multiply it by an amount of time (despite the fact that CPR 3 PD E 7.3 already disavowed this process).

D. Variation of budgets

4–19 There is an apparent tension between CPR 3.15(3), which requires the court to control the parties' budgets once a costs management order has been made, and CPR 3 PD E 7.6, which suggests that where there is a significant development in the litigation that necessitates a variation to the budget, the parties should seek to agree this between themselves and only involve the court if agreement is not possible.

What is clear is that the budget may only be varied if there is a significant development in the litigation. Perhaps the dissipation of the tension lies here. It is hard to imagine a 'significant development' that does not require consequential case management. If further case management directions are proportionate, then inevitably, budgets will have to be re-visited and it is no surprise that the parties are encouraged to agree these. Of course, the court may take the view, informed by the revised budgets, that the directions sought are disproportionate and refuse them and the budget variation that accompanied them.

CPR 3 PD E 7.6 envisages both downward and upward budget revision. Examples of the former may be where a claimant discontinues part of a claim or where a defendant withdraws part of a defence and of the latter where a final prognosis in a personal injury claim provides a bleaker outlook than expected with a significant increase in future loss and the evidence in support of this. Clearly all of these are significant developments, affect the proportionality assessment under CPR 44.3(5) and respectively are likely to result in lesser or increased costs being expended. A failure to seek a variation in respect of additional costs means that at least one party may have to rely upon 'good reason' to depart from the budget at any subsequent standard basis assessment (the paying party when the variation ought to have resulted in lesser expenditure and the receiving party when the variation has resulted in increased expenditure, unless appropriate concessions are made). A cross application of *Mitchell* suggests that an oversight is unlikely to be a 'good reason'. If a party fails to vary downwards when it should there is no obvious 'sanction' (treating any downward variation as an inevitability of reduced work rather than as a sanction). However, plainly if costs have to be assessed simply because a party has failed to vary downwards or make an appropriate

[32] *Confronting costs management* May 2015 para. 3.4.

concession when it ought to have done, that raises issues in respect of the costs of the assessment under CPR 47.20(3).

If there was any doubt that the court may only permit variation in respect of costs 'to be incurred' (and it is hard to see why there should have been any doubt given the wording of CPR 3 PDE 7.6 expressly refers to 'future costs'), this was dispelled in *Yeo v Times Newspapers Ltd*[33].

CPR 3 PD E 7.9 makes it clear that discrete applications that were reasonably not included in the budget shall be treated as additional to the budgets. In such cases, the court will make an award of costs and, if that is for one party to pay the costs of another, undertake a summary assessment and order payment in the usual way (subject to any consideration of qualified one way costs shifting or indemnity issues deferring an immediate entitlement to costs) with this having no impact on the budget. If the order is for 'costs in case', then these costs fall outside the budget, and are additional to it, at any subsequent assessment once an award of the costs of the case is made.

E. The effect of a costs management order on subsequent assessment

CPR 3.18 clearly sets out that on a standard basis assessment, the court will **4–20**
not depart from the last approved or agreed budget for each phase without 'good reason'. Accordingly:

This provision applies to summary and detailed assessments. Unless there is 'good reason', the budgeted costs will be assessed as budgeted and any assessment will focus on the non-budgeted costs. What constitutes 'good reason'? There is no guidance in the rules.

The only reported case so far directly on CPR 3.18 and departure from a budget presents more questions than answers. In *Simpson v MGN Ltd & anor*[34] it was argued that where a party had exceeded its budget and there was no good reason for this, the inevitability was that under CPR 3.18(b) the costs over and above the budget would not be recoverable. However, the court concluded that neither CPR 3.18 nor CPR 3 PDE prescribed an automatic sanction in this circumstance. Instead, the court adopted what it described as a just and proportionate sanction which involved *'an assessment which makes every assumption against the party which has failed to submit an amended budget, and properly compensates the defendant for the additional costs involved'*. It is arguable that whether or not CPR 3.18(a) and (b) include a sanction is of academic interest only, as, on a simple construction, they combine to preclude departure from the agreed/approved budget for any phase in the absence of good reason. This is considered further in the Q&A section of this chapter.[35]

The provision at CPR 3.18 does not apply to costs assessed on the indemnity basis. There was initially some suggestion within the pilot schemes that the budgets still formed the starting point for an assessment on the indemnity

[33] *Yeo v Times Newspapers Ltd [2015] EWHC 2132 (QB) para. 47.*
[34] *Simpson v MGN Ltd & anor [2015] EWHC 126 (QB).*
[35] See further consideration of this decision in ***Q51*** below.

basis (see *Elvanite Full Circle Ltd v Amec Earth & Environmental (UK) Ltd*,[36] which advanced this proposition and *Kellie v Wheatley & Lloyd Architects Ltd*[37] which disagreed with that approach). This is not the position as proportionality has no place in an indemnity basis assessment and budgets have been produced and set by specific reference to proportionality. Any doubt was resolved by the Court of Appeal in *Denton v T H White*.[38] When referring to the consequence of an indemnity--based costs order, the Master of the Rolls described it as follows:

> *"If the offending party ultimately loses, then its conduct may be a good reason to order it to pay indemnity costs. Such an order would free the winning party from the operation of CPR rule 3.18 in relation to its costs budget."*[39]

The intention is plain—assessments, whether of a summary or detailed nature, will be both less time-consuming and more proportionate, because the court will be concerned only with determining the reasonableness of those costs that have not been budgeted and the overall proportionality cross check under CPR 44.3(2)(a). An illustration of the ease of summary assessment where a budget has been set can be found in *Slick Seating Systems v Adams*,[40] where the trial judge concluded that the sum sought was within the budget for each phase, assessed in that sum and commented that detailed assessment had been rendered 'otiose'.

4–21 The fact that an order for indemnity costs sees 'escape' from the constraints of the budget is not a reason for an increase in applications for such orders. The principles surrounding when the court will make an order for indemnity costs have not altered (save by the identification in *Denton* of a specific type of conduct that might merit such an award).

However, an indemnity costs award arising under CPR 36.17(4)(b) presents unique challenges. A claimant is entitled to indemnity costs from "the date on which the relevant period expired" (relevant period is defined in CPR 36.3(g)). However, this means that for some part of the litigation costs are constrained by the budget (absent 'good reason') and, for another part, the budget becomes irrelevant. However, the chance of the date when this transition takes place falling neatly at the end of a phase of Form H so it is clear which parts of the budget remain wholly relevant is slim (not non-existent, e.g. if the relevant period expired just before trial it may be possible to identify the phases clearly).

What happens in this situation where only part of the phase falls to be assessed on the standard basis? Sadly the answer is not clear. It is arguable that as the court is not looking at a phase exclusively on the standard basis, then CPR 3.18 has no application or if it does, then this is a 'good reason' to depart

[36] *Elvanite Full Circle Ltd v Amec Earth & Environmental (UK) Ltd* [2013] EWHC 1643 (TCC) Coulson J.
[37] *Kellie v Wheatley & Lloyd Architects Ltd* [2014] EWHC 2886 (TCC) HHJ Keyser QC.
[38] *Denton v T H White* [2014] EWCA Civ 906.
[39] para.43 majority judgment.
[40] *Slick Seating Systems v Adams* [2013] EWHC 1642 (QB) HHJ Simon Brown QC.

from the budget. However, this potentially presents a windfall to the receiving party beyond the ordinary benefit of an indemnity costs order. Even if this is the position, the court is still required to undertake an assessment in part on the standard basis and in part on the indemnity basis and the proportionality cross check pursuant to CPR 44.3(2)(a) continues to apply to the standard basis costs. Does this mean that bills where there is a relevant CPR 36 offer will need to be split between dates as well as, within the new format bill, phases matching the Precedent H? Certainly the new Precedent Q of the Costs Precedents provides no assistance with the division of phases between those on a standard and those on an indemnity basis. At the moment questions abound and there are no clear answers.

Those accepting a CPR Pt 36 offer, but then seeking an order for costs on the indemnity basis (in order to escape from the confines of a budget) should take note of the decision in *Courtwell Properties Ltd v Greencore PF (UK) Ltd*,[41] in which Akenhead J stated:

> *"In cases where the parties have settled through the Part 36 procedure or otherwise but leave the judge to decide costs, particularly where indemnity costs are claimed, parties must act in a proportionate way. There can be few if any cases in which there should in effect be a trial of all or some of the settled issues in the case. Where the indemnity cost application depends on evidence which is likely to involve material conflicts of evidence, the applicant party needs to think long and hard about whether it is appropriate to pursue the application."*[42]

Case and costs management in harmony

Having identified the key case management amendments and the costs management provisions, the practical link between the two becomes obvious. By requiring the court to costs manage by phases (which broadly equate to the procedural steps on the way to trial), the court is able to tailor the directions to the reasonable and proportionate cost of the respective phases. This should result in the court: 4–22

- Selecting the appropriate form of disclosure from the options at 31.5(7), which includes the possibility of dispensing with disclosure altogether.
- Controlling the number of witnesses, the issues they may address and the length of their statements (CPR 32.2(3)).
- Controlling the extent of expert evidence by number, by reliance on jointly instructed experts, by specific identification of the issues upon which they may report and by the use of concurrent evidence at trial.
- Conducting ongoing case and costs management preventing claims changing fundamentally in nature without court intervention. Any variation in the budget is linked to 'significant developments in the litigation'. It is hard to imagine any such developments that do not require

[41] *Courtwell Properties Ltd v Greencore PF (UK) Ltd* [2014] EWHC 184 (TCC) Akenhead J.
[42] para.42.

further court case management directions. At such a stage the ongoing control of the parties' budgets required by CPR 3.15 and the requirement at CPR 3.17 for the court to take account of the costs in each procedural step, combine so that the court must determine the extent, if at all, to which it is prepared to permit the claim to change course.

- Limiting the trial length. In a sense one should start here, for the assessment of proportionality dictates the trial length and all other directions must then be crafted to ensure that the trial can be completed within that period. Inevitably this informs the court's decisions on the matters listed above.
- Conducting a summary rather than detailed assessment at the conclusion of the trial. In some cases the 'costs of the costs' are disproportionate. One way to avoid this is for the court to undertake more assessments on a summary basis.

What is clear from the consideration of case and costs management above is that this presents new challenges to both the judiciary and court users. All must now be astute to ensure that rules, practice directions and orders are followed and to 'cut the cloth' proportionately. For the court this may mean deciding cases on more limited evidence than might previously have been available. For the professions this, inevitably, places a far greater emphasis on compliance with timetables and the management of client expectations. For the parties they have to co-operate with timescales and temper their expectation of a case being dealt with justly to what outcome can be achieved at a proportionate cost.

Questions and answers

Q1. How prescriptive is the wording of CPR 3.12(1) and (1A)? In particular can the court costs manage cases that fall within the definition of those outside the scheme and when may the court exclude cases from the regime under CPR 3.12(1)(e)?

4–23 The wording of 3.12(1) and (1A) allows the court flexibility, both of an inclusionary and exclusionary nature.

Under CPR 3.12(1A) it may bring into the costs management regime other proceedings. Although a case involving consideration of the provisions in force from 1 April, 2013 until 22 April, 2014, Coulson J considered the question of extension of the regime in *CIP Properties (AIPT) Ltd v Galliford Try Infrastructure Ltd.*[43] In this case the claim was put in the region of £18,000,000—so in excess of both the £2,000,000 cut off in place until 22 April, 2013 and the £10,000,000 cut off since that date. He concluded that the provision at CPR 3.12(1A), and in particular the reference to 'any other proceedings', did indeed extend to multi track claims worth £10,000,000 or more, stating:

[43] *CIP Properties (AIPT) Ltd v Galliford Try Infrastructure Ltd* [2014] EWHC 3546 (TCC) Coulson J.

> *"I take the view that the exercise of the court's discretion under CPR 3.12(1) is unfettered. There is nothing in the CPR to suggest otherwise. This discretion extends to all cases where the claim is for more than £2 million (old regime) and £10 million (new regime) There is no presumption against ordering budgets in claims over £2 million or £10 million, and no additional burden of proof on the party seeking the order."*[44]

Coulson J recognised that to have concluded otherwise would have left the court's hands tied and the system open to abuse by claimants wishing to avoid the costs management regime simply valuing their claims at £1 more than the cut off.

The fact that the regime is sufficiently flexible to permit costs management in cases not strictly within the provisions is, in any event, borne out by the express provision in CPR 3 PD E 2. This allows the court, whether on the application of a party or of its own initiative, to costs manage in those cases where the parties are not required to file budgets under CPR 3.12 and 3.13. CPR 3 PD E 5 sets out examples of cases strictly outside the regime where it may be particularly appropriate to costs manage. The fact that the £10 million limit is not a bar is reinforced by the inclusion in CPR 3 PD E 5 of personal injury and clinical negligence cases where the value exceeds that sum.

The reverse position is envisaged by CPR 3.12(1)(e), which permits the **4–24**
court to disapply the regime in multi track Part 7 claims that would otherwise fall within the provisions.

If the court does not do so prior to the deadline for filing and exchanging budgets then the court must make a decision not to costs budget based on CPR 3.15(2)—namely that it is satisfied that the litigation can be conducted justly and at proportionate cost in accordance with the overriding objective without a costs management order.

Cases where the court disapplies the regime before the filing and exchange of budgets ought to be rare (save for example where temporary exclusions are given, such as that for clinical negligence before the Queen's Bench Masters). The reason for this is that it is hard to see how the court can reconcile the obligation imposed on it by the overriding objective and, more specifically by CPR 3.17 (to take into account the costs of each procedural step) without any information about costs.

If the parties wish to persuade the court that a case is not suitable for costs management then they should apply <u>before</u> the expiry of the time for filing and exchanging budgets both to disapply the regime and, in the alternative, for an extension of time to file and exchange budgets until a date after the determination of the application in the event that the primary application is refused. If they do this and the court dismisses the application to disapply the costs management provisions, then the parties are dealing with an application to extend time and not an application for relief from the sanction under CPR 3.14 (see consideration of *Hallam Estates v Baker*[45] in **Q2** below).

---

[44] para.27.
[45] *Hallam Estates v Baker* [2014] EWCA Civ 661.

In *Sharp (and the other claimants detailed in the GLO Register) v Blank & ors*[46], the court had to grapple with whether or not a claim fell within the costs management regime. The situation was where a claimant indicated on the Claim Form that the claim had a value of over £25,000 (and so complied with CPR 16.3(2)(b)(iii)), gave no value in the 'amount claimed' box on the Claim Form, but it subsequently transpired the claim had a value in excess of £10 million. On the face of the rules, the court concluded this type of case was strictly caught by the costs management provisions, even though it was known by the time of the case management hearing that the claim value exceeded £10 million. Nugee J concluded that it might be useful for CPR 16.3 to require confirmation of whether or not a claim exceeds £10 million, which would avoid this situation arising, but then used *'unless the court otherwise orders'* in CPR 3.13 to dispense with budgets in the particular case.

Q2. Can parties agree to dispense with costs management?

4-25 Whilst it is open to parties to agree to dispense with costs management, they will still need to persuade the court to do so. If they are to avoid preparing, filing and exchanging Precedent H they must apply to dispense with/defer costs management before the date prescribed for compliance or find themselves caught by the provisions of CPR 3.14. For the reason given in **Q1** above in relation to the court's obligation under CPR 1 and 3.17, it is difficult to see any situation where the court would dispense with Precedents H. Once Precedents H are filed and exchanged, then the parties will have to satisfy the court under CPR 3.15(2) (see **Q1** above). If successful in persuading the court at this stage, the parties should remember that CPR 44 PD 3 then applies in respect of the costs budgets that were filed.

Q3 Does costs management apply to the disposal stage of a claim after the entry of a default judgment for damages to be decided by the court?

4–26 Strictly a disposal hearing is defined in CPR 26 PD 12.4 as a hearing that will not exceed 30 minutes and at which the court will not take oral evidence. Such claims are not allocated to track (unless they are within the small claims limit and are allocated to that track — see CPR 26 PD 12.3(2)). Accordingly, claims listed for disposal are not allocated to the multi track and they do not fall within the costs management regime under CPR 3.12.

However, parties often refer to a disposal hearing when, in fact, they mean a trial on quantum where the final hearing will exceed 30 minutes and at which oral evidence will be given. These cases should be allocated. If they are allocated to the multi track, then, as CPR 7 multi track cases, the costs management provisions apply. In such cases there may not be any requirement to file directions questionnaires under CPR 26.3. Instead the file may be referred to the District Judge on entry of the judgment for damages to be decided to give directions. Prior to the introduction of costs management, the District

[46] *Sharp(and the other claimants in the GLO Register) v Blank & ors [2015] EWHC 2685 (Ch).*

Judge might have ordered the filing of directions questionnaires, listed the claim for case management conference or given directions as a paper exercise. The likelihood now is that the last of those options is unlikely to occur in cases where allocation is to the multi track. Accordingly, parties should be astute to when a Precedent H is triggered under the provisions of CPR 3.13 in these cases. Q7 below provides more detailed consideration of relevant time limits, but this does not cover the situation where the statement of value of the claim is for less than £50,000, but there is no requirement to file a directions questionnaire as neither CPR 3.13 (1)(a) nor (b) appear to envisage this situation. It seems that if the court still requires a directions questionnaire by express order then CPR 3.13(1)(a) will apply in this situation, but if it does not, then there is no direct provision, but if the court orders a case management hearing without expressly ordering a Precedent H, it would still be prudent to comply with CPR 3.13(1)(b). If the statement of value of the claim is for £50,000 or more, then CPR 3.13(1)(b) certainly applies.

Q4 Do the provisions apply to a claim brought under CPR 8, where the court has expressly listed a case management conference?

No, unless the court has also expressly made an order requiring the parties to file and exchange costs budgets. As set out in the text above the costs management provisions from April 2014 do not apply to CPR 8 claims (see CPR 3.12(1)). Whilst the court retains a discretion under CPR 3.12(1A) and CPR 3 PD E 2 to bring claims that would not otherwise be subject to costs management into the regime, this would require an express order. 4-27

The court may convene a directions hearing before giving directions in CPR 8 claims (see CPR 8 PD 6.4). If no order for costs budgets has been made, the description of the hearing as a 'case management conference' rather than as a directions hearing carries no significance other than to distinguish the hearing from a final one.

Q5. What should parties do when the notice of provisional allocation under CPR 26.3 is to the multi track, but one or more parties believe that the appropriate allocation is to the fast track?

The risk of ignoring the consequence of the provisional allocation to multi track in claims where the statement of value of the claim is less than £50,000 and simply filing a directions questionnaire with proposed directions seeking allocation to the fast track but without a Precedent H, or, in claims with a stated value on the Claim Form of £50,000 or more, failing to file one 21 days before the CCMC, is that if the court concludes that the provisional allocation was appropriate, then there is a breach of CPR 3.13 and the consequences of CPR 3.14 apply. A more prudent approach is to file a consent application (if all parties agree that the provisional allocation is inappropriate) or an on notice application (if all parties do not agree that the provisional allocation is inappropriate) prior to the date for filing and exchanging costs budgets, seeking an extension of the time for so doing until a date to be fixed after determination 4–28 of the appropriate track at an allocation hearing. This avoids the potentially wasted expense of producing a Precedent H if subsequently the court allocates other than to the multi track, but means that the argument is one of extension of time for compliance under CPR 3.13 and not relief from the sanction of 3.14 if the court maintains the provisional allocation to multi track.

However, one of the major criticisms of the costs management regime is that there is a significant delay between the listing and hearing of a CCMC. If there is an argument on appropriate allocation the court will need to convene an allocation hearing and then, if it decides to allocate to the Multi Track, at that juncture list a CCMC. The scope for delay is obvious. One way to ameliorate this without pre-determining what the decision of the court may be on allocation is to suggest that the court lists a short allocation hearing as soon as possible and, in the same request, ask it to list a separate full CCMC as soon as possible after the allocation hearing (allowing time for Precedents H to be filed and exchanged in the meantime). If the allocation hearing results in allocation to the fast track, then the CCMC may be vacated. If the allocation hearing results in allocation to the multi track, there will only be a short delay between this decision and the CCMC. This may be easier to arrange in some courts than others (as quite often the time can be backed or there is always box work so the vacation of a CCMC does not result in a disproportionate waste of court time). Certainly some courts are already adopting this approach in this situation.

Q6. Does the fact that a party has a contractual right to indemnity costs against the other party mean costs management is not applicable or pointless because the claimant has a contractual right to claim costs under *Gomba Holdings (UK) Ltd v Minories Finance Ltd (No.2)*?[47]

4–29 Whilst the position of the contractual costs of a mortgagee may be somewhat different from those parties holding contractual rights to costs in other situations, this question seems directed to those cases where, in one form or another, there is a contractual right to costs on an indemnity basis between the parties in favour of one party, which is known about at the time that costs management would ordinarily arise.

The position is really a matter for the court. Whilst there is merit in avoiding the time and expense of budgeting by not costs managing the costs of the party who will rely upon the contractual obligation, the court still has a duty to case manage proportionately. Knowing what that party sees as the proportionate expenditure for the directions it advances will assist the court in determining the proportionate procedural approach to adopt. By so doing the court may, incidentally, reduce the costs due under the contract, as the directions proposed may not be proportionate and the effect of a different procedural route to trial may well limit what is reasonably incurred and reasonable in amount under the contractual entitlement.

[47] *Gomba Holdings (UK) Ltd v Minories Finance Ltd (No.2)* [1993] Ch 171.

Q7. In respect of those cases where the value of the claim is less than £50,000 and a party fails to file and exchange Precedent H by the date set out in the CPR 26.3(1) notice, but does file and exchange it by the extended date given in the further notice under CPR 26.3(7A), does CPR 3.14 apply? Is CPR 3.8(4) of any relevance in this situation?

Until the April 2016 amendments to the provisions of CPR 3.13, this situation posed a procedural trap for the unwary. This was because the time for filing and exchanging budgets was set by reference to the date in the CPR 26.3(1) notice and not, more generally, to the date for filing the directions questionnaire. Whilst CPR 26.3(7A) provided a further period for the filing of the directions questionnaire it did not provide any linked extension to the date for filing and exchanging Precedent H. Accordingly on a strict interpretation a represented party that failed to respond to the CPR 26.3(1) notice, but complied with the CPR 26.3(7A) notice, avoided the striking out of its statement of case under CPR 26.3(7A)(b), but fell foul of CPR 3.14 and was treated as having filed a budget comprising applicable court fees only. **4–30**

That trap has now gone because:

- In respect of claims where the statement of value of the claim is less than £50,000, the trigger for filing and exchanging budgets is the filing of the directions questionnaire and so any extension of time for filing the directions questionnaire provides an automatic extension of time for filing of the Precedent H; and
- In respect of claims where the statement of value of the claim is £50,000 or more the trigger for filing and exchanging is 21 days before the first CCMC.

Can the parties agree to extensions of these time limits whether by use of CPR 3.8(4) or otherwise?

Again it is easiest to look at the two 'triggers' for filing and exchanging Precedents H separately as follows:

- In respect of claims where the statement of value of the claim is less than £50,000 the position is not straightforward and produces a different outcome depending upon whether it is the notice under CPR 26.3(1) or that under CPR 26.3(7A) that the parties wish to vary.

  i) **CPR 26.3(1) notice** CPR 26.3(6A) states categorically that the time for compliance with a notice under CPR 26.3(1) may not be varied by agreement between the parties. CPR 3.8(4) only applies where a party is required to do something within a time specified by a rule and that rule imposes a sanction for failure to comply. In this situation there has been non compliance with 26.3(1) and the sanction is imposed by 26.3(7A). Is the rule CPR 26.3 and are 3(1) and 3(7A) sub-rules within it? The answer seems to be yes. Although there is no definition of 'rule' in the CPR, when it refers to a rule it seems to do so to, for example, all of 26.3. However, does the provision permitting agreement under CPR 3.8(4) take precedence over the bar to agreement in CPR 26.3(6A)? The answer is that specific rules take precedence over general rules. CPR 26.3(6A) is a specific rule and CPR 3.8(4) is a general rule. As such it would seem that the period cannot be extended by agreement and that CPR 3.8(4) does not apply to the time for compliance with CPR 26.3(1). However, see **Q8** below in respect of Chancery proceedings. The fact that the Chancery Division felt it necessary to issue a Practice Note on this topic may suggest that it shared the interpretation above.

ii) **CPR 26.3(7A) notice** CPR 26.3 contains no bar to an extension of the time provided under CPR 26.3(7A) and, therefore, it seems to fall squarely within the provisions of CPR 3.8(3) and (4) and the parties may agree to an extension. However, parties so doing would be well advised to notify the court as otherwise the court may well respond to any subsequently filed directions questionnaires and Precedents H with a letter saying that the claim, defence and any counterclaim has been struck out.

- In respect of claims where the statement of value of the claim is £50,000 or more where the trigger for filing and exchanging is 21 days before the first CCMC, no sanction applies and so CPR 3.8(3) and (4) do not apply. The parties' ability to agree a variation is governed by the more general 'agreement to vary' provisions at CPR 2.11. However, this is qualified by CPR 29.5. Whilst it is arguable that at this stage the claim may not have been formally allocated (as opposed to provisionally allocated), the reality is that court approval will be required if the variation that the parties agree impacts upon the date fixed for the CCMC (CPR 29.5(1)(a)). Parties should also be astute to the fact that the ability to agree a variation for Precedents H is also constrained by the provision at CPR 3.13(2) to file a 'budget discussion report' seven days before the CCMC.

Q8. What effect, if any, does the Practice Note released in the Chancery Division in July 2015 have on the time for filing and exchanging Precedents H? If there is any effect, does this apply outside the Chancery Division?

4-31 Paragraph 3 of the *Chancery Division – Extending time limits and Sealing Tomlin Orders* practice note dated 20 July 2015 expressly permits parties to agree to an extension of time of the date specified in Form N149C (the notice under CPR 26.3(1)) for the filing and serving of Directions Questionnaires) and for the exchange of Precedents H for up to 28 days without reference to the court. As discussed in **Q7** above, the amendments to CPR 3.13(2) as to when Precedent H must be exchanged and filed has altered the position, and has done so after the publication of the Practice Note. As there are unlikely to be claims in the Chancery Division High Court (as the practice note is limited to Part 7 claims in the Chancery Division of the High Court) where the statement of value of the claim is less than £50,000, these case will now, ordinarily, be governed by the provisions set out in the final bullet point of **Q7**. As a result the specific provision in the Practice Note relating to extensions for Precedent H based on the date in the notice under CPR 26.3(1) has been rendered obsolete, save in respect of any cases in the Chancery Division of the High Court where the statement of value is less than £50,000. If there are any such cases, then it would seem that the Practice Note is intended to override CPR 26.3(6A).

It is important to stress that, in so far as this Practice Note has any residual application, it is only to CPR 7 cases in the Chancery Division of the High Court in any event.

Q9. The Shorter Trial Pilot Scheme available for certain claims issued after 1 October 2015 under CPR 51 PD N disapplies CPR 3.12 and the costs management regime unless the parties agree otherwise (CPR 51 PD N 2.58). Why might parties wish to opt in?

Ignoring the larger debate raised by this question of the merits of the costs 4-32 management regime generally (and for those interested in this, Jackson LJ set out seven benefits in his *'Confronting costs management'* lecture in May 2015[48]), there may be case specific reasons for departure from the general rule in the Shorter Trial Scheme pilot. Certainly the scheme is designed to avoid protracted disputes and ensure proportionate directions (e.g. as to disclosure, witness statements, experts, interim applications, trial, summary assessment and appeals), by robust prescribed case management and determination at various stages on paper, where appropriate. These address some of the perceived 'ills' that costs management is designed to prevent and the general rule avoids the expense of the costs management exercise. However, there may still be valid reasons that parties opt for costs management. The three most significant seem to be:

- The clients may wish this to ensure that the shorter trial scheme provides 'up front' certainty as to potential costs exposure.
- Linked to this, reinforcing the lack of certainty, is that no costs management exposes all the costs to the CPR 44.3(2)(a) proportionality cross check on summary assessment after the costs have been incurred. This may result in the receiving party recovering a lesser amount than expected as proportionality 'trumps' both reasonable and necessary expenditure. In other words, whilst work may have been reasonably or necessarily incurred under a specific direction, if the total, when judged retrospectively against the relevant factors at CPR 44.3(5), is deemed disproportionate, the costs will be reduced to that sum which is determined to be proportionate.
- CPR 51 PD N 2.59 and 2.60 require parties to file and exchange costs schedules containing 'sufficient detail of the costs incurred in relation to each applicable phase identified by Precedent H to the costs budgeting regime. . .'. In other words the parties must record time by phase in any

[48] *'Confronting costs management'* May 2015 paras 2.2–2.12.

event so that they can produce this detail at the conclusion of the claim. As such the only real saving is the initial costs of budgeting and the costs of managing expenditure under the budget. In some cases this saving may not seem proportionate when viewed against the uncertainty referred to in the two points above.

Q10. Should a party file its Precedent H on the basis of the way in which it thinks the claim should progress, e.g. if it thinks a split trial is appropriate should the budget be completed on that basis?

4–33 CPR 3 PD E 6 is clear on this. The court may direct that budgets are limited initially to part of the proceedings and subsequently extended to cover the whole of proceedings. Accordingly, unless the court has so directed, the budget must cover the entire proceedings. This means that any party which proposes to seek costs management of part only of the proceedings has two options. The first is to file and exchange a budget of the whole proceedings and then seek a direction before the case management conference that budgets are filed and exchanged on the additional alternative basis. The second is to apply before the time expires for budgets to be filed and exchanged under CPR 3.13 for an extension of time to file budgets and for a direction that budgets should be limited initially to a discrete part of the proceedings.

The advantage of the first approach is that the party has complied with CPR 3.13 and does not face sanction under CPR 3.14. The disadvantage is that if the court agrees that the claim proceeds with budgeting of part only, then the parties may have incurred the cost of preparing two budgets instead of one.

The advantage of the second approach is that if the court agrees with it, then one or both parties may have saved the cost of preparing two budgets at this stage. The disadvantage is that whilst a prospective application will be treated as one for an extension of time and not as one involving relief from sanctions (see *Hallam Estates v Baker*[49]), in this age of robust case management, it is a brave course to adopt. However, there is no doubt that it is better than filing and exchanging a full budget and raising the possibility of limited costs management only at the case management hearing when the court will then have difficulties deciding whether that is proportionate (without knowing the cost of so doing) and costs managing if it agrees (e.g. the court accepts that it is just and proportionate that there should be a preliminary trial on liability, but the budgets are not readily divisible between costs on liability and costs on quantum).

Interestingly, the Precedent H guidance suggests that the trial of a preliminary issue may be dealt with as a contingency in the budget. In practical terms it is hard to see how this could be done in an informative way, as to do so would have the court budgeting one figure under one contingency phase for all the work to be incurred to the end of the preliminary point, rather than by the identified phases in Precedent H. As such it would be difficult, if not

[49] *Hallam Estates v Baker* [2014] EWCA Civ 661.

impossible, for the court to determine the proportionality by phases to enable it to manage the steps to be incurred in the preliminary issue proportionately.

Q11. Is it better for a party to over-estimate costs in the budget filed and exchanged, on the basis that it is then likely to see a higher budget set and less likely to need to go back to the court asking for the budget to be varied under CPR 3 PD E 7.6? Conversely, if a party recognises that it is likely to be the paying party is underestimation better, trying to persuade the court to reduce the budgets of all parties to that level to limit the potential liability for costs or limit the work that can be undertaken, making the outcome of the claim less certain as a result?

The simple answer to the related questions above is that the parties must complete Precedent H in a fashion that enables them to sign the statement of truth set out in CPR 22 PD 2.2A. As is clearly set out in CPR 22 PD 5 and, by cross reference, CPR 32.14, the consequence of verifying the budget by statement of truth knowing that the Form H does not give a fair and accurate statement of incurred and estimated costs that it would be reasonable and proportionate for the client to incur, is possible proceedings for contempt of court. Representatives should be extremely wary of adopting 'tactical budgets'—whether high or low. **4–34**

Q12. If one party puts in an absurdly low budget is it advisable for the other party to agree it or will this suggest an acceptance that any costs above that level are not reasonable and proportionate and so prejudice its own budget which is significantly higher?

Yes it is advisable to agree it. This will not prevent submissions being made to the court that such a budget is artificially low, that it has been agreed because that is in the other party's best interest to limit potential exposure to 'between the parties' costs in the event of a subsequent adverse costs order, but that budget has no relevance whatsoever to what the reasonable and proportionate costs of the other party may be. Courts will be astute to the possibility of tactical budgeting (whether high or low). **4-35**

Q13. If a defendant brings an additional claim against a party other than the claimant, does the defendant need to produce two budgets—one for the defence of the claim and one for the pursuit of the additional claim—or will one total budget suffice?

There is no clear guidance upon this. However, the situation did arise and was considered by Coulson J in *CIP Properties (AIPT) Ltd v Galliford Try Infrastructure Ltd*[50] (see **Q1** above). In that case one of four additional parties suggested that the defendant should provide separate costs budgets for the defence of the claim and for the discrete claims against each additional party. The response of the defendant was that the costs overlapped, with some costs **4–36**

[50] *CIP Properties (AIPT) Ltd v Galliford Try Infrastructure Ltd* [2014] EWHC 3546 (TCC) Coulson J.

being common costs, and that to do separate budgets would be "unworkable, impractical and expensive". Coulson J concluded that as it was a case where it would be difficult to identify what of the overall costs would be spent on the defence and what on the additional claims, it would be unfair and disproportionate to order separate budgets. He cited with approval the judgment of Master Kaye QC in *Lotus Cars Ltd v Mechanica Solutions Inc.*[51] In multi party litigation the Master had concluded that:

> *" . . . where the management of cases is to be treated as common and is dealt with accordingly, there is no sensible reason why the costs budgeting should always be considered separately and some good reasons why it should not".*

What seems clear is that each case is likely to be fact specific, but that where the issues overlap inextricably then the court is unlikely to order separate budgets.

Q14. Does the budget have to be on Precedent H or can parties produce their own forms provided that they recognisably contain the same information?

4-37 CPR 3PD E 6 is clear: a budget must be in the form of Precedent H annexed to CPR 3PD E. This degree of prescription contrasts with the more flexible language adopted by the CPR when 'suggesting' the use of a particular Form e.g. in CPR 44 PD 9.5(3) *'The statement of costs should follow as closely as possible Form N260.* This interpretation is supported by the fact that CPR 3 PD E 6 refers expressly to Page 1 of Precedent H when considering budgets below £25,000 or where the statement of value is below £50,000. Note also that the same PD provision requires the Precedent H to be in landscape format and an easily legible typeface. A final and more general point on this topic, is that experience shows that even when use of a particular form is recommended, but not mandatory, problems often arise for those who devise and use their own version. Unless there is a very good reason, counsel of caution is to adopt the recommended version of a form – this avoids the risk of omitting an essential piece of information.

Q15. How detailed should be the assumptions upon which the budget is based?

4–38 The length of assumptions accompanying Precedent H is an acknowledged area of contention. The minutes of the July 2015 meeting of the Civil Procedure Rules Committee revealed that *'An attempt should be made to limit the amount of detail provided by way of schedules of assumptions'.* The result is a clearer steer to proportionality in the revised Precedent H guidelines, which parties are obliged to follow pursuant to CPR 3 PDE 6(b). The amount of detail falling within those guidelines depends upon the case.

What is clear is that attached breakdowns of costs that rendered the Precedent H far more akin to a bill for a prospective detailed assessment are

[51] *Lotus Cars Ltd v Mechanica Solutions Inc* [2014] EWHC 76 (QB) Master Kaye QC.

clearly contrary to requirements and are things of the past. The guidelines have made it clear that the purpose of the assumptions is so that other parties and the court can readily understand the case plan upon which the budget is predicated, e.g. how many witnesses, what type of disclosure, how many experts and whether party or jointly instructed and the length of trial. Remember that the court is also likely to have both the directions questionnaire and draft directions from all parties, which should also provide clear indications as to the assumptions under which the parties propose to progress the claim.

Q16. The guidance for completion of Precedent H is brief and it is not always clear where certain items of work should be included. Is there any sanction for inserting items in what the court may regard as the wrong phase of the budget?

The decisions in *Bank of Ireland v Philip Pank Partnership*[52] and *Americhem* 4–39
Europe Ltd v Rakem Ltd[53] suggest that the court may treat insertion of items in the wrong place in the budget as irregularities rather than things that render the budget a nullity.

Obviously parties should follow the Precedent H guidance but where it is not clear there is a real danger that the process of completing the Precedent H becomes one of form rather than substance. The document should inform the parties and the court to enable the parties to reach agreement or raise any issues of contention and to enable the court to case and costs manage properly. If it is not clear where to insert specific work and the cost incurred and to be incurred on that (e.g. on an interim application that has already been made and so arguably is not a contingency, but does not fit happily into any other phase) the key is to ensure that wherever it is included it, and the costs attributable to it, are clearly identified. In the example given, it may be best to insert the application as a contingency, even though it creates the oddity that work has already been undertaken and costs spent on something that comes in a phase that the guidance refers to as 'anticipated'. At least by so doing the expenditure is in the budget and the costs attributable to it are set out separately—assisting the court under CPR 3 PD E 7.4 as what has already been spent informs what costs should be budgeted going forward.

Q17. The Precedent H guidance notes have been amended to include a specific reference to CPR 44.3 (5) and 44.4(3) and state that when deciding the reasonable and proportionate costs the court will include in its consideration *'where and the circumstances in which the work was done as opposed to where the case is heard'*. What is the significance of these amendments?

The reference to the two CPR provisions is because these are, respectively, 4-40
the procedural provisions that define whether costs are proportionate and

[52] *Bank of Ireland v Philip Pank Partnership* [2014] EWHC 284 (TCC) Stuart-Smith J.
[53] *Americhem Europe Ltd v Rakem Ltd* [2014] EWHC 1881 (TCC) Stuart-Smith J.

whether costs are reasonable. Although they have been put in chronological order, as they follow a reference to reasonable and proportionate costs, it may have made this link easier to understand if they had been inverted so it was clear that 44.3(5) referred to proportionality and 44.4(3) to reasonableness.

The words at the end are an extension of CPR 44.4(3)(g). However, the tenses used do not sit happily with the task of budget setting, which is about prospective costs, and seem to resonate more with a retrospective assessment of costs. However, as these words appear in the guidance notes for completion of a form for use in prospective costs budgeting they should be interpreted purposively. Doing so, it seems likely that these words have been inserted to deal with the possibility of forum shopping -- where representatives are based in one location, but issue proceedings out of another, where, for example, guideline hourly rates are higher or lower, resulting in a budget that is artificially high or low. However, as budgets are not set by reference to hourly rate and as the court is astute to tactical budgeting arguments[54], forum shopping should not result in any benefit in any event. Linked to this, it is worth remembering that amendments inserted at CPR 29 PD 2.6A already compel parties in claims in specialist lists to justify in detail why these should be heard in London and not in regional specialist courts where the dispute arises in a region outside London.

Q18 Should the costs of surveillance evidence be included in a budget? If not, if surveillance evidence is subsequently obtained, should applications be made under CPR 3 PD E 7.6 to amend the budgets?

4-41 In *Purser v Hibbs & anor*[55] the court concluded that, contrary to the note at 3.15.3 of the 2015 *White Book*, a defendant should be allowed to recover the costs of surveillance evidence, notwithstanding that those costs had not been included in the costs budget on the basis there was 'good reason' for those costs not to have been included In the budget at all. The court referred to the absence of any reference to this type of evidence in either Precedent H or the guidance upon it. The rationale for the decision was that alerting a fraudulent claimant to the possibility of covert surveillance evidence would discourage judicious use of such evidence and the court did not wish to do so. As a result when the evidence showed the claimant to be exaggerating injuries there was 'good reason' to allow recovery in excess of the budget figure. In fact, the court had already decided to award these costs on the indemnity basis, rendering their lack of inclusion in the budget of academic interest only for, as a result, the requirement for 'good reason' under CPR 3.18 did not arise on subsequent assessment anyway as it only applies to a standard basis assessment. Accordingly the defendant would not have been constrained by the budgeted figures (see para **4-20** above). It is also arguable that the guidance and the Precedent H do cover this situation without requiring express reference as this type of evidence falls within both disclosure and witness statement evidence.

[54] See for example *CIP Properties (AIPT) Ltd v Galliford Try[2015] EWHC 481 (TCC)* para.24.
[55] *Purser v Hibbs & anor* unreported 19.5.2015 QBD HHJ Moloney QC.

In any event *Purser* only deals with half the story (this is not intended to be a criticism, because it only had to do so). The reason for this is that the court in *Purser* was determining the award of costs after the claimant accepted the defendant's CPR 36 offer on receipt of the surveillance evidence, but outside the relevant period for acceptance. As the parties could not agree the incidence of costs, the court had to determine them under what is now CPR 36.13(4) and (5). However, what of the situation where surveillance evidence is served, but the claim continues? Clearly the case/costs managing judge cannot budget retrospectively, but the admission of the evidence is surely a significant development in the litigation pursuant to CPR 3 PD E 7.6.and as a result that provision requires parties to revise budgets. At this stage there is no 'secrecy' requirement – the evidence has been served. In that situation one would expect both parties to apply for a prospective variation of budgets (regardless of the obligation to do so under CPR 3 PD E 7.6), because they want prospective approval of additional costs, rather than find themselves arguing 'good reason' under CPR 3.18 at a later date. The claimant's solicitor will want to view the evidence and take instructions, parties will want to put the evidence to experts, ask questions and review answers, counsels' views may be sought, the evidence may impact on any settlement work and it is likely to affect the trial time estimate. Accordingly service of surveillance evidence should be accompanied (by the defendant) and swiftly followed (by the claimant) by service of revised budgets, an attempt to agree these, and, failing that, by applications to the court for variation of the budgets set. If revision is not sought it seems unlikely that the court will conclude that the costs related to surveillance after disclosure of it either fall outside the budget or that there is a 'good reason' to depart from the original budget at any subsequent assessment on the standard basis as there seems no logical explanation for why parties would not seek prospective variation.

How does the court approach this evidence and any costs budget variation going forward, assuming, if the evidence is served outside the time set for disclosure and witness statement evidence, that the court permits the 'late' evidence by any appropriate grants of relief from sanction or retrospective extensions of time and the parties seek budget variation? This involves consideration of CPR 1.1 (to manage cases justly and at proportionate cost), CPR 3.17 (taking into account the cost of any procedural step), CPR 3.15(3) (if a costs management order has been made the court will thereafter control the parties' budgets) and CPR 3 PD E 7.6 (the court may approve, vary or disapprove the proposed variations to the budget). When undertaking this exercise the court will be astute to the fact that any previous determination of the relevant proportionality factors under CPR 44.3(5) may require revision because this evidence may engage 44.3(5)(c) and (e) – a timely reminder that proportionality is a flexible concept and may vary during the lifetime of a claim. The court will then determine, against the proportionality factors, the extent to which it is just and proportionate to permit the evidence and, if so, the reasonable and proportionate costs that should be added to the relevant phases of the budgets.

Q19. Will the introduction of 'J--Codes'[56] lead to Precedent H being completed to include all costs—including those of a solicitor/client nature?

4–42 No. The court has no role in budgeting solicitor and client costs—those remain a matter of contractual retainer. J-Codes will enable representatives to record time against the specific phases of the Precedent H and should simplify both the production of Precedent H and the management of any budget set by a costs management order. So far as the court is concerned the use of these codes should enable easier comparison of the budget and the sum spent on each phase budgeted if there is a challenge on any subsequent assessment—although this will require practitioners to separate out 'solicitor and client' costs from costs recoverable 'between the parties' if the retainer is not limited to budgeted costs.

J-Codes should also make it easier for a party to identify the costs attributable to any free standing application that falls outside a budget under CPR 3 PD E 7.9.

The voluntary pilot in the SCCO from 1 October 2015, with, the intention that at some stage this will become a compulsory pilot, should provide further information.

Q20. Do the costs allocated to contingencies count when determining whether or not a budget exceeds £25,000 and, in consequence, in determining whether only page 1 of the Precedent H needs to be completed?

4–43 As the budget is in Precedent H and that includes contingencies and, as any contingencies that the court includes in the costs management order it makes plainly form part of the budget, it follows that the sums included by parties as contingencies in Precedent H count towards the total budget and even if, absent these, the budget would be less than £25,000, the full Precedent H must be completed.

Q21. Does the introduction of costs management mean that the court is rarely likely to dispense with a case/costs management conference and deal with directions and budgets as a paper exercise?

4–44 Clearly having a case/costs management hearing introduces delay and expense to cases. If the court is able to undertake this work as a paperwork exercise that would be the preferable course (indeed Jackson LJ in the final report was at pains to stress that only case management hearings that had a purpose should be listed). However, unless the case management directions and budgets are agreed and the court is prepared to approve both, then it is difficult to envisage

[56] For more information on J-Codes, see Jackson Review Drafting Group, *Civil Litigation J-Code Set Overview and Guidelines*, 4 August, 2014.

how a hearing can be dispensed with at this stage. Even the optional provisional paper budget scheme introduced for certain work in the Manchester Civil Justice Centre envisages an oral hearing if any party wishes after the provisional setting of the budget. It is hoped that as the regime settles in and the experience of practitioners and judges alike grows, then an increasing number of budgets and proposed directions will lend themselves to a paper determination. In the meantime, parties should seek to narrow as many issues as possible and the insertion of 'discussion reports' at CPR 3.13(2) will assist in this process and enable the judge to 'target' preparation in advance of the CCMC. If there is early and significant agreement the parties should inform the court of this as early as possible as that will reduce the required hearing time for a case management conference and that may both expedite the listing of the hearing (as a shorter time estimate ought to lead to earlier court availability) and reduce the cost of the hearing. It is fair to observe that the amendment to CPR 3.13 means that in many cases Precedents H will be filed and exchanged later and this means that CCMC time estimates will have to be set on a 'worst case assumption', allowing sufficient time for both case and costs management and the chances of the court dealing with the matter as a paper exercise are reduced.

Parties should remember, in any event, that they are under a duty to endeavour to agree appropriate directions anyway (CPR 29.4).

Where it is not possible to dispense with a hearing, the parties should, at least, consider whether a telephone case/costs management hearing is feasible (subject to the court being prepared to accommodate this). In many cases there is an argument to be made that a hearing by telephone is more proportionate (e.g. where the advocates are not local to the hearing centre). However, whilst CPR 23 APD.6.2(c) suggests that a case management conference will be by telephone unless the court orders otherwise, this is in respect of hearings up to an hour long. Many case/costs management hearings are listed for longer than this.

Q22. A number of courts are issuing detailed directions when listing a CCMC. Are these necessary and should they be standardised?

This was a topic considered by Jackson LJ in his May 2015 *Confronting costs* **4-45**
management lecture[57]. He concluded that it ought to be possible to create a standard order, distilling the best from those orders that have emerged from the 2 3/4 years' experience acquired by the judiciary. What is essential is that any order is proportionate to the needs of the specific case. In many cases a light touch only will be needed e.g. those judges who budget and create case management orders electronically will require the Precedents H and draft directions in electronic and alterable form (and self calculating in respect of the budgets). Even when there is a 'standard order' only those parts of it pertinent to the individual case should be used. The danger of a tick box form

[57] *Confronting costs management* May 2015 para 8.1.

is that there is a temptation to tick all the boxes in every case. If concerns over the costs of the costs management process are to be addressed, directions must be targeted proportionately.

Q23.Does CPR 3.14 apply to any failure to file a costs budget?

4-46 A strict interpretation of CPR 3.14 reveals that it applies to failure to comply with any requirement to file a budget and not just to the preliminary requirement to do so under CPR 3.13 -- *'as required by the rules or as the court otherwise directs'*. Accordingly, any order of the court requiring the filing of a costs budget carries the sanction of CPR 3.14. The practical outcome where this occurs before any costs management order has been made is simple – the defaulting party is limited in the terms of CPR 3.14. However, what if the failure arises after a costs management order has been made e.g. where the court orders amended budgets to determine the effect on proportionality of any proposed further direction or after there is a discontinuance or admission of part of the claim and the costs will reduce?

This presents a number of options and to date there is no guidance on this. The options are:

- The sanction applies only to all costs from the date of the breach -- so any budgets set are varied to reduce them from the date of breach to future court fees only. However, this may be a complicated exercise when the breach arises in mid stage of many of the phases and there will need to be agreement or assessment of how much of the permitted budget had been spent at the time of default. This increases the likelihood of detailed assessment – defeating one objective of costs management. In addition this has the effect of 'varying' a previous order, as applying the sanction to future costs, means that any budget the court may have already set for those phases is reduced.
- The sanction applies only to the costs directly linked to the significant variation in the litigation. This is simple if the development would ordinarily lead to increased budgets. The defaulting party's budget is only increased by any further and additional court fees. However, this approach does not work where the significant development should result in a reduction in costs -- not only because there are unlikely to be any further court fees, but, more importantly, because the purpose of the amended budgets was to enable the court to revise budgets downwards in the light of the development that alters the reasonableness and proportionality assessment going forward anyway. Accordingly the failure to file the budget leads to no sanction as the outcome should be the same as if the party had filed a reduced budget removing these costs anyway (albeit that the court is deprived of the clear information to make this decision).
- The sanction applies retrospectively and the previously set budgets are void, This sanction would appear to breach the provisions of 3.12 and 3.15 that costs management can only be of costs 'to be incurred'.

On balance the first option appears both the most logical and the one that seems to fit the closest with the costs management mechanism, but higher court authority appears inevitable at some stage.

Q24. Should the discussions that the parties have when attempting to agree the costs budgets be without prejudice?

The amended CPR 3.13 requires the parties to file an agreed 'budget discussion report' at least seven days before the CCMC. However, as with any discussions, there is nothing to prevent both 'open' and 'without prejudice' proposals being made in an attempt to reach agreement over budgets or certain phases within the budgets. **4-47**

Q25 Does the court give the directions first and subsequently costs manage?

As costs management and case management go hand in hand, the two cannot be separated. If the case management directions are set without reference to the costs, with the budgeting exercise conducted afterwards, then all the court is doing when costs managing is pricing directions that have been given. The consequence is that if the court subsequently determines that a particular direction cannot be budgeted proportionately, there is nothing it can do as the direction has already been given. In contrast, if the two are done hand in hand the proportionate expenditure informs the appropriate direction. In simple terms, the danger of setting the directions and then costing them is that the directions ordered are those that the court determines are needed in the particular case. However, CPR 44.3(2)(a) makes it clear that proportionality trumps need and the overriding objective 'to deal with a case at proportionate cost' applies to any case management decision. The court should be giving directions that see the case dealt with proportionately and that assessment can only be made by dealing with the directions and the relevant phase of the budget simultaneously. This was a theme to which Jackson LJ returned in *'Confronting costs management*[58]*'* concluding that the proportionate cost for a phase inevitably determined the proportionate case management direction for that phase. This might mean that the court's preliminary view of the proportionate direction would need to be revised if the cost associated with it was not proportionate e.g. a more limited disclosure order may have to be adopted to ensure proportionality of spend on that phase. **4–48**

Q26. Should costs lawyers attend CCMCs?

This must be for the client to decide. In principle there is no reason why a costs lawyer/costs draftsman should not attend provided that this person has rights of audience. Anecdotally it seems that some CCMCs are attended by counsel/solicitor and a costs lawyer/draftsman. Views differ, but, provided only one of the advocates addresses the court on each point, there appears to **4-49**

[58] *Confronting costs management* May 2015 paras 7.4 -7.6.

be nothing wrong with this approach. Indeed there has long been a history of costs counsel and a costs lawyer/draftsman attending detailed assessment with the former addressing the court on substantive points of principle and then handing over to the costs lawyer/draftsman for the minutiae of assessing actual sums. This begs the question of whether a costs lawyer/draftsman is necessary at the CCMC as the court will not be undertaking anything approaching an assessment and the appropriate person to attend is the one best able to address the court on proportionality and how this translates into the reasonable and proportionate directions and budget for each phase.

Q27. The court has suggested that costs already incurred at the time of the costs management order can be the subject of a costs management order. Is this correct?

4-50 This issue arose in *SARPD Oil Ltd v Addax Energy S.A & anor*[59]. This was a case concerning security for costs, but the question of budgeting arose in the context of the amount that might be ordered as security. Ultimately the court made no order for security. However, the court concluded that CPR 3.15(2) contemplates that a costs management order refers to the whole budget (both incurred and estimated costs). However, the judgment makes no reference to CPR 3.15(1), which expressly limits the management of costs to those *'to be incurred'*. Accordingly the judge's concern that CPR 3.18 makes no express distinction between incurred and estimated costs is simply addressed – it does not need to, as only 'to be incurred' costs can be budgeted under 3.12 and 3.15(1) and so CPR 3.18, by definition, can only refer to those costs. CPR 3 PDE 7.4 also makes it clear that 'incurred' costs cannot be the subject of a costs management order.

Q28. The court seems to have adopted a number of approaches to dealing with incurred costs. Is it possible to discern clear guidance on the treatment of these costs in the budgeting exercise?

4-51 There is no doubt that the treatment of incurred costs is difficult and that the court has adopted different approaches to try to address this. The difficulty is that the court cannot budget 'incurred costs' (see **Q27** above), but is required to take these into account when considering the reasonableness and proportionality of all subsequent costs. This presents a number of problems, the most obvious of which are:

- What if the incurred costs already exceed the sum that the court considers a reasonable and proportionate sum for the entire claim?
- What if the incurred costs on a certain phase which is incomplete exceed the sum that the court considers a reasonable and proportionate sum for the entire phase?
- What if the court sets the budget for a phase by determining the reasonable

[59] *SARP Oil Ltd v Addax Energy S.A & anor [2015] EWHC 2426 (Comm).*

and proportionate sum for that phase, deducts from it the amount that has been incurred and budgets the difference for the 'costs to be incurred', but at assessment the assessing judge allows less than the full amount of the incurred costs?

These specific problems are addressed in more detail in the answers to **Qs 29, 30** and **31**, below. However, they have caused the court to grapple with how best to treat incurred costs against the backdrop of case specific situations.

In *Yeo v Times Newspapers Ltd* the court considered the position when it was presented with substantial costs incurred prior to the costs management hearing. It set out CPR 3 PD E 7.4 and concluded that comments on those costs, 'briefly recorded at the time the budget is approved' would greatly assist the parties and the court at the conclusion. At the time of writing this case has just concluded and reports suggest that the parties have agreed the amount the losing party is to pay for costs without need for an assessment.

The problem was more acute in *CIP Properties (AIPT) Ltd v Galliford Try Infrastructure Ltd*. The court was confronted by a budget that it considered 'unreliable', that had been 'deliberately manipulated' and which revealed both the incurred and estimated costs to be disproportionate. Challenged by the extent of the incurred costs, but to ensure that the overall costs were limited to those that he determined to be reasonable and proportionate, Coulson J. adopted a mechanism that enabled him to control all the costs whilst recognising the problem of the assessing judge taking a different view to his in respect of incurred costs. His solution was to limit the recoverable incurred costs per phase, but to devise an off-setting calculator so that if the assessing judge allowed more than that sum, then an equivalent amount should be deducted from the estimated spend budgeted. In other words, regardless of how ultimately the costs are divided between those incurred and those budgeted, the claimant will be limited to the overall sum permitted by this mechanism. This raises a number of issues e.g. can the costs managing judge prospectively limit recoverable costs on a subsequent assessment of costs (para.98 plainly refers to 'assessed costs'), the extent to which, if at all, the costs managing judge may off-set incurred costs in one phase against budgeted costs in another phase (para.97(a) expressly offsets incurred costs on the pre-action phase against future costs generally), the extent to which the court can effectively set a budget for a phase to include both incurred and estimated costs by adopting the set off formula used by the court when CPR 3.12 and 3.15 are clear that budgets are in respect of 'costs to be incurred' and whether the effect of setting a total sum (para.98) precludes arguments under 'good reason' or the exercise by the assessing judge of discretion on 'good reason' for the budgeted sums to be increased on assessment (the effect of which anyway would seem simply to be a £ for £ off-set against incurred sums). This approach has subsequently been adopted in *GSK Project Management Ltd v QPR Holdings Ltd*.

The simple answer to the question is that 'guidance' on the treatment of incurred costs comes from CPR 3 PD E 7.4. However, it is clear from the above that the court is still grappling with the question of how to implement this fairly on a practical level, Further authority seems inevitable. In the meantime the answers to the subsequent three questions attempt to address some of the issues that arise.

Q29. Are incurred costs relevant to the overall costs at the budgeting stage or only relevant on a phase by phase basis?

4-52 This picks up on the previous answer. CPR 3 PD E 7.4 refers to incurred costs without reference to specific phases. Although the judgment does not overtly say so, it may be that it is the absence of an express link between 7.4 and individual phases that was relied upon by the court in *CIP Properties (AIPT) Ltd v Galliford Try* (see above) to justify off-setting of the incurred expenditure on one phase against the 'to be incurred' budget on another phase (e.g. the off-set at paragraph 97(a) of any pre-action costs subsequently assessed above £680,000 against the prospective budgeted figures in other phases – albeit without specifying any particular phase). Difficulties with adopting this approach have been mentioned above. However, this narrower question highlights what appear to be insurmountable procedural hurdles to the adoption of a general off- set. These are that:

- Costs managements orders are made in respect of budgets which are set by what is reasonable and proportionate for individual phases. Accordingly a formula that may operate, albeit retrospectively, to reduce what has been determined as the reasonable and proportionate sum for a specific phase to a sum less than that by an off-set of incurred costs from another phase, means that in those instances where the off-set operates, the court has not set the budget as required under CPR 3 PD E 7.3.
- At assessment on the standard basis, by a combination of CPR 44.3(1) and (2)(a), the receiving party may only recover those costs which are reasonable and proportionate. CPR 3.18 is clear that the court looks at whether there should be a departure from the budget by reference to the last agreed/approved sums for each phase. As the agreed/approved sums for those phases budgeted have been expressly determined by reference to the same criteria (under CPR 3 PD E 7.3), how can it be a 'good reason' under CPR 3.18 (or, indeed, correct under CPR 44.3) to reduce budgeted costs on one phase by an off-set from another phase.

Although it did not arise in *CIP Properties (AIPT) Ltd v Galliford Try*, it is conceivable that this situation could arise in reverse adopting this formula. This would happen where a party actually recovers less at subsequent assessment for incurred costs than the court had assumed it would when ordering the general inter phase off-set. The same problems arise, albeit in reverse. The budget for a particular phase would be retrospectively varied to a sum over that which was reasonable and proportionate for that phase or the court would have to assess the sum for the budgeted costs for that phase in excess of the reasonable and proportionate sum.

As stated above, depending upon how the court articulates its decision and with properly drafted recitals reflecting this in the costs management order, there is a possibility of applying a later off-set between incurred and budgeted costs within a phase, resulting in either an addition or a deduction to the budgeted sum for 'good reason' if the assessing judge is so minded, However, for the reasons set out above these options are not available when the off-set is between different phases.

However, this does not mean that overall incurred costs have no relevance. Clearly when the court undertakes its initial determination of overall proportionality, to inform the proportionate case management directions and budgets for the discrete phases, the total 'incurred costs' will determine how much of the overall proportionality figure remains.

Q30. What happens if the total incurred costs means that even with the most proportionate case management possible it is not possible to budget costs 'to be incurred' at a level that when added to those 'incurred costs', comes within the court's overall assessment of proportionality?

As discussed in response to the previous two questions this is a real, rather than merely theoretical problem. There are a number of possible outcomes as follows: 4-53

- The court declines to make a costs management order (as was the decision of Coulson J. in *Willis v MRJ Rundell and Associates Ltd & anor*[60]). Whilst this leaves all of a budget exposed to the subsequent proportionality cross check at any subsequent assessment under CPR 44.3(2)(a), it does mean that the court has lost one of the vital tools out of its robust case management armoury. In reality, even with robust case management and the provisions of CPR 44 PD 3 (which deals with the relevance of filed budgets in cases where no costs management order is made), the costs incurred by the end are likely to be even higher than those in the budget and it will be more challenging to manage the case in accordance with the overriding objective. The one occasion where this may be less challenging is if the case managing judge is also to be the assessing judge on any subsequent assessment (an option for the District Bench). As trenchant comments and recitals to the case management order justifying the fact no costs management order has been made and giving a view of what the case managing judge determined to be the overall proportionate figure, coupled with the fact both parties know that the same judge will conduct any subsequent detailed assessment, may encourage greater cost control going forward, recognising the inevitability of outcome on assessment of increased expenditure. This may also avoid the need for an assessment as

[60] *Willis v MRJ Rundell and Associates Ltd & anor [2013] EWHC 2923 (TCC).*

the parties will know what is likely to happen at any subsequent assessment when the assessing judge undertakes the CPR 44.3(2)(a) proportionality cross check at the end (a figure not dissimilar to that indicated at the case management conference).

- The court adopts the approach of Warby J. in *Yeo v Times Newspapers Ltd*[61] and records as recitals comments on 'incurred costs'. He adopted this route adding, by way of explanation that to do so *'. . .is likely to help the parties reach agreement without detailed assessment later on if these reasons are briefly recorded at the time the budget is approved'*
- The court adopts the approach of Coulson J as set out above. In *GSK Project Management Ltd v QPR Holdings Ltd*[62] this is precisely what the court did. As noted above this approach does raise interesting challenges. It is right to record that the problems of 'incurred costs' in *CIP* presented far more of a challenge on costs management than they did in *Yeo*. In *CIP* the 'incurred costs' totalled £4,226,768.16. At the end of the costs management exercise, adopting his off-set formula across the phases, the total that the court decided would ultimately be recoverable was £4,280,000. As the pre-action phase spend was over £1.3 million and as the total sum Coulson J 'allowed' overall in those phases where there was an incurred sum was always less than the incurred sum, the extent of his difficulty in costs management is obvious.
- Another way is a variation of the *CIP* approach, but one that may be seen to sit more comfortably within the existing rules. It extends the recitals approach advocated in *Yeo*. Under this approach the court first indicates and recites its view of overall proportionality of each party's costs. The court then case and costs manages by phases. In those phases where the 'incurred costs' already equal/exceed what the court decides is the proportionate sum for that phase, nothing is budgeted and the court recites its finding on the proportionate overall sum for the phase. In those phases where the 'incurred costs' do not equal or exceed the overall proportionate figure for that phase, the court budgets the difference and recites its view on the overall proportionate sum for that phase. This does leave matters to the assessing judge and, as such, is less prescriptive than the *CIP* approach, but provides a formula that sits happily with the budgeting by phase requirement, does not remove the assessing judge's discretion on arguments on 'good reason', provides clarity of intended outcome from the costs managing judge to the assessing judge and provides a mechanism to ensure that the overall costs are ultimately proportionate. Remember that the assessing judge will apply CPR 44.3(2)(a) as a cross check at the end of any assessment. Whilst this cannot apply to budgeted costs, as they have already been set by reference to proportionality, all costs incurred at the time of the costs management order are subject to the cross check. Armed

[61] *Yeo v Times Newspapers Ltd [2015] EWHC 209 (QB).*

[62] *GKN Project Management Ltd v QPR Holdings Ltd [2015] EWHC 2274 (TCC).*

with this clear order and forewarned of the likely outcome of any assessment it will be a brave party or one armed with genuine 'good reason' on any particular phase who accepts the challenge of an assessment.

Q31. If there has been a significant front loading of the costs so that by the time of the costs management hearing the costs already spent exceed what the court regards as the proportionate expenditure on the claim, can the court set a budget going forward of nil?

No. As set out above, the reason for this is that the budget is not set as an overall sum. It is set by phase under CPR 3 PD E 7.3. Accordingly, even if the court concludes that the incurred sum to date exceeds that which is proportionate to have dealt with the entire claim, it must look at the budget on a phase by phase basis. This may mean that the budget for certain phases may be set at nil if the court thinks the incurred sum under that phase already equals or exceeds the reasonable and proportionate cost for the entire phase. This is because CPR 3 PD E.7.4 requires the court to take costs already incurred 'into account when considering the reasonableness and proportionality of all subsequent costs'. However, there will be other phases, such as PTR, trial preparation and trial, where plainly there will be no incurred costs at the CCMC stage and it would be wrong, as the budget is set by reference to the reasonable and proportionate costs for each phase, for the court to budget these phases at nil. **4–54**

Of course, as noted in the answers to **Qs 28-30** above, the court may also record its comments on the costs incurred before the date of any budget to assist the court at any later assessment when it considers the non budgeted costs.

Q32. What can be done to avoid the potential injustice of the court setting a phase budget by basing this on an overall view of the proportionate sum for that phase, deducting the incurred costs and budgeting the difference, only for the assessing judge then to reduce the incurred costs undermining the basis upon which the budget was set?

This has already been identified above as a real risk of setting budgets by reference to the overall proportionality of a phase. However, the final suggested approach in the answer to **Q30** (above) may provide the solution. If the court adopts that approach, then it will be clear to the assessing judge the basis upon which the budget was set, both within the context of overall proportionality and on a phase basis. Of course, the assessing judge is not bound by the costs managing judge's recitals, but if the assessing judge allows less for the incurred costs than the costs managing judge included when setting the budget this may open the door for the receiving party to argue that there is a 'good reason' under CPR 3.18 to depart from the budget for that phase. The 'good reason' being that the budget sum was calculated on the basis that £w had already been spent of the overall proportionate sum for that phase of £x and so the budget for the phase is £x-w, but as the assessing judge has only allowed £w-y for the incurred costs, to achieve the outcome the costs **4-55** managing judge envisaged requires the budget for that phase to be £x-w+y. This preserves the discretion of the assessing judge, which it is arguable that the *CIP* approach does not.

Q33. Should the court set hourly rates as part of the budgeting exercise?

4–56 There still appears to be a divergence of approach on this topic. The straightforward answer is that the court is not required to set hourly rate when costs managing because CPR 3 PD E 7.3 specifically states that the court sets 'total figures for each phase of the proceedings'. This has now been reinforced by CPR 3 PD E 7.10 (which is considered below in **Q34**). There are those who still favour the setting of hourly rates and suggest that the court can only set a total figure by reference to an hourly rate. However, hourly rate in isolation is worthless. It is only relevant if it is multiplied by an amount of time. However, hours multiplied by time smacks of what is 'needed', which brings us back to CPR 3 PD E 7.3 as the court is <u>not</u> charged with setting a budget to allow necessary work—instead it is charged with setting a budget for each phase that is reasonable and proportionate.

There are a number of other reasons why setting the budget by reference to an hourly rate is inappropriate for those still attracted to this approach despite the clear and reinforced provisions of CPR 3 PD E. These reasons are:

- It is too prescriptive. It is for the legal representatives and the client to determine how to spend the sum budgeted for a phase. If the budget is set by a specific hourly rate, then the court is effectively saying that that particular fee earner must do that amount of work. This is micro management taken to an extreme. Setting a total figure enables the representatives and, more importantly, the client, to decide who does what work and what work is contracted out to counsel.
- If the budget is set by reference to hourly rate it opens doors for arguments at assessment as to whether, in fact, a fee earner commanding that rate actually undertook the phase work in question. If the answer is no, then that may be 'good reason' to depart from the budget. These arguments do not arise if the budget is simply a total sum for the phase.
- If an hourly rate is set and at the end of the case, on assessment a different hourly rate is set for the non budgeted work (as the hourly rate set for the budget cannot be determinative in respect of the non budgeted costs as the court has no power to budget them under CPR 3.12 and 3.15), then immediately that opens the door to one or other party to argue 'good reason' to depart from the budget, submitting that the budget was set on the 'wrong' hourly rate.
- Setting rate and then determining the time by which to multiply it has all the hallmarks of a detailed assessment, which CPR 3 PD E 7.3 specifically cautions the court against undertaking when costs managing.
- The amount of court time taken to determine rate and then the time by

which to multiply it renders the budgeting exercise disproportionate—both for the parties and for the court.

- There is a very real risk that parties/representatives will 'forum shop' in cases with no requirement to proceed in a particular court venue.

In summary, CPR 3 PD E 7.3 and 7.10 do not require the court to set hourly rates – indeed 7.10 makes it perfectly plain that the position is quite the reverse – it is expressly not the role of the costs manager to fix or set hourly rates. The emphasis is on a far simpler, less time-consuming and more proportionate process. One aim of costs management is to reduce the incidence of, and time taken on, subsequent assessments of costs. Setting a rate within the budget seems designed to encourage more contested assessments and to defeat this aim.

Q34. If the court does not set the budget by reference to hourly rates and time, then why does Precedent H require this information and, linked to this, what does *'the underlying detail in the budget for each phase used by the party to calculate the totals claimed is provided for reference purposes only to assist the court in fixing a budget'* in CPR 3 PD E 7.10 mean?

This is a very fair point. Whilst this text has always maintained that CPR 3 PD E 7.3 was clear that the court does not set hourly rate and this has been bolstered by CPR 3 PD E 7.10, why does Precedent H require a breakdown, which simply serves to reinforce the 'old' approach to costs - set a rate and multiply it by an amount of time? It is arguable that a form that makes those completing it focus on reasonableness and proportionality in the round is more likely to achieve the desired effect. On that basis Precedent H could be reduced to just the first page in all cases as some have suggested. **4-57**

However, that is not the position, and CPR 3 PD E 7.10 considers the 'underlying detail'. This suggests that some courts may be assisted by this detail. An example of this may be where the parties' budgets are poles apart, but their proposed directions are similar and the court is endeavouring to discern a reason for this. In other words there may be cases where some of the detail assists, but at the end of the day the court will not set rates, will not prescribe the amount of time to be taken, but will simply budget a reasonable and proportionate sum and leave it to the parties to manage the budgets. A review of CPR 3 PD E 7.3 suggests that this was always an option for the court. However, given the apparent inconsistency of approach, notwithstanding that provision, the iteration in CPR 3 PD E 7.10, that the court does not set rate is a welcome one and should reduce some CCMC hearing times significantly.

Q35 How can the court set the budget without assessing prospectively the work that is required and the appropriate hourly rate(s) at which that work should be done?

The court is not charged when setting a budget with 'assessing', giving the word its customary meaning in a costs context. The court is also not charged with determining what work is required. What the court <u>is</u> charged with doing, is **4–58** determining the proportionate case management directions and whether the budgeted costs for a phase of these directions 'fall within the range of reasonable and proportionate costs'. This inevitably involves a decision based on the definition of proportionality at CPR 44.3(5). It is against the backdrop of this definition that the court determines whether the sum sought for a phase is reasonable and proportionate and, if it is not, whether there is a more suitable case management direction and what total sum should be substituted. When looked at in these stark terms, it is clear why a detailed analysis of hourly rate and time does not inform the outcome. The court simply determines the work to be done by reference to proportionate expenditure. It is for that reason that case and costs management have to go hand in hand, so that the directions ordered only permit work that can be undertaken at proportionate cost.

Q36. If the court is budgeting only be reference to a global sum and not taking account of the respective hourly rates, surely this means that a party who has agreed a lower hourly rate retainer will be able to do more work than one with a higher hourly rate? If so this appears unfair.

4–59 Yes—a party with a lower hourly rate retainer is, in theory, able to undertake more work than one with a higher hourly rate. However, there are relevant factors that militate against the apparent unfair consequence:

- The court determines the appropriate proportionate case management directions. These inevitably define the extent of work that may be undertaken, e.g. limits on the number of factual witnesses, the amount of disclosure, the length of trial, etc.
- If the budget is set globally, then it is for a party to determine how to spend that money. Remember, costs are the client's and the budget is the client's to spend—**see Chapter 9 below**. The budget 'set' by the court will have to be explained to the client. Professional obligations on legal representatives may dictate that the way that sum is spent necessitates that the case plan is re-visited (e.g. does the client wish the work to be done by a lower level fee earner or is the client happy to have the higher level fee earner for less time or for the same amount of time, but in the knowledge that some of that cost will, inevitably be irrecoverable from the other party? Does the client want a less expensive expert/counsel or lesser input from the expert/counsel?). In certain instances this may mean that the client seeks alternative representation. What this does highlight is the importance of the retainer, both at the outset and on any variation, in defining precisely what work will be done for what remuneration. There is no doubt that the introduction of budgets reiterates the ongoing importance of managing client expectation, particularly in terms of any restraints that the case and costs management orders impose on a client's instructions.

However, at the end of the day it is for each client to negotiate the retainer with the legal representatives. If one negotiates a lower rate than another, then any consequences based on the differential rate stem from the choice of retainer and not from any costs management order.

Q37. If the court does set the hourly rate in the budget what happens if, at assessment, the assessing court sets a different hourly rate for the non budgeted work?

See the answer to **Q33** above. This may open the door to arguments that there is 'good reason' to depart from the budget. The possible consequences are that the length of summary assessments may be increased, that this persuades the trial judge to order a detailed assessment instead of assessing summarily in a fraction of the time and at a fraction of the cost and that there is an increased incentive for a paying party to take its chances on a detailed assessment. All fly in the face of a desire to make decisions about 'the costs of the costs' simpler and proportionate. **4–60**

Q38. Upon taking over instructions for a client from another firm it is clear that the 'incurred costs' for the pre-action phase in the Precedent H filed and exchanged by that firm are considerably lower than the amount of costs that the client paid that firm for work done during that period. Whilst estimating future costs may be somewhat speculative, is there any explanation for why the incurred costs in Precedent H differ from 'actual costs' incurred?

Yes, there is an explanation, although whether it applies to a particular budget is fact specific both as to the terms of the solicitor and client retainer and as to whether the costs incurred are reasonable and proportionate. The explanation is that the Precedent H is meant to be prepared as a fair and accurate statement of incurred and estimated costs which it would be reasonable and proportionate for the client to incur. This is the wording of the statement of truth under CPR 22 PD 2.2A that appears on the Precedent H. In other words, regardless of the costs actually incurred by the client at the time of the preparation of Precedent H, only those that are reasonable and proportionate should be included. Of course, this does not preclude the actual billed/incurred costs and those appearing in the Precedent H coinciding, but that should only occur if the representative signing the statement of truth on that form are satisfied that those costs are reasonable and proportionate. **4-61**

Q39. Is the budget 'without prejudice' to any subsequent assessment?

CPR 3.18 is clear. On a subsequent standard basis assessment (whether summary or detailed) in a case where the receiving party's costs have been subject to a costs management order, then the court will not depart from the budgeted sums for those phases budgeted unless there is 'good reason' to do so. **4–62**

There is no provision in the rules for applying a 'without prejudice' qualification beyond 'good reason' to a costs management order, it is not part of the costs management regime and seems, simply to add time and costs to the case management process for no purpose—other than possibly assisting the court to identify the proportionate case management directions that should be given (by virtue of setting the budget in the normal way), but in a thoroughly disproportionate way if the budget is qualified other than by CPR 3.18.

Adopting this approach seems to deprive the parties of the certainty that CPR 3.18 provides, involves everyone in an exercise that may well prove futile and seems to act as a clear encouragement to pursue costs issues further at assessment. Accordingly, such an approach seems contrary to the specific costs management provisions and the overriding objective.

Q40. What, if anything, can the court do when the parties agree budgets or phases of the budgets in sums that the court thinks are disproportionate? Is there a potential tension between CPR 3.15(3) and CPR 3 PD E 7.6?

4–63 This is one of the curiosities of the costs management regime. CPR 3.15 clearly envisages that the parties may agree all or part of the budgets and that if they do so, the court is left with the options of making no costs management order at all or making a costs management order recording the extent of the agreement (and approving a budget in respect of those phases not agreed).

However, CPR 3.12(2) makes it clear that the function of the court is to manage both the steps and the costs to be incurred. Accordingly, if the court takes the view that the case management approach of the parties upon which the budget agreement is based is not proportionate, then the court must give proportionate directions. This is reinforced by the duty on the court imposed by CPR 3.17 to take account of the cost of any procedural step and by the overriding objective.

It is unlikely that an agreed budget will remain so if the assumptions upon which the agreement was reached are altered, e.g. if the disclosure phase is agreed on the basis of an order for standard disclosure, but the court permits only a more limited form of disclosure, is a party really likely to maintain the agreement? This means that representatives at court must have ready access to the client during the case management hearing (if the client is not present) so that further instructions may be taken. Of course, if the parties have agreed what the court perceives to be proportionate case management directions, but have simply agreed figures more than the court thinks are proportionate, then there genuinely is nothing that the court can do to interfere with the agreement.

The position becomes even more curious if there is a variation of the budget. CPR 3 PD E 7.6 provides that in such circumstances the parties need only involve the court if they cannot agree the budget variation. This seems to sit unhappily with CPR 3.15(3), which imposes on the court the obligation to control the parties' budgets once it has made a costs management order. How can it do so if the parties may vary the budget by agreement (and, it seems, without any requirement that the agreed varied budget is even filed at the court)? The answer, perhaps, lies in the first sentence of CPR 3 PD E 7.6. The parties may only revise budgets if 'significant developments in the litigation warrant such revisions'. It is hard to think of such developments that will not require consequential case management directions. As already stated, as soon as the court is concerned with case management CPR 3.17 applies and the court must determine whether the procedural step is worth the candle. This may mean that if court determines that the costs the parties have agreed as a consequence of the further directions necessitated by the 'significant developments' are disproportionate, then the directions will not be given. This leaves the parties with the options of proceeding on the basis of the case that was originally budgeted or revisiting the varied budget to try to reach a figure at which the court will determine the significant developments can be dealt with at proportionate costs.

Q41. How important is the breakdown between disbursements and solicitors' fees in an approved/agreed budget?

Whilst the format of Precedent H requires a division between profit costs and **4–64**
various types of disbursement, CPR 3 PD E.7.3 simply requires the court to set the budget for a phase by way of a total figure. Accordingly, many courts are not breaking down the sum budgeted for a specific phase between profit costs, counsel, experts and other disbursements, and for good reason. The rationale for this is that it is for the solicitor and the client to agree how the sum for a phase is to be spent. Solicitors may model this in many ways for the client to choose, e.g. where the proposed budget has been reduced by the court, the client may agree to place less reliance than had been envisaged on counsel or the same amount of reliance, but with the solicitors then using a less expensive fee earner.

Another difficulty of the court being too prescriptive about how the total sum for a phase is spent, is that it reduces the flexibility for the solicitor and client, e.g. if the budget for the pre-trial review is based on a division between solicitor and counsel on the assumption that counsel will attend the PTR and, in fact, the solicitor and the client agree that the solicitor will conduct that hearing, is that then 'good reason' to depart from the budget that was based on counsel attending? As one aim of costs budgeting is to reduce the number of assessments, this is better achieved by the court setting one figure for each phase and leaving the solicitor and client to decide how to spend that sum. Remember that the court is not sanctioning, for example, use of counsel or a fee earner with a set hourly rate at a specific stage: it is instead simply determining what is the reasonable and proportionate' sum of costs for each phase.

Having said all the above, there is no doubt that the breakdown in the Form H may inform the court of the case plan upon which the filed budget is predicated and so influence the decision as to what is the reasonable and proportionate overall sum for a phase.

Q42. To which sum do the percentages in CPR 3 PD E 7.2 apply—the total sum in the Precedent H after the budget has been set or just those parts of the Precedent H that the court has budgeted?

4–65 There appears to be some debate about this, with anecdotal evidence that some take the view that the percentage is to be applied to the 'Grand Total' sum in the bottom right hand box of page 1 of the Precedent H after the budget has been set and others taking the stance that the percentage applies only to the sums budgeted for costs to be incurred in those phases of the Form H that have been costs managed. CPR 3 PD E 7.2 states:

> *"i) that the costs of initially preparing Precedent H are the greater of £1,000 or 1% of the approved and agreed budget;*
> *ii) all other recoverable costs associated with the budgeting and costs management process shall not exceed 2% of the approved or agreed budget."*

The definition of budget in the Glossary to the CPR does not help as it can be read in a way that suits either interpretation. It is this:

> *"Budget - An estimate of the reasonable and proportionate costs (including disbursements) which a party intends to incur in the proceedings"*

'in the proceedings' suggest overall, but 'intends to incur' suggests in the future However, and of greater significance, is that there is no definition in the glossary of what is an 'approved or agreed budget'.

Those arguing for the former interpretation can point to the fact that 'throughout CPR 3.12–3.18, and the accompanying CPR PD E, the budget is described as being in the format of Precedent H. As such, reference to the budget is to the entire Form H. Whilst these points have some resonance, they seem to miss the point that CPR 3 PD E 7.2 refers to the percentage as being set by reference to the 'approved or agreed budget' and not 'the budget'. The only costs within Precedent H that can be approved by the court or agreed by the parties as part of the costs management exercise are those to be incurred. Indeed the specific reference to approval or agreement of the budget is in CPR 3.15(2) and is directly linked to costs to be incurred. This leads inexorably to the conclusion that the percentage can only apply to those parts of the budget in respect of which the court makes a costs management order.

There are three other valid reasons why the interpretation adopted above may be preferred: the first two are by specific reference to the rules and the third is one of common sense:

i) CPR 3.18 expressly uses the words 'approved or agreed budget' and it is clear that in doing so it refers only to those parts of the Precedent H in respect of which the court has made a costs management order, suggesting that there is a difference between the respective definitions of 'budget' and 'last approved or agreed budget'.
ii) If the words 'approved or agreed budget' apply to the entire precedent H total after the costs management exercise then, for the purpose of continuity under CPR 3.18, the court has costs managed incurred costs (which is impermissible) and the CPR 3.18 provisions would apply

to all the costs in the Precedent H and so any subsequent assessment would be on 'good reason' alone.

iii) There would be nothing that the court could do to prevent a party over-estimating 'incurred' costs within the Precedent H to ensure that whatever happened on those parts costs managed, the percentage still came to an inappropriately high sum, even if, at a subsequent assessment of the 'incurred' costs, most were assessed to be irrecoverable as unreasonable and/or disproportionate. It seems utterly illogical that in rules designed to ensure both reasonableness and proportionality of costs, the percentage should be set by reference to a figure, over much of which the court has no control.

Q43. Should parties re-file budgets after the CCMC when a costs management order has been made under CPR 3.15?

Whilst the answer is simple, as CPR 3 PD E 7.7 imposes an obligation upon the parties to do precisely this, it is worth stressing that if the court has made a costs management order that makes it plain from the face of the order, or any attached pages 1 of the budgets, which phases of the Precedent H have been budgeted, and in what amount, the court should be asked, if it does not automatically so do, to dispense with the requirements of CPR 3 PD E 7.7 as they are superfluous and disproportionate in that situation. **4-66**

Q44. Can the parties agree to vary their budgets from that recorded by the court in a costs management order, where there has been no 'significant development' in the litigation, but both are unhappy with the amount budgeted by the court?

No. Once a costs management order has been made by the court, it may only be varied where there are significant developments. The fact that all parties may be unhappy with the costs management order made is not a significant development. The remedy of the parties in such a situation would be to seek to appeal the costs management order. This is reinforced by CPR 3.15(3) which places an obligation upon the court having set a budget to control the parties' budgets thereafter. **4–67**

Q45. Once a budget has been set, should solicitors be monitoring the budgets?

Although the answer to this question is so obvious it ought not to need answering, it leads to a slightly different and more important issue. The answer to the basic question is yes. However, merely monitoring the budget is insufficient in isolation. The more important issue arises if one substitutes the word 'managing' in place of 'monitoring'. Simply watching as the budget for a phase dissipates is largely purposeless, it simply identifies when the money has been spent regardless of whether there has been compliance with the phase direction. What is needed is a planned expenditure within **4-68** the budget. This requires consideration immediately after the CCMC of how the directed phase work is to be undertaken within the budgets set for the phases (assuming that the client is not prepared to fund additional work over and above the budget in the knowledge that it will be irrecoverable 'between the parties'). This must be followed by management to ensure that the directed phase work is completed within budget as planned. Accordingly, it comes as no surprise that some firms are/are considering engaging project managers accustomed to delivering work within budgetary constraint.

Q46. What if a client still wants the legal representatives to incur costs that the court has not allowed within the budget?

4–69 Remember that the costs management exercise is concerned with recoverable costs 'between the parties' only. The basis of retainer remains a contractual issue between the solicitor and the client – **see Chapter 9**. To that extent, provided that the retainer permits it and the expenditure is agreed, the client is not constrained in what costs are actually incurred by the budget set by the court. So, for example, the client may still choose to engage counsel whose brief fees will mean that the client inevitably exceeds the budgeted sum for the trial phase. This is entirely the prerogative of the client provided /he/she realises that there will be a shortfall between expenditure incurred and recovery of costs even if he/she is awarded the costs—see **Q52** and the reference to CPR 46.9(3)(c) below.

However, clearly the case management directions that the court has given do impose an inevitable constraint. For example, if the court has limited a party to a set number of named expert witnesses, then there is no purpose in the client insisting upon the instruction of further experts as their evidence cannot be relied upon in court.

In summary, as Jackson LJ stated in his *Preface and Guide to the Civil Justice Reforms* in the *White Book* 2014:

> *"Within the confines of the directed procedure any party is free to waste its own money if it wishes to do so"*

Q47 What effect will a 'costs sanction' for unreasonable conduct, as suggested by the Court of Appeal in Denton v T H White,[63] have on a costs budget?

4–70 At para.42 of the majority judgment the Court of Appeal said this:

> *"The court will be more ready in the future to penalise opportunism . . . Heavy costs sanctions should, therefore, be imposed on parties who behave unreasonably in refusing to agree extensions of time or unreasonably oppose applications for relief from sanctions. An order to pay the costs of the application under rule 3.9 may not always be sufficient. The court can, in an appropriate case, also record*

[63] *Denton v T H White* [2014] EWCA Civ 906.

in its order that the opposition to the relief application was unreasonable conduct to be taken into account under CPR rule 44.11 when costs are dealt with at the end of the case. If the offending party ultimately wins, the court may make a substantial reduction in its costs recovery on grounds of conduct under rule 44.11. If the offending party ultimately loses, then its conduct may be a good reason to order it to pay indemnity costs. Such an order would free the winning party from the operation of CPR rule 3.18 in relation to its costs budget."

Accordingly, it is clear that the 'costs sanction' envisaged may be relevant to budgets set in two scenarios:

1) If the offending party subsequently becomes the receiving party on an assessment, then the unreasonable opposition may be a 'good reason' to depart from the budget relying upon the provisions at CPR 44.11(1)(b) and 44.11(2)(a).
2) If the offending party subsequently becomes the paying party, then an award of costs on the indemnity basis may follow and, as has already been stated, this means that the provisions of CPR 3.18 do not apply (as that rule is limited to where the court is assessing on the standard basis).

In both situations the effect may be substantial—in the first limiting and in the second increasing costs recovery.

Q48. Can you explain how an award of costs on the standard basis differs from an award of costs on the indemnity basis in circumstances where a costs budget is in place?

The difference stems from the respective definitions of standard basis and indemnity basis costs in CPR 44.3. Under the former costs will only be allowed if costs are reasonably incurred and reasonable and proportionate in amount. Under the latter costs will be allowed if they are reasonably incurred and reasonable in amount. In other words there is no consideration of the proportionality of the costs under an award of indemnity basis costs. As costs budgets are set under CPR 3 PD E 7.3 on the basis of setting a figure within the range of reasonable and proportionate costs, it immediately becomes apparent that a budget cannot be relevant on an indemnity basis assessment as it has been set taking account of something that does not arise under the indemnity basis. This is why CPR 3.18 expressly only applies to standard basis assessments. Accordingly on a standard basis assessment CPR 3.18 applies and there may only be departure from those costs budgeted if there is 'good reason', whilst on an indemnity basis assessment CPR 3.18 does not apply, the budget does not operate as any constraint on recovery of costs and the court simply allows those costs reasonably incurred and reasonably in amount, with the benefit of any doubt going to the receiving party. It is obvious that the potential differential between costs on the standard basis and those on the indemnity basis **4-71** in budgeted cases may, where the costs incurred exceed the budgeted sum, be significant.

Q49 If an award of indemnity costs is made and CPR 3.18 does not apply, does the budget still form the starting point for the assessment of costs?

4-72 No – see para.*4-20* above. The starting point is that CPR 3.18 only applies on standard basis assessments. In effect this provides the explanation for the short answer given. However, to provide greater clarity there are two obvious justifications linked to the same underlying principle. These are:

- The statement of truth on the Precedent H makes it clear that the form should only include 'incurred and estimated costs which it is reasonable and proportionate' for that party to incur. However, on an indemnity basis assessment proportionality has no part to play and, so, using a budget based on a Precedent H, which was prepared taking account of proportionality, as the starting point for an assessment which takes no account of it is immediately and obviously flawed.
- Under CPR 3 PD E 7.3, any budget set by the court will be one within the range of 'reasonable and proportionate costs'. Accordingly the budgeted figures have been set taking account of proportionality which has no place on an indemnity basis assessment.

If there remained any doubt, the comments of Dyson MR cited in para.*4-20* should dispel it.

Q50. What guidance is there on what may constitute 'good reason' under CPR 3.18 to enable a departure from a budget at assessment?

4–73 At the moment there have been no reported authorities on the current provisions in respect of what might constitute good reason. However, as is clear from the text of this chapter, Moore-Bick LJ in *Henry v News Group Newspapers Ltd*,[64] a case within the defamation pilot scheme, clearly envisaged that 'good reason' was intended to present a high hurdle and that the court would not lightly permit departures from the budget. Although in a different context (CPR 3.9), the Court of Appeal has already reinforced the view that the 'good reason' definition bar is set high.

Some 'good reason' departures from the budget are obvious, e.g. where a budgeted contingency does not arise or where a claim is resolved before a specific phase has commenced. Beyond these, counsel of caution must be to seek prospective variation under CPR 3 PD E 7.6 whenever it is appropriate, rather than to run the gauntlet of arguing 'good reason' at assessment.

Whilst *Simpson v MGN Ltd & anor*[65] saw a departure from the budget, this

[64] *Henry v News Group Newspapers Ltd* [2013] EWCA Civ 19.

[65] *Simpson v MGN Ltd & anor [2015] EWHC 126 (QB).*

case provided no guidance on 'good reason' as the court found that there was no 'good reason' – **see para. 4-20** above and **Q51** below.

Q51. Does CPR 3.18(b) prescribe an automatic sanction where the receiving party has failed to amend its budget prospectively and can show no 'good reason' for this failure or, as is suggested in *Simpson v MGN Ltd & anor* (see above), is it for the court, applying the overriding objective, to determine what the just and proportionate sanction should be?

This depends entirely upon the construction of the wording at CPR 3.18(b). In **4-74**
Simpson the court concluded that this provision did not provide a sanction and so, even where there was no 'good reason' to depart from the last approved or agreed budget, that did not mean that the receiving party was automatically precluded from recovering in excess of the budgeted sum.

An alternative view is advanced at para.**4-20** above. This is that the inclusion of the words *'unless satisfied that there is good reason to do so'* in CPR 3.18(b) provide a sanction, which is that absent 'good reason' there is no departure from the budget. We prefer this interpretation. It also seems better to meet two of the objectives of costs management, namely:

- Increased certainty of costs exposure between the parties at the earliest possible juncture so that they make informed decisions about pursuit of a claim or a defence and settlement.
- Increased certainty of costs outcome, resulting in fewer detailed assessments (occupying both court time and resulting in increased expenditure for the parties).

The lesser the clarity as to where the bar to departure from agreed or approved budgets is positioned, the greater both of uncertainty of outcome and of the costs incurred in locating its position.

What does seem certain, is that as more costs managed cases come to assessment, further authority on both the interpretation of the effect of the rule itself and what constitutes 'good reason' is likely to emerge.

Q52. Does the statement of truth on the budget prevent a solicitor recovering more than the budget from the client?

No, subject to the appropriate wording of any specific solicitor and client fee **4–75**
retainer (the qualification is because in County Court proceedings, s.74(3) of the Solicitors Act 1974 limits costs to those which could have been recovered from another party in the absence of any agreement to the contrary).

CPR 22 PD 2.2A makes it clear that the budget is concerned with reasonable <u>and proportionate costs</u>. Proportionality has no place in solicitor/client assessments (which are effectively on the indemnity basis).

However, plainly a solicitor should inform the client of the budgeted sum so that the client is aware of the limit on those costs that may be recovered from another party in the event a costs order is made in the client's favour.

This should enable the client to give informed instructions after the budget has been set. CPR 46.9(3)(c) makes clear that on any assessment of solicitor and client costs, costs are assumed to be unreasonably incurred if they are of an unusual nature or amount and the solicitor did not tell the client that as a result they might be irrecoverable.

Q53. Can a trial judge ordering a detailed assessment of the costs of a party subject to a costs management order, give guidance to the assessing judge on what may be 'good reason' to depart from the budget set.?

4-76 This issue was mentioned in passing in *Capital for Enterprise Fund A LP and another v Bibby Financial Services Ltd (HHJ Pelling QC unreported, 18 November 2015)*. The judge concluded that even if, which he doubted, the trial judge had jurisdiction to indicate that it would be appropriate for there to be a departure from a budget, such power should only be used in exceptional circumstances. This immediately creates an inconsistency if an assessing judge is not assisted by any indication that the trial judge, but if the trial judge conducts a summary assessment then information from the trial relevant to departure for 'good reason' under CPR 3.18 will be before the court. It is arguable that the court in *Capital for Enterprise Fund ALP* took too narrow a view of its function. If it could have used 'trial information' to assist it on a summary assessment, why should that not be before the assessing judge on a detailed assessment: it is the same information and surely carries the same relevance whoever assesses the costs? This view is supported by established authority that trial judges should assist assessing judges with relevant information (e.g. in the context of the application of the conduct provisions under CPR 44.2 [trial judge] and 44.4 [assessing judge] – see for example *Northstar Systems Limited & ors v Fielding & ors*[66] and *Drew v Whitbread Plc*[67]) and there appears no discernible reason why the position should be any different in this situation.

Q54. Can the budgeted sum exceed the sum due from that party to the solicitor under the contractual retainer, and, if so, is this a permitted breach of the indemnity principle?

4–77 The budgeted sum may exceed the sum provided for within the retainer. However, the fact that the court makes a costs management order does not mean that those costs are recoverable from another party regardless of the indemnity principle. Indeed the amendment to the statement of truth on Form H was, in part at least, to address the problem where specific fee retainers made completion of the budget difficult (e.g. in house lawyers, fixed fee cases, etc.).

Breach of the indemnity principle would be a 'good reason' under CPR 3.18 to depart from the budget. However, this may prove a more challenging exercise than it seems at first sight. Imagine the case where the fee retainer is a fixed fee for all work or a Damages Based Agreement where there is simply

[66] *Northstar Systems Limited & ors v Fielding & ors[2006] EWCA Civ 1660 para.34.*
[67] *Drew v Whitbread Plc [2010] EWCA Civ 53.*

'the payment' which cannot be calculated until the end of the claim. How does the solicitor apportion between the phases of Precedent H in those situations? Client retainers may need to be drafted in creative fashion to enable this apportionment and to meet any challenge under 'good reason', e.g. that apportionment of the overall fixed fee/the payment is a matter for the solicitor provided that the work that has been agreed to be done under the retainer is undertaken. It is likely that as these cases work through the system, the court will be confronted with the challenges that they present and authority will emerge.

Q55. What is the position if a Part 7 claim commences as a fast track claim, but subsequently it becomes apparent that the claim is undervalued and needs to be re-tracked to the multi track, but it is not within one of the costs management exceptions in CPR 3.12(1)?

This is not an uncommon scenario—particularly in personal injury proceedings where the prognosis is uncertain at the time of allocation. Whilst the court is not constrained by a statement of value or allocation as to what sum it may award (see CPR 16.3(7)), plainly the claimant must apply to amend the statement of value and to seek re-allocation. In any event, the increase in value is likely to result in a need to be linked with an application for further substantive directions (e.g. change of trial time estimate/trial window/further expert evidence, etc.). **4–78**

As the costs management provisions apply to all multi track CPR 7 claims (subject to the exceptions detailed in CPR 3.12(1)), then the effect of any re-allocation is to bring the claim within the costs management provisions. As such, it would be prudent for the claimant to attach a Precedent H to the application (and if the application is by consent for the defendant to do likewise). In any event, expect the court to order Precedent H to be filed and exchanged when listing the application or before it considers any consent order if the parties have not already provided them. This is not only because the court wishes to consider costs managing, but also because of the provisions of CPR 3.17. Re-allocation is a case management decision and the court will need to know the cost consequence of any decision it takes.

If the application comes very late in the claim and the only variations to the existing case management directions are the amendment to statement of value, re-allocation and fresh trial window, it may be appropriate to include in the application a request that the court exercises its power under CPR 3.12(1)(c) not to costs manage. This would be on the basis that the cost of the exercise may, in context, be disproportionate as the costs and steps to be incurred at that stage are limited. Of course this argument is something of a double-edged sword, as the court may take the view that as such, the costs management exercise will not occupy much court time and can be dealt with promptly and proportionately and as preparation for trial and trial are usually two of the most expensive phases of the budget (if not the most expensive), the exercise is still worthwhile and necessary. In the case of *Hegglin v Person(s)*

Unknown, Google Inc.[68] the court was confronted with an application to cap costs ten days before the commencement of the trial. Edis J declined to do so, based on the late stage of the proceedings and the procedural threshold for making such orders, but, instead, exercised costs management powers under CPR 3.15 to budget the trial and some outstanding work on an expert's report.

Q56. Is a party who was acting in person at the costs management conference (and so has no budget), but who subsequently instructs solicitors, required to exchange and file a Precedent H?

4-79 Strictly the answer is that there is no procedural provision that requires the party to serve and file a budget in this situation. However, in practice the position is not quite as simple as this initial answer suggests as there are a number of potential triggers for a Precedent H in this situation. These are as follows:

- Whilst the court file is unlikely to be referred to a judge simply because a party has become represented and a Notice of Acting is filed, experience suggests that frequently solicitors coming on record make applications for directions at the same time. If the file is referred to the judge to consider listing of any such application it is likely that the court will take the opportunity to order the filing and service of a Precedent H, triggering the possibility of costs management.
- It is arguable that the instruction of solicitors by a party previously unrepresented is a significant development in the litigation for any other party who is subject to a costs management order already (e.g. representation may shorten the trial or any application made by the new representatives, If successful, would have an effect on the budget previously set). This would engage CPR 3 PDE.7.6 for the budgeted party and it is hard to see that if the court had to be involved in respect of any variation of budgets it would not also wish to budget the costs of the party who had previously been a litigant in person.
- Any other party who was subject to a budget might apply to the court to make a costs management order in respect of the previously unrepresented party's costs under CPR 3.16 (convening a hearing solely for costs management). This seems likely as otherwise any budgeted party may feel prejudiced by having to conduct litigation within the parameters of a budget, whilst the previously unrepresented party would not be so constrained.
- The represented party may want a budget set so that the 'recoverable costs' are known at this stage and that party may then make decisions about the litigation fully informed about the costs consequences i.e knowing what, if anything, will be the shortfall between recoverable and solicitor/client costs if a costs order is secured.

[68] *Hegglin v Person(s) Unknown, Google Inc.* [2014] EWHC 3793 (QB) Edis J.

Q57. Is a further Precedent H required with a pre-trial checklist ("PTCL") as CPR 29 imposes no such requirement and yet the wording of the Precedent H guidance still suggests this is work included at the PTR stage?

CPR 29 PD 8.1(1) requires a PTCL to be in Form N170. Form N170 no longer refers to a budget at **Section F**. Instead it refers to an estimate of costs. However, guidance at the beginning of the N170 suggests that in cases not costs managed an estimate of costs is required. However, it is clear from the wording used (reference to costs estimates and reference to these being provided in accordance with the provisions of the CPR) that the guidance is an unhappy and unwelcome failure to take account of the revised CPR. The only provisions relating to budgets are to be found at CPR 3.1(7)(ll), 3.12–3.18, 3.20, 3 PD E, 3 PD F and CPR 44 PD 3. These do not contain any requirement for an estimate at the time of PTCL (and neither does CPR 29—other than by cross reference to Form N170 in the PD as referred to above). **4–80**

The only requirement to file a further budget actually arises in costs managed cases where a party seeks revision of the budget and cannot agree that revision and so applies to the court.

Whether because of the confusion in the wording of Form N170, because the parties have not understood the significance of CPR 3 PD E 7.6 or because of the reference in the Precedent H guidance on the PTR phase, most Precedents H filed under CPR 3.13 contain within the assumptions in the PTR phase 'Updating of the budgets'. This is wrong as there is no automatic right to update. The only provision is CPR 3 PD E 7.6 which permits revision only in specific circumstances. Expect the court to examine the PTR phase closely and reduce it where it contains the assumption set out above as work updating the budget is not time routinely reasonable and proportionate. There is also a danger that including this will make the court concerned as to what else has been included in the budget that ought not to have been and lead to a far closer scrutiny of all of the assumptions.

As an aside there appears little reason for the reference to 'an estimate of costs' in case not costs managed in Form N170 By this stage directions will have been given and so the estimate is unlikely to inform the route the claim takes to trial. In addition the provisions of CPR 44 PD.3 do not apply as the estimate is not 'a budget in accordance with' CPR 3 PDE. It is also not clear what form the estimate should take as one is not prescribed.

Q58. Can a party make repeated agreed variations or, in default of agreement, applications to the court to vary a budget?

Yes, if that is appropriate. Under CPR 3 PD E 7.6 a party shall revise its budget in respect of future costs if significant developments in the litigation warrant this. Accordingly, provided that there are a number of significant developments then there is no reason why there should not be repeated attempts to agree variations to the budget or, if agreement is not forthcoming, repeated applications to vary. What a party may not do is to make repeated applications **4-81** to vary in respect of the same alleged significant developments. If there is no agreement and an application is made, but the court finds that there is, in fact, no significant development or the court finds that there is a significant development but either that this does not justify revision of the budget or not to the level that the party wishes, any dissatisfied party may appeal the decision of the court in the usual way under CPR 52 (recognising that it will be rare indeed for an appellate court to interfere with a discretionary case management decision).

Q59. It seems that some parties are not applying to vary budgets, but instead prefer to wait to argue 'good reason' to depart from the budget at any subsequent assessment. Is this because it is easier to depart from a budget retrospectively when the work may be easier to justify than to vary prospectively when the work may be seen to be speculative?

4-82 As noted under **Q56** above, a party is obliged to try to agree a budget variation or, in default of agreement, apply to the court for variation where there is a significant development in the litigation. CPR 3 PD E 7.6 is prescriptive – *'Each party shall revise its budget In respect of future costs upwards or downwards. . .'* Accordingly any party choosing to ignore this and seek to argue 'good reason' at any subsequent assessment does so contrary to mandatory requirements in the CPR. Whilst it is for the court in each individual case to determine whether the 'good reason' requirement for departure from a budget under CPR 3.18 is met, it is difficult to imagine that a deliberate decision to defer could ever constitute 'good reason'.

It is also challenging to imagine a significant development in the litigation that does not require court intervention by way of further case management decision. As the court is under an obligation pursuant to CPR 1.1, CPR 3.15(3) and 3.17 to control costs and ensure that case management decisions are made against a backdrop of whether or not a step is proportionate, it should not be possible for directions that result in or follow a significant development in the litigation to be determined without consideration of the budgetary implications at that juncture. It follows from this that any application for any additional case management directions that will result in or follow a significant development in the litigation, after a budget has been set, should be accompanied by a revised budget setting out the implications on the budget set, if the additional direction/s is/are granted. Any respondent to such an application, whether opposing it or not, should also file and submit any revised budget. This is true even if the parties have agreed the budget revision as the court will still want to know potential cost implications of any decision, to inform it when determining under the provisions set out above, whether to make the order sought.

The suggestion that work (and, more precisely, the costs associated with it) may be easier to justify with the benefit of hindsight, also risks overlooking the provisions of CPR 44 3(2)(a) – namely that considerations of proportionality trump both reasonable and necessary work. Accordingly, unless the application of CPR 44.3(5) leads to a different conclusion than it did when the budget was set, the fact that more work might have been necessary or reasonable is irrelevant.

Q60 If a costs management order has been made in a case but not long afterwards a party makes a potentially determinative application for summary judgment ("SJ"), should the parties apply promptly for the budgets to be revised? Suppose that they do, but the hearing for SJ is likely to come on before the application to revise costs budgets can be heard what should they do? Could the potential respondent to the SJ application not justifiably seek, in such circumstances, an order that the costs thrown away by this change of tack by the applicant be paid by it in any event?

These questions raise two issues. The first relates to contingencies and the second to the relationship between budgets and CPR 3 PD E 7.9. Dealing with those in turn: **4-83**

1) Depending upon the temporal proximity the position may be different for the applicant and the respondent to the application.
   - **The applicant** This seems to be an example of when something (the application) was more likely than not to occur at the time of the budget, and so ought to have been included as a contingency. If it ought to have been in the budget as a contingency, it raises the interesting question of whether the failure to include it means that the applicant to the application can neither seek budgetary variation because it is not, for that party, a significant development in the litigation (as it knew at budget setting time it was going to issue the application imminently) nor, if successful on the application, seek a freestanding order for costs of the application outside the budget (considered in more general terms below) as it is not an interim application made that, reasonably, was not included in the budget. The fact that the application itself may fall within a fixed costs regime (e.g. a CPR 24 application) offers no assistance either, as it is only if the proceedings (as opposed to the application) are subject to fixed costs that there is an exclusion from costs management under CPR 3.12(1)(c).
   - **The respondent** Obviously the respondent's budget did not include in it anything for the application, as it was not in a position to determine whether it was more likely than not to occur. As a result CPR 3 PD E 7.9 applies (**see below**) to any costs to which the respondent may become entitled, as it reasonably did not include this in the budget.
2) If the application was not 'more likely than not to occur' at budget setting time and so was reasonably not included in either budget, then CPR 3 PD E 7.9 applies. As such costs of the application will be dealt with at the end of the application and fall outside the budget. In other words, any costs

awarded to a party will be in addition to, and freestanding of, any costs under the budget.

Q61. What sort of applications fall within the provisions of CPR 3 PD E 7.9? How does this link with the provision for contingencies in the budget?

4–84 CPR 3 PD E 7.9 (considered above)) and the Precedent H guidance give very clear steers in respect of those costs that will fall outside the budget. CPR 3 PD E 7.9 refers to interim applications 'which reasonably were not included in a budget'. The guidance provides some distinction between those costs and ones that fall within CPR 3 PD E 7.6 (significant developments requiring variation), defining the latter as those "costs which are not anticipated but which become necessary later". These comments link to the definition of contingent costs in the Precedent H guidance. The definition is that these are "costs which are more likely than not to be incurred". The result is this:

- If something is more likely than not to occur at the time of the costs management order, but is not certain and so does not fit into another phase under estimated costs, it should be included as a contingency. Parties need to be astute to whether or not a budgeted contingency becomes a reality as otherwise they may overlook that some of the contingencies never came to fruition for the purpose of 'good reason' to depart from the budget (as the fact that a contingency for which budgetary provision was made did not occur, must surely be a 'good reason' for departing from the budget).
- If the cost relates to an application that was not reasonably included in the budget at the time of the costs management order, it falls within CPR 3 PD E 7.9 e.g. an application to enforce compliance with directions, and that cost is outside the budget and the costs of that application fall to be determined and then assessed as part of the determination of the application, which is entirely free standing and independent of the budget.
- If something represents a significant development in the litigation arises (other than an application which is either more likely than not to occur at the time of costs management or which it was reasonable not to include in the budget), then the costs fall to be dealt with under CPR 3 PD E 7.6 as a revision to the budgets.

Q62. Can the court costs manage detailed assessment proceedings?

4–85 Some see it as curious that claims worth £25,001 are subject to the full rigour of the costs management regime and yet detailed assessments, where the costs claimed may run into many millions and the 'costs of the costs' proceedings are substantial, fall outside the provisions. We say 'fall outside' as Precedent H specifically excludes the costs of detailed assessment (although this does not seem to stop some parties erroneously including these costs as a contingency).

However, there seems to be no reason why the court cannot exercise its power under CPR 3.12(1A) to costs manage detailed assessment proceedings where that is appropriate. CPR 47.1 clearly implies that the substantive proceedings are over by the time of assessment and CPR 47.6 expressly refers to detailed assessments as 'proceedings'—both suggesting that detailed assessments are 'proceedings' in their own right (an interpretation supported by *Crosbie v Munroe*[69]) and capable of consideration under CPR 3.12(1A).

The difficulty with costs management of detailed assessment proceedings is when and how it is undertaken. This raises many of the same arguments as to the inability of the court to costs manage 'incurred costs' (and particularly pre-action costs) in substantive proceedings. Does the court decide to budget whenever it makes an order for detailed assessment so that costs are managed from the inception of the process even though this will require a significant time and costs investment when most costs are settled without there even being a request for a detailed assessment hearing under CPR 47.14? If not there is a real danger in most cases, that by the time the court does step in all that remains is the assessment hearing itself and significant costs have already been incurred in settlement skirmishes, preparation of the bill, drafting of the Points of Dispute and any Replies to them. This is against a backdrop of repeated concern expressed by the judiciary about the 'costs of the costs'.

Inevitably, the consideration above leads to the conclusion that costs management is an option in detailed assessment proceedings, but that its suitability is entirely case specific. It will require robust costs and case management by the costs judge or costs officer and an early identification of those cases where costs management is purposeful—which essentially means that it is, in context, a proportionate exercise. In practice complex assessment proceedings are already the subject of robust case management, with the resolution of preliminary issues often leading to settlement.

Q63. If an appeal is launched against a decision on an interim application that falls within a discrete phase (e.g. against an order in respect of permission for expert evidence) does CPR 3 PD E 7.6 apply and should budgets be revised with a view to agreement or an application to vary?

Precedent H itself makes it clear that the costs of any appeals are excluded. **4-86**
Accordingly, unless the appellate court decides to costs manage the appeal under the provisions of CPR 3.12(1A) and so orders, there is no requirement either to file and exchange budgets for the appeal itself or to seek revision of the existing budget in the substantive proceedings simply to budget the appeal. However, where the substantive appeal requiring determination raises issue of proportionality (e.g. should an additional expert have been permitted) the appellate court may require revised budgets to enable it to determine the issue. In any event, if the consequence of the appeal, whether allowed or dismissed, is to have an effect on the budgets set for the substantive litigation,

[69] *Crosbie v Munroe* [2003] EWCA Civ 350.

then variation of those existing budgets does arise e.g. the appeal results in permission for another expert, for strike out of or judgment on part only of the claim. This latter point raises the issue of whether the appellate court undertakes any budget revision required or refers this back to the first instance case managing court. If the appeal allowed is one such as in respect of additional expert evidence, the appellate court has had the revised budgets to enable it to determine the issue of proportionality, then it is likely to be proportionate for it to undertake the revision. If the appeal is one such as summary judgment in part, that does not require consideration of the costs consequences and which, in any event, completely alters the complexion of the case (and, inevitably in consequence, the budget set), then adjourning the revision to the case managing judge, seems more appropriate.

Q64. Does the decision of the Court of Appeal in *Denton v T H White*[70] mean that relief from sanction will be granted provided that there is no prejudice to any other party that cannot be compensated by a costs order and that a trial date can still be met?

4–87 No, not necessarily. All cases will be fact specific. The Court of Appeal has set out a clear three-stage approach to applications under CPR 3.9 and it is the application of that which will determine the outcome of each specific application for relief. As such that may mean that in some cases the fact that there is no prejudice to the other party and a trial date can be met will, in all the circumstances, result in relief and in others it will not.

Whilst *Denton* clearly provides those seeking relief with a greater prospect of success than *Mitchell*, it is clear from the phraseology adopted by the court in *Denton* that there is not to be a return to the approach of pre 1 April, 2013 as set out in the quote from the judgment in the text. Instead, as is stated in the judgment of the majority, what is required "is a more nuanced approach . . . Anything less will inevitably lead to the court slipping back to the old culture of non-compliance which the Jackson reforms were designed to eliminate"[71]. It is also important to remember that whilst *Denton* may have clarified and amplified the judgment in *Mitchell*, much of what that latter case determined remains pertinent and the actual facts of *Mitchell*, and the conclusion reached on those facts, still represents a far more robust approach to non compliance than prior to 1 April, 2013.

The fact that a lack of prejudice is not determinative (rather than simply a circumstance to take into account under stage 3 of *Denton)* was confirmed by the Court of Appeal in *R (on the application of Idira v The Secretary of State for the Home Department*[72] when it stressed:

> *"At para.43 in Denton, this court said that parties should not "adopt an uncooperative attitude in unreasonably refusing to agree extensions of time and in*

[70] *Denton v T H White* [2014] EWCA Civ 906.

[71] para.38.

[72] *R (on the application of Idira) v The Secretary of State for the Home Office [2015] EWCA Civ 1187.*

> *unreasonably opposing applications for relief from sanctions". It added: "it is unacceptable for a party to try to take advantage of a minor inadvertent error. . . ..". I would emphasise the words "unreasonably" and "minor inadvertent". A party is not required to agree to an extension of time in every case where the extension will not disrupt the time-table for the appeal or will not cause him to suffer prejudice. If the position were otherwise, the court would lose control of the management of the litigation."*

Similarly the fact that refusal to grant relief will cause significant prejudice to the party in default does not mean that relief should be granted. In *Sinclair & anor v Dorsey & Whitney & ors*[73] a professional negligence claim said to be valued at £30 million was struck out for breach of an unless order to provide security for costs. An application for relief was dismissed on application of the *Denton* 3 stage test. The fact of prejudice (in terms of the lost opportunity to pursue such a claim) was insufficient when considered in all the circumstances and giving particular weight to the two factors in CPR 3.9.

Q65. What is the purpose of the reference in CPR 36.23 to CPR 36.17(4)(b)?

CPR 36.23 provides a limited 'automatic' relief from the sanction of CPR 3.14 **4-88** if an offerer pursuant to CPR 36 is subject to the constraints imposed by CPR 3.14. In the three situations set out in CPR 36.23 (namely under CPR 36.13(5)(b), 36.17(3)(a) and 36.17(4)(b)), the offeror may still be able to recover 50 per cent of the costs assessed for those costs otherwise subject to the sanction and any other recoverable costs (i.e. those that were incurred at the time of the failure to file Precedent H). The rationale is clear. It is to provide the offeree with an incentive to accept the offer (the incentive being some adverse costs risk if the offer is a good one).

However, why does CPR 36.23 expressly refer to CPR 17(4)(b) because that provision is one specifically awarding the claimant costs on the indemnity basis? Having secured such an award of costs one might think that the sanction under CPR 3.14 falls away anyway, because the constraints imposed on recoverable costs as a result of an approved or agreed budget by CPR 3.18 expressly only apply to costs awards 'between the parties' on the standard basis (**see para 4-20** and **Q48** above). Accordingly one might assume that any budget set on the basis of what is deemed under CPR 3.14 to be in the budget (namely future court fees) ceases to be relevant on an indemnity basis award of costs. On this interpretation the provision seems designed to cover the period from the date the budget is set at future court fees only until the date from which the indemnity basis costs order runs. However, if that is the intention why link the provision to CPR 36.17(4)(b) expressly, which already offers a solution for the particular period covered by that provision and not to CPR 36.17(1) more generally?

Another construction is that CPR 36.23 is a 'freestanding' procedural

[73] *Sinclair & anor v Dorsey Whitney & ors unreported QBD 20.11.15.*

sanction designed to constrain the effect of an award of indemnity costs where there has been a breach of CPR 3.13, so that the award of indemnity costs under CPR 36.17(4)(b) does not provide an unqualified escape route for a claimant. In other words, it is a specific rule, the 50 per cent is not expressed to be 50 per cent of what would have been budgeted and therefore CPR 3.18 is not engaged at all. This would mean that CPR 36.23 provides a benefit where the offeror comes before the court under either CPR 36.13(5)(b) or 36.17(3)(a), but a sanction if the offeror is a claimant coming before the court under CPR 36.17(4)(b). However, this would mean that a claimant who secures an indemnity basis costs award outside the CPR 36 regime is in a better situation than one who secures the award under CPR 36.17(4)(b) – a curious outcome when CPR 36 is designed to promote settlement.

On balance, given that CPR 36.23 does not refer to the 50 per cent being linked to what would have been budgeted, instead being an assessed sum outside of the budget, and because it expressly refers to a specific rule for indemnity costs that the rule makers would have realised gives 'relief' from CPR 3.14 without the need for any further provision, the arguments for the latter of these two constructions appear more compelling. However, with an increasing number of 'costs managed' cases coming to fruition and with this provision having been in place for approaching a year, it cannot be long before some authorities emerge from the Higher Courts to provide guidance on the purpose of this discrete provision.

A final option is that the reference to CPR 36.17(4)(b) in 36.23 is one made in error. However, it must be assumed that this is not so and that it reflects the intention of the rule makers. Unless and until it is removed it raises the issues set out above.

Q66. Does the emphasis on proportionality impact on the situation where a claim falls within fast track financial limits, but the number of witnesses is such that the time needed for trial exceeds one day?

4–89 Indeed it does. Many of these cases would have been allocated to the multi track based on the trial time estimate prior to 1 April, 2013. Since that date, allocation must be viewed against the revised overriding objective and the court must determine whether allocation to the multi track is proportionate. It will do so by reference to the revised overriding objective and the CPR 44.3(5) factors. The mere fact that the number of witnesses that the parties wish to call would mean that the trial will exceed one day is not determinative in isolation. If there is that number of witnesses because of the complexity of the claim or because there are issues of public importance or reputation, then that may justify allocation to the multi track as proportionate. If no such factors exist, then the court is likely to allocate to the fast track. This will be in conjunction with effective case management using the powers that the court has under CPR 32.2(3) to control the extent of witness evidence permitted and its powers under CPR 39.4 to timetable the trial to ensure that the trial does not exceed one day. In such a case parties may expect the trial timetable to limit the time allocated for opening the case (if permitted), cross examination, closing submissions and judicial consideration, judgment delivery, award of costs and summary assessment under any award. In other words, parties may have to select their 'best' evidence and their 'best' cross examination points. As Jackson LJ stated in the Final Report:

> *"The essence of proportionality is that the ends do not necessarily justify the means."*[74]

Remember that not only will allocation to the multi track incur the parties in further expenditure, but also that CPR 1.1(2)(e) expressly includes in the definition of "dealing with a case justly and at proportionate cost" the allocation of court resources and the express requirement to take account of the resource needs of other cases. Allocation to multi track simply to accommodate a longer trial time erodes the judicial time available for other cases.

Q67. Do the case management rules apply as much to litigants in person as to represented parties?

Prior to 1 October 2015 the answer was yes, with the exception of the costs management provisions (as litigants in person are not required to prepare Precedents H under CPR 3 PD E 7.8). However, from 1 October CPR 3.1A has added a discrete provision relating to case management and the taking of evidence in claims involving litigants in person. The rule applies where at least one party is unrepresented (3.1A(1)) and requires the court to have regard to the fact that at least one party is unrepresented when exercising any case management function. This includes the court adapting the standard directions under CPR 29.1(2) (**para.4-08 above**) and adopting any procedure that it considers appropriate to further the overriding objective. When taking evidence the court may ascertain from an unrepresented party matters about which a particular witness may be able to give evidence and upon which that witness should be cross examined and may put to that witness or cause to be put to that witness such questions as appear to the court to be proper. What this means in practice remains to be seen. However, it seems likely that in terms of case management, properly interpreted, any alterations to usual procedure'/directions in any particular case by the application of this rule will apply equally to represented and unrepresented parties in that particular claim. **4-90**

Q68. Will cost capping be ordered more rarely?

It seemed that costs capping had run its course. In his May 2015 '*Confronting costs management*' lecture there is a record of one question put to Jackson LJ that evening. It is, *"Is there now any place for costs capping?"*. His answer was unequivocal *"No. In my view the costs capping rules should be repealed"*. Reports of the Civil Procedure Rules Committee meeting in July 2015 suggested that **4–91**

[74] Ch.3.para 5.3.

this was to happen. However, it appears they were granted an 11th hour reprieve and remain.

However, it is difficult to see how costs capping has a future in those cases where the costs management regime applies (see *Hegglin v Person(s) Unknown, Google Inc.*[75]). By definition, a costs management order ensures that the costs budgeted are proportionate, as that is the basis upon which they have been set under CPR 3 PD E 7.3. As the court in the costs capping regime can only apply a cap to future costs, then where costs management is available a party will never be able to satisfy the requirement of CPR 3.19(5)(b), that without a cap there is a substantial risk that costs will be disproportionately incurred.

It would be nonsensical to look at costs capping in those cases where the court exercises its discretion under CPR 3.12(1)(e) to exclude cases that would otherwise fall within the costs management regime. This would fly in the face of the decision not to costs manage in the first place.

The relevance of costs capping in cases where the court chooses not to make a costs management order or which fall outside the regime is, at first blush, unaltered by costs management. However, in cases outside the regime where the court is concerned at the level of costs and the likelihood of these being adequately controlled by case management and subsequent assessment, the court may choose to exercise its discretion under CPR 3.12(1A) to costs manage, rather than to costs cap. As the budget to be filed and served in an application for costs capping will be in the format of Form H (see CPR 3 PD F 2) and as the court will have to assess the quantum of the costs for the purpose of imposing a cap anyway (CPR 3 PD F 4.1), it may determine that costs management is preferable to costs capping. This also avoids the difficulty presented by the 'exceptional circumstances' threshold set for costs capping. As a result it may be that a party seeking a costs cap may wish to link the application to one for costs management.

Obviously, if the court is to consider costs management as an alternative to costs capping it will require Precedents H from all parties and will need to exercise its discretion under CPR 3.20 to ensure that this is the case when dealing with a multi party claim.

A point of interest arises in respect of the subsequent relevance of budgets where a claim is not subject to the costs management regime, but where, in the course of an unsuccessful application for costs capping, Precedents H are filed and served. Are these budgets of relevance at any subsequent assessment of costs? Strictly under CPR 44 PD 3.1 only budgets filed under 3 PD E are relevant when considering the provisions relating to a 20 per cent or more difference between budget and eventual costs claimed. As the budget in a costs capping application has been filed under CPR 3 PD F it seems that these provisions do not apply. It does seem curious that the provisions of CPR 44 PD 3 have been limited and do not apply to all budgets filed under any rule, practice direction or court order.

[75] *Hegglin v Person(s) Unknown, Google Inc.* [2014] EWHC 3793 (QB) Edis J.

CHAPTER 5

Part 36 and Other Settlement Offers Including ADR and Costs Consequences

Introduction

This Chapter deals both with Part 36 Offers and with other methods of achieving settlement; and is divided into two sections, the first dealing with Part 36 and the second with methods of settlement other than Part 36.

Section 1 Part 36

Background to Part 36

Part 36 has undergone significant changes in recent years. With effect from 6 April, 2007, CPR Part 36 was completely revised. Payments into court were no longer permitted. These reforms came about following two Court of Appeal decisions: *Crouch v Kings Healthcare NHS Trust*[1] and *Trustees of Stokes Pension Fund v Western Power Distribution (South West) Plc.*[2] 5–01

The changes foreshadowed by these decisions were brought about by the Civil Procedure (Amendment No.3) Rules 2006 which came into force on 6 April, 2007. The earlier version of Part 36 was replaced by an entirely new Part 36, together with a new Practice Direction. The Civil Procedure (Amendment No.8) Rules 2014,[3] which came into force on 6 April, 2015, contain another, entirely new, version of Part 36 in Sch.1. There are also consequential amendments to other Parts.

Reform of Part 36

The Civil Procedure Rule Committee (CPRC) set up a sub-committee to consider reforms to Part 36 with a view to simplifying and clarifying it by, for example, allowing offers by counterclaiming defendants and discouraging "cynical claimant offers". The Forum of Complex Injury Lawyers (FOCIS) reacted to the sub-committee's report in relation to "cynical claimant offers" and suggested that wider amendments could risk undermining the Jackson Reforms and create greater disparity. The CPRC's sub-committee examining Part 36 felt that it was too technical and offers under it were failing on technical grounds. The intention of the new Part 36 is to align the rules with the case law developed since the Part was last amended. 5–02

[1] *Crouch v Kings Healthcare NHS Trust* [2004] EWCA Civ 1332; [2005] 1 W.L.R. 2015.
[2] *Trustees of Stokes Pension Fund v Western Power Distribution (South West) Plc* [2005] EWCA Civ 854; [2005] 1 W.L.R. 3595.
[3] SI 2014 No.3299.

Transitional provisions

5–03 The new Part 36 applies only in relation to Part 36 Offers made on or after 6 April, 2015, save that rr.36.3 (definitions), 36.11 (acceptance of a Part 36 Offer), 36.12 (acceptance of a Part 36 Offer in a split trial case) and 36.16 (restriction on disclosure of a Part 36 Offer) also apply in relation to any Part 36 Offer where the offer is made before 6 April, 2015, but a trial of any part of the claim or any issue arising in it starts on or after 6 April, 2015.[4]

CPR Part 36 after 5 April, 2015

5–04 Section I of Part 36 contains a self-contained procedural code about offers to settle made pursuant to the procedure set out in that Part. Section I contains general rules about Part 36 Offers. Section II contains rules about offers to settle where the parties have followed the Pre-Action Protocol for Low Value Personal Injury Claims in Road Traffic Accidents ("the RTA Protocol") or the Pre-Action Protocol for Low Value Personal Injury (Employers' Liability and Public Liability) claims ("the EL/PL Protocol") and have started proceedings under Part 8 in accordance with Practice Direction 8B.[5]

Under Section I, any party to an action may make an offer to settle in whatever way that party chooses, but if the offer is not made in accordance with r.36.5 (form and content of a Part 36 Offer) it will not have the consequences specified in Section I.[6] Where an offer does not comply with the requirements set out in r.36.2, it is not a Part 36 Offer.[7]

A Part 36 Offer may be made in respect of the whole or part of any issue that arises in a claim, counterclaim or other additional claim, or an appeal or cross-appeal from a decision made at a trial.[8] Counterclaims and other additional claims are treated as claims, and references to a claimant or a defendant include a party bringing or defending an additional claim.[9]

In proceedings following a road traffic accident, the defendant, who alleged contributory negligence, made an offer, under the previous regime, to settle that issue on the basis of a 25 per cent reduction, three weeks before the trial was due to start. The claimant accepted the defendant's offer one week before trial. Neither the offer nor the acceptance made any mention about the costs of the contributory negligence issue. The judge at first instance found that the defendant was in fact the claimant for the purposes of the contributory negligence issue, and ordered the claimant to pay the defendant's costs in relation to it. On the claimant's appeal, it was held that the defendant's offer amounted to an offer solely in relation to liability. It fell within old r.36.2(5) (which provided that "An offeror may make a Part 36 Offer solely in relation to liability"—this provision has been omitted from the new rule, presumably because it was superfluous), and the fact that the context was contributory

[4] Civil Procedure (Amendment No.8) Rules 2014, rr.18(1) and (2).
[5] r.36.1.
[6] r.36.2.
[7] See *Thewlis v Groupama Insurance Co Ltd* [2012] EWHC 3 (TCC); [2012] BLR 259.
[8] r.36.2(3).
[9] rr.20.2 and 20.3.

negligence did not affect that. The defendant's offer was, and was intended to be, a Part 36 Offer and the claimant's entitlement to costs arose under old r.36.10(1) (now r.36.13). In the light of the settlement at 75 per cent to 25 per cent liability split, it was wholly artificial to describe the claimant as anything other than the winner.[10]

The definition section of Part 36 makes it clear that a trial means any trial in a case whether it is a trial of all the issues or a trial of liability, quantum or some other issue in the case. A trial is in progress from the time when it starts until the time when judgment is given or handed down. A case is decided when all issues in the case have been determined, whether at one or more trials.[11]

Part 36 Offers in appeal proceedings

Except where a Part 36 Offer is made in appeal proceedings, it has effect only in relation to the costs of the proceedings in respect of which it is made and not in respect of any appeal in those proceedings. If a Part 36 Offer is made in appeal proceedings the references in the rules to, e.g. claimant/defendant are replaced by corresponding terms, e.g. appellant/respondent (r.36.4(1) and (2)). 5–05

The Court of Appeal held that an appeal is an independent regime, so far as Part 36 is concerned. In an appeal where the defendant chose to resist a claimant's new point without having made any offer, the defendant was at risk of paying the costs of the appeal. On the facts it would not be right to order the defendant to pay the costs of the claimant's new point when considerable costs were expended fighting the preliminary issue on a different basis in the court below, and those costs had been reserved to the trial judge. It would be better if the costs were looked at in the round after the trial had taken place. The costs of the appeal were accordingly reserved to the trial judge as well.[12]

Form and content of a Part 36 Offer

A Part 36 Offer must: 5–06

(a) be in writing;
(b) make clear that it is made pursuant to Part 36[13];
(c) specify a period of not less than 21 days within which the defendant will be liable for the claimant's costs, where a Part 36 Offer is accepted in accordance with r.36.13 or, where Section IIIA of Part 45 applies, in accordance with r.36.20 if the offer is accepted;
(d) state whether it relates to the whole of the claim or part of it or to an issue that arises in it and if so, to which part or issue; and
(e) state whether it takes into account any counterclaim.[14]

---

10 *Onay v Brown* [2009] EWCA Civ 775; [2010] 1 Costs LR 29 CA.
11 r.36.3.
12 *RTS Flexible Systems Ltd v Molkerei Alois Muller GmbH & Co AG* [2009] EWCA Civ 26.
13 This is a change from the earlier version of the rule which required the offer to "state on its face if it was intended to have the consequences of Section I of Part 36".
14 r.36.5(1).

Where a defendant had made what purported to be a claimant's Part 36 Offer in respect of the defendant's counterclaim, "the proceedings in respect of which" it was made included the claim and the proposed counterclaim, but were not restricted only to the counterclaim. A Part 36 Offer may be made before the commencement of proceedings (under old r.36.3(2), now r.36.7) so the fact that the defendant's counterclaim had not been formulated or pleaded did not of itself matter.[15]

A Part 36 Offer may be made at any time including before the commencement of proceedings. Such an offer is made when it is served on the offeree.[16] The period of 21 days specified in (c) above or such longer period as the parties agree in the case of an offer made not less than 21 days before trial, is known as "the relevant period". Where an offer is made less than 21 days before a trial, the relevant period is the period up to the end of the trial.[17] A Part 36 Offer may be made using Form N242A. If the other party is legally represented the notice must be served on the legal representative.[18]

Withdrawing or changing the terms of a Part 36 Offer generally

5–07 A Part 36 Offer may only be withdrawn or its terms changed if the offeree has not previously served notice of acceptance. The offeror may withdraw the offer or change its terms by serving written notice of the withdrawal or change of terms on the offeree.[19] Rule 36.10 makes provision about when permission is required to withdraw or change the terms of an offer before the expiry of the relevant period. Subject to that, notice of withdrawal or change of terms takes effect when it is served on the offeree.[20]

Provided that the offeree has not previously served notice of acceptance, after expiry of the relevant period the offeror may withdraw the offer or change its terms without the permission of the court, or the offer may be automatically withdrawn in accordance with its terms. Where the offeror changes the terms of the offer to make it more advantageous to the offeree, the improved offer will be treated not as the withdrawal of the original offer, but as the making of a new Part 36 Offer on the improved terms, and provided that the new offer is not made less than 21 days before the start of the trial, the relevant period will be 21 days or such longer period (if any) identified in the written notice of change of terms.[21]

Rule 36.9(4)(b) provides that an offer may be automatically withdrawn after the expiry of the relevant period in accordance with its terms. This is both the effect and apparent intention of the rule—a Part 36 Offer can now include within it a provision by which the offer is automatically withdrawn (and

[15] *AF v BG* [2009] EWCA Civ 757. Contrast *Van Oord UK Ltd v Allseas UK* Ltd [2015] EWHC 3385 **Q13** below.
[16] r.36.7.
[17] rr.36.3(g) and 36.5(2).
[18] Now amended to reflect the changes in Part 36. PD36A para 1.2.
[19] See r.36.17(7) as to the costs consequences following judgment of an offer which is withdrawn.
[20] r.36.9(1), (2) and (3).
[21] r.36.9(4) and (5).

therefore time limited)—though it must still usually be open for a minimum of 21 days and CPR 36.9(4)(b) cannot be used until that relevant period has passed. This alters the position under the previous version of Part 36, as confirmed in *C v D*.[22]

Part 36 is to be treated as prescriptive. Its requirements have to be complied with clearly by a party seeking to secure its benefits. A Part 36 Offer can only be withdrawn by a notice in writing by the offeror to the offeree (or, after the expiry of the relevant period, automatically in accordance with its terms (r.36.9(4)(b)). It is irrelevant whether the offer has been rejected or even ignored by the offeree. Withdrawal cannot be implied by conduct. It does not automatically follow that a claimant's costs should be payable by a third party in the same proportion as any apportionment of liability established by the Court as between a defendant and a third party. The Court has an overall discretion which is not circumscribed by the Civil Liability (Contribution) Act 1978.[23]

A claimant in libel proceedings made a Part 36 Offer which was not accepted and was withdrawn after 21 days. At trial the claimant beat her own Part 36 Offer and sought indemnity costs on the grounds of the defendant's failure to beat the Part 36 Offer and on the basis of the defendant's unreasonable conduct during the proceedings. The court decided that the procedural matters carried little weight and did not amount to unreasonable conduct sufficient to justify an award of costs on the indemnity basis. In considering that the withdrawn Part 36 Offer had not been beaten, the judge decided that to award indemnity costs on that basis would involve the introduction of such an award for behaviour which was not necessarily unreasonable[24].

A building contractor sued a householder for work done. The householder counterclaimed for losses alleging poor workmanship. The defendant made a Part 36 Offer, inclusive of interest, and subsequently made increased offers. The claimant made counter-offers, but the parties did not reach agreement. The defendant withdrew all the offers, except the original one. At trial before the District Judge the claimant recovered some £300 more than the defendant's original Part 36 Offer. The defendant appealed against the costs order, arguing that the judgment was not materially more advantageous to the claimant than the original Part 36 Offer. On appeal the Court of Appeal held that the provisions of Part 36 state clearly how an offer may be made, how it may be varied and how it may be accepted. Unlike ordinary common law principles they do not provide for an offer to lapse or become incapable of acceptance on being rejected by the other party. Once made, a Part 36 Offer remains open for acceptance until the start of the trial or its withdrawal in the manner set out in previous r.36.3(7) (now r.36.9(4)). Where a party makes

[22] *C v D* [2011] EWCA Civ 646.
[23] *Carillion JM Ltd v PHI Group Ltd, Carillion JM Ltd v Robert West Consulting Ltd* [2011] EWCH 1581 (TCC); 2011 BLR 504, Akenhead J.
[24] *Gulati and Others v. MGN Limited* [2015] EWHC 1805 (Ch.) Mann J.

several offers in different terms, a later offer does not revoke or vary an earlier offer, and all of them may be capable of acceptance at any one time.[25]

Following a collision at sea, the claimant offered to settle liability 60/40 in favour of the claimant. The offer was said to be made in accordance with CPR Part 61.4(10)–(12) and/or Part 36. The offer was subsequently withdrawn two months before trial, when the claimant offered to settle on a two thirds/one third basis. At trial, liability was apportioned 60/40 in favour of the claimant. In relation to costs, the court decided that there was a line of authority starting before the CPR but continuing after it, indicating that where an offer had been withdrawn which should have been accepted, it would not be unjust to award the offeror all of its costs, because, had the offer been accepted, no further costs would have been incurred thereafter (see *Bristol and West Building Society v Evans Bullock & Co*[26]). The mere fact that an offer had been withdrawn did not necessarily deprive the offer of effect on the question of costs. The defendant should have accepted the offer when it was available, or should have appreciated the costs risk and taken protective steps by making a realistic Part 36 Offer itself. The fact that the offer was withdrawn two months before trial did not make it unjust to order that the claimant should get all their costs from 21 days after the offer was made. Prior to that the defendant should pay 60 per cent of the claimant's costs, and the claimant should pay 40 per cent of the defendant's costs.[27]

Withdrawing or changing the terms of a Part 36 Offer before the expiry of the relevant period

5–08 Where the offeree has not previously served notice of acceptance and the offeror serves notice of withdrawal of the offer or changes in its terms to be less advantageous to the offeree before the expiry of the relevant period, if the offeree has not served notice of acceptance of the original offer by the expiry of the relevant period, the offeror's notice has effect on the expiry of that period; if the offeree serves notice of acceptance of the original offer before the expiry of the relevant period, that acceptance has effect unless the offeror applies to the court for permission to withdraw the offer or to change its terms within seven days of the offeree's notice of acceptance, or, if earlier, before the first day of trial. If such an application is made, the court may give permission for the original offer to be withdrawn or its terms changed if satisfied that there has been a change of circumstances since the making of the original offer and that it is in the interests of justice to give permission.[28]

Where the offeror seeks permission of the court to withdraw a Part 36 Offer or to change its terms to be less advantageous to the offeree before expiry of the relevant period, the permission of the court must, unless the parties agree

[25] *LG Blower Specialist Bricklayer Ltd v Reeves* [2010] EWCA Civ 726.
[26] *Bristol and West Building Society v Evans Bullock & Co* Unreported February 5, 1996 CA.
[27] *Owners and/or Bareboat Charterers and/or Sub Bareboat Charterers of the Ship Samco Europe v Owners of the Ship MSC Prestige* [2011] EWHC 1656 (Admlty) Teare J.
[28] r.36.10.

otherwise, be sought by making a Part 23 application which must be dealt with by a judge other than the trial judge or at a trial or other hearing provided that it is not to the trial judge.[29]

Acceptance of a Part 36 Offer

Acceptance of a Part 36 Offer is effected by serving written notice of acceptance on the offeror. Except where the permission of the court is required (see below) or in a split trial case, a Part 36 Offer may be accepted at any time unless it has already been withdrawn, whether or not the offeree has subsequently made a different offer.[30] **5–09**

A claimant who was already in breach of an unless order requiring him to serve certain documents purported to accept a Part 36 Offer. On appeal it was held that a claim that had been struck out (under the unless order) was at an end, therefore the claimant could not have accepted the Part 36 Offer once he was in breach of the order, as his claim had, in substance, been brought to an end.[31]

Acceptance of a Part 36 Offer made by one or more but not all defendants

The Court's permission is required to accept a Part 36 Offer where: **5–10**

- an offer is made by one or more but not all defendants (subject to the exceptions set out below);
- a defendant in personal injury claims who has made a Part 36 Offer has stated that it is intended to include any deductible amounts, the relevant period has expired and further deductible amounts have been paid to the claimant since the date of the offer;
- an apportionment is required under Rule 41.3A in proceedings under the Fatal Accidents Act 1976 and Law Reform (Miscellaneous Provisions) Act 1934; or
- a trial is in progress.

Where the Court gives permission, unless all the parties have agreed the costs, the Court must make an order dealing with costs and may order that the costs consequences set out in r.36.13 (costs consequences of acceptance of a Part 36 Offer) apply.[32]

In the case of Part 36 Offers made by one or more, but not all, of a number of defendants, if they have been sued jointly or in the alternative the claimant may accept the offer, if the claimant discontinues the claim against those defendants who have not made the offer, and those defendants give written consent to the acceptance of the offer. If the claimant alleges that the defendants have a several liability, the claimant may accept the offer, and continue **5–11**

[29] Practice Direction 36A, para.2.
[30] r.36.11(1) and (2).
[31] *Joyce v West Bus Coach Services Ltd* [2012] EWHC 404 (QB) Kenneth Parker J.
[32] r.36.11(3) and (4).

with the claims against the other defendants if entitled to do so. In any other case the claimant must apply to the court for an order permitting acceptance of the Part 36 Offer.[33]

Acceptance of a Part 36 Offer in a split-trial case

5–12 Where there has been a trial but not all the issues in the case have been determined,[34] a Part 36 Offer, which relates only to parts of the claim or issues that have already been decided, can no longer be accepted. Subject to that proviso, and unless the parties agree, any other Part 36 Offer cannot be accepted earlier than seven clear days after judgment is given or handed down in that trial.[35]

Costs consequences of acceptance of a Part 36 Offer

5–13 Subject to the exceptions set out below, where a Part 36 Offer is accepted within the relevant period, the claimant will be entitled to the costs of the proceedings (including their recoverable pre-action costs) up to the date on which notice of acceptance was served on the offeror[36].

Where a defendant's Part 36 Offer relates to part only of the claim and the claimant abandons the balance of the claim at the time of serving notice of acceptance within the relevant period, the claimant will only be entitled to the costs of that part of the claim unless the Court orders otherwise.[37]

Where a Part 36 Offer which was made less than 21 days before the start of the trial is accepted; or, which relates to the whole of the claim and is accepted after expiry of the relevant period; or, subject to the previous paragraph, a Part 36 Offer which does not relate to the whole of the claim is accepted at any time; the liability for costs must be determined by the Court unless the parties have agreed the costs.[38] Where the offer has been accepted after expiry of the relevant period but the parties are unable to agree the liability for costs, the Court must unless it considers it unjust to do so, order that the claimant be awarded costs up to the date on which the relevant period expired and that the offeree pay the offeror's costs for the period from the date of expiry of the relevant period to the date of acceptance. In considering whether it would be unjust to make the orders specified, the Court must take into account all the circumstances of the case including the matters listed in r.36.17(5) (**see paragraph 5–16** below, costs consequences following judgment). The claimant's costs include any costs incurred in dealing with the defendant's counterclaim if the Part 36 Offer states that it takes it into account.[39]

---

[33] r.36.15(1)–(4).
[34] Within the meaning of r.36.3(e).
[35] r.36.12 and also see r.36.3.
[36] r.36.13(1).
[37] r.36.13(2).
[38] r.36.13(4).
[39] r.36.13(5) to (7).

Despite the variation in wording between old CPR Rule 36.10(5) and the new Rule 36.13(5) and in particular the new reference to whether it is "unjust" to disapply the normal costs consequences, the new Rule has not materially changed the proper approach to be taken by the court when deciding how to deal with costs where there has been a late acceptance of a Part 36 Offer. The appropriate test is whether, bearing in mind the factors listed under r.36.17(5), the usual costs rules should be departed from because it would be unjust to apply it in the particular circumstances of the case. In the particular case, the claimant was found to have grossly exaggerated her damages claim and the court ordered that the costs payable by the claimant to the defendant should include the defendant's reasonable costs of collecting the surveillance evidence, even though this had not been included in the defendant's approved budget. The court did not agree with the note at paragraph 3.15.3 of the White Book, which suggests that some allowance should be made in budgets for surveillance (see **Chapter 4 Q18** for further consideration of this topic).[40]

Unaccepted offers

Restriction on disclosure of a Part 36 Offer

A Part 36 Offer is treated as being *"without prejudice except as to costs"*. The fact that such an offer has been made must not be communicated to the trial judge until the case has been decided. This restriction does not apply where: **5–14**

- the defence of tender before claim has been raised;
- the proceedings have been stayed following the acceptance of a Part 36 Offer;
- the offeror and offeree agree in writing that it should not apply; or
- although the case has not been decided, any part of it or issue in it has been decided, and the Part 36 Offer relates only to parts or issues which have been decided.

Where a part or issue has been decided, the trial judge may be told whether or not there are Part 36 Offers other than those relating to the parts or issues which have been decided, but must not be told any of the terms of the other offers unless any of the above exceptions apply to them.[41]

[40] *Purser v. Hibbs* [2015] EWHC 1792 (QB) HHJ Moloney QC.

[41] r.36.16(1)–(4). For cases which led to the revision of this Rule, see *Experience Hendrix LLC v Times Newspapers Ltd* [2008] EWHC 458 (Ch) Warren J; *Beasley v Alexander* [2012] EWHC 2715 (QB) Sir Raymond Jack; *Ted Baker Plc v Axa Insurance UK Plc* [2012] EWHC 1779 (Comm) Eder J.

Costs consequences following judgment

5–15 Save where Section IIIA of Part 45 applies,[42] where, upon judgment being entered, (i) a claimant fails to obtain a judgment more advantageous than the defendant's Part 36 Offer, or (ii) judgment against the defendant is at least as advantageous to the claimant as the proposals contained in the claimant's Part 36 Offer, the court must, unless it consider it unjust to do so, where (i) applies: order that the defendant is entitled to costs (including any recoverable pre-action costs) from the date on which the relevant period expired, and interest on those costs.[43] The provision does not apply to a soft tissue injury claim to which r.36.21 applies.

Where (ii) applies the court must, unless it considers it unjust to do so, order that the claimant is entitled to—

(a) interest on the whole or part of any sum of money (excluding interest) awarded, at a rate not exceeding 10 per cent above base rate for some or all of the period starting with the date on which the relevant period expired;
(b) costs (including any recoverable pre-action costs) on the indemnity basis from the date on which the relevant period expired;
(c) interest on those costs at a rate not exceeding 10 per cent above base rate; and
(d) provided that the case has been decided and there has not been a previous order under this provision, an additional amount, which may not exceed £75,000, calculated by applying the prescribed percentage set out in the ruke to an amount which is—
    (i) the sum awarded to the claimant by the court; or
    (ii) where there is no monetary award, the sum awarded to the claimant by the court in respect of costs.[44]

The prescribed percentage where the amount awarded by the court is up to £500,000 is 10 per cent of the amount awarded. Where the amount awarded by the court is above £500,000, the prescribed percentage is 10 per cent of the first £500,000 and (subject to the limit of £75,000) 5 per cent of any amount above that figure.[45]

Neither of these consequences apply to a Part 36 Offer which has been withdrawn, which has been changed so that its terms are less advantageous to the offeree—where the offeree has beaten the less advantageous offer, or made less than 21 days before trial unless the court has abridged the relevant period.[46]

In a claim for damages for an accident at work, the defendant accepted

[42] See r.36.21.
[43] In relation to any money claim or any money element of a claim, "more advantageous" means better in money terms by any amount however small and "at least as advantageous" is to be construed accordingly—r.36.17(1)–(3).
[44] r.36.17(3) and (4).
[45] r.36.17(4).
[46] r.36.17(7) and (8).

liability and made a Part 36 Offer for "£18,500 net of CRU and inclusive of interim payments in the sum of £18,500". The defendant also stated that the offer was made "without regard to any liability for recoverable benefits". The claimant obtained judgment for £29,550 made up of £4,000 general damages and the balance for loss of earnings. A CRU certificate was issued for £16,262. This was subsequently revised down to £6,760 because some of the benefits paid were not attributable to the accident. At first instance the Recorder decided that the claimant's had failed to beat the defendant's Part 36 Offer. On appeal, the court held there was no contradiction between the concept of the offer being made "net of CRU" and it's being made "without regard to any liability for recoverable benefits". The natural ruling of "net of CRU" was "remaining after all necessary deductions of benefits".

The words "without any liability for recoverable amounts" did not mean that the court was to have no regard to the amount of recoverable benefit when deciding whether the claimant had obtained a judgment more advantageous than the offer. The offer was for £18,500 leaving aside any liability in respect of recoverable benefits once such liability had crystallised. The real measure of whether, after the CRUs revised certificate was issued, the claimant had bettered the offer, was whether the total payment he actually received was more or less than the amount of the offer. On that basis the claimant had beaten the Part 36 Offer.

The Court of Appeal has dealt with a case where the claimant had failed to beat the defendant newspaper's Part 36 offer at trial. At first instance the judge found that the newspaper's wrongdoing was far more extensive than it was prepared to admit and concluded that, since the newspaper had made limited admissions and had denied any liability until shortly before the trial, the claimant had some justification for proceeding. The claimant could not recover his costs from the defendant but the judge did not order him to pay the defendant's costs using his powers under r.36.17. On appeal by the defendant the Court found that the trial judge had correctly decided that, where a claimant rejected a Part 36 Offer because it reasonably wished to have the facts investigated at trial, that did not normally make it unjust for the normal costs consequences to follow; there had to be some further element: implicitly unjustness. The onus was on the person who had failed to beat the offer to show that it would be unjust for the normal consequences to apply. The appeal was dismissed.[47]

A defendant accepting a claimant's Part 36 Offer outside the 21 day period but before the offer had been withdrawn was not entitled to an order under r.36.14 (now r.36.17) as the issue of liability had been compromised and judgment had not been entered. The appropriate regime was under r.36.10 (now r.36.13) and r.36.11 (now r.36.14).[48]

The claimant's additional award under r.36.17(4)(d) has come about as **5–16**
a result of Jackson LJ's recommendation in his Final Report that, where a

[47] *Yentob v MGN Ltd* [2015] EWCA Civ 1292.
[48] *Jolly v Harsco Infrastructure Services Ltd* [2012] EWHC 3086 (QB) Cranston J.

defendant rejects a claimant's offer, but fails to do better at trial, the claimant's recovery should be enhanced by 10 per cent.

In considering whether it would be unjust to make the order described above, the court must take into account all the circumstances of the case including:

(a) the terms of any Part 36 Offer;
(b) the stage in the proceedings when such an offer was made including, in particular, how long before the trial started the offer was made;
(c) the information available to the parties at the time when the offer was made;
(d) the conduct of the parties with regard to the giving of or refusal to give information for the purposes of enabling the offer to be made or evaluated; and
(e) whether the offer was a genuine attempt to settle the proceedings.

Where the court awards interest under these provisions and also awards interest on the same sum and for the same period under any other power, the total rate of interest must not exceed 10 per cent above base rate.[49]

The Court has considered the correct application of former r.36.14(3) (now r.36.17(4)). It was agreed between the parties, following judgment at the end of a split trial on liability in favour of the claimant, that the judgment the claimant was awarded was more advantageous than the offer that he had made and which had been rejected. It was also agreed that Part 36 is to be read as a self-contained code and not to be confused with contractual notions or general costs discretion under Part 44 or non-Part 36 Offers such as Calderbank type offers. The cases which support that proposition are *Gibbon v. Manchester City Council*[50]; *Fox v. Foundation Piling Limited*[51]; and *Coward v. Phaestos*[52]. The claimant had made an offer to settle of 80 per cent of the damages to be awarded in the split trial case. The defendant did not accept the offer within the relevant period so that r.36.14 (now r.36.17) applied. The judge in his draft costs order awarded indemnity costs to run throughout. He also ordered interest on those costs but at a lower rate than the maximum, from the end of the relevant period. The judge expressly made no order under r.36.14(3)(a) (interest on the whole of or any part of any money awarded) or under r.36.14(3)(d) (an additional amount not exceeding £75,000). Counsel for the claimant argued that the judge did not have the power to take that course given that Part 36 was not only a complete code but was "as it were a menu all of whose courses must be delivered". It was argued that the judge was not free to choose between the relevant features of sub-rule (3) or to find that to apply one would be unjust and to apply another would not. The judge held, reading the plain

49 r.36.17(5) and (6).
50 [2010] 1 WLR 2081.
51 [2011] EWCA Civ.790.
52 [2014] EWCA Civ.1256.

language of the Rule, that he was required to consider each stage of the sub-paragraph and ask whether the application of the particular sub-paragraph to this case with its own particular circumstances would be unjust. Having heard the argument, the judge amended his draft order so that the provision that the defendant should pay the claimant's costs relating to the issue of liability on the indemnity basis should be restricted expressly to the costs incurred or recoverable after the expiry of the relevant period.[53]

The Court is willing to impose sanctions on a defendant who seeks to avoid his liabilities and abuse the Court's process. The defendant had sought an adjournment on the grounds that the Malaysian receiver needed time to decide whether or not to defend the summary judgment proceedings. The judge found that it could not be right that, if a defendant decided to petition for his own bankruptcy, at a time when he did not have to, the court must forget about the defendant and focus instead on the receiver. That would allow any defendant to avoid or delay proceedings. Further, an adjournment would serve no purpose from the Malaysian receiver's point of view. The judge also found that there was no real prospect of a successful defence and no other compelling reason for a trial. The judge awarded:

- The capital sums invested by the claimants through the defendant, together with interest at a rate "in the region of 20 per cent", being the sort of return expected on the claimants' investment.
- The claimants' costs on the indemnity basis, given that the defendant's conduct in these proceedings had been *"nothing short of abusive"* and he had failed to beat the claimants' Part 36 offer.
- An additional amount under r.36.17(4)(d). Although the judge had jurisdiction to award up to £75,000, he considered a more *"modest"* sum appropriate, bearing in mind that the Part 36 offer was in relation to a simple application for summary judgment, rather than, say, a lengthy trial, and that the interest rate already awarded was high.[54]

Where a claimant who had made a Part 36 Offer under the Rules prior to 6 April 2015 and obtained judgment for almost three times the amount of the offer, the court held that it was not appropriate to reduce the costs award, because, although the claimant had not succeeded on every single issue, it had been overwhelmingly successful on the points which mattered most in terms of financial recovery. The defendant was ordered to pay costs on the standard basis up to the date upon which the court considered it was in a position to take an informed view of the quantum of the claim. Thereafter the defendant was ordered to pay costs on the indemnity basis together with enhanced interest for the same period at the rate of 8 per cent[55].

[53] *RXDX v. Northampton Borough Council* [2015] EWHC 2938 (QB), Sir Colin Mackay.
[54] *Bataillon and another v Shone and another* [2015] EWHC 3177 (QB) HHJ Waksman QC.
[55] *Thai Airways International Public Company Limited v. KI Holdings Co. Limited* [2015] EWHC 1476 (Comm) Leggatt J.

The High Court has clarified that the additional amount which can be awarded under r.36.17(4)(d) should be calculated as a percentage of the basic monetary award but should not be applied to any award of interest. The Court awarded a Liquidator £360,000, plus statutory interest at 3 per cent above base rate. The defendant was also ordered to pay all the costs on the indemnity basis. The Court expressed the view that this was a case that should never have been defended. The Liquidator had beaten its own Part 36 Offer of £325,000 inclusive of interest and the judge also awarded an enhanced rate of interest of 10 per cent above base rate on the sum awarded from the end of the relevant period until the date of judgment, interest at 10 per cent above base rate on the costs and the additional amount allowed under r.36.17(4)(d).

This decision illustrates the potential advantages for claimants of making a Part 36 Offer and also clarifies that where the claim includes a money claim, the additional amount is calculated as a percentage of the basic monetary award exclusive of interest.[56] The additional amount was not allowed in a case where, having made a Part 36 Offer just before trial, the claimant beat her offer and sought payment of the additional amount under r.36.17(4)(d). The court declined to make such an order, because she had raised a matter of fundamental importance to her case only in the course of opening, and other important information was disclosed only on the eve of the trial.[57]

The Court of Appeal has dealt with the tension between the provisions of CPR Part 45 IIIA (r.45.29B) and Part 36 (r.36.14A) (now r.36.21) where a claimant obtains judgment at least as advantageous as her Part 36 offer. The particular appeals were dealt with under the rules as they were before 6 April 2015, but the Master of the Rolls made it clear that the underlying provisions remain the same.

The question for the Court was whether rule 36.14(3) (now r.36.17(4)) Costs consequences following judgment, applies where a claimant makes a successful Part 36 offer, or whether the recoverable costs are limited to the fixed costs set out in Table 6 of r.45.29C.

Rule 45.29B provides: "the only costs allowed are—(a) the fixed costs in rule 45.29C; (b) disbursements in accordance with rule 45.29I". In 2013 a new rule 36.14A (r.36.21) was introduced to prescribe the costs consequences following judgment in section IIIA cases. While it modified some aspects of rule 36.14 (r.36.17) in fixed costs cases, it left rule 36.14(3) (39.17(4)) unmodified.

In the two appeals before the Court one, Broadhurst, had been limited to the fixed costs in Table 6 whilst in the other, Smith, the Judge had not limited the costs to Table 6.

The Court was referred to the Explanatory Memorandum to the 2013 Amendment Rules:

> *". . . If a defendant refuses a claimant's offer to settle and the court subsequently*

[56] *Watchorn v Jupiter Industries Ltd* [2014] EWHC 3003 (Ch) HHJ Purle QC.
[57] *Feltham v Bouskell* [2013] EWHC 3086 (Ch) Charles Hollander QC.

awards the claimant damages which are greater than or equal to the sum they were prepared to accept in the settlement, the claimant will not be limited to receiving his fixed costs, but will be entitled to costs assessed on the indemnity basis in accordance with rule 36.14."

The Master of the Rolls giving judgment with which the other members of the Court agreed said:

"23 rule 45.29B does not stand alone. The need to take account of Part 36 offers in section IIIA cases was recognised by the draftsman of the rules. Indeed, rule 36.14A is headed "costs consequences following judgment where section IIIA of Part 45 applies". Rule 45.29F (8) provides that, where a Part 36 offer is accepted in a section IIIA case, "rule 36.10A [36.20] will apply instead of this rule". And rule 45.29F(9) provides that, where in such a case upon judgment being entered the claimant fails to obtain a judgment more advantageous than the claimant's Part 36 offer, "rule 36.14A [36.21] will apply instead of this rule". Rule 45.29F does not, however, make provision as to what should happen where the claimant makes a successful Part 36 offer.

25 The effect of rules 36.14 [36.17] and 36.14A [36.21] when read together is that, where a claimant makes a successful Part 36 offer, he is entitled to costs assessed on the indemnity basis. Thus, rule 36.14 [36.17] is modified only to the extent stated by 36.14A [36.21]. Since rule 36.14(3) [36.17(4)] has not been modified by rule 36.14A [36.21], it continues to have full force and effect. The tension between rule 45.29B and rule 36.14A [36.21] must, therefore, be resolved in favour of rule 36.14A [36.21].

31 Where a claimant makes a successful Part 36 offer in a section IIIA case, he will be awarded fixed costs to the last staging point provided by rule 45.29C and Table 6B. He will then be awarded costs to be assessed on the indemnity basis in addition from the date that the offer became effective. This does not require any apportionment. It will, however, lead to a generous outcome for the claimant."[58]

More advantageous

Sub-paragraph 72(vii) of the judgment in *Multiplex Construction (UK) Ltd v Cleveland Bridge UK Ltd*[59] (dealing with the effect of *Carver v BAA*) should be disregarded. *Carver* had effectively been reversed by the rule change in previous r.36.14(1A) (now r.36.17(2))—a change that was recommended by Lord Justice Jackson in his *Review of Civil Litigation Costs: Final Report*. The judge making a Costs Order under r.44.2 is exercising a broad discretion, not just deciding who the winner on each issue was, but taking into account the conduct of the parties and all the circumstances of the case. The judge is the best person to exercise that discretion having been immersed in the trial details.[60] **5–17**

In a successful claim for dilapidations, it was common ground that there

[58] *Broadhurst (1) Taylor (2) v Tan (1) Smith(2)* [2016] EWCA Civ 94.
[59] *Multiplex Construction (UK) Ltd v Cleveland Bridge UK Ltd* [2008] EWHC 2280 (TCC) Jackson J.
[60] *Dufoo v Tolaini* [2014] EWCA Civ 1536.

was no offer under CPR Part 36 which had any automatic costs consequences. The defendant had however made a Part 36 Offer by letter dated 23 December, 2011 in the sum of £1,000,000. When interest was added to the sums awarded of £900,000 and £20,320.40 up to 13 January, 2012, the last date for acceptance of the Part 36 Offer, the sum awarded to the claimant exceeded the defendant's Part 36 Offer by £3,637.90, which represented a very small percentage of the sum offered.

The court noted that previous r.36.14, had been amended on 1 October, 2011, by the insertion of r.36.14(1A) (now r.36.17(2)). The claimant had not failed to obtain a judgment more advantageous than the defendant's Part 36 Offer and therefore r.36.14 (r.36.17) did not apply. Ramsey J stated:

> *"The Part 36 Offer made in this case could be said, in principle, to come within the wording of CPR 44.2(4)(c). It is an admissible offer to settle and is not an offer to which costs consequences under Part 36 apply. However I do not consider, even in a case such as this, where [the claimant] has only received a very small amount more than the sum which [the defendants] offered in its Part 36 Offer, the court should approach CPR 44.2(4)(c) on the basis that this could lead to an order that a claimant should pay the defendants' costs. In my judgment, to do so would be to seek to use the provisions of CPR 44.2(4)(c) to give a similar effect to a Part 36 Offer and thereby introduce the same uncertainty into Part 36 Offers which are near to but below the sum awarded, as led to the criticism of Carver and the subsequent amendment introduced in CPR 36.14(1A) [now r.37.17].*
> *In my judgment the principle in sub-paragraph (vii) of [72] in Multiplex, derived as it was from Carver, is no longer a principle which applies to Part 36 and should not be applied as a special 'near miss' rule through CPR 44.2(4)(c). If there is an unreasonable refusal to negotiate then that is a matter which comes within the circumstances which the court can take into account under CPR 44.2(4) and sub-paragraph (a) in particular. I am doubtful that, on analysis, a 'near miss' offer can generally add anything to what otherwise would be conduct in the form of unreasonable refusal to negotiate . . ."*[61]

The court considered issues of conduct by both parties and the relative success and failure on various issues. In the light of those circumstances the court assessed costs by reference to the factors in r.44.2(4)(a) and (b). The claimant was awarded 80 per cent of its costs.[62]

5–18 At a trial on quantum, the claimant succeeded in beating the defendant's Part 36 Offer. The judge when considering what order for costs to make, took into account, as a matter of discretion, the Part 36 Offer which had been beaten. Eder J made it clear that he was not introducing a 'near miss' rule for Part 36 Offers by the back door.[63] In the judge's view the circumstances indicated that the claimant had insisted unreasonably on a higher figure than

[61] paras 26 and 36.
[62] *Hammersmatch Properties (Welwyn) Ltd v Saint-Cobain Ceramics & Plastics Ltd* [2013] EWHC 2227 (TCC) Ramsey J.
[63] See *Hammersmatch Properties (Welwyn) Ltd v Saint-Cobain Ceramics & Plastics Ltd* [2013] EWHC 2227 (TCC) Ramsey J.

that offer, the claim had been much exaggerated and delays regarding disclosure and evidence had caused the defendant real difficulties in taking appropriate precautions to protect its position.[64]

The Claimant appealed. The Court of Appeal found that the judge had erred in his approach to the Part 36 offer and in mischaracterising S's conduct as unreasonable. He had effectively characterised S's pursuit of a business interruption claim in excess of £600,000 after receipt of the Part 36 letter as misconduct. In doing so, he had converted what was not an offer to compromise the business interruption claim at £600,000 into just such an offer. It could not be misconduct simply to pursue a claim greater than the amount accepted by the defendant; something more was required to render pursuit of the claim unreasonable. The matters discussed by the judge did not justify the characterisation of S's conduct as unreasonable. The main judgment had not described the claim or any part of it as exaggerated. Significant parts of the business interruption claim had failed, but that did not mean that it had been exaggerated.

At first instance the Claimant had been awarded 70 per cent of its costs up to 21 days after the defendant's offer and was also ordered to pay the defendant's costs of the assessment of damages. The Claimant had therefore been penalised twice for the same shortcoming. There was no basis on which it was appropriate to deprive the Claimant of its costs after the offer, still less to require it to pay the defendant's costs. Its failure to succeed on all its claim was adequately reflected in the deduction of 30 per cent of their costs (para.31).

There are numerous reported cases where offers which did not comply with r.36.5 have been held not to be Part 36 Offers. In these circumstances however, the Court is not precluded from considering the fact that an offer has been made as part of the circumstances which it is required to take into account when considering what order for costs to make.[65] The Court has held that Part 36 should be construed as designed to protect defendants from claims being pursued, on the basis that a claimant might be able to persuade a defendant to pay more than the legal entitlement, or to pay the legal entitlement more quickly than would otherwise be the case, where the costs of contesting the entitlement would not be worth incurring. Part 36 is not intended to reward in costs, claimants who pursue their claims on such a basis.[66]

Where an offer was expressed to relate to an additional claim which the defendants had set out in draft Amended Particulars of Claim, that claim was not yet part of the claim for the purposes of previous r.36.2(2)(d) (now Rule 36.5(1)(d)) therefore the offer was not a Part 36 Offer and the normal costs consequences did not apply. Although the claimant argued that it was possible to make a Part 36 Offer before the commencement of proceedings

64 *Sugar Hut Group Ltd & Ors v A J Insurance* [2016] EWCA Civ 46.

65 For example, *Rowles–Davies v Call 24-7 Ltd* [2010] EWHC 1695 (Ch) Bernard Livesey QC; *Carillion J M Ltd v PHI Group Ltd* [2012] EWCA Civ 588; [2012] CP Rep 37.

66 *D Pride & Partners v Institute for Animal Health* [2009] EWHC 1617 (QB); [2009] 5 Costs LR 803, Tugendhat J.

and the references to the whole or part of a claim should be taken to include references to a claim that had not yet been brought but which was brought after the offer was made, the judge held that Part 36 is a highly prescriptive and self-contained code and it would not be right to add in further provisions on the basis that it would have an analogous effect to an existing express provision.[67]

In a case where the claimant had achieved judgment against the defendant which was more advantageous than the proposal set out in its Part 36 Offer, the defendants argued that it would be "unjust" to apply the previous r.36.14(3)(b) and (c) (now r.36.17(4)(b) and (c)). It was argued that the claimant had only succeeded as a result of material that had come to light since the Part 36 Offer had been made. The argument was rejected by the Court of Appeal on the basis that the defendants were experienced litigators in the field and must have appreciated that there was a very serious risk that there would be a significant recovery above the interim payment which had already been made. The defendants had enough information to evaluate the Part 36 Offer which they had rejected.[68]

5–19 It is for the offeree to satisfy the court that it is unjust for the court to make the normal order. The court must take into account all the circumstances of the case including the matters set out in previous r.36.14(4) (now r.36.17(5)). They are not the only matters to be considered. Anything which is relevant must be considered as well, including uncertainty as to the developing condition and prognosis of a claimant under a disability.[69] There is no limit to the circumstances which could make it unjust that the ordinary consequences under r.36.14 (now r.36.17) should follow. Where an action had been about restoration of reputation and the conduct of the defendant's disciplinary procedures the court ordered the costs to lie where they fell.[70]

Where a claimant obtained judgment materially in excess of the figure proposed by way of settlement in the claimant's Part 36 Offer, which had been rejected by the defendant company, the claimant applied to add the husband and wife directors as defendants in order to obtain an order for costs against them under s.51 of the Senior Courts Act 1981. A third party costs order was made. The question then arose as to the appropriate rate of interest on the claimant's costs in respect of the Part 36 Offer. The court held that previous r.36.14 (now r.36.17) dealt with the position which applied when judgment was entered. The relevant judgment was that against the defendant company and interest at 6 per cent above base rate was awarded from the date of the refused Part 36 Offer until the date of judgment. In respect of the costs of the s.51 proceedings, which were governed by r.44.3(6)(g) the court awarded interest at one per cent above base rate.[71]

---

[67] *Hertel and Another v. Saunders and Another* [2015] EWHC 2848 (Ch), Morgan J.
[68] *Bent v Highways and Utilities Construction & Allianz Insurance* [2011] EWCA Civ 1539.
[69] *SG (a child) v Hewitt* [2012] EWCA Civ 1053.
[70] *Smith v Trafford Housing Trust* [2012] EWHC 3320 (Ch) Briggs J.
[71] *Chantrey Vellacott v The Convergence Group plc* [2007] EWHC 1774 (Ch) Rimer J.

In personal injury proceedings, the court, having found in favour of the claimant, ordered that the costs should be on the standard basis, save that the costs attributable to dealing with the evidence of the defendant's expert witnesses should be assessed on the indemnity basis.[72] The defendant contended that it had made a written offer on costs, with a better outcome than the claimant had obtained. The court held that it was not possible to conduct a preliminary assessment of costs to establish arithmetically whether the defendant's offer was better on a pound for pound basis than the outcome achieved by the claimant. The justice of the case required the defendant to pay the claimant's costs of the oral hearing, together with the costs of the subsequent dispute as to costs of that hearing on the standard basis.[73]

Costs in the case and Part 36

In a libel action brought by three claimants against three defendants in respect of emails sent in January and July 2012, the claimants each accepted offers of settlement which had been made by the third defendant. At the same time, the claimants gave notice of discontinuance of their claims against the first and second defendants. 5–20

The court had to determine the appropriate final orders in respect of damages and costs to give effect to the settlements and the discontinuance. The main issues were: whether such costs orders as were made against the claimants should be on the standard or the indemnity basis; whether the claimants should be jointly and severally liable for costs ordered in favour of the third defendant; and whether—and if so to what extent—costs and damages due to the claimants should be set off against costs due to the third defendant. There was also an issue in respect of the effect of an order for costs in the case in respect of the third defendant's strike out application.

The court explained:

> *"The 'general effect' of an order for costs in the case is that 'the party in whose favour the court makes an order for costs at the end of the proceedings is entitled to that party's costs of the part of the proceedings to which the order relates': PD44 paragraph 4.2. Here, that general rule cannot be very readily applied; at the end of the proceedings the court has made orders for costs in favour of each party, save for [one].*
>
> *The action has concluded by settlement via Part 36 and without prejudice save as to costs offers. All the claimants have obtained judgment for damages. [Two of the claimants] have recovered substantial damages, sums which on [the third defendant's] case are the maximum they could possibly have obtained. Yet it is said that they are the losers because their recovery is but a fraction of what they*

[72] Such an order would be extremely difficult to assess, and would probably not result in any significant difference in the amount of costs awarded.

[73] *Williams v Jervis* [2009] EWHC 1838 (QB) Roderick Evans J.

claimed. Views could differ about that conclusion, in this case and in others. It is easy to see that if [that] criterion were adopted there could often be lengthy argument as to which party has in reality 'won'.

A simpler and better criterion is to hand for a case like this, which is to have regard to when in the proceedings the relevant costs were incurred and which party has obtained an order for costs in relation to that phase of the proceedings. As a starting point I would suggest that acceptance of a Part 36 Offer, which will ordinarily lead to an order for the costs up to the relevant date, should also carry with it any costs incurred within that period which are the subject of an order for costs in the case. Equally, if an offer is accepted 'out of time' and an order is made, in the ordinary way, for the offeree to pay costs since the expiry of the relevant period that order should carry with it any costs incurred in that period which are the subject of an order for costs in the case."[74]

The court ordered the third defendant to pay the two claimants' costs of the strike out application.[75]

Cases in which the offeror's costs have been limited to court fees

5–21 Where, because of failure to file a costs budget on time or otherwise, the offeror is limited to applicable court fees, "costs"[76] means, in respect of the costs subject to any such limitation, 50 per cent of the costs assessed without reference to the limitation together with any other recoverable costs (see **Chapter 4 Q63**. for further consideration of this).[77]

RTA Protocol and EL/PL Protocol offers to settle

5–22 Section II of Part 36 applies to an offer to settle where the parties have followed the RTA Protocol or the EL/PL Protocol, and started proceedings under Part 8, in accordance with Practice Direction 8B (the Stage 3 procedure). Parties may make an offer to settle in whatever way they choose, but any offer which is not made in accordance with Section II will not have any costs consequences.[78]

A Protocol offer under Section II must be set out in the Court Proceedings Pack (Form B) Form, and contain the final total amount of the offer from both parties. The offer is deemed to be made on the first business day after the Court Proceedings Pack is sent to the defendant.[79]

A Protocol offer is treated as exclusive of all interest, and has costs consequences only in relation to the fixed costs of the Stage 3 procedure (as provided for in r.45.18), not in relation to the costs of any appeal from the final decision in those proceedings. The amount of a Protocol offer must not be

[74] paras 89–91.
[75] *Ontulmus v Collett* [2014] EWHC 4117 (QB) Warby J.
[76] In rr.36.13(5)(b), 36.17(3)(a) and 36.17(4)(b).
[77] r.36.23. This provision is intended to mitigate the effect of the claimant being unable to recover more than the applicable Court fees.
[78] r.36.24.
[79] rr.36.25, 36.26.

communicated to the court until the claim is determined. Any other offer to settle must not be communicated to the court at all.[80]

Costs consequences following judgment

Rule 36.29 applies where on any determination by the court, the claimant obtains judgment against the defendant for an amount of damages that is: 5–23

(a) less than or equal to the amount of the defendant's Protocol offer;
(b) more than the defendant's Protocol offer, but less than the claimant's Protocol offer; or
(c) equal to or more than the claimant's Protocol offer.

Where (a) applies, the court must order the claimant to pay the fixed costs in r.45.26, and interest on those fixed costs from the first business day after the deemed date of the Protocol offer under r.36.26.Where (b) applies, the court must order the defendant to pay the fixed costs in r.45.20.

Where (c) applies, the court must order the defendant to pay interest on the whole of the damages awarded at a rate not exceeding 10 per cent above base rate for some or all of the period, starting with the date specified in r.36.26, the fixed costs in r.45.20, interest on those fixed costs at a rate not exceeding 10 per cent above base rate, and an additional amount calculated in accordance with r.36.17(4)(d).[81]

Deduction of benefits

For the purposes of (a) above, the amount of the judgment is less than the Protocol offer where the judgment is less than the offer once deductible amounts identified in the judgment are deducted.[82] 5–24

Costs of detailed assessment proceedings

Rule 47.20(4) clarifies that the provisions of Part 36 apply to the costs of detailed assessment proceedings with certain modifications. Where an offer to settle is made whether under Part 36 or otherwise, it should specify whether or not it is intended to be inclusive of the costs of preparation of the bill, interest and VAT. Unless the offer makes it clear that the position is otherwise, it will be treated as being inclusive of all those matters.[83] 5–25

In proceedings for detailed assessment, the paying party wrote to the receiving party, setting out what they described as Part 36 Offers, which were stated to be open for 21 days, and offered a proportion or fixed sum in respect of the receiving party's costs. The offers were rejected, and the paying

[80] rr.36.27, 36.28.
[81] r.36.29(1)–(4).
[82] r.36.30.
[83] Practice Direction 47 para.19.

party made a further offer in respect of a third receiving party, if the other receiving parties were willing to accept the Part 36 Offers. These offers were accepted, but the costs hearing still took place because the paying party contended they were entitled to costs in respect of the period from the expiry of the 21 days referred to in the original offers, until the point when the offers had been accepted. The court made no order for the costs in respect of that period. The court held, on the facts, that the earlier offer was not a Part 36 Offer, because it specifically excluded the offerors from recovering all of their costs, and it could not, by its very terms, comply with r.36.10(1) (now r.36.13(1)).

The subsequent offer was indistinguishable from that in *C v D*,[84] and the subsequent offer should be treated as a Part 36 Offer, particularly since all the parties treated the offers as having been made under Part 36. The overriding objective, and common sense, suggested that an offer which was expressed to be a Part 36 Offer, and which otherwise appeared to comply with Part 36, had to be given substantially the same effect as a Part 36 Offer. The offer which was accepted was significantly better than the original offer, and the allocation of liability for costs for the period between the expiry of the 21 days and acceptance was a matter for the Judge's discretion, without the presumption in favour of the paying party inherent in r.36.10(4) and (5) (now r.36.13(4) and (5)). The right order to make was that each party should bear its own costs from the expiry of the 21 days.[85]

Section 2 Settlement other than under Part 36.

5–26 In Chapter 36 of his Final Report Jackson LJ wrote:

> *"4.2 I recommend that:*
> *(i) There should be a serious campaign (a) to ensure that all litigation lawyers and judges are properly informed about the benefits which ADR can bring and (b) to alert the public and small businesses to the benefits of ADR.*
> *(ii) An authoritative handbook should be prepared, explaining clearly and concisely what ADR is and giving details of all reputable providers of mediation. This should be the standard handbook for use at all JSB seminars and CPD training sessions concerning mediation."*

There is growing pressure from the judiciary and court users for greater use of ADR. The Jackson ADR Handbook was published in January 2013, written by three distinguished authors[86] under the banner of the Judicial College, the Civil Justice Council and the Civil Mediation Council.

The Book deals with the general principles of Alternative Dispute Resolution (ADR) as well as the range of ADR options. These include: Offer and Acceptance (offers other than under Part 36); Negotiation; Mediation;

[84] *C v D* [2011] EWCA Civ 646.
[85] *Howellv Lees-Millais* [2011] EWCA Civ 786.
[86] Susan Blake, Julie Browne and Stuart Sime.

Early Neutral Evaluation; Expert Evaluation; Adjudication; and Arbitration. All of these processes may be used in connection with the resolution of costs disputes.

The Court of Appeal has firmly endorsed the advice given in the ADR Handbook to the effect that, as a general rule, silence in the face of an invitation to participate in ADR is itself unreasonable, regardless of whether a refusal to engage in ADR might have been justified. There might be rare cases where ADR is so obviously inappropriate that to characterise silence as unreasonable would be pure formalism, or where the failure to respond was a result of a mistake, in which case the onus would be on the recipient of the invitation to make that explanation good. The court stated that the reasons for extending the guidelines set out in *Halsey v Milton Keynes General NHS Trust*[87], were: first, because an investigation of the reasons for refusing to mediate advanced for the first time at a costs hearing, perhaps months or years later, posed forensic difficulties for the court concerning whether those reasons were genuine. Second, a failure to provide reasons for refusal was destructive of the objective of encouraging parties to consider and discuss ADR. Any difficulties or reasonable objection to a particular ADR proposal should be discussed so that the parties could narrow their differences. Third, it would also serve the policy of proportionality. The court held it would be perverse not to regard silence in the face of repeated requests for mediation as anything other than a refusal. A finding of unreasonable conduct by a refusal to mediate did not produce an automatic result in terms of a costs penalty. The judge has a broad discretion.[88]

A defendant police commissioner who successfully defended proceedings was found to have refused to engage in the alternative dispute resolution process without adequate justification. The Court found that the claimants could have obtained some level of damages. There were issues of fact to be resolved from which both parties ran the risk of adverse findings. The defence was not so strong as to have justified a refusal to engage in ADR. The commissioner did not make any offers to settle before ADR was suggested and ADR would not have delayed the trial of the action. The commissioner was awarded two thirds of his costs.[89]

When the Court exercises its discretion under r.44.2, it has to have regard to all the circumstances including the conduct of the parties both before and during the proceedings. "Conduct" includes a refusal to agree to ADR. The factors to be taken into account include: the nature of the dispute; the merits of the case; the extent to which other settlement methods have been attempted; whether the costs of ADR are disproportionately high; whether any delay in setting or attending the ADR would be prejudicial; and whether ADR has a reasonable prospect of success.[90]

---

87 [2004] EWCA Civ 576, [2004] 1 W.L.R. 3002.

88 *PGF II SA v OMFS Co 1 Ltd* [2013] EWCA Civ 1288.

89 *Laporte v Commissioner of Police of the Metropolis* [2015] EWHC 371 (QB) Turner J.

90 See *Halsey v Milton Keynes General NHS Trust* [2004] EWCA Civ 576; [2004] 1 WLR 3002.

The Advantages of ADR

5–27 The advantages of ADR include: lower costs (provided that the ADR process is entered into sufficiently early); the speed of resolution of the issues; the choice of forum and process; the flexibility of process (the parties may agree how they wish to proceed; a wider range of issues/outcomes may be considered; and shared future interests may be protected. In litigation there will usually be a winner and a loser with damages and costs being paid by one party to another. In ADR the parties may have been unable to agree on the contentious issues but may wish to maintain a potentially lucrative business relationship.

Offers other than Part 36 Offers

5–28 It is open to either party in litigation to make offers which do not comply with the requirements of Part 36. These may be open offers or offers without prejudice save as to costs. The latter are generally known as Calderbank offers, which arose in the Family Division where there was no provision for payment into Court, but the parties could be at risk as to costs, particularly in respect of financial arrangements.

In deciding what order to make about costs the Court is required to have regard to all the circumstances including the conduct of all the parties, whether a party has succeeded on part of its case and if not wholly successful, the extent to which that party has succeeded and any admissible offer to settle which is drawn to the Court's attention and which is not an offer to which the costs consequences of Part 36 apply.[91] The question of who was the successful party or the unsuccessful party to an action can be determined by who ultimately wrote the cheque at the end.[92]

Fraud and dishonesty in making offers

5–29 Where parties in family proceedings had entered into a consent order compromising the wife's financial claims, it subsequently came to light that the husband had failed to disclose arrangements being made to float a software company in which he had a substantial shareholding. The judge at first instance found that the husband's evidence had been dishonest but did not set aside the consent order as the initial public offering had not taken place and was not likely to do so in the future. This decision was upheld by the Court of Appeal but overturned by the Supreme Court. The Supreme Court endorsed the broad approach to dishonesty that "*fraud unravels all*". The Court emphasised the fundamental principle that parties have a duty to provide full and frank financial disclosure to one another and the Court in financial remedy proceedings. The Court and the parties must have all relevant information before them to enable an informed decision to be made about what

[91] r.44.2(4), Practice Direction 44, paras 4.1–4.2.

[92] *Day v Day* (Costs) [2006] EWCA Civ 415; [2006] CP Rep 35.

constitutes a fair financial outcome.[93] This principle will clearly apply in all negotiated settlements.

Negotiation

Negotiation needs no explanation. It is the method by which the majority of civil cases are still settled. Negotiation may be between the parties themselves; between their lawyers; between experts, reporting back to the lawyers/clients; or any combination of the above. **5–30**

Mediation

Mediation is conducted by an independent third party (who is normally an accredited mediator) who is independent of the parties and whose function it is to try to bring the parties together so that a settlement or compromise may be achieved. It is a confidential process, which can usually be arranged to take place within a reasonably short timescale. Lord Justice Jackson, in Chapter 36 of his Final Report, stated[94]: **5–31**

> *"Mediation is not, of course, a universal panacea. The process can be expensive and can on occasions result in failure. The thesis of this chapter is not that mediation should be undertaken in every case, but that mediation has a significantly greater role to play in the civil justice system than is currently recognised."*

There are several types of mediation, the most usual being facilitative and evaluative. In facilitative mediation the mediator tries to help the parties reach a position with which they can live. There is often a matter of pride which prevents a party from compromising for fear of appearing weak. The cloak of confidentiality helps in this regard.

Evaluative mediation requires a rather more robust approach by the mediator. The writer has found that although one starts out on the facilitative track one finds that one ends up going down the evaluative route. Each party ultimately asks: "What do you think would happen on assessment?" or "What do you think it is worth".

Many mediation agreements contain a clause to the effect that if the parties fail to agree, the mediator may be asked to give a non-binding opinion as to the final outcome.

The main benefits are that a neutral third party may be able to help each side see the strengths and weaknesses of its case. A skilled mediator may help parties step outside the adversarial framework and entrenched positions so the mediation may work even where a negotiation has failed. A skilled mediator may make possible offers and concessions look more acceptable. A robust and experienced mediator can help to find a way forward even in a relatively intractable dispute. The structure of a mediation allows a lawyer and a client time to review offers and options in a way which may not be

---

[93] *Sharland v. Sharland* [2015] UKSC 60.

[94] Paragraph 3.2.

possible in negotiation. Mediation can be used to allow a party to make a statement about something of particular personal importance. Experience suggests that mediation generally achieves good success rates and party satisfaction.

The Mediator needs to be selected with care as regards expertise, experience etc. to ensure the parties have confidence in the process. The most obvious advantages of mediation are that, provided the parties are able to agree the process, a mediation can be set up quickly rather than having to wait 9 to 12 onths for a court hearing. The parties may choose their Mediator. Parties are not permitted to choose the judge where a matter proceeds to litigation. The process is confidential, whereas in the absence of a specific Order, all hearings in courts are in public.

The Court of Appeal has addressed the question of ADR in greater detail.[95] The Court indicated that the burden was on the unsuccessful party to show why there should be a departure from the general rule on costs, in the form of an order to deprive the successful party of some or all of his costs on the grounds that he refused to agree to ADR. A fundamental principle was that such a departure was not justified unless it had been shown that the successful party had acted unreasonably in refusing to agree to ADR. In deciding whether a party had acted unreasonably the court should bear in mind the advantages of ADR over the court process and have regard to all the circumstances of the particular case. The factors that could be relevant include:

(i) the nature of the dispute;
(ii) the merits of the case;
(iii) the extent to which other settlement methods have been attempted;
(iv) whether the costs of ADR are disproportionately high;
(v) whether any delay in setting up and attending the ADR would have been prejudicial;
(vi) whether the ADR had a reasonable prospect of success.

Where failure to mediate was due to the attitudes taken on either side it was not open to one party to claim that the failure should be taken into account in the order as to costs. A party who agreed to mediation but then took an unreasonable position in the mediation was in the same position as a party who unreasonably refused to mediate. That was something which the court should take into account in its costs order.[96]

Where a party reasonably considered that it had a strong case and where a party was faced with an unfounded claim and wished to contest it rather than buy it off, the Court should be slow to characterise that as unreasonable

[95] *Halsey v Milton Keynes General NHS Trust* [2004] EWCA Civ 576; [2004] C.P. Rep.34.
[96] *Carleton (Earl of Malmesbury) v Strutt & Parker (A Partnership)* [2007] EWHC 424 (QB). 118 Con. L.R. 68, Jack J.

conduct. The fact that a party reasonably believed that it had a watertight case might well be sufficient justification for refusal to mediate.[97]

The Court has to look beyond the polarised positions of the parties. A skilled mediator might be able to find middle ground by analysing the parties' position and making each reflect on its own and the other's position. By bringing other commercial arrangements or disputes into the discussion or by finding future business opportunities, a mediator might find solutions that the parties had not considered. On the facts of the particular case, the defendant's refusal to mediate had deprived the parties of the opportunity of resolving the case without a hearing, as had the claimant's failure to accept the defendant's offer. The fair and just outcome was that neither party's conduct should modify the general rule on costs. The claimant was accordingly ordered to pay the whole of the defendant's costs on the standard basis.[98]

In *Garritt-Critchley v Ronnan*[99] the defendants accepted the claimant's Part 36 Offer just before judgment was about to be given following a four day trial. The judge did not criticise the late acceptance of the Part 36 Offer but penalised the defendants in costs because he considered that they had been wrong in consistently refusing to mediate. The defendants had refused to mediate because they were confident of their position and believed that the parties were too far apart. The judge stated that the claim involved a question of fact which was a classic case for mediation and parties did not know whether they were too far apart until they sat down and explored settlement. Mediation also costs less than trial[100]. If the defendants had accepted the claimant's last offer of mediation, the difference in costs might have been almost £100,000. The judge applied *Halsey*, which held that in deciding whether a party had acted unreasonably in refusing ADR, the court should bear in mind the advantages of ADR over the court process and have regard to all the circumstances of the particular case.[101]

A defendant in person who unsuccessfully opposed a grant of probate in favour of the claimants, having lost at trial, argued that he should not have to pay the claimant's costs as they had initially refused to mediate. The Court held that a successful party's unreasonable refusal to mediate might warrant a reduction in the amount of costs. In the instant case, however, the claimants had subsequently changed their attitude to mediation, but it did not take place because the defendant was not ready to take part. There was, therefore, no reason why the defendant should not face the usual order as to costs. The order was made on the standard basis since, although the defendant should not have challenged the will, the case did not cross the threshold for ordering costs on the indemnity basis. An order for payment on account was also made. Another issue was whether the claimant's counsel was entitled to a

[97] See *Halsey* (above) and *Daniels v Commissioner of Police of the Metropolis* [2005] EWCA Civ 1312; [2006] CP Rep.9.

[98] *Northrop Grumman Mission Systems Europe Limited v BAE Systems (AL Diriyah C41) Limited* [2014] EWHC 3148 (TCC); [2014] TCLR 8, Ramsey J.

[99] *Garritt-Critchley v Ronnan* [2014] EWHC 1774.

[100] Unless the mediation fails.

[101] In *Reid v Buckinghamshire Healthcare NHS Trust* [2015] EWHC B21 Master O'Hare in the SCCO ordered the losing defendant to pay the costs of detailed assessment from the date they unreasonably refused an offer of mediation.

separate brief fee in respect of the defendant's late application to amend his defence to include a claim for forgery. The court did not specifically disallow the claim for a separate brief fee, but directed the Costs Judge to pay particular attention to the matter and to consider whether there would be any element of double recovery.[102]

Where a defendant had agreed to a mediation but then failed to attend the mediation itself without giving any reason, the Court took the view that this was a very serious matter both because of the expenditure incurred and more importantly because the defendant had shown himself unwilling to engage in a serious attempt to resolve the litigation. In the view of the Court this was serious misconduct that the Court could take into account in an application where that party asked for relief on the basis that it was just to make the order sought. In the particular case, the defendant was seeking an order for security for costs under r.25.13(2)(c). The application was refused and the Court noted that the defendant's misconduct would itself have been sufficient justification for dismissing the application.[103]

In a building dispute the claimant made a Part 36 Offer to settle, and also suggested mediation. At trial the judge awarded damages which were less than the claimant had claimed, and less than their Part 36 Offer. The judge made no order for costs up to the expiry of the period for acceptance of the Part 36 Offer, and ordered the claimant to pay the defendant's costs thereafter. The Court of Appeal held that the judge had erred fundamentally in his appreciation of the significance of the claimant's Part 36 Offer. There was nothing in Part 36 which stated that an offeror was to be prejudiced as to costs because she expressed her willingness to accept less than her formal claim. An order for no order as to costs did substantial justice between the parties. The claimant was the winner but only just. On an issues-based approach she had failed on three issues, but succeeded on one issue which had taken a substantial amount of time. The defendants' rejection of offers to enter into settlement negotiations or mediation was unreasonable, and conduct which ought to be taken into account.[104]

While mediation is not compulsory, it is now well established that the courts may robustly encourage parties to embark on it and an unreasonable failure to do so places a party at risk of being penalised in costs. This decision is a reminder that refusing mediation is a high risk strategy, and lawyers and their clients should consider their position carefully.

Mediation in the Commercial Court

5–32 The Commercial Court normally strongly encourages the parties to attempt to resolve their dispute by ADR. The parties are required to co-operate with each other by exchanging the names of three mediators, who are available to

[102] *Murray and Another v. Bernard* [2015] EWHC 2395 (Ch.) Mann J.
[103] *Gresport Finance Limited v. Battaglia* [2015] EWHC 2709 (Ch.), Chief Master Marsh.
[104] *Rolf v De Guerin* [2011] EWCA Civ 78.

conduct the mediation by the date fixed by the Court. If the parties cannot agree, the Court will give directions. In the event that the mediation fails the parties are required to explain why the mediation failed.

Early Neutral Evaluation

Early Neutral Evaluation (ENE) is carried out by an independent person, who is normally experienced in the particular field of the issue under dispute. That person may be appointed by one or all parties. **5–33**

The Technology and Construction Court Guide and the Commercial Court Guide both deal with ENE.[105] ENE may be carried out by the Court with the consent of the parties. In *Seals v. Williams*[106] Norris J concluded that the wide jurisdiction provided by r.3.1(2)(m), to the effect that the Court can make any order to manage cases and further the overriding objective, provided the power to order ENE. This did not therefore require the consent of the parties. Following this, r.3.1(2)(m) was amended to read:

> *"Except where these rules provide otherwise, the court may . . . (m) take any other step or make any other order for the purpose of managing the case and furthering the overriding objective, including hearing an early neutral evaluation with the aim of helping parties to settle the case".*

This Rule is not limited to Chancery proceedings but is of general application. It is expected that its use in appropriate cases in the Chancery Division, the Queen's Bench Division and the County Court is likely to become increasingly common. To date there is no dedicated ENE Practice Direction. General guidance (excluding the need for party consent) can be obtained from the TCC and Admiralty and Commercial Court Guides.

ENE is intended to be an advisory and evaluative process. ENE can take place within the Court system in which case it is usually carried out by a judge. There is no requirement for proceedings to be in progress, any party may appoint an independent third party to carry out an ENE. It is of course preferable and more conducive to settlement if all the parties can agree to the appointment.

Expert Evaluation

Expert evaluation may take different forms. This may be an evaluation similar to Early Neutral Evaluation or a Determination. As the name implies one or more neutral experts are appointed by the parties to evaluate or determine the issues between the parties. The evaluation/determination may be agreed to be binding between the parties or merely advisory, leaving the parties to proceed further if they so decide. Expert evaluation/determination is most commonly employed in cases of a technical nature (e.g. costs). The way in which matters proceed will be governed primarily by the terms of the contract by which the **5–34**

[105] See Technology and Construction Court Guide paragraphs 7.5.1–7.5.4; the Admiralty and Commercial Court Guide, paragraphs G2.1–G2.5.
[106] [2015] EWHC 1829 (Ch), Morris J.

expert is appointed. The parties will usually agree that the determination will be final and binding and this is usually recorded in the contract.

Adjudication

5–35 Adjudication usually takes place in a specialist commercial field where the parties prefer a system adapted to the needs of their industry or business. It is most frequently used in construction disputes. It is used to resolve specific issues and is usually agreed by the parties to a contract as a means of resolving disputes which may arise by a process agreed to be binding on the parties.

Construction industry adjudication is a creature of statute which requires all construction contracts to have a provision for adjudication.[107] The statutory requirement is for adjudication by an independent third person who produces a decision on the dispute which is binding on an interim basis until finally determined as appropriate by the Court, arbitration, or agreement. The adjudicator is required to give a decision within a limited time. The decision is enforceable through the courts and appeal is only possible on the grounds of lack of jurisdiction or breach of the rules of natural justice.

In a construction dispute, the defendant made an open offer in the sum found by the adjudicator. The claimant believed it was entitled to more than the adjudicator had found and brought court proceedings. The claimant did not accept the offer and it was withdrawn. The claimant company applied for judgment on the basis that the offer was a formal admission of liability under r.14.1. The Court held that the open offer contained a package of terms that the claimant could accept or reject. It would run contrary to the basis of the offer if the claimant could accept part of it as being an admission of liability but then reject other terms. The Court had to encourage the making of offers which was in accordance with the overriding objective. If a party were able partially to accept an offer and to reject other parts which ensured that the litigation continued, the purpose of making offers would not be met. The defendant's offer letter did not refer to r.14.1, nor did it admit the truth of the claimant's case. It did not in any way admit that any of the defendant's points were bad. To be a formal admission under r.14.1, it needed to be clear and unequivocal. The alleged admission was neither. The claimant had had to seek clarification and had been told that there was no admission in respect of early payment discounts. If there had been any admission at all, it was in respect of the sums identified by the adjudicator which was the opposite of the claimant's case.[108]

Arbitration

5–36 Arbitration is effectively a trial process outside the Court system. Arbitrations may be domestic or international. They may be conducted under the

[107] Housing Grants Construction and Regeneration Act 1996 as amended by Part 8 of the Local Democracy, Economic Development and Construction Act 2010.

[108] *Dorchester Group Limited (T/A Dorchester Collection) v. Kier Construction Limited* [2015] EWHC 3051 (TCC), Coulson J.

Arbitration Act 1996 or under the rules of any of the numerous arbitration providers. In many commercial contracts there are clauses providing terms for arbitration should a dispute arise. Arbitrators may be appointed by agreement between the parties or, if no agreement is possible, by the President of the relevant professional body. If the arbitration requires three arbitrators, each side usually nominates one arbitrator and the third will be appointed by a neutral person e.g. the President of the professional body.

The agreement to arbitrate may be made before or after the relevant dispute has arisen. There is a strong public policy in favour of upholding arbitration agreements, which is supported by the idea that an arbitration clause in a contract is separable from the rest of the substantive contract[109] and so continues to apply even if the substantive contract is avoided. Where Court proceedings are commenced in breach of an arbitration agreement, the defendant may apply to the Court to stay those proceedings.[110]

It is worth looking at some of the provisions of the Arbitration Act 1996: S.1, S.4, S.61, and S 63. It is clear from the extracts below that the terms of any arbitration agreement are very much in the hands of the parties. Apart from the mandatory provisions (which are basically common sense), the terms may be agreed in whatever form the parties wish. The Act provides certain long stop provisions, e.g. in section 61, the powers of the Tribunal where the parties have not agreed.

1. General principles.
The provisions of this Part are founded on the following principles, and shall be construed accordingly—

(a) the object of arbitration is to obtain the fair resolution of disputes by animpartial tribunal without unnecessary delay or expense;
(b) the parties should be free to agree how their disputes are resolved, subject only to such safeguards as are necessary in the public interest;
(c) in matters governed by this Part the court should not intervene except as provided by this Part.

4. Mandatory and non-mandatory provisions.

(1) The mandatory provisions of this Part are listed in Schedule 1 and have effect notwithstanding any agreement to the contrary.
(2) The other provisions of this Part (the "non-mandatory provisions") allow the parties to make their own arrangements by agreement but provide rules which apply in the absence of such agreement.
(3) The parties may make such arrangements by agreeing to the application

[109] Arbitration Act 1996, Section 7.
[110] Arbitration Act 1996, Section 9.

of institutional rules or providing any other means by which a matter may be decided.

(4) It is immaterial whether or not the law applicable to the parties' agreement is the law of England and Wales or, as the case may be, Northern Ireland.

(5) The choice of a law other than the law of England and Wales or Northern Ireland as the applicable law in respect of a matter provided for by a non- mandatory provision of this Part is equivalent to an agreement making provision about that matter.

For this purpose an applicable law determined in accordance with the parties' agreement, or which is objectively determined in the absence of any express or implied choice, shall be treated as chosen by the parties.

61. Award of costs.

(1) The tribunal may make an award allocating the costs of the arbitration as between the parties, subject to any agreement of the parties.

(2) Unless the parties otherwise agree, the tribunal shall award costs on the general principle that costs should follow the event except where it appears to the tribunal that in the circumstances this is not appropriate in relation to the whole or part of the costs.

63. The recoverable costs of the arbitration.

(1) The parties are free to agree what costs of the arbitration are recoverable.

(2) If or to the extent there is no such agreement, the following provisions apply.

(3) The tribunal may determine by award the recoverable costs of the arbitration on such basis as it thinks fit.

If it does so, it shall specify—

(a) the basis on which it has acted, and

(b) the items of recoverable costs and the amount referable to each.

(4) If the tribunal does not determine the recoverable costs of the arbitration, any party to the arbitral proceedings may apply to the court (upon notice to the other parties) which may—

(a) determine the recoverable costs of the arbitration on such basis as it thinks fit, or

(b) order that they shall be determined by such means and upon such terms as it may specify.

(5) Unless the tribunal or the court determines otherwise—

(a) the recoverable costs of the arbitration shall be determined on the basis that there shall be allowed a reasonable amount in respect of all costs reasonably incurred, and
(b) any doubt as to whether costs were reasonably incurred or were reasonable in amount shall be resolved in favour of the paying party.

(6) The above provisions have effect subject to section 64 (recoverable fees and expenses of arbitrators).
(7) Nothing in this section affects any right of the arbitrators, any expert, legal adviser or assessor appointed by the tribunal, or any arbitral institution, to payment of their fees and expenses.

There are no budgeting requirements in arbitration, unless the parties agree. This is unlikely to happen, although commercial clients are bound to want to keep strict control of expenditure. There should be no problems of the sort generated by *Mitchell v NGN Ltd*[111] and *Denton v White*[112].

Questions and answers

Section 1 Part 36

Q1. Is there anything in CPR Part 36 or the Privy Council Rules which prevents a Part 36 offer being made in costs proceedings before the Privy Council? (Rule 2.1).

CPR 2.1 states that the rules apply to all proceedings in the County Court, 5–37
the High Court and the Civil Division of the Court of Appeal. There is no mention of the Privy Council. The Judicial Committee (Appellate Jurisdiction) Rules 2009 set out the procedure before the Judicial Committee but make no mention of Part 36 or anything equivalent to it. A party wishing to make an offer may make a Calderbank type offer. Rule 43(1) of the 2009 Rules provides "the Judicial Committee may make such orders as it considers just in respect of the costs of any appeal, application for permission to appeal or other application to or proceeding before the Judicial Committee".

Q2. My firm needs to serve an expert's report out of time. The Defendants are Objecting to relief from sanctions. How does this affect potential Part 36 Offers? (Rule 3.9).

It depends on the particular facts of your case but this decision may 5–38
help. The Claimant applied to serve its expert report late, accepting that it was out of time and that the default was serious and without good reason. The

[111] *Andrew Mitchell MP v News Group Newspapers Limited* [2013] EWCA Civ 1537.
[112] *Denton v T H White Ltd* [2014] EWCA Civ 906 [2014] CP Rep 40.

issue for the court was whether it was appropriate to grant the claimant relief from sanctions. The defendant submitted that there would be prejudice if relief were granted as the date for making a Part 36 Offer giving rise to costs consequences had passed. The defendant had already seen the expert report in draft and it was reasonable to suppose that it would be similar to the final version of the report. Therefore if the defendant was influenced by the report to make a Part 36 Offer, it would most probably have done so before service of the final report. The court found that there was minimal prejudice to the defendants and granted relief from sanctions on very strict terms including that the claimant could not recover from the defendant any of its costs relating to the expert's report.[113]

Q3. Can a valid Part 36 offer include settlement terms which (if accepted), impose conditions; require a defendant to do something other than pay money; or provide for interest to run after the end of the relevant period? Rule 2.1; Rule 36.2(2), (Rule 36.5(4)).

5–39 Rule 36.2(2) states *"Nothing in this Section prevents a party making an offer to settle in whatever way that party chooses, but if the offer is not made in accordance with Rule 36.5, it will not have the consequences specified in this Section."* Rule 36.5 sets out the form and content of a Part 36 Offer. Provided therefore that Rule 36(5) is complied with, the terms of an offer may be in whatever terms the offeror chooses.

Q4. If a defendant makes a Part 36 Offer which does not take into account its counterclaim and the offer is then accepted, what happens to the counterclaim? (Rule 36.5).

5–40 "Counterclaim" is defined by the CPR glossary as 'a claim brought by a defendant in response to the claimant's claim which is included in the same proceedings as the claimant's claim'. A counterclaim is treated for certain purposes as if it were a claim (r.20.3). Rule 36.2(3) provides that a Part 36 Offer may be made in respect of the whole, or part of, any issue that arises in a claim, counterclaim or other additional claim, and state whether it takes into account any counterclaim (r.36.5(1)(e)). Rule 36.14(3) provides that if a Part 36 Offer which relates to part only of the claim is accepted, the claim will be stayed as to that part upon the terms of the offer. The question which has to be decided is whether the counterclaim is 'part only of the claim' or is a claim in its own right. Whilst the rules provide for a Part 36 Offer to take into account the existence of a counterclaim if so desired, there is no requirement to do so and it is accordingly arguable that a counterclaim is a claim in its own right and would continue notwithstanding any Part 36 Offer accepted in respect of the claim. The options for a party making a Part 36 Offer, where a counterclaim exists, appear to be: either to ensure that

[113] *Art and Antiques Limited v. Magwell Solicitors* [2015] EWHC 2143 (Ch) Klein J.

the offer takes into account the counterclaim or to make an offer without prejudice save as to costs, i.e. a Calderbank offer.

Where a defendant had made what purported to be a claimant's Part 36 Offer in respect of the defendant's counterclaim, "the proceedings in respect of which" it was made included the claim and the proposed counterclaim, but were not restricted only to the counterclaim. A Part 36 Offer may be made before the commencement of proceedings under r.36.7 so the fact that the defendant's counterclaim had not been formulated or pleaded did not of itself matter.[114]

Q5. When considering whether a claimant has failed to obtain a judgment more advantageous than a defendant's Part 36 offer how do you deal with any interest element that the judge awards the claimant at trial? Assuming that the defendant's offer was inclusive of interest until the expiry of the relevant period do you compare that figure with the principal sum that the judge awards at trial plus any interest awarded too up to the date of judgment? Or can you argue that for the purposes of working out whether the judgment is more advantageous you should only take into account the principal sum awarded and interest up to the date of expiry of the Part 36 offer?

Rule 36.5(4) provides that a Part 36 Offer which offers to pay or offers to accept a sum of money will be treated as inclusive of all interest until the date on which the relevant period expires; or, if the offer is made less than 21 days before the start of the trial, a date 21 days after the date the offer was made. When the judge gives judgment, any interest awarded in the judgment is part of that judgment. There appears to be no basis upon which, when considering whether or not the judgment is more advantageous, one should only take into account the principal sum awarded and ignore the interest element. 5–41

Q6. What is the position when a Part 36 offer is made pre-action and accepted after the issue of proceedings, but before the proceedings have been served on the defendant, where service has been reserved for up to four months? Rule 36.7.

CPR r.36.7 permits a Part 36 Offer to be made at any time including before the commencement of proceedings. If the offer is not made in accordance with rule 36.5, it will not have the consequences specified in Section I of Part 36. If the offer is not a valid Part 36 Offer r.44.2 requires the court to consider any offer to settle, that does not have the costs consequences set out in Section I, in deciding what order to make about costs. 5–42

R.7.2(1) provides that proceedings are started when the court issues a claim form at the request of the claimant. The fact that the proceedings have not been served or that service has been reserved for a period is immaterial. The

[114] *AF v BG* [2009] EWCA Civ 757.

purpose of Part 36 is to enable and encourage parties to settle cases at an early stage, without the need for a trial.

Q7. If an offeree serves a notice of acceptance during the relevant period, when does that acceptance take effect, given that the offeror may apply for permission to withdraw or vary its offer within seven days of the notice of acceptance (or, if earlier, before the first day of trial)? If the offeror's application is unsuccessful, it is not clear when the notice of acceptance will be treated as having been accepted. (Rule 36.9; 36.10).

5–43 A Part 36 Offer can only be withdrawn or its terms changed if the offeree has not previously served notice of acceptance (Rule 36.9(1)). If the offeree serves notice of acceptance before the expiry of the relevant period, that acceptance has effect unless the offeror applies to the Court for permission to withdraw the offer or to change its terms within seven days of the offeree's notice of acceptance; or, if earlier, before the first day of trial. Where the offeror makes such an application, the Court may give permission for the original offer to be withdrawn or its terms changed if satisfied there has been a change of circumstances since the making of the original offer and that it is in the interests of justice to give permission (r.36.10).

As to when the acceptance takes effect if the offeror's application is unsuccessful, the answer may be fact sensitive but the starting point must be the date of the notice of acceptance. This has the slightly odd result that the case will then be deemed to be settled and stayed from a date before the hearing of the offeror's application.

Q8. What is the position where a Part 36 Offer is withdrawn at the same time as the claimant purports to accept it? (Rule 36.9, 36.10).

5–44 The rules governing the withdrawal of offers are rr.36.9 and 36.10. The following decision still holds good. An NHS Trust made a Part 36 Offer to a claimant which stated that if it was accepted within 21 days, the Trust would be responsible for the claimant's costs. The offer pointed out that it could be withdrawn before the expiration of that period with permission of the Court. Before the expiration of the relevant period the Trust obtained permission to withdraw its offer but did so without serving any notice or evidence on the claimant who had accepted the offer on the day it was withdrawn. Leggatt J held that an application should not be made without notice unless that would enable the respondent to take steps to defeat the purpose of the application or there had been no time to give notice before the urgent assistance of the Court was required. It was wrong in principle for the Trust to make its application for permission without notice to the claimant and for the Court to entertain the application. It was all the more wrong to conceal from the claimant the grounds on which the order had been made. The making of orders which determined questions of substantive rights between the parties without notice could only be justified if that party had the right to apply to set aside the order. The test to be applied, when considering whether to grant a party permission to withdraw a Part 36 Offer, was whether there had been a sufficient change of circumstances to make it just to do so.[115] The only new circumstances which could make it just were circumstances which the Trust was able and willing to make known to the claimant at the time of serving notice of withdrawal.[116]

Under r.36.10(3), where the offeree serves notice of acceptance of the offer before the expiry of the relevant period and the offeror applies to court for permission to withdraw or change its terms within seven days of the offeree's notice (or, if earlier, before the first day of trial), the court will only give permission if satisfied that there has been a change of circumstances and that it is in the interests of justice.

Q9. Where there has been a split trial or a trial of preliminary issues, what is the position with regard to Part 36 Offers which may have been made? (Rule 36.12)

Where there has been a trial but all the issues in the case have not been 5–45 determined,[117] any Part 36 Offer, which relates only to parts of the claim or issues that have already been decided, can no longer be accepted. Subject to that proviso, and unless the parties agree, any other Part 36 Offer cannot be accepted earlier than seven clear days after judgment is given or handed down in that trial.[118]

Where an offer, which relates to the whole of the claim, is accepted after the expiry of the relevant period, the court must, unless it considers it unjust to do so, order that the claimant be awarded costs up to the date on which the relevant period expired, and, that the offeree pay the offeror's costs for the period from the date of the expiry of the relevant period to the date of acceptance. In considering whether it would be unjust to make such orders the court must take into account all the circumstances of the case including the matters set out in r.36.17(5) (see Costs consequences following judgment above). The claimant's costs include any costs incurred in dealing with the defendant's counterclaim if the Part 36 Offer states that it takes the counterclaim into account.[119] Rule 36.16 deals with restrictions on disclosure in such cases.

It is open to the Court to depart from the normal costs rule in r.36.13(5). Where a young boy had suffered frontal lobe damage in a road traffic accident, it was material that the inherent uncertainty in prognosis would have resolved well before the limitation period expired so that the child did not need to commence proceedings before the position was clear. The defendant had made a pre-action Part 36 Offer in full and final settlement; the claimant accepted the offer after the date of its expiry. The Court

115 *Cumper v Pothecary* [1941] 2 KB 58.
116 *Evans v Royal Wolverhampton Hospitals NHS Foundation Trust* [2014] EWHC 3185 (QB) Leggatt J.
117 Within the meaning of r.36.3(e).
118 r.36.12 and also see r.36.3.
119 Rule 36.13(5)–(7). For cases which led to the revision of this rule, see *Fitzpatrick Contractors Ltd v Tyco Fire & Integrated Solutions (UK) Ltd* [2009] EWHC 274 (TCC) Coulson J; *Thompson v Bruce* [2011] EWHC 1730 (QB) John Leighton Williams QC; *Kunaka v Barclays Bank Plc* [2010] EWCA Civ 1035; *Sutherland v Turnball* [2010] EWHC 2699 (QB) Stadlen J.

approved the settlement, but at first instance it was held that the defendant should be entitled to its costs from the date of acceptance. The Court of Appeal held that the judge's conclusion did not give weight to the particular features of the claimant's case, the consequence of omitting to give weight to the matters that were in the claimant's favour was that the normal rule dominated when it should not have done. In the circumstances it was unjust to make the normal costs order, and the claimant was awarded his costs throughout.[120]

There was previously no general rule that in the case of a split trial the Court should ordinarily reserve the costs until the end of the case. Mr Justice Eder stated that there was an urgent need for the rule to be reviewed and possibly reformulated in order to address the question of split trials. In the particular case, due to the substantial level of costs, costs were reserved.[121]

Eder J eventually gave three main judgments. The first dealt with the outcome of the preliminary issues (Part 1); the one cited above he referred to as "Part 2"; and the third dealt with further issues concerning claims co-operation and also quantum (Part 3). The costs by this time had "spiralled out of all proportion" to the amount which was then in dispute.

During the course of the proceedings the defendants made various offers of settlement. Although the claimants had succeeded in relation to the preliminary issues (Part1), they had failed to obtain a money judgment more advantageous than any of the defendants' settlement offers. The claimants' success on Part 1 resulted in no ultimate financial benefit to them; they would have been enormously better off if they had accepted any of the offers.

Relying on previous r.36.14 (now r.36.17) the Court held that the rule meant that "the Court will make the order there specified 'unless it considers it unjust to do so'". The burden of showing such injustice is a "formidable obstacle".

Eder J stated:

> *"It follows that the real question, in my view, is whether the claimants can show any relevant 'injustice' so as to displace the general rule, bearing fully in mind that the burden of doing so is a 'formidable obstacle'. In this context and without seeking to lay down any hard and fast rules, it seems to me that where a claimant fails to 'beat' a Part 36 Offer made by a defendant, the mere fact that such defendant may fail on certain issues would not necessarily of itself make it 'unjust' to displace the general rule under Part 36 and to require the claimant to pay the costs from the date on which the relevant period expired and interest on such costs under Part 36.14(2)* [now r.36.17(3)]. *However, on the other hand . . . it seems to me that the fact that a defendant may make a Part 36 Offer does not give such defendant carte blanche to run any defence whatsoever so as to*

[120] *SG v Hewitt* [2012] EWCA Civ 1053.
[121] *Ted Baker Plc v Axa Insurance UK Plc* [2012] EWHC 1779 (Comm) Eder J.

entitle such defendant necessarily to expect that the CPR Part 36 consequences will automatically to apply to those issues on which such defendant lost."[122]

In the light of the above and bearing in mind that the claimants had succeeded on Part 1, the defendants were awarded 25 per cent of their costs on Part 1. They were awarded all their costs on Part 2.[123] This decision remained case-specific until the introduction of the new rules.

In a different case, the judge decided that success on the preliminary issue did not mean that the claimant would ultimately establish any claim in contract at all, and the incidence of costs should therefore be the same as if it had been tried as part of that claim. The judge did not think that this was a reason for departing from the general rule. The defendants had asked for a preliminary issue. They did so because it was thought to be helpful to the parties, and to the Court, for the question of proper law to be determined as a discrete issue. The judge agreed, but the corollary of this was that the question did not arise as part and parcel of the trial but was tried separately. That necessarily involved a separate hearing with separate preparation and the incurring of separate costs on that issue. It is in general a salutary principle that those who lose discrete aspects of complex litigation should pay for the discrete applications or hearings which they lose, and should do so when they lose them rather than leaving the costs to be swept up at trial.[124]

Q10. I act for a proposed claimant in a dispute where legal proceedings have yet to be issued. The proposed defendant has served a Part 36 offer by form N242A which states that the defendant will be liable for the claimant's costs in accordance with Part 36.13. Part 36.13 states the claimant will be entitled to the Costs of proceedings including their recoverable pre-action costs. Does this mean my client can only recover pre action costs as part of the costs of any proceedings? If this is so, can I agree that the pre-action costs are recoverable and if so, if the amount cannot be agreed can I issue costs only proceedings pursuant to Part 8A to have the court adjudicate upon costs? (Rule 36.13).

Part 8 Costs Only proceedings are the way forward. 5–46

In a road traffic case where a Part 36 offer had been made and accepted before proceedings had been issued, the claimant contended that a deemed order for costs would have arisen providing a sufficient basis for commencing a detailed assessment. The court held that an order for costs:

"...cannot exist in a vacuum divorced from any substantive proceedings, and accordingly an order for costs cannot be deemed to have been made under rule [44.9(1)(b)] if a Part 36 offer is made and accepted before any proceedings have been commenced."

---

[122] para.17.
[123] *Ted Baker Plc v AXA Insurance UK Plc* [2014] EWHC 4178 (Comm) Eder J.
[124] *Merck KGAA v Merck Sharp & Dohme Corp* [2014] EWHC 3920 (Ch) Nugee J.

The court stated:

"18. On the face of it, the procedure in rule [46.14 (Costs Only Proceedings)] is apt to refer to cases that fall within Part [36.13(1)] as well as to those" that do not . . .it provides for Section II of Part 45 to take precedence in cases to which it applies: see rule [46.14(5) and (6)]. In my view the mechanism provided by rule [46.14] is intended to apply both to cases settled through the operation of Part 36 and to those settled without recourse to it.

The court commented that it was not easy to see why a claimant who proceeds under r.46.14 should be subject to a more restrictive costs regime, than one who started proceedings under Part 7 to recover his costs:

"The whole purpose of introducing Section II of Part 45 was to impose a somewhat rough and ready system in a limited class of cases. . ."

If the claimants' argument was correct, the acceptance of a Part 36 offer would always result in an order for costs on the standard basis in low value road traffic accident cases which would undermine the fixed costs regime and provide a powerful incentive for defendants not to make Part 36 offers in such cases. The court concluded that, subject to any agreement between the parties to the contrary, neither could recover more or less by way of costs than is provided for.[125]

Q11. If a defendant accepts a claimant's Part 36 offer after proceedings have been issued, is a consent order to dispose of the proceedings necessary? (Rule 36.13(1)

5–47 No. Under CPR PD 36A 3.1 a copy of the acceptance must be filed at court. CPR 36.14(1) provides that the claim will be stayed.

In the event that a defendant accepts a claimant's Part 36 Offer, r.44.9(1)(b) provides that where a cost arises under r.36.13(1) or (2), a costs order will be deemed to have been made on the standard basis. This provision does not apply where the Part 36 Offer is accepted before the commencement of proceedings. The existence of the deemed order for costs enables the claimant to commence detailed assessment proceedings under Part 47.

Q12. Where there is a Part 36 offer, what is the position where the offeree seeks clarification of the offer?

5–48 Where there had been a settlement agreement of the substantive claim, one party asserted that the other was in repudiatory breach and terminated the agreement. The party against whom breach was alleged, claimed damages from the other. The defendant (later appellant) made a Part 36 offer of £200,000. The offer stated that it did "not take into account any counterclaim". The claimant (later respondent) requested clarification as to whether

[125] *Solomon v Cromwell Group Plc* [2011] EWCA Civ 1584; [2012] 1 W.L.R. 1048; [2012]. C.P. Rep. 14.

it was intended to bring a counterclaim and the defendant stated that he did not intend to. The claimant sought further information about the valuation of the claim but that was not provided.

The claimant refused the offer and issued proceedings, and the defendant filed a defence and added a counterclaim. The claimant then served a Part 36 offer which offered to accept £185,000 and stated that it "took account of the entire claim and counterclaim". The defendant accepted that offer outside the 21 day period to avoid an automatic costs order.

The defendant sought an order that the claimant pay his costs from 21 days after the first Part 36 offer. The claimant sought an order that the defendant pay her costs up to the date of his acceptance. At first instance the Master held that she could not regard the offers as being on similar terms, as the claimant was proposing to settle the claim and counterclaim, thereby bringing finality, whereas an acceptance of the defendant's offer would not necessarily have done so. In light of the fact that the first Part 36 offer did not state whether it took into account any counterclaim, as required by CPR r.36.2, (now r.36.5) she declined to 'order otherwise' pursuant to CPR r.36.10(4) (now r.36.13(4)) and ordered that the defendant pay the claimant's costs of the claim.

On appeal the Court held that the Master had taken account of the clarification but had concluded that it did not modify it and she was entitled to that view as a matter of law. However, in construing the first Part 36 offer, the subsequent clarification had to be taken into account. The Master had failed to adopt that approach and should have seen that, had the respondent (claimant) accepted the first Part 36 offer, the appellant (defendant) would have been bound. The Master had wrongly construed the first Part 36 offer as excluding any counterclaim without having regard to the whole of the correspondence. The first Part 36 offer had been modified in correspondence so as to encompass any counterclaim.

The counterclaim that had later been brought was not in fact a discrete claim but no more than a claim for a declaration as to the repudiation of the settlement agreement and therefore no more than a mirror image of the defence. The fact of the later counterclaim did not therefore alter the court's conclusion. Even if the first Part 36 offer had been capable of comparison with the second, the respondent had not initially acted unreasonably in refusing it. She had made reasonable requests for information that the appellant had not thought were relevant. The purpose of the Part 36 regime was to encourage early settlement and allow the offeror costs if their offer was not accepted within 21 days. The appellant's letter and first Part 36 offer clearly explained the valuation of the respondent's claim. It was reasonable for the respondent to seek further clarification. However, she had misunderstood the valuation. There was no doubt that that misunderstanding had been corrected by the appellant and the respondent had received all the information needed to understand the official valuation shortly after the original offer.

The further information that the respondent requested was not relevant and it was not unreasonable of the appellant not to provide it. The respondent's questions had been answered by the letter accompanying the first Part 36 offer and she could have made an informed decision on that basis. It was not unreasonable conduct for the appellant to refuse to give further information and his actions were not unreasonable or obstructive. It would be unjust for the appellant to pay costs past the 21 day period following the first Part 36 offer.[126]

Whilst Part 36 requires an offer to state whether it includes a counterclaim or not, provided the position is clear or is made clear by way of clarification, it therefore appears the court will give effect to the offer.

Q13. If a defendant makes a Part 36 offer in relation to its counterclaim, which is accepted within the relevant period, does that mean that the defendant is automatically "entitled to the costs of the proceedings" (that is, the costs relating to both the original claim and the counterclaim) under CPR 36.13(1)? What about the situation where the defendant makes a Part 36 offer in relation to its counterclaim and the original claim too? Again, if it is accepted within the RP, does that mean that the defendant is automatically entitled to the costs of the proceedings under CPR 36.13(1)? Or can the court look at the reality of the situation and, in particular, at whether the offer leads to a net payment being made to the defendant/counterclaimant. (Rule 36.13(7)).

5–49 There have been numerous questions covering more or less the same ground. Coulson J in the TCC has recently dealt with this situation.[127] A defendant contractor was sued by a sub-contractor for £10 million damages and interest on the basis of disruption and prolongation. The defendant counterclaimed in relation to interim payments made in relation to the claims. The judgment resulted in the claimant having to repay the defendant almost £2.8 million.

The defendant had made and beaten a Part 36 offer and the question arose whether this was a claimant's Part 36 offer attracting the enhancements in Rule 36.17(4).

The Court held that the offer was a defendant's Part 36 offer. Although the Court of Appeal in *AF v BG* (**see Q4 above**) had held that the offer was a claimant's offer, that case could be distinguished. The defendant's offer did not say expressly that it was a claimants' offer; it did not offer to accept an amount of money in settlement of claim and counterclaim (instead, it offered to pay an amount to the claimants); it offered to pay the claimants' costs; further, it did not spell out the enhanced consequences of non-acceptance. Instead, the offer had all the hallmarks of a defendant's Part 36 offer. It offered to pay a sum in settlement of the litigation (taking into account the counterclaim). The defendant stated that the claimants could retain the sums already paid.

[126] *Bailes v Bloom* [2015] EWHC (QB) 23 November Simler J, unreported.
[127] *Van Oord UK Ltd v and Anor v Allseas UK Ltd* [2015] EWHC 3385 (TCC) Coulson J.

The defendant offered to pay the claimants' costs up to the date of acceptance, for a maximum period of 21 days after the date of the offer. And when the offer letter stated that "for the avoidance of any doubt" the defendant would seek an order that the claimants pay its costs from the date of the expiry of the offer if the claimants failed to do better than the offer at trial, that was classically in accordance with a defendant's Part 36 offer. No separate, stand-alone counterclaim had been asserted by the defendant at the time of the offer, and no sum was set out in the offer as representing the liquidated amount of any such counterclaim. The Court made an award of costs on the indemnity basis since the claim should not have been pursued.

The CPR do not give a great deal of guidance in relation to Part 36 Offers where there is a counterclaim. Nothing in s.1 of Part 36 prevents a party making an offer to settle in whatever way that party chooses, but if the offer is not made in accordance with Rule 36.5, it will not have the consequences specified in the Section. A Part 36 Offer may be made in respect of the whole, or part of, or any issue that arises in – (a) a claim, counterclaim or other additional claim (r.36.2(2)(3)). A Part 36 Offer must (a) be in writing; (b) make clear that it is made pursuant to Part 36; (c) specify a period not less than 21 days within which the defendant will be liable for the claimant's costs in accordance with r.36.13 (costs consequences of acceptance of a Part 36 Offer) or r.36.20 (costs consequences of acceptance of a Part 36 Offer where Section IIIA of Part 45 applies); (d) state whether it relates to the whole of the claim or to part of it or to an issue that arises in it and if so to which part or issue; and (e) state whether it takes into account any counterclaim (r.36.5(1)). Subject to certain exceptions (**explained in paragraph 5–15 above**), where a Part 36 Offer is accepted within the relevant period, the claimant will be entitled to the costs of the proceedings (including their recoverable pre-action costs) up to the date on which notice of acceptance was served on the offeror (r.36.13(1)). The claimant's costs include any costs incurred in dealing with the defendant's counterclaim if the Part 36 Offer states that it takes it into account (r.36.13(7)).

The topic of offers in claim and counterclaim has also been examined by the Court of Appeal. A landlord sued a tenant for rent arrears and the parties agreed that approximately £6,000 in arrears were due. The landlord also claimed for physical damage to the property and consequential loss of rent both of which claims were disputed. The tenant counterclaimed for breach of the covenant of quiet enjoyment and for the landlord's failure to address the property's state of disrepair which far outweighed any sum claimed by the landlord. The landlord made what purported to be a Part 36 Offer offering to withdraw the claim for the rent arrears if the tenant also discontinued the disrepair claim with each party paying its own costs. The offer specified a relevant period under r.36.5(1)(c) of 21 days, but did not state that the tenant would be liable for the landlord's costs if the offer was accepted.

At trial the landlord was awarded the rent arrears and interest amounting to £16,000. The tenant was awarded damages for discomfort and inconvenience in the sum of about £7,000. The tenant was ordered to pay the costs of the landlord's claim on the standard basis until the date of the offer and on the indemnity basis with 8 per cent interest after expiry of the relevant period. On appeal to the Court of Appeal, the Court held that Part 36 had been carefully drafted and meant what it said. It is open to a party to make an offer in whatever way the party chose but an offer not made in accordance with r.36.2 would not have Part 36 consequences. The Court held that the landlord's offer had not complied with r.36.2(2)(c) which was a mandatory requirement that the offer specified a period within which the defendant would be liable for the claimant's costs. Under Appendix 2 to RSC Order 62The offer had only specified the relevant period. Notwithstanding the fact that it was the tenant's counterclaim which determined the issue, the landlord and the tenant had been claimant and defendant respectively for the purposes of the rule. Accordingly, Part 36 did not apply, the correct approach was under r.44.2 under which the unsuccessful party would generally pay the successful party's costs. The Court did not encourage issue-based costs orders and an appellate Court would normally be slow to intervene with costs orders made by judges who were best placed to have a feel for the case. In the instant case, the judge at first instance had taken a mistaken starting point. Where much time had been taken by a party unsuccessfully taking numerous points, the Court could give less weight to the fact that on balance that party had been ultimately successful. The case had not only been about the amount of equitable set-off versus the rent arrears. The landlord had sued for substantial damages and had failed on many issues. The judge had insufficiently considered the parties' conduct and partial successes. The tenant had substantiated his allegation as to the state of the property and had been entitled to vindicate his claim even if the damages awarded were small. The landlord's offer had been very realistic and the tenant should have considered it more. The tenant had however received no response to his many requests for mediation. No dispute was too intractable for mediation and silence towards an invitation to engage an alternative dispute resolution was in itself unreasonable.[128] The tenant had won more issues than the landlord even if the latter had succeeded financially. A fair and balanced approach was to make no order as to costs. The fact that the landlord had incurred costs of £85,000 and the tenant of £100,000 made a stronger case as was possible that there should be some form of limitation on the costs recoverable in such cases.[129]

Q14. Are costs recoverable if a claimant's Part 36 Offer is accepted in circumstances where the claimant's costs budget has not been filed on time? (Rule 36.13)

5–50 This question was originally raised after the decision in *Mitchell* but before the Court of Appeal decision in *Denton*. Given the more measured approach of the Court in *Denton*, it would seem that if the Part 36 Offer has been accepted

[128] See *PGF II SA v. OMFS Co. 1 Ltd* [2013] EWCA Civ.1288; [2014] 1 WLR 1386.
[129] *N J Rickard Ltd v Holloway and Ors* [2015] EWCA Civ 3 November unreported.

within the relevant period, the claimant will be entitled to the costs of the proceedings up to the date on which notice of acceptance was served on the offeror (r.36.13(1)). If the acceptance of the offer is after the expiry of the relevant period and the parties are unable to agree the liability for costs, liability for costs must be determined by the Court (r.36.13(4)). The outcome may, however, depend on how late the budget was—if, indeed, it has been filed—and all the circumstances because the canny defendant might argue that the offer was only made because it knew it had only a very limited costs liability after the date the budget fell due and r.3.14 applied. On the other hand the consequences of the Court requiring the claimant to apply for relief from sanction and then refusing such relief would merely be to generate further satellite litigation, an outcome which the Court in *Denton* was at pains to avoid. Rule 36.23 somewhat ameliorates the draconian effect of r.3.14.

Q15. In a claim by a claimant (C) against two separate defendants (D1 and D2), where separate allegations are advanced against each defendant, if C makes a Part 36 offer to settle the whole of his claim which is addressed to both D1 and D2 as "the offeree", and only D1 accepts the offer, is the claim against D2 stayed, even though D2 did not accept the offer? (Rule 36.14)

The answer will depend on the exact wording of the offer. Rule 36.14 is clear: 5–51

"(1) If a Part 36 Offer is accepted the claim will be stayed.
(2) In the case of acceptance of a Part 36 Offer which relates to the whole claim the stay will be upon the terms of the offer."

Since the offer to settle in this question was an offer in respect of the whole claim, which has been accepted, it must follow that the whole claim is stayed. Had the offer been differently worded, r.36.14(3) would apply "if a Part 36 Offer which relates to part only of the claim is accepted the claim will be stayed as to that part upon the terms of the offer."

Rule 36.15 deals with acceptance of a Part 36 Offer made by one but not all defendants. The rule does not cover the circumstances described in this question.

Q16. Can you explain how an award of costs on the standard basis (e.g. under CPR 36.17(3)(a)) differs from an award of costs on the indemnity basis (e.g. under CPR 36.17(4)(b)) in circumstances where a costs budget is in place? The definition of 'standard basis' and 'indemnity basis' appear to be hard to reconcile with the concept of costs budgets, because there should be no doubts about reasonableness to resolve in anyone's favour if the costs are within the court-approved costs budget. (Rule 36.17(4).

See **Chapter 4 Qs. 48** and **49** on this topic. 5–52

Q17. Is it appropriate to award a lower additional amount under CPR 37.17(4)(d) than the prescribed amount because the proceedings were

determined early, for example, as a result of summary judgment being given, rather than going to full trial?

5–53 Defendants will not always be penalised. Where a claimant's Part 36 Offer which had been refused, but not bettered at trial, expired days before the trial commenced and the defendants had not received its witness statements until the final day of the expiry of the offer, the High Court ruled that making a defendant who rejected a Part 36 Offer pay an additional 10 per cent of the sum awarded for costs, pursuant to r.36.17(4)(d), would introduce a 'penal' element and be unjust. The ruling was made after an injunction had been granted to the claimant restraining the defendant from joining another company before the end of his 12 month notice period.[130]

Q18. Is the following case still good law—*Hammersmatch Properties (Welwyn) Ltd v Saint Gobain Ceramics and Plastics Ltd*[131]? Is Eder J's costs decision in *Sugar Hut etc. v AJ Insurance*[132] reintroducing *Carver* by the back door? (Rule 36.17).

5–54 The general view is that *Hammersmatch* is still good law, but the decision in *Sugar Hut* has caused confusion. In the latter, Eder J found that he was entitled to take the defendant's Part 36 Offer into account as a matter of conduct and in accordance with the wide discretion of the court, even though it was narrowly beaten by the claimant, when ordering the successful claimant to pay the defendant's costs from a certain date. This ran counter to Ramsay J's warning against allowing CPR r.44.2(4)(c) to be used as a basis for making an order for the claimant to pay the defendant's costs where there is a "near miss" Part 36 Offer. Ramsay J was concerned that this would introduce the same degree of uncertainty as led to the criticism of Carver. CPR Rule 44.2(4) requires the court, when making a costs order, to have regard to "all the circumstances"—this includes the conduct of all the parties (CPR r.44.2(4)(a)) and any admissible offer to settle drawn to the court's attention which is not an offer to which the Part 36 costs consequences apply (CPR r.44.2(4)(c)).

Although Eder J made it clear that he was not introducing a "near miss" rule by the back door and went to significant lengths to emphasise that *Sugar Hut* could be distinguished from Hammersmatch; The Court of Appeal took a different view as explained at paragraph **5–18** above.

Q19. Do you agree that it may be difficult to decide who has obtained the more advantageous result in a detailed assessment? Also, does r.36.17(4)) about enhancing claimants' recovery by 10 per cent apply in detailed assessments? (Rule 36.17).

[130] *Elsevier Ltd v Munro* [2014] EWHC 2728 (QB) Warby J. See also *Feltham v Bouskell* [2013] EWHC 3086 (Ch) Charles Hollander QC; and see: *Bataillon and another v Shone and another* [2015] EWHC 3177 (QB) HHJ Waksman QC. **Paragraph 5–54** above.

[131] *Hammersmatch Properties (Welwyn) Ltd v Saint Gobain Ceramics and Plastics Ltd* [2013] EWHC 2227 (TCC) Ramsey J.

[132] *Sugar Hut etc. v AJ Insurance* [2014] EWHC 3775 (Comm).

Where a Part 36 Offer has been made in detailed assessment proceedings, it will be for a specified amount. When the bill is totalled at the end of the detailed assessment there should be no difficulty in ascertaining whether or not the offer has been beaten. The power of the Court under r.36.17(4) to award interest not exceeding 10 per cent above base rate on the sum awarded; to award indemnity costs; to award interest on those costs at a rate not exceeding 10 per cent above base rate; and, an additional amount in accordance with r.36.17(4)(d) is certainly exercisable. In detailed assessment proceedings, the receiving party made a Part 36 Offer to settle for £152,500. At the detailed assessment the bill was allowed at £173,693 which was more advantageous to the receiving party than the Part 36 Offer. The Costs Judge declined to award the 10 per cent additional amount stating that in circumstances where there had been a significant reduction in the claimant's bill, it would be unjust to reward the claimant with the additional amount prescribed by Rule 36.17(4). On appeal, the court found that the Costs Judge was in error in relying on the degree of reduction on assessment. That approach penalised the appellant for making a reasonable Part 36 Offer. It was the terms of the Part 36 Offer not the level of the sums claimed in the bill of costs which were to be considered. Accordingly, the appellant was entitled to the additional award.[133] 5–55

Q20. How does the cap on damages in the IPEC apply where there is also a claim for costs? (Rule 36.17(4).

In the Intellectual Property Enterprise Court (IPEC) the cap on the maximum value permitted for a claim for damages on an account of profits is £500,000. A claimant in IPEC proceedings obtained judgment for an amount well in excess of its rejected Part 36 Offer. The question was whether the 'additional amount' payable by the defendant under r.36.17(4) should be treated as further damages (subject to the £500,000 cap) or whether it was a separate payment unaffected by the cap. The Court held that it appeared to be clear from the note to r.36.14 in the White Book and the authorities there mentioned that the 'additional amount' had nothing to do with compensating a claimant for any wrong committed by the defendant in the substantive dispute. It was solely intended to serve as an incentive to encourage claimants to make and defendants to accept appropriate Part 36 Offers.[134] 5–56

Q21. We represent a client in a case where we feel that the client is bound to succeed. We are considering making a claimant Part 36 offer to settle at 100 per cent liability plus costs. This would save the Defendant the time and cost of preparing for trial and the trial itself. Will this succeed? (Rule 36.17).

Every case is fact sensitive, but, in the light of the decision below caution is advisable with what you propose. 5–57

---

[133] *Cashman v. Mid-Essex Hospital Services NHS Trust* [2015] EWHC 1312 (QB) 2015 3 Costs LO 411, Slade J.

[134] *000 Abbott v Design and Display Ltd* [2014] EWHC 3234 (IPEC) HHJ Hacon.

Prior to a trial, one of the issues in which was the claimant's age (i.e. whether the claimant was a child), the claimant made what purported to be a Part 36 Offer stating that the defendant should accept the claimant's age and agree to pay the claimant's costs. The claimant was successful at trial and the issue arose as to whether the indemnity costs and interest on costs consequences set out in r.36.17(4) should apply in view of the terms of the offer made. The defendant argued that the offer made by the claimant was not a genuine offer to settle as understood by r.36.17(5)(e) and that it would be unjust to make the order sought. The defendant's counsel relied on *AB v. CD and Others*[135] and also *East West Corporation v. DKBS*[136] arguing that there was no give and take involved in the offer made. It was a total capitulation offer. It did not assist the claimant to contend that the Part 36 Offer was genuine because had the defendant accepted it, it would have gained by saving the costs of the hearing. There was no obvious answer to the matter in issue in the present case and the Court's jurisdiction in disputed age cases was inquisitorial not adversarial.[137] The Court held that the claimant's offer was not a give and take offer, as the claimant was offering to take "nothing short of what he was claiming in the proceedings". It was not a settlement offer in any real sense but a "tactical ploy". It did not constitute a concession on the claimant's part but, had the defendant accepted the offer, the defendant would have saved costs. Accordingly, the claimant failed to obtain an order for enhanced interest, indemnity costs, enhanced interest on those costs and an additional amount under r.36.17(4). Instead the defendant was ordered to pay costs on the standard basis.[138]

Q22. If I make a successful Part 36 Offer am I sure to recover all my costs? (Rule 44.2).

5–58 The existence of a Part 36 Offer does not, in principle, insulate the offeror from a proportionate costs order. The fact that there has been a Part 36 Offer does not mean that the court is unable to make an issue based or proportionate costs order. Part 36 is a self contained regime and the rule itself makes no reference to such orders. Nevertheless, insofar as such an order is necessary to avoid injustice, it is permissible for the court to make it[139].

Q23. When the question of costs is being decided is it possible for a party to refer to without prejudice correspondence in order to establish that the other party did not respond to Part 36 Offers? (Rule 44.2).

5–59 A defendant who had been found liable for misusing the claimants' confidential information made two Part 36 Offers during the course of an inquiry as to damages. The claimants did not respond to either offer and made no

[135] [2011] EWHC 602 (Ch.), Henderson J at 22.
[136] [2002] All ER (D) 361, Thomas J.
[137] See *R (CJ) v. Cardiff* [2011] EWCA Civ.1590.
[138] *R (MVN) v. London Borough of Greenwich* [2015] EWHC 2663 Admin, Picken J.
[139] *Webb v. Liverpool Women's NHS Foundation Trust* [2015] EWHC 449 (QB) HHJ Saffman.

counter-offer. When the court was dealing with the costs of the inquiry the defendant criticised the claimants' conduct and served a witness statement which referred to an exchange of without prejudice correspondence between solicitors attempting to settle the question of costs. The claimants sought an order to strike out those passages which referred to the without prejudice correspondence.

The court stated that there was a strong public policy justification for denying the ability to rely on without prejudice correspondence at any stage in the proceedings including costs assessment. Where a without prejudice offer was made the recipient was free to make a without prejudice response. The response might be to make a counter-offer, ask for more information, reject the offer or simply ignore it. All these responses were protected by privilege. The fact that the claimants were seeking costs on the indemnity basis did not amount to a waiver of privilege but was based on criticism of the defendant's conduct.[140]

Q24. Where a Part 36 offer is accepted in a small claim that has not yet been allocated to the small claims track, is it the case that the fixed costs regime will generally apply? (Rule 46.13).

Rule 46.13(3) is a new provision following the Jackson Reforms and the decision of the Court of Appeal in *O'Beirne v. Hudson*[141]. The Rule provides that where the Court is assessing costs, on the standard basis, of a claim which concluded without being allocated to a track, it may restrict those costs to the costs that would have been allowed on the track to which the claim would have been allocated if allocation had taken place. The position is further explained in para.8.2 of Practice Direction 46. The Court of Appeal has since decided that in relation to Rule 46.13(2) (Allocation and Re-Allocation), the Court has power to backdate the reallocation for costs purposes if the Court is satisfied that there were good reasons for doing so.[142] **5–60**

Where a mother and two children were passengers in a car and claimed damages, following an accident, and instructed the same solicitor, a District Judge decided that it was appropriate for all three claims to be issued on the fast track (the claims of the children were small claims). Liability had been denied and the claims had left the portal. Costs were provisionally assessed rather than being fixed costs.[143]

Q25. What is the requirement for open offers in detailed assessment proceedings meant to achieve and how they will co-exist with Part 36 Offers? (PD47 para 8.3).

Practice Direction 47 para.8.3 sets the matter out clearly: **5–61**

[140] *Vestergaard Frandsen v Bestnet Europe Ltd* [2014] EWHC 4047 (Ch) Iain Purvis QC.
[141] [2010] EWCA Civ. 52; [2010] 1 WLR 1717; [2010] CP Rep. 23.
[142] *Conlon v. Royal Sun Alliance Insurance Plc* [2015] EWCA Civ. 92.
[143] *Dilip v Paynes Dairies Ltd. Case No: A53YJ800 Leicester County Court.*

> *"The paying party must state in an open letter accompanying the points of dispute what sum, if any, that party offers to pay in settlement of the total costs claimed. The paying party may also make an offer under Part 36."*

Lord Justice Jackson's objective in inserting this requirement was to ensure that the parties were not in fact arguing over an insignificant amount of money. It is clearly open to the paying party to make an open offer of 0 per cent. This would presumably only be done if there were an arguable point of principle which might well result in the receiving party recovering nothing. There is no requirement that the open offer and any Part 36 Offer should be in the same terms.

If a paying party fails to make an open offer as required by the Practice Direction, it would clearly be within the power of the costs judge to strike out the points of dispute or if that were felt to be too draconian, to rely only on the written points of dispute and not permit any further oral argument.

The Court of Appeal expressly considered provisions of the CPR which contain mandatory language, but where no sanction is provided for any failure to comply in *Altomart v Salford Estates (No.2) Ltd.*[144] The court accepted the proposition that there might be implied sanctions which were capable of engaging r.3.9 and equally there might be cases not analogous with r.3.9 and where it was a matter for the court to determine the consequence of non-compliance. It is clear that the open offer does not form part of the Points of Dispute (it merely accompanies that document) and therefore it is difficult to see how any argument suggesting that the Points of Dispute should be struck out would find favour (indeed there is a risk it would be seen as an attempt to turn the rules into 'tripwires' and invoke possible costs sanctions). Perhaps a more measured approach would be to identify the failure to comply to the paying party promptly, suggesting a short period for rectification, and, in default of compliance reserve the position to the question of costs of the assessment, if relevant, under 'conduct' within r.47.20(3)(a).

Section 2 Settlement other than under Part 36

Q26. How are Calderbank offers treated in relation to costs? (Rule 44.2(4)).

5–62 The Court of Appeal has made it clear that the effect of a Calderbank offer is not to be assessed by analogy with the terms of r.36.17(2) which defines a 'more advantageous' judgment as one that is 'better in money terms by any amount, however small' than the relevant offer. Parts 36 and 44 of the CPR are separate regimes with separate purposes. Part 36 is a self-contained procedural code which specifies particular consequences in the event that such offers are not accepted. Those consequences include features which go far beyond that which might be ordered by way of costs under Part 44. Whilst Part 36 is highly prescriptive and highly restrictive of the exercise of any discretion by the Court, Part 44 confers on the Court a discretion in almost the widest

[144] *Altomart v Salford Estates (No.2) Ltd* [2014] EWCA Civ 1408.

possible terms. It contains no rules as to the way in which the Court has to have regard to offers and there is no equivalent to the 'more advantageous' test in Part 36.[145]

Q27. Does anyone/any kind of company (for example) have to use ADR because the law says so? If so I would be grateful if you would direct me to that law or illuminate what kind of people MUST use ADR.

In short: Yes. The Alternative Dispute Resolution for Consumer Disputes (Competent Authorities and Information) Regulations 2015 (2015 No. 542) which came into force for the purposes of Parts 1 to 3 on 7 April 2015 and for the purposes of Parts 4 & 5 on 9 July, 2015, as amended by The Alternative Dispute Resolution for Consumer Disputes (Amendment) Regulations 2015 (2015 No 1392) together implement the provisions of Directive 2013/11/EU of the European Parliament and of the Council of 21 May 2013 on alternative dispute resolution for consumer disputes. Regulation 2(3) of the amending regulations substitutes a new coming into force date for Parts 4 and 5, the effect of which is to postpone the commencement of the trader information requirements until 1 October 2015. **5–63**

"Consumer" and "trader"

"Consumer" means an individual acting for purposes which are wholly or mainly outside that individual's trade, business, craft or profession.

"Trader" means a person acting for purposes relating to that person's trade, business, craft or profession, whether acting personally or through another person acting in the trader's name or on the trader's behalf.[146]

This includes those providing legal services.

Schedule 1 lists the Competent Authorities: the Financial Conduct Authority; the Financial Ombudsman Service; the Legal Services Board; and the Office for Legal Complaints. Others are being added from time to time.

Consumer information by traders

The Regulations provide:

"19.—(1) Where, under an enactment, rules of a trade association, or term of a contract, a trader is obliged to use an alternative dispute resolution procedure provided by an ADR entity or EU listed body the trader must provide the name and website address of the ADR entity or EU listed body— (a) on the trader's website, if the trader has a website; and (b) in the general terms and conditions of sales contracts or service contracts of the trader, where such general terms and conditions exist. (2) Where a trader has exhausted its internal complaint handling procedure when considering a complaint from a consumer relating to a sales contract or a service contract, the trader must inform the consumer, on a durable

[145] *Coward v Phaestos Ltd* [2014] EWCA Civ 1256.

[146] Regulation 3, The Alternative Dispute Resolution for Consumer Disputes (Competent Authorities and Information) Regulations 2015 (2015 No. 542).

medium— (a) that the trader cannot settle the complaint with the consumer; (b) of the name and website address of an ADR entity or EU listed body that would be competent to deal with the complaint; and (c) whether the trader is obliged, or prepared, to submit to an alternative dispute resolution procedure operated by an ADR entity or EU listed body. (3) The trader information requirements set out in paragraphs (1) and (2) apply in addition to any information requirements applicable to traders regarding out-of-court redress procedures contained in any other enactment.

Consumer information by online traders and online marketplaces regarding the ODR platform.

19A.—(1) Where under an enactment, rules of a trade association, or term of a contract, an online trader is obliged to use an alternative dispute resolution procedure provided by an ADR entity or EU listed body, the trader must— (a) provide a link to the ODR platform in any offer made to a consumer by email; and (b) inform consumers of— 5 (i) the existence of the ODR platform; and (ii) the possibility of using the ODR platform for resolving disputes. (2) The information in (1)(b) must also be included in the general terms and conditions of online sales contracts and online service contracts of the trader, where such general terms and conditions exist. (3) An online trader must on its website— (i) provide a link to the ODR platform; and (ii) state the online trader's email address. (4) An online marketplace must provide a link to the ODR platform on its website. (5) The online trader requirements set out in paragraphs (1) to (3) apply in addition to the trader information requirements set out in regulation 19. (6) The online trader and online marketplace requirements in paragraphs (1) to (4) apply in addition to any information requirements regarding out-of-court redress procedures contained in any other enactment. (7) In this regulation— 'online marketplace' has the meaning given in Article 4(f) of the Regulation (EU) No 524/2013 of the European Parliament and of the Council of 21 May 2013 on online dispute resolution for consumer disputes and amending Regulation (EC) No 2006/2004 and Directive 2009/22/EC; 'online sales contract' means a sales contract where the trader, or the trader's intermediary, has offered goods on a website or by other electronic means and the consumer has ordered such goods on that website or by other electronic means; 'online service contract' means a service contract where the trader, or the trader's intermediary, has offered services on a website or by other electronic means and the consumer has ordered such services on that website or by other electronic means; 'online trader' means a trader who intends to enter into online sales contracts or online service contracts with consumers."

The Law Society in its advice dated 10 September 2015 advises:

"The Law Society has changed its advice for firms on compliance with UK regulations which transpose the EU Directive on consumer alternative dispute resolution (ADR Directive).

This is in response to the unexpected withdrawal of the Legal Ombudsman's (LeO) application to the Legal Services Board (LSB) to become certified as an ADR approved body for the purposes of the ADR Directive. Although the Legal

Ombudsman has withdrawn its application, solicitors must still comply with the government regulations. New requirements will apply from 1 October 2015 in relation to the information solicitors are required to provide to clients at the end of a solicitor's internal complaints process.

In order to be as comprehensive as possible, this advice provides:

1. *a description of the requirements*
2. *suggested text to be included in letters at the end of first-tier complaints, from 1 October 2015*
3. *information on further changes that are likely to be made*
4. *web links to further information*
5. *frequently asked questions (FAQs)"*[147]

In short, from 1 October, 2015, solicitors must: continue to provide information on the Legal Ombudsman as the statutory complaints scheme for solicitors, and provide information on an additional ADR entity certified under the EU Consumer ADR Directive[148]. Solicitors will be under no obligation to use such a scheme and information need only be provided at the end of the complaints process. Given the clear indications from the Courts that unreasonably refusing ADR is likely to have costs consequences, it is in the interests of those providing legal services to have an appropriate procedure in place and to utilise it.

Q28. When we suggest mediation on behalf of clients we are often met with a variety of reasons why there should be no mediation. Have you any suggestions?

Parties can be reluctant to mediate for various reasons. The following are some **5–64**
common misconceptions and ideas to address them[149]:

Mediating is a sign of weakness. Mediation is, in fact, usually a sign of strength; the strength of knowing what the lawyer and the client want to achieve, and pursuing that objective through a negotiated outcome. The key to negotiating from a position of strength is the ability to identify what the client and the opponent really need to achieve. The CPR including the Pre-Action Protocols and the Practice Direction—Pre-Action Conduct require parties to consider mediation before commencing proceedings. Failure to comply with this can lead to costs sanctions. Referring to this may help to focus the parties' minds. In *Jane Laporte and another v Commissioner of Police of the Metropolis*[150], a police commissioner was found to have failed, without adequate justification, to have engaged in the alternative dispute resolution process, despite successfully defending the proceedings and, after taking into account the factors listed in *Halsey*, that was to be reflected in the costs order made.

Lawyers and clients can negotiate directly so mediation is unnecessary. There can

[147] The full advice can be found at: *www.lawsociety.org.uk/support-services/advice/articles/changes-to-client-care-information-and-leo-time-limit/*. See also: *www.tradingstandards.uk/advice/AlternativeDisputeResolution.cfm*.

[148] The Department for Business, Innovation and Skills has confirmed that the following ADR entities are currently available to deal with disputes in the legal services sector: Ombudsman Services, ProMediate and Small Claims Mediation.

[149] With acknowledgements to The Practical Law Company.

[150] [2015] EWHC 371 (QB) Turner J.

be barriers to effective communication when negotiations are direct (between lawyers or between clients). The intervention of a neutral third party can change the dynamics and help to overcome these barriers. The mediator can use several techniques to manage the negotiating process, free up communications, encourage a problem-solving approach or brainstorming of options, and overcome deadlock. Parties tend to be unwilling to disclose information about their view of the case to an opposing party during direct negotiations.

Direct negotiations have failed so mediation will not succeed. Direct negotiations may become positional, with each party assuming entrenched and unrealistic positions and becoming increasingly defensive. A mediator can focus each party on a problem-solving approach, directing energy away from threats, attacks, or challenges to the credibility or good faith of a party in the dispute, towards a focus on the issues to be resolved and the potential implications of a failure to settle the problem.

The mediator is just a messenger. A mediator's task is considerably more sophisticated. It includes coaching, developing strategies and reality testing. The mediator is an active participant in the mediation process, and will use a range of techniques to engage people in the process and encourage them to consider a range of settlement options.

You cannot mediate until full disclosure is provided. Lawyers especially tend to argue that early mediation, before the disclosure process has been completed, is not appropriate. In practice, mediation simply requires knowledge of enough information (about the facts and the relevant law) for the lawyer to be able to advise the client on:

- the strengths and weaknesses of the case;
- the alternatives to settlement; and
- any options for settlement of the dispute.

The earlier that mediation takes place and an agreement is reached, the lower the costs will be.

Mediation will be a waste of time and money if the case does not settle at mediation. Even a failed mediation can help to narrow the issues and increase the likelihood that the case will settle without the need for trial. The parties will certainly have a better understanding of each other's positions and perspectives, and the potential barriers to settlement. A failed mediation can also generate options and opportunities that can be discussed after the mediation. In practice, a large proportion of cases that do not settle during a mediation settle shortly afterwards.

Mediation only delays the progress of litigation. Agreeing to attempt mediation does not stop court proceedings unless the parties agree and the court stays the proceedings. Awareness of the implications of failing to reach settlement during the mediation (for example, in terms of the costs and management time that would be incurred going to trial) can help to focus the parties' minds, and encourage them to engage positively in the mediation process.

Q29. There must be drawbacks to Mediation – What are they?

There are possible drawbacks to mediation. A successful conclusion may depend, to a certain extent, on the abilities of the mediator. Costs may be increased if the mediation fails. The mediator may need to handle the parties with some skill and firmness if a party tries to misuse the process, for example to obtain an unjustified offer in a weak case. Mediation may simply not work if the parties are deeply antagonistic. One can reach a point where each side complains that the other is "not engaging". Sometimes this is true and it becomes clear that one or possibly both parties have come to the mediation with the view that they are willing to negotiate provided that the other side will agree to everything they seek. Trying to get it through to them that a successful settlement may involve some pain on both sides is sometimes very difficult. The process may be more difficult where one or both parties are not represented or not fully advised in advance. Some mediators say that the presence of lawyers can prevent settlement, because the lawyers are programmed to litigate not to compromise. The situation is even worse when the parties are lawyers arguing about their own costs. There are no winners or losers in mediation and it can be difficult to get this altered mind-set across to the parties and their lawyers. 5–65

Q30. Can you please advise on the available options where the parties to an on-going case have essentially agreed on every issue other than costs. It is at an early stage (just post CCMC). Both sides are saying that the other should pay their costs. Both parties are alleging that the other's conduct has been in breach of the pre-action protocol. Because of the circumstances it is uncertain which party (if any) will be deemed to have "won" the case. What are the options available to the parties? It doesn't seem correct that the main case should proceed as everything other than costs is essentially agreed. I see from the practice note that costs only proceedings are not available where it is not decided as to who is paying who's costs. So, for example, could the parties make an application to end the current proceedings and just deal with costs, or go straight to assessment?

Where proceedings are already in existence, costs only proceedings are not available. Where the parties have agreed the substantive issues between them, there appears to be no reason why an application should not be made to the Court to decide the one remaining issue namely which party should be liable for the costs. It is not possible to go straight to assessment since there is no authority to assess i.e. there is no judgment or order under which the costs can be assessed. The question asks what the options available to the parties are and these, of course, include mediation and expert evaluation. The prospects for a successful mediation seem good given that the parties have managed to agree all the other issues. 5–66

Q31. I have a matter in which my client has successfully sued for professional negligence. The opponent made a Part 36 offer which was accepted and the damages settled. The issue remaining is our costs. The Part 36

offer included an offer to pay reasonable expenses. Having assessed our costs schedule the opponent has made a Part 36 offer significantly less than our costs. How does one challenge the offer made by the opponent for costs? This is a matter in which we do not want this to go to court for a detailed assessment but would certainly want a better offer than is currently being made.

5–67 It is not possible to *"challenge the offer made by the opponent"* since it is entirely up to the opponent what offer they are prepared to make. The options include a counter offer and one would normally allow the matter to proceed to detailed assessment where the Costs Judge would deal with the costs of the assessment as well as the assessment itself. Given that the questioner does not wish to go for a detailed assessment, expert evaluation and/or mediation are the obvious answers.

Q32. Are you aware of any cases where a refusal to mediate a small claims track claim has resulted in the court making an adverse costs award against the refusing party? It is settled that refusal to accept an offer which is not beaten at trial is not "unreasonable behaviour" for the purposes of CPR Part 27 and will not lead to adverse costs consequences, but it is unclear what effect, if any, refusal to mediate might have on the usual "no costs" rule.

5–68 There do not appear to be any reported cases on this point. The reason for this may well be that the Small Claims Track was originally intended to be lawyer free and to have a (virtually) no costs regime. If the parties go to mediation there will inevitably be a charge for the mediator and possibly room hire, even if no lawyers are instructed. The only possible justification seems to be the saving of court time if the matter goes to mediation, but that rather defeats the objective of the small claims track.

Q33. What is the proper approach to assessing costs in an Arbitration?

5–69 The form of words used in Section 61 of the 1996 Act is derived from the Rules of the Supreme Court which were in force between 1986 and 1998. RSC Order 62 r. 3(3) states:

> *"If the Court in the exercise of its discretion sees fit to make any order as to the costs of any proceedings, the Court shall order costs to follow the event, except where it appears to the Court that in the circumstances of the case some other order should be made as to the whole or any part of the costs."*

Section 63(5) of the Act states that the successful party shall be allowed a reasonable amount in respect of all costs reasonably incurred. Again the wording is very similar to RSC Order 62, Rule 12 (in force between 1986 and 1998) which reads:

> *"(i) On the taxation of costs on the standard basis there shall be allowed a reasonable amount in respect of all costs reasonably incurred and any doubt which*

the taxing officer may have as to whether the costs were reasonably incurred or were reasonable in amount shall be resolved in favour of the paying party and in these rules the term 'the standard basis' in relation to the taxation of costs shall be construed accordingly."

It is clear that the Parliamentary Draftsman was ensuring consistency between the Rules and the 1996 Act.

As to the correct approach to deciding whether costs have been reasonably incurred and are reasonable in amount, RSC Order 62 Appendix 2 (in force between 1986 and 1998), paragraph 1 provides:

"Amount of Costs
1-(1) The amount of costs to be allowed shall . . . be in the discretion of the taxing officer.
2. In the exercise of his discretion the taxing officer shall have regard to all the relevant circumstances, and in particular to
(a) the complexity of the item or of the cause or matter in which it arises and the difficulty or novelty of the questions involved;
(b) the skill, specialised knowledge and responsibility required of, and time and labour expended by, the solicitor or counsel;
(c) the number and importance of the documents (however brief) prepared or perused;
(d) the place and circumstances in which the business involved is transacted;
(e) the importance of the cause or matter to the client;
(f) where money or property is involved its amount or value;
(g) any other fees and allowances payable to the solicitor or counsel in respect of other items in the same cause or matter but only where work done in relation to those items has reduced the work which would otherwise have been necessary in relation to the item in question."

Under Appendix 2 to RSC Order 62, the taxing officer is required to have regard to "*all the relevant circumstances*" and in particular to the seven headings set out above. Conduct of the parties should be considered as part of "the relevant circumstances", when assessing the reasonableness of costs. Reasonableness, rather than proportionality, is the proper test to apply in assessing the costs of an arbitration under the 1996 Act.

CHAPTER 6

Qualified One-Way Costs Shifting

Introduction

The introduction of a system of one-way costs shifting (QOCS) in personal injury litigation was the subject of close and detailed scrutiny and debate during Lord Justice Jackson's review. Amongst its primary attractions was that it was seen to provide a possible solution to the problem and costs of the 'indefensible' regime of After the Event Insurance (ATE) in such cases,[1] particularly given that claimants were perceived as being successful in the majority of personal injury claims. 6–01

In clinical negligence claims where the success rate of claimants was lower, the relatively higher costs of ATE premiums in such cases provided a counter-balancing justification for the consideration of one way costs shifting.

Accordingly, the firm recommendation was made that a system of one-way costs shifting should be introduced in all such cases with the specific aim of reducing the costs of personal injury litigation, in particular by removing the need for ATE. One way costs shifting was part of a package, therefore, along with the restrictions in recoverability of ATE introduced by s.46 of LASPO.

Jackson LJ, however, was alive to the need to deter frivolous or fraudulent claims and to encourage acceptance of reasonable offers, aims which would be undermined by wholesale protection to claimants from the risk of adverse costs orders no matter what. Accordingly, the proposed system of one way costs shifting was to be qualified to address these requirements, hence QOCS.

To avoid undue complexity and impracticality, QOCS was to be introduced for all personal injury claims, rather than merely being restricted to low value claims or claims run on Conditional Fee Agreements. In fact, the definition in CPR 44.13(1) makes clear that QOCS applies (at least in part) not merely to a 'pure' personal injury claim, but to any proceedings which include such a claim. When introduced, the only absolute exception was for cases where a claimant had entered into a pre-commencement funding arrangement (considered below).

Jackson LJ's proposal was for a system which provided a "broadly similar degree of protection against adverse costs" to that which applied to publicly funded litigants through what was then s.11 of the Access to Justice Act 1999.[2] 6–02

The proposal involved a broad test, based on the test applicable in such cases, whereby the costs ordered against a claimant in such cases would not exceed:

[1] Final Report, pp.184 and 188.
[2] Now s.26 of LASPO—see Final Report, p.189.

"... the amount, if any, which is a reasonable one for him to pay having regard to all the circumstances including (a) the financial resources of all parties to the proceedings; and (b) their conduct in connection with the dispute to which the proceedings relate."

The proposal would firstly have allowed the courts to address concerns in relation to frivolous and fraudulent claims. Secondly, it would have ensured that QOCS could be limited where the claimant's means were such that it would be unjust not to require the claimant to pay costs. It would also have allowed for the possibility of a 'football pools' type application, whereby a defendant who was not allowed to enforce a costs order might, in limited circumstances, reapply to do so where the claimant finances subsequently and substantially improved.

Whilst Jackson LJ's general proposal for a system of qualified one-way costs shifting was adopted, his proposed test was not and a more rigid approach, which does not include any limitation by reference to the claimant's financial resources, was introduced.

In order to address Jackson LJ's second concern, that of incentivising claimants to make Part 36 offers despite QOCS protection, Jackson LJ proposed the 10 per cent increase in general damages which did come into effect, in relation to cases where there was no pre-commencement funding arrangement,[3] as a result of the Court of Appeal's second bite of the cherry in *Simmons v Castle*.[4]

The new rules

6–03 The new rules are set out in CPR 44 Part II and CPR 44 PD 12.1.

The scope of the new rules

6–04 The rules apply to all proceedings which include a claim for damages for personal injuries or under the Fatal Accidents Act 1976 or claims under the Law Reform (Miscellaneous Provisions) Act 1934 (CPR 44.13(1)) (this includes claims arising out of clinical negligence (see the broad definition of 'claim for personal injuries' in CPR 2.3). Pre action disclosure applications are excluded (CPR 44.13(1)).

QOCS does not apply to proceedings 'ancillary' to personal injury claims—that is to say claims such as Civil Liability (Contribution) Act 1978 claims by a defendant to a personal injury action against a third party alleging that that third party was responsible for the claimant's injuries, even where such claims are brought as Part 20 claims within the claimant's personal injury action. 'Proceedings', in CPR 44.13, is intended to refer to the claimant's claim for damages for personal injury.[5]

There is no exception for appeals (arising from claims within the scope of CPR 44.13) and therefore QOCS applies to such appeals.

[3] As defined in CPR 48.2.
[4] *Simmons v Castle* [2012] EWCA Civ 1288; [2013] 1 WLR 1239.
[5] *Wagenaar v Weekend Travel Ltd* [2014] EWCA Civ 1105, at 34–46.

Importantly, there is no restriction on the application of QOCS by reference to the date on which proceedings were brought. Although the new rules only came into effect on 1 April, 2013, they apply to all claims involving a claim for damages for personal injury (subject to one exception below) whether or not proceedings were issued prior to 1 April, 2013.

This has the somewhat unexpected, but possibly intended, effect that not only did defendants who were involved in litigated personal injury claims which had been issued prior to 1 April, 2013 find that the risks the claimant faced in the claim had shifted mid litigation[6], but that even in claims which had concluded prior to 1 April, 2013 and where the defendant had obtained a costs order in its favour, its ability to enforce that costs order was now restricted by virtue of QOCS.

This effect was tolerably clear from the face of the rules, but has been affirmed by the Court of Appeal's decision in *Wagenaar*, where Vos LJ considered that the rules were clearly intended to operate 'retrospectively' in this way.[7]

There is a single operative transitional provision—CPR 44.17—which provides that QOCS does not apply where the claimant has entered into a pre-commencement funding arrangement as defined in CPR 48.2. 6–05

That definition broadly covers Conditional Fee Agreements (but not any other kind of retainer) or ATE policies entered into before 1 April, 2013 in relation to the matter that is the subject of the proceedings in which the cost order is made.[8]

Accordingly, where a claimant has entered into either a CFA or has taken out ATE in respect of the claim before 1 April, 2013, QOCS is not available at all. There may be cases where the claimant has taken out one, but not the other (for example has entered into a CFA pre-April 2013 but did not take out ATE, perhaps because none could be found before the deadline). In such cases, it may seem harsh that the claimant is denied QOCS protection when QOCS was intended, primarily, to be a quid pro quo for not taking out ATE and the claimant has not taken ATE. However, such apparent injustices in individual cases are arguably an inevitable consequence of broad based procedural reform.

There may be scope for arguments as to what the position would be if the 6–06
claimant had entered into a pre-April 2013 CFA, for example, but chose to 'abandon' that arrangement pre-issue (whether because of a change of solicitors

[6] Although from the Claimant's perspective this may often have been theoretical since many such Claimants in pre April 2013 issued cases will have been insulated against adverse costs orders by virtue of After the Event Insurance.

[7] *Wagenaar v Weekend Travel Ltd* [2014] EWCA Civ 1105, at 29–30.

[8] There are technical complexities to the definitions which are addressed in the section on funding arrangements. Note that the taking out of a post 31 March, 2013 ATE policy does not affect the availability of QOCS, even where part of that ATE premium may remain recoverable in principle between the parties in a clinical negligence claim pursuant to the Recovery of Costs Insurance Premiums in Clinical Negligence Proceedings Regulations 2013. Note also that by virtue of the definitions in CPR 48.2, where the case is in one of the categories where there is a LASPO 'exemption', allowing for continued between the parties recoverability of success fees and ATE premium, then QOCS will not apply. The only such category which involves claims which will also satisfy the definition of being 'personal Injury claims' is a mesothelioma claim. Accordingly a mesothelioma claimant who funds their case by way of CFA (with a success fee) or ATE policy (even if taken out after April 2013) will not have the benefit of QOCS.

or otherwise) and to enter into a new funding arrangement. CPR 44.17 provides that QOCS is unavailable 'where the claimant has entered into' such an arrangement and would, therefore, appear to exclude the ability to gain QOCS protection by later abandoning that arrangement. The factual question upon which the availability of QOCS is predicated appears to be simply whether or not such an arrangement has ever been entered into in connection with the case, and not whether or not that is the operative arrangement at the time any application of QOCS is being considered.

This approach seems to have been adopted by Master Haworth in the SCCO in the case of *Landau v The Big Bus Company*[9] where, in a situation where the claimant (acting in person by this point) had entered into a pre-commencement funding arrangement in relation to matters at first instance, but not in relation to an appeal from the first instance judgment, the court held that QOCS was not available in respect of the costs of the appeal, firstly because the appeal related to the same 'matter' which was the subject of the proceedings (and therefore the first instance CFA was a pre-commencement funding arrangement per CPR 48.2(1)(i)(aa)) and secondly that, in any event, the appeal was part of the same 'proceedings' for the purposes of CPR 44.17. The latter issue is a point that seems arguable, not least in light of the Court of Appeal's decision in *Hawksford Trustees*[10] where the Court of Appeal treated an appeal as separate proceedings in relation to a different funding issue, namely the recoverability of ATE premiums—an argument considered, but dismissed, by the Master.

However, in *Casseldine*[11], Regional Costs Judge Phillips took a more purposive approach. In that case, the Claimant had entered into a pre-April 2013 CFA with success fee and had taken out an ATE policy. However, those solicitors had terminated the CFA pre-issue. The Claimant found new solicitors who took the case on a post-April 2013 CFA. The claim was dismissed at trial. In considering whether QOCS applied, the judge took into account that because it was the Claimant's solicitor that had ended the agreement (and, under the terms of that agreement, the solicitor had no right to payment of base costs or success fee), there were no circumstances whereby the Claimant could, in the issued claim, have sought to recover any additional liability under the pre-April 2013 arrangements from the Defendant. Accordingly, applying the rules purposively, it would be unfair to deny the Claimant QOCS protection.

Whether that analysis is correct is likely to require a decision of a higher court. In any event, the *Casseldine* type situation is likely to be a relatively rare one and whether a similar reasoning would apply in circumstances where a claimant and her solicitor simply abandoned existing arrangements before then entering into new, post LASPO, arrangements between the same parties in order to obtain QOCS protection (particularly if this was done at a time

[9] *Landau v The Big Bus Company* Unreported 31 October, 2014.
[10] *Hawksford Trustees Jersey Ltd v Stella Global UK Ltd* [2013] EWCA Civ 987; [2012] 1 WLR 3581.
[11] *Casseldine v Diocese of Llandaff Board for Social Responsibility* (Cardiff County Court, unreported, 3 July 2015).

when the Claimant or the solicitor had just appreciated that the case was likely to be lost) appears very much open to argument.

The effect of the new rules

QOCS does not prevent the making of a costs order against a personal injury claimant. Any question of whether to make such an order falls to be decided on 'usual' principles by reference to CPR 44.2. 6–07

By the same token, it is a mistake for claimants to regard QOCS as a guarantee of an award of costs in their favour in a successful case. The court's discretion under CPR 44.2 remains entirely untrammelled and unaffected by QOCS and regardless of the impact of QOCS, a claimant may still find their costs being disallowed or reduced in a case where they have won if their conduct or other circumstances warrant it.

The effect of QOCS is limited to the defendant's ability to enforce any costs order that has been made.

In practice, however, it can be anticipated that the presence of QOCS, as with the presence of adverse costs protection for publicly funded litigants, will, in certain circumstances, have an effect on the frequency with which defendants seek adverse costs orders where the option might be open to them to do so. This is particularly so given the absence of a 'football pools' or 'lottery win' provision allowing the defendant to return to seek enforcement of an order is an otherwise impecunious claimant's resources drastically improve. As noted, financial resources (present or future) are (probably) immaterial to any question of the application of QOCS.

Because the QOCS rules operate on enforcement of orders, where a claim comes within the scope of CPR 44 Part II any issue of the enforcement of any costs order (including interim orders) against a claimant is deferred until after the conclusion of the proceedings, including after any agreement or assessment of costs (CPR 44.14(2)). Note, this does not mean that the assessment or agreement itself is deferred, merely the enforcement. Quite the opposite. These still take place at the usual time and must be concluded before any issue of enforcement, and therefore whether QOCS prevents enforcement, falls to be considered. However, again in practice it is to be anticipated that in many cases parties will wish to deal with any question of whether QOCS applies and, if so, to what extent, before spending time and money on the assessment of costs that might never be payable.

Where there are interim awards of costs, which may well take place at a time when the application of QOCS is yet to be decided, a Defendant would be well advised in most cases to pursue an order for interlocutory costs and the summary assessment of any such costs as If QOCS did not apply. To assume QOCS does not apply, and to allow the opportunity to obtain such an order would be to risk losing an entitlement to costs which might be of benefit either (i) to set off against any damages or interest awarded to the Claimant if the claim succeeds, even if QOCS applies and/or (ii) to seek against the Claimant in the event QOCS is disapplied for some reason.

The wording of CPR 44.14(2) also supports the argument that the assessment of costs is not to be regarded as 'proceedings' within the meaning of that word for the purposes of QOCS.

6–08 The basic operation of the rules, where QOCS applies, may be summarised as follows:

(i) Any adverse costs order may be enforced in full to the extent that it does not exceed the damages and interest awarded to the claimant (CPR 44.14(1)).

(ii) Where the claimant's claim has been struck out on the basis that it: (i) discloses no reasonable grounds; or (ii) was an abuse of process; or (iii) the conduct of the claimant or someone acting on his behalf (and with the claimant's knowledge of their conduct) was likely to obstruct the just disposal of the proceedings, then the costs order may be enforced in full (CPR 44.15(1)). In such a situation, of course, the claimant will not have been awarded any damages, so this provision simply allows full enforcement of any costs orders made in the defendant's favour in the proceedings, as if QOCS did not exist.

(iii) Where the claimant's claim is found, on the balance of probabilities, to have been 'fundamentally dishonest', then the order for costs may be enforced to its full extent with the permission of the court (CPR 44.16(1)). This, of course, covers a number of possibilities. The claim may have failed, but not been struck out per CPR 44.15, in which case the defendant will need permission to enforce the costs order at all. The claim may have succeeded and some damages may have been awarded, but the claim may still be found to have been fundamentally dishonest, in which case the defendant can enforce without permission to the extent of the damages and interest awarded, but requires permission to enforce any further. This latter position is considerably less likely following the introduction of s.57 of the Criminal Justice & Courts Act 2015, with effect from the 13 April 2015 (and only applying to claims issued on or after that date). This requires the court to dismiss any claim in its entirety where the Claimant has been fundamentally dishonest In relation to it or a related claim, even though the primary claim has succeeded in whole or part. The only qualification Is that the court has a discretion not to do so if it considers that to do so would cause substantial Injustice.

Accordingly, in respect of post April 2015 claims, where the claimant has been fundamentally dishonest, the claim as a whole is likely to be dismissed and the Claimant is likely to be denied QOCS protection in whole or part. There may still be a benefit to Defendants in seeking to strike out such claims as being abusive or on the basis that the Claimant's conduct is obstructing just disposal, since this will give rise to an automatic disapplication of QOCS in its entirety, removing any question of judicial discretion.

(iv) Where the claim is brought in whole or part for the benefit of a person other than the claimant or a dependant in a Fatal Accidents Act case, or where the claim is only in part a personal injury claim, the defendant may enforce the order up to the full extent with the permission of the court (CPR 44.16). Again, in such cases, the defendant will be entitled to enforce in part without permission if damages have been awarded, but needs permission to go beyond the level of damages and interest (if any).

Each of these provisions warrants a little further examination. In relation to the basic operation of QOCS by restriction on enforcement (CPR 44.14), perhaps the single most interesting question is what is meant by 'enforcement'. The defendant's right to 'enforce' a costs order in its favour is restricted.

It is restricted to the limit of damages and interest awarded to the claimant. There is no mention of the claimant's costs.

However, the very section of the CPR which precedes QOCS deals with the ability of a party to 'set off' one costs order against another. Is a set off enforcement? If it is not, then it would appear that the QOCS rules do not prevent a defendant setting off its costs against any costs awarded to the claimant, in addition to enforcing the costs order to the extent of damages awarded (subject, of course, to the total limit of the costs awarded to the defendant).

If, however, a set off of costs against costs does amount to enforcement, then the defendant's rights are limited to those under CPR 44.14.

The issue is undecided, at least in the specific context of QOCS. In *Vava*,[12] 6–09
Andrew Smith J declined to allow a set off of one costs order against another in circumstances where parties had entered into a QOCS like arrangement (but where QOCS did not in fact apply). He did so on the grounds that it would be 'unfair' in the circumstances to do so.

Existing authority in the not dissimilar area of costs protection for publicly funded litigants indicates that an order for set off of costs is not to be regarded as enforcement of the order because it does not place the claimant under any obligation to pay, but merely reduces the amount that they can recover.[13] This would appear to support an argument that a defendant can firstly seek to set off costs awarded to it against those awarded to a claimant and, if thereafter, there remains a net liability to the defendant, seek to set this against damages and interest under CPR 44.14, rather than being limited to the CPR 44.14 set off. The issue will no doubt be the subject of specific argument and authority in due course in the QOCS context.

CPR 44.15 requires relatively little further discussion. The categories of strike out referred to therein mirror those in CPR 3.4(2)(a) and (b) and issues as to when such a strike out is appropriate are beyond the scope of this section. The only real gloss to note is that where the strike out is on the basis

[12] *Vava v Anglo American South Africa Ltd* [2013] EWHC 2326 (QB); [2013] 5 Costs LR 805.
[13] *R (Burkett) v London Borough of Hammersmith & Fulham* [2004] EWCA Civ 1342, at 50.

that the conduct of the proceedings was such as to be likely to obstruct the just disposal of the proceedings, in order to disapply QOCS it is necessary, in addition, that the court concludes that such conduct was that of the claimant himself or that he knew of the relevant conduct on the part of the person so acting on his behalf. A defendant seeking a strike out on this basis in a personal injury claim should take care to ensure that this additional aspect is specifically addressed in any judgment given on the strike out (and ideally recited in the order).

However, the case of *Brahilika*[14] illustrates that the court may be prepared to apply a relatively wide interpretation of the conduct likely to obstruct the just disposal of proceedings. In that case, the relevant conduct was the failure of the Claimant to attend trial, due to being on holiday (It not being known whether the holiday was booked before or after the trial date was fixed).

6–10 CPR 44.16 and the introduction of a test of 'fundamental dishonesty' had given rise to much debate, which has been added to by the introduction of s.57 of the Criminal Justice and Courts Act 2015.

What does 'fundamentally dishonest' mean? It is relatively early days, but some guidance is available. 'Dishonesty' is a concept the courts are extremely familiar with and there is clear judicial guidance as to the issues a court must consider in deciding in a personal injury context whether a claimant has been dishonest.[15] More contentious is the 'fundamentally' aspect, which has troubled parliamentarians in recent debates in relation to the use of the term in s.57 of the new Act.

6–11 There have been a number of first instance cases where the issue has arisen. One of the most thoroughly argued earlier cases was that of *Gosling*,[16] which was a classic case of a successful, but dishonestly exaggerated, claim, though with an added complication that the claimant succeeded only against one defendant and discontinued against a second. In that case, the judge held that a claim was not fundamentally dishonest merely because he had been dishonest in respect of some collateral matter or some minor, self contained head of damage, but that where the dishonesty went to the root of a substantial part of the claim the test was made out.

The case appears to confirm, though only at first instance level, a number of propositions. Firstly, that CPR 44.16(1) may apply where the dishonesty does not infect the entire claim, but goes only to a substantial part of it—the classic exaggerated claim case. Secondly, where the test in CPR 44.16(1) is made out, the court is not bound to allow the defendant to enforce the costs order to its full extent, but is then given a discretion to decide to what extent to allow such enforcement.

Both propositions appear logical interpretations of the rule, though there will no doubt be further argument on these and related topics.

---

[14] Unreported, Romford County Court, 30 July 2015.

[15] See, for example, *Brighton & Hove Bus v Brooks* [2011] EWHC 2504.

[16] *Gosling v Hailo & Screwfix Direct* Unreported 29 April, 2014 CC (Cambridge).

The first proposition—that a claim may be seen as being fundamentally dishonest as a whole even where the dishonestly only relates to part of the claim—is, of course, supported by the approach taken in s.57 of the 2015 Act, requiring the dismissal of the entire claim even where there are elements of that claim in respect of which the Claimant has not been dishonest (see s.57(3)). It is also consistent with the Court of Appeal's approach to the issue of fraud in personal injury claims, as seen in *Hayward v Zurich Insurance Company PLC*[17] where, despite the fortuitous outcome for the appellant, it is clear from the judgments that the court regarded the whole claim as being fraudulent, despite the fact that there was no doubt that the appellant had been injured and his dishonesty related to the claim that the injury was continuing and had not resolved.

CPR 44 PD 12 contains clear guidance in relation to arguments under CPR 44.16(1) and in particular that where parties settle proceedings the court will not, 'save in exceptional circumstances' order that issues relating to fundamental dishonesty be tried (12.4(b)) and that such issues will normally be determined at trial (12.4(a)). The logic is obvious and needs little explanation, but the point should not be overlooked by defendants. Settlement of a claim will usually be an effective bar to taking this point.

A claimant cannot, however, escape such scrutiny (at least in relation to fundamental dishonesty) by discontinuing the claim (CPR 44 PD 12.4(c)).

CPR 44.16(2) has attracted less debate. However, its impact should not be overlooked.

CPR 44.16 applies in two types of claims. The one which has received less **6–12**
attention is the second (CPR 44.16(2)(b)), namely where a claim is made "for the benefit of the claimant other than a claim to which this Section applies". This is intended to cover claims where the beneficiary of the claim is the claimant, but the claimant's claim is only partially a personal injury claim (the classic example being a housing disrepair claim where there may be a claim for personal injuries as part of a wider claim).

By virtue of CPR 44.16(2) the mere fact that procedurally, the claim as a whole is deemed a personal injury claim, because it includes a claim for damages for personal injury, does not prevent the court disapplying QOCS, to the extent just. Commonly, this is likely to be used so that the court can allow full enforcement of adverse costs orders in relation to that part of the claim which was not a personal injury claim, and is likely to be used in cases where the personal injury claim is viewed as being the more modest or less complex part of the claim. An example might be a professional negligence claim which included an ancillary claim for damages for personal injury.

More contentious is CPR 44.16(2)(a), which allows the court to disapply QOCS where the claim in whole or party is for the financial benefit of a third party.

[17] [2015] EWCA Civ 327.

The Rule itself gives only limited guidance as to the circumstances where it will apply. The Practice Direction is more specific and provides examples of where the claim is "made for the financial benefit of a person other than the claimant", including credit hire claims and subrogated claims (PD 12.2).

6–13 Whilst this seems to be the clear intention of the rulemakers, there is likely to be argument in the future as to whether or not claims, such as credit hire or subrogated claims are properly claims brought for the financial benefit of another party, a wording which appears to cut across the traditional and well established legal status of claims by such parties where the involvement of the third party is seen as being *res inter alios acta* (that is to say something which is considered not to be the court's business when considering the claim between the parties), particularly in the context of costs, save in particular and unusual circumstances.[18]

The fact that the 'examples' are given in the Practice Direction rather than forming part of the rule might be said to provide greater scope for such arguments.

The clear intention of CPR 44.16(2) is that where QOCS is disapplied in this situation, it is not the claimant that should suffer. CPR 44.16(3) contains a clear point to the making of a costs order directly against the third party in such a circumstance, subject to consideration of the usual rules for such orders under CPR 46.2. Whilst such a third party costs order would not remove the order against the claimant, it is to be anticipated that in such cases the court's likely approach would be to decline to allow enforcement (beyond damages and interest) against the claimant, but to make a third party costs order for the relevant sum or percentage or issues against the third party for whose benefit that part of the claim was brought, and CPR 44 PD 12.5 clearly points in this direction, indicating that it will be 'exceptional' that (further) enforcement will be allowed against the claimant.

Whether the working of CPR 44.16(3) (and CPR 44 PD 12.5) is intended to and does in any way relax the established common law as to the circumstances in which a third party costs order is available is a moot point and will no doubt be argued in due course.

A wider use of QOCS

6–14 The Ministry of Justice published detailed proposals for the extension of a version of QOCS to defamation and privacy claims, such proposals being put out to consultation which closed in November 2013. Although the original intention was for QOCS to be introduced in this area with effect from April 2014, no implementation date has yet been given and it is not clear if, when or if so in what final form QOCS will be introduced in this area.

Given the uncertainty, the proposals are not considered in any detail here, save to note that the proposals were for a rather different model of QOCS, whereby QOCS would be available to both claimants and defendants

[18] See the classic case of *TGA Chapman v Christopher* [1998] 1 WLR 12 in the context of subrogated claims.

and organisations and parties with significant financial resources would be excluded from the scheme, with full costs protection only being available to those who would suffer 'severe financial hardship' if forced to pay adverse costs. Whether that model remains and is implemented in due course remains to be seen.

The Civil Justice Council's Working Group on the impact of the Jackson reforms is also considering arguments for and against the extension of QOCS to other categories of cases which are said to be characterised by an asymmetric relationship between the parties, such as actions against the policy and professional negligence claims against solicitors arising out of personal injury claims. Nuisance claims are also under consideration. What the final recommendations will be and whether they will be taken forward by the Government will have to be awaited.

There have been calls for the wider extension of QOCS, most notably from Ramsey J,[19] including to actions against the police, but there are no firm proposals in this regard and the delays and difficulties with the privacy and publication extension suggest that it will be some considerable time before any such extension might materialise. It is reasonably to be anticipated that if and when the LASPO exemptions for privacy and publication claims and mesothelioma claims are removed that QOCS will be extended to those areas. In the mesothelioma case, this can reasonably be anticipated to be a simple extension of the existing QOCS provisions (subject to the Government taking the operation to revise those provisions at the same time). In respect of privacy and publication claims, there is far greater scope for a different scheme to be introduced, not least in light of the complex and competing political pressures surrounding reform in that area.

Questions and answers

Q1. How will QOCS apply where a claim comprises both a personal injury and a non-personal injury element?

This will have to be the subject of judicial guidance in due course. The rule 6–15
expressly allows the court to disapply QOCS to the extent that it considers just where this situation arises (CPR 44.16) and the Practice Direction envisages that where this arises the court will normally order the claimant to pay costs notwithstanding that they exceed the level of damages and interest awarded (i.e. will allow enforcement beyond the limit in CPR 44.14, which is what CPR 44.16 expressly envisages). There is, however a degree of tension and some lack of clarity in the rules as to precisely how this will operate.

In practice, it is likely that the court will seek to identify the true nature of the claim. Where the personal injury claim was dominant and the 'additional claim' a modest ancillary part which is unlikely to have significantly increased the costs then the court may decide not to allow any enforcement beyond

[19] In his speech to the Compass Law Commercial Litigation Conference: *http://www.litigationfutures.com/news/extension-qocs-key-true-jackson-says-ramsey* [Accessed 29 January, 2015].

CPR 44.14. Where the 'additional claim' was dominant, and the court may be reasonably satisfied that the Defendant would have had to incur broadly the same level of costs to meet that claim alone, then the court may allow full enforcement. Perhaps more commonly, the court may seek to identify, by percentage, date or in some other way, the 'additional claim' and allow enforcement in that regard accordingly.

Given that the claimant in this scenario will already probably have suffered some costs deduction against damages (CPR 44.14) and given that the quantum of costs may have been assessed (CPR 44.13(3)) the court may simply make an order that enforcement of a certain sum above the level of damages is just. The Court of Appeal is unlikely to be keen to interfere with a broad exercise of discretion here unless the outcome is manifestly unjust.

Q2. Will QOCS be extended to other areas in due course?

6–16 This seems highly likely. If the mesothelioma exemption from the ending of between the parties recoverability of additional liabilities is ended, then QOCS for such cases is likely to be introduced at the same time, on the current lines. The extension of QOCS to publication and privacy claims was anticipated. However, the process is slow and it seems highly likely that in that area at least any model of QOCS introduced will differ significantly from the model in CPR 44 Part III. Other areas, in particular claims against the police, may benefit from a QOCS extension and in those cases at least it is likely that the QOCS regime will follow the current model.

Q3. Do parties still have to costs budget where QOCS applies and, if so, is the agreeing of budgets in such cases likely to be more difficult?

6–17 In answer to the first part of the question, the answer is a simple 'yes', assuming the case is within CPR 3.12. QOCS relates to enforcement only. Until a case is concluded, a defendant will not know whether or not the case is one where there might be good grounds to seek a disapplication of QOCS. In any event, the defendant may be in a position to enforce a costs order against damages without needing to seek to disapply QOCS. There are a wide range of situations where the defendant may be entitled to, and able to enforce, some or all of its costs. In any and all of these situations, the defendant will need to be able to quantify its costs and, if it has failed to file a costs budget, is likely to find those costs (at least post the date on which a budget should have been supplied) limited to court fees only pursuant to CPR 3.18 or to suffer some other form of costs penalty or reduction.

As to agreeing budgets in such cases, there is no reason in principle why the budget should be more or less difficult to agree. QOCS also applies, for example, in publicly funded claims, where a not dissimilar form of costs protection exists. In both types of case, the budgeting rules apply without amendment. In practice, there will be concerns in such cases that defendants will be inclined to underestimate their own costs (because they are unlikely to be recovering them in many cases, or recovering them in full even in cases where some success is achieved), with a view to painting the claimant's budgeted costs as disproportionate by comparison. Also, that in such cases the perceived greater likelihood that the claimant will be recovering costs at the end of the case may make the defendant more inclined to take every opportunity to limit those costs, and therefore to take a more aggressive approach at the budgeting stage.

Anecdotally, it appears to be the case that the most regularly contested CCMCs relate to personal injury claims, including clinical negligence and there appears to be a greater willingness to agree budgets between the parties in commercial claims. Whether this has anything particularly to do with QOCS or is merely a reflection of the fact that personal injury has long been the hotbed of satellite costs litigation is a moot point.

Q4. Is QOCS excluded where the claimant has Before The Event Insurance?

No. Provided the claim is within CPR 44.14, and provided that the claimant **6–18** has not entered into a CFA or ATE prior to 1 April 1 2013 in relation to the claim, then the method of funding is irrelevant. QOCS is available.

This applies even where the claim was commenced prior to 1 April, 2013—and even where the costs order was made prior to 1 April, 2013 but has not yet been enforce. It is the presence of a funding model which contains provision for recoverable additional liabilities which leads to the loss of availability of QOCS. Whether the Claimant is otherwise indemnified for the costs liability is irrelevant.

Q5. Does QOCS apply to costs incurred prior to 1 April, 2013?

Yes. Provided the claim is within CPR 44.13 and provided the claimant has **6–19** not entered into a pre-commencement funding arrangement (CPR 48.2), then QOCS applies and the defendant's ability to enforce a costs order is restricted accordingly. Although there is scope for argument beyond that raised in *Wagenaar*, the Court of Appeal's decision in that case disposed of the primary argument that COCS could not operate retrospectively in this way.

Q6. Is QOCS excluded where the claimant has entered into a pre-commencement funding arrangement, even if the claimant then is advised not to pursue the claim by the initially instructed solicitor but later does so under a post April 2013 funding arrangement with a different firm?

In the previous edition of this supplement, it was stated that these issues **6–20** needed to be resolved, but that the wording of CPR 48.2 and CPR 44.17 suggested that the answer to this is 'yes'. In *Casseldine* (supra), the regional costs judge concluded to the contrary on the facts of the case before him.

Authoritative resolution of this point will only be possible at a high appellate level. As was acknowledged in *Casseldine*, the strict wording of the provisions points to the conclusion that the fact that there has been a pre-commencement funding arrangement in respect of that claim, even if as a matter of fact that arrangement no longer operates and as a matter of fact there will not and could not have been any claim for additional liabilities if the claim succeeded, will mean that QOCS is not available.

This undoubtedly seems harsh. Whether the correct answer is that this is simply an unfortunate consequence of the introduction of a broad brush provision where there will be individual harsh decisions which are necessary as part of a wider desire to ensure consistency, simplicity and to avoid satellite litigation (as with the Court of Appeal's reasoning In *Wagenaar*) or whether the correct approach is the more purposive one remains a matter of argument in respect of which there is no binding authority.

Q7. The claimant has incurred costs unnecessarily in an unmeritous claim. They have now served a notice of discontinuance and, as QOCS applies, they are not liable for the defendant's costs (unless an exception applies). In the above circumstances, is it possible for the defendant to apply for a wasted costs order even though a notice of discontinuance has been filed by the claimant?

6–21 This question covers a number of issues.

Firstly, the assumption that the claimant is not liable, in principle, for the defendant's costs is wrong. CPR 38.6 is not disapplied merely because QOCS applies. As discussed above, the defendant is entitled in principle to the same costs order whether QOCS applies or not. QOCS only addresses the enforcement of that order. Of course, as with publicly funded claims, it may be the case that the difficulties with enforcement mean that, save where the costs order is automatic (which, of course, it is under CPR 38.6(1) unless the court orders otherwise), there will be cases where the defendant chooses not to spend money arguing for a costs order which serves little practical benefit. However, in the example given, the defendant will by default have a costs order in its favour.

As to exceptions, CPR 44 PD 12.4(c) must not be overlooked. A claimant cannot (automatically) escape the risk of a finding of fundamental dishonesty by discontinuing the claim.

An interesting issue arises where the claim is one which was arguably abusive or in relation to which it could be argued that there were no reasonable grounds for bringing the claim, but the claimant has beaten the defendant to the point by discontinuing the claim before an application could be heard to have the proceedings struck out. CPR 44 PD 12.4(c) does not address this. Under CPR 38.4 it would be possible to apply to have the notice of discontinuance set aside in order for the court to hear an application to strike out which, if successful, would allow for full enforcement of the costs order without permission. It is likely that the court will only permit this in exceptional circumstances—perhaps where a claimant has been repeatedly warned as to the abusive nature of the claim, but has persisted, but then responds to a formal application to strike out by discontinuing. However, it remains to be seen in practice how the court approaches such issues.

Accordingly, the defendant is not left entirely without remedy in this situation (though in practice, whether even an enforceable costs order is of any value against an impecunious claimant is a question which must be considered).

This approach, which was noted in the previous edition, appears similar to that following in *Kite*[20]. In that case, the judge concluded that in the rather unusual circumstances of that case—where a Claimant had obtained judgment in default, which was set aside and the Defendant applied for a strike out on the basis that there were no reasonable ground for bringing the claim—an attempt by the Claimant to avoid the strike out and therefore the risk of an automatic loss of QOCS, by discontinuing his claim, was prevented by the court readily setting aside the notice of discontinuance so that it could deal with the strike out application. Although only a first instance decision, the outcome appears logical and the ability of the court to set aside such a notice whether under CPR 38.4, which expressly provides for this, or under CPR Part 3 (relied on by the judge in *Kite*) is clear. Discontinuance is unlikely to be an effective remedy to prevent the loss of QOCS where the court considers that it is simply a tactical ploy to avoid an otherwise likely application of CPR 44.15 or 44.16.[21]

As to the possibility of seeking a wasted costs order, the ability to make such an application is not ousted by the fact of the discontinuance. However, as is the case with publicly funded claimants (see the guidance in *Symphony Group PLC v Hodgson*[22]) the court will be very astute to guard against the risk that the wasted costs application is motivated by an inability to recover costs against the claimant, rather than being a properly founded application for wasted costs against a solicitor. Wasted costs orders will not be made against a solicitor merely because they acted for a claimant in respect of a claim which is doomed to fail. The courts will assume, unless it can be established to the contrary, that the solicitor will have properly advised the client and will have been acting on instructions.

Q8. I need to discontinue proceedings against a number of defendants in an action. Obviously, when I file a notice of discontinuance, there will be a deemed order for costs against the claimant unless the court orders otherwise (CPR 38.6(1)). However, my understandings of QOCS (from CPR 44.14, 44.15 and 44.16) is that an order for costs may only be enforced if the claim has been struck out (no court permission needed) or if it is fundamentally dishonest (court permission needed). We do not have sufficient time to obtain written consent from each and every defendant in

[20] *Kite v Phoenix Pub Group* (unreported).

[21] The case of *Akhtar & Khan v Ball* (unreported, HHJ Gregory, 10 July 2015) raises further interesting issues. In that case, not only was QOCS disapplied, but the Defendant mounted a counterclaim, which was successful to the sum of £3,000 in exemplary damages, relying on *Kuddus v Chief Constable of Leicestershire* [2001] UKHL 29, where the Claimant's claims were held to have been entirely fraudulent (and therefore fundamentally dishonest). Although unusual, this does suggest that a dishonest Claimant may not merely be exposed to the loss of QOCS and now the dismissal of the claim, but also a risk of paying damages—and of course any risk of contempt or criminal proceedings.

[22] *Symphony Group PLC v Hodgson* [1993] 3 WLR 830, 842.

a consent order but in any event consider that we would be QOCS protected even by serving a Notice of Discontinuance.

6–22 This is largely answered in the previous answer. A costs order will be deemed to be made against the claimant unless the court orders otherwise, pursuant to CPR 38.6. Assuming the claim is within CPR 44.13 and no other exception applies, then QOCS protection will be available. However, if the claim is one which might be said to have been brought in a 'fundamentally dishonest' fashion, the defendants will still be able to ask the court to grant permission to enforce some or all of the costs order.

There is also a risk that the defendants might be able to persuade the court to set aside the notice of discontinuance and ask the court instead to strike the claim out, to avail themselves of the exceptions under CPR 44.15. The circumstances in which this will be allowed remain to be seen, but it is likely to require an exceptional case.

Q9. Can a personal injury claimant who had a pre-action CFA (entered into before 1 April 2013) with a 100 per cent success fee, and who wishes to proceed with the claim with the benefits of QOCS protection, terminate the existing CFA, on the basis that the law firm will waive its success fee, and enter into a new post-Jackson CFA? Would the claimant then be able to benefit from QOCS, even though the pre-action base costs are covered under a CFA entered into before 1 April 2013? Alternatively, could the client and or the solicitor agree to end the existing CFA, but enter into a new, post LASPO CFA, with any success fee payable by the client only, but with the CFA expressly covering all work done since first instruction and thereby benefit from QOCS?

6–23 This is a variant of the *Casseldine* type situation discussed above. On a strict interpretation of CPR 44.17, the Claimant 'has' entered into a pre-commencement funding arrangement in respect of the claim and QOCS is not available. However, *Casseldine* is an illustration of the scope for a wider, more purposive, approach to be adopted. In particular, if the abandonment of the success fee and the use of a post LASPO CFA take place before the issue of proceedings and if the abandonment of the success fee (or at least the ability to claim it on a between the parties basis) / the ending of the earlier CFA is done in some irrevocable way, such that the court could conclude that there was no possibility of the defendant being required to pay the success fee (or any ATE premium) then the point would be arguable. However, such cases perhaps serve to illustrate the difficulties with adopting a purposive approach.

Ultimately, until such matters receive higher judicial attention, it is not possible to provide a definitive answer to this question. Given that in any case which reached the stage of a letter before action (at the latest) the Defendant should have been notified of the existence of a CFA with a success fee in the case then there must be a substantial risk that the Defendant will be alive to the point and will seek to challenge the application of QOCS if the claim is defeated.

Q10. Will qualified one way costs shifting apply where a personal injury claimant entered into a CFA pre Jackson reforms but did not enter into an after the event insurance policy until after the introduction of QOCS?
No. Whilst the broad intention behind the introduction of QOCS was to act as a quid pro quo for the loss of between the parties recoverability of ATE premiums, the transitional provision at CPR 44.17 expressly provides that QOCS does not apply to proceedings where the Claimant has entered into a pre commencement funding arrangement. These are defined in CPR 48.2. They include a CFA with a success fee. Accordingly where either or both of a CFA with a success fee or an ATE policy have been entered into prior to the 1 April 2013, QOCS will not be available. 6–24

Q11. Does QOCS apply to just personal injury? We have a commercial litigation matter for breach of contract so nothing to do with personal injury.
Yes, at present QOCS only applies to personal injury—see CPR 44.13(1). The main body of the text identifies some areas where QOCS might be introduced, whether in the same form as at present or in a revised form. It is not presently anticipated that general commercial litigation will be one of these areas. 6–25

Q12. Does QOCS apply to claims for damages for clinical negligence?
Yes—see the definition of a claim for personal injuries at CPR 2.3(1). 6–26

Q13. Where a claimant is currently subject to an 'old style' CFA (pre-April 2013 whereby QOCS would not apply) but the client seeks the protection of QOCS, would the previous presence of the old style CFA prevent the claimant ever obtaining the benefit of QOCS under the workings of CPR 44.17 If the claimant was to continue as a litigant in person would she then obtain the benefit of QOCS?
On the strict wording of the transitional provision, CPR 44.17 provides that the fact of the pre- April 2013 CFA (assuming it had a success fee) would mean that QOCS is not available. However, cases such as *Casseldine* (supra) suggest that a more purposive approach might mean that if the Claimant in some way conclusively abandoned her pre-April 2013 funding arrangements she may benefit from QOCS after all. *Casseldine* is a first instance County Court decision and care should be exercised before placing relying on the reasoning therein. 6–27

CHAPTER 7

Fixed Costs; Indemnity Costs; Litigants in Person

Background

Part 45 of the Civil Procedure Rules deals with fixed costs and is divided into sections. The topics dealt with are as follows: 7–01

- Section I—Fixed Costs in the normally accepted sense, i.e. costs which are payable in a given set of circumstances.
- Section II—Road Traffic Accidents—fixed recoverable costs.
- Section III—Pre-Action Protocol for Low Value Personal Injury Claims in Road Traffic Accidents and Low Value Personal Injury (Employers' Liability and Public Liability) Claims.
- Section IIIA—Claims Which No Longer Continue Under the RTA and EL/PL Pre-Action Protocols—Fixed Recoverable Costs.
- Section IV—Scale Costs for Claims in the IPEC.
- Section V—Fixed Costs: HM Revenue & Customs.
- Section VI—Fast Track Trial Costs.
- Section VII—Costs Limits in Aarhus Convention claims.

Section I of Part 45 sets out the amounts which are to be allowed in respect of solicitors charges in cases to which it applies unless the court otherwise orders.[1] The fixed costs provisions apply where the only claim is a claim for a specified sum of money exceeding £25 and certain circumstances apply.[2]

The provisions of r.45.3 operate to apply the costs fixed by Section I of Part 45 unless the court otherwise orders. The Court refused to exercise its discretion to allow more than the fixed costs, on the particular facts of the case, stating, among other reasons:

> *". . .this Court has recognised the importance of a summary and prompt procedure to secure enforcement of adjudicators' decisions properly reached".*
>
> *"A party which makes a 'without prejudice save as to costs' offer is not entitled in some way to have it responded to or to assume that threatened proceedings against it will or might be withheld. It would be different if the without prejudice correspondence had revealed some agreement by which the claimant undertook, at least temporarily, not to issue proceedings . . . It would not be fair to limit a*

[1] r.45.1(1) and see PD 45, paras 1.1–1.3.

[2] The provisions apply where: (i) judgment in default is obtained under r.12.4(1); (ii) judgment on admission is obtained under r.14.4(3); (iii) judgment on admission on part of the claim is obtained under r.14.5(6); (iv) summary judgment is given under Part 24; (v) the Court has made an order to strike out a defence under r.3.4(2)(a) as disclosing no reasonable grounds for defending the claim; or (vi) r.45.4 applies (defendant only liable for fixed commencement costs).

successful claimant which complied with the steps called for in the rule and the [TCC] Guide".

The claimant was justified in issuing proceedings and the Part 24 application following a threatened defence and an unqualified admission on the part of the defendant after issue.[3] Where the claimant claims fixed commencement costs and judgment is entered (in certain specified circumstances[4]), the amount to be included in the judgment in respect of the claimant solicitor's charges is the aggregate of the fixed commencement costs and the relevant amount set out in the table depending on the particular type of judgment.[5] Section II of Part 45 sets out the costs allowable in proceedings relating to certain road traffic accidents. The provisions apply to road traffic accident disputes,[6] where the accident giving rise to the dispute occurred on or after 6 October, 2003. The fixed costs provisions are intended to meet the case where the parties have been able to agree damages within certain limits but have been unable to agree the amount of costs. The agreed damages include damages in respect of personal injury, damage to property or both. The total value of the agreed damages must not exceed £10,000 or be within the small claims limit.[7] The provisions of this section do not apply where the claimant is a litigant in person, or where Section III or IIIA of Part 45 applies.[8]

Section III: Pre-Action Protocols for Low Value Personal Injury Claims in Road Traffic Accidents and Low Value Personal Injury (Employers' Liability and Public Liability) Claims is in two distinct parts.

The RTA Protocol Scheme

7–02 The provisions of the RTA Protocol apply to a claim for damages exceeding £1,000, but not exceeding £10,000, arising from a road traffic accident occurring on or after 30 April, 2010, and before 31 July, 2013, or a claim for damages not exceeding £25,000 arising from a road traffic accident occurring on or after 31 July, 2013. Claims which fall within the scope of the scheme must follow the process, although a claimant is entitled to settle directly with an insurer/defendant without using the process. The process may be adopted by agreement for claims arising from an accident prior to the implementation date, but the claimant's solicitor will only be allowed the fixed recoverable costs applicable to the new process.

The rules and practice directions are unusual, in that they relate to work done in accordance with the RTA and EL/PL Protocols, rather than (except in relation to Stage 3) to proceedings in court. The case will no longer continue under the Protocol if there is fraud at any stage, and under Stage 1 if there is no admission of liability or there is an allegation of contributory negligence; under

[3] *Amber Construction Services Ltd v London Interspace HG Ltd* [2007] EWHC 3042 (TCC); [2008] B.L.R. 74, Akenhead J.
[4] Under r.45.2.
[5] The circumstances are as set out in r.45.1(2)(a) or (b).
[6] "Road traffic accident", "motor vehicle" and "road" are defined in r.45.9(4).
[7] r.45.9(2), r.26.8(2) sets out how the financial value of a claim is assessed for the purposes of allocation to track.
[8] r.45.9(3).

Stage 2 if damages cannot be agreed. Stage 3 applies where quantum cannot be agreed; application is then made to the court to determine the quantum.

The Pre-action Protocol for Low Value Personal Injury (Employers' Liability and Public Liability) Claims

This protocol deals with low value personal injury employers' liability and public liability claims. An employers' liability claim is a claim by an employee against the employer for damages arising from a bodily injury sustained by the employee in the course of employment, or a disease that the claimant is alleged to have contracted as a consequence of the employer's breach of its duty of care in the course of the employee's employment, other than a physical or psychological injury caused by an accident or other single event. A public liability claim is a claim for damages for personal injuries arising out of a breach of duty of care made against a person other than the claimant's employer, or the claimant's employer in respect of matters arising other than in the course of the claimant's employment, but it does not include a claim for damages arising from a disease that the claimant is alleged to have contracted as a consequence of breach of a duty of care, other than a physical or psychological injury caused by an accident or other single event.[9] The protocol sets out the behaviour which the court expects of the parties prior to the start of proceedings where a claimant claims damages not exceeding £25,000 in an EL or PL claim.[10] The EL/PL Protocol applies where either the claim arises from an accident occurring on or after 31 July, 2013, or in a disease claim no letter of claim has been sent to the defendant before that date. The claim must include damages in respect of personal injury and must not exceed the upper limit of £25,000 on a full liability basis, including pecuniary losses but excluding interest. The claim must not be one in which the small claims track would be the normal track (i.e. the claim must be for more than £1,000). The protocol ceases to apply to a claim where at any stage the claimant notifies the defendant that the claim has now been re-valued at more than the upper limit.[11] The protocol does not apply to a claim: 7–03

(i) where the claimant or defendant acts as personal representative of a deceased person;
(ii) where the claimant or defendant is a protected party[12];
(iii) in a public liability claim—the defendant is an individual;
(iv) where the claimant is bankrupt;
(v) where the defendant is insolvent and there is no identifiable insurer;
(vi) in the case of a disease claim, where there is more than one employer defendant;

[9] EL/PL Protocol 1.1.
[10] EL/PL Protocol 2.1.
[11] EL/PL Protocol 4.1–4.2.
[12] As defined in r.21.1(2).

(vii) for personal injury arising from an accident or alleged breach of duty occurring outside England and Wales;
(viii) for damages in relation to harm, abuse or neglect of or by children or vulnerable adults;
(ix) which includes a claim for clinical negligence;
(x) for mesothelioma; or
(xi) for damages arising out of a road traffic accident.

The fixed costs in r.45.18 apply in relation to a claimant only where a claimant has a legal representative.[13]

7–04 With effect from 31 July, 2013, Section IIIA applies where a claim is started under either the RTA or EL/PL Protocol, but no longer continues under the relevant protocol or the stage 3 procedure. This section does not apply to a disease claim which is started under the EL/PL Protocol.[14]

The fixed recoverable costs scheme under r.45.29A is not intended to be implemented only in relation to fast-track claims but is capable of applying to a low value personal injury claim arising out of a road traffic accident which has been started under the RTA protocol but which has proceeded on the multi-track due to allegations that the accident has been fraudulently induced. Although the nature and ambit of the fraud allegations were different from the type of allegation often made in cases of commercial fraud, the overall nature of the case still answered the description of low value personal injury claim arising out of a road traffic accident, albeit proceeding on the multi-track. The nature of the underlying proceedings were such that the implementation of fixed recoverable costs would not offend against the overriding objective. The provisions of r.45.29J provide a material safeguard against injustice. Applications under that provision were to be made at the end of proceedings which ensured that any decision on costs reflected actual events.[15]

Indeed on a strict interpretation, the fixed costs regime under CPR 45 Section IIIA applies to all claims that start under the RTA or EL/PL Pre-Action Protocols, exit it and a claim is issued which is subsequently allocated to the multi-track and not just to the 'fraud' type case considered above. This appears to be in contrast to a claim that starts under the protocols, exits it and settles pre–issue for more than £25,000, as Table 6B Section A only provides fixed costs where the agreed damages are up to £25,000.

Section IV of Part 45 sets out the scale costs for claims in the IPEC. The provisions do not apply where the court considers that a party has behaved in a manner which amounts to an abuse of the court's process or the claim concerns the infringement or revocation of a patent or registered design, the validity of which has been certified by a court in earlier proceedings.[16]

[13] EL/PL Protocol 4.3, 4.4.
[14] r.45.29A. Nothing in Section IIIA prevents the Court from making an order under r.45.24.
[15] *Qader and Others v. Esure Services Limited* [2015] EWHC B18 (TCC), HHJ David Grant, permission to appeal.
[16] r.45.30(1) and (2).

The court will make a summary assessment of the costs of the party in whose favour any order for costs is made. Rules 44.2(8), 44.6(b) and Pt 47 do not apply to s.IV.[17] The court will reserve the costs of an application to the conclusion of the trial when they will be subject to summary assessment. Where a party has behaved unreasonably the court may make an order for costs at the conclusion of the hearing. Where the court makes a summary assessment of costs it will do so in accordance with Section IV of Part 45.[18]

Section V of Part 45 sets out the amounts which are to be allowed in respect of HMRC charges in specified cases, unless the court orders otherwise.[19] Part 8 applies where the only claim is a claim conducted by an HMRC officer in the County Court for recovery of a debt, and the Commissioners obtain judgment on the claim. Any appropriate court fee will be allowed in addition to the costs set out in Tables 9 and 10 and the claim may include a claim for fixed commencement costs.[20]

Table 9 sets out the fixed costs on commencement of the County Court claim conducted by an HMRC officer, the amount claimed in the claim form is used to determine which band in Table 9 apples. Table 10 sets out fixed costs on entry of judgment in a County Court claim conducted by an HMRC officer. The total to be included in the judgment for HMRC charges is the total of the fixed commencement costs, and the amount in Table 10 relevant to the value of the claim. In cases where the only claim is for a specified sum of money, and the defendant pays the money claimed within 14 days after service of the particulars of claim, together with the fixed commencement costs stated in the claim form, the defendant will not be liable for any further costs unless the court orders otherwise.[21]

Section VI of Part 45 governs the amount of fast track trial costs and their application. "Fast track trial costs" means the cost of a party's advocate for preparing for and appearing at the trial. It does not include any other disbursements, or any VAT payable on the advocate's fees. The "trial" includes a hearing where the court decides an amount of money or the value of goods. "Trial" does not include the hearing of an application for summary judgment, or the court's approval of a settlement or other compromise by, or on behalf of, a child or protected party.[22] **7–05**

Section VII of Part 45 limits the amount of costs recoverable in Aarhus Convention claims.[23] The provisions of Section VII do not apply where

[17] r.45.30(3).
[18] r.63.26.
[19] r.45.33. "HMRC charges" are claimed as "legal representative's costs" on relevant Court forms and means the fixed costs set out in Tables 9 and 10 of Section V.
[20] r.45.33(3)–(6).
[21] r.45.34, 35 and 36 and Tables 9 and 10.
[22] Under r.21.10; r.45.37(1) and (2) and Practice Direction 45, paras 4.1–4.3.
[23] An Aarhus Convention claim means a claim for judicial review of a decision, act or omission all or part of which is subject to the provisions of the UNECE Convention on Access to Information Public Participation in Decision Making and Access to Justice in Environmental Matters done at Aarhus, Denmark on 25 June, 1998, including a claim which proceeds on the basis that the decision, act or omission or part of it is so subject—r.45.41(2).

the claimant has not stated in the claim form that the claim is an Aarhus Convention claim, or has stated that it is not an Aarhus Convention claim, or, although it is such a claim, the claimant does not wish those rules to apply.[24] If the claimant has stated in the claim form that the claim is an Aarhus Convention claim, the limits on costs apply unless the defendant has in the acknowledgment of service denied that the claim is an Aarhus Convention claim and has set out the grounds for that denial and the court has determined that the claim is not an Aarhus Convention claim. In such a case, the court is required to determine the issue at the earliest opportunity. If the court holds that the claim is not an Aarhus Convention claim it will normally make no order for costs in relation to those proceedings. If it holds that the claim is an Aarhus Convention claim, it will normally order the defendant to pay the claimant's costs of those proceedings on the indemnity basis and the order may be enforced notwithstanding that this would increase the costs payable by the defendant beyond the amount to which such Convention claims are limited.[25] Subject to the above, a party to an Aarhus Convention claim may not be ordered to pay costs exceeding £5,000 where the claimant is claiming only as an individual and not as or on behalf of a business or other legal person, or £10,000 in all other cases.[26] Where a defendant is ordered to pay costs the amount recoverable is limited to £35,000.[27]

The availability of protective costs orders for environmental cases falling within the Aarhus Convention had been deliberately limited to judicial review claims and did not extend to statutory appeals or applications. Accordingly, it was not appropriate for the Court to exercise its discretion to grant cross-protection in respect of an application to quash planning permission under the Town & Country Planning Act 1990 s.288, as this would side-step the limitation deliberately enacted in the CPR to give effect to a convention which had not been directly incorporated into domestic law. Legislative action was necessary to remedy r.45.41's non-compliance with the Convention (it applies only in relation to judicial review proceedings).[28]

The Ministry of Justice launched a consultation on its proposals to adjust the costs protection for environmental claims under the Aarhus Convention on 17 September 2015. The proposals include amending the current costs regime under Part 45 to:

- Extend the types of case for which costs protection is available beyond judicial review to include similar statutory reviews including under s.288 of the Town and Country Planning 1990.

[24] r.45.42.
[25] r.45.44.
[26] r.45.43, PD 45, para.5.1.
[27] r.45.43, PD 45, para.5.2.
[28] *Secretary of State for Communities & Local Government v Venn* [2014] EWCA Civ 1539.

- Reduce the level of costs protection for financially well-resourced claimants.
- Reduce a defendant's liability for costs when it unsuccessfully challenges whether a claim is an Aarhus Convention claim under Part 45. The consultation closed on the 10 December 2015.

Costs on the indemnity basis

The basis of assessment

Where the court assesses costs, whether by summary or detailed assessment, it will (subject to any statutory provisions relating to, e.g. legal aid costs) assess those costs on either the standard basis or the indemnity basis. In either case the court will not allow costs which have been unreasonably incurred or which are unreasonable in amount. Where the court is assessing costs on the standard basis it will in addition only allow costs which are proportionate to the matters in issue and will resolve any doubt which it may have as to whether costs were reasonably incurred or reasonable and proportionate in amount in favour of the paying party. Where the amount of costs is to be assessed on the indemnity basis there is no proportionality requirement but the court will resolve any doubt which it may have as to whether the costs were reasonably incurred or were reasonable in amount in favour of the receiving party.[29] Where the court makes an order about costs without indicating the basis upon which costs are to be assessed or purports to make an order on a basis other than the standard or indemnity basis the costs will be assessed on the standard basis.[30] 7–06

When the Court may order costs on the indemnity basis

The Court awarding costs on the indemnity basis should be satisfied that there is something in the conduct of the action or the circumstances of the case which takes the case out of the norm in a way which justifies an order for indemnity costs.[31] Following *Excelsior Commercial & Industrial Holdings*[32] it is appropriate to award costs on the indemnity basis where the conduct of a party has taken the situation away from the norm. It is not always necessary to show deliberate misconduct, in some cases unreasonable conduct to a high degree would suffice. The claimant's refusal of two reasonable offers to settle would have been enough in itself to warrant an order on the indemnity basis.[33] 7–07

The power to award costs on the indemnity basis may extend to the manner in which a party's expert had prepared and given evidence. In the particular case the defendant was ordered to pay the claimant's costs of having to

[29] r.44.3(1)–(3).
[30] r.44.3(4).
[31] *Excelsior Commercial & Industrial Holdings Ltd v Salisbury Hammer Aspden & Johnson* [2002] EWCA Civ 879; [2002] C.P. Rep. 67.
[32] [2002] EWCA Civ 879; [2002] C.P. Rep. 67.
[33] *Franks v Sinclair (Costs)* [2006] EWHC 3656 (Ch); [2007] W.T.L.R. 785, David Richards J.

recall its own expert, on the indemnity basis.[34] In another case involving an expert who was "inexperienced and overenthusiastic" the claimants, having put forward a figure at which they were prepared to settle, refused to settle at that figure when the defendants offered it. No explanation for the refusal was given. Akenhead J awarded costs on the indemnity basis against the claimants. Because of the claimants' unwillingness to accept the amount offered by the defendants in settlement, an enormous amount of time, costs and Court resources had been wasted, and the defendants were entitled to costs on the indemnity basis.[35]

The Court of Appeal has held that there should be no general principle applicable to all applications under r.31.22 (concerning subsequent use of disclosed documents) to the effect that indemnity costs would be awarded against the applicant. There are many different kinds of such applications and the general rules as to costs ought to be applicable to them as to any other application before the Courts. On the facts of the case the Judge at first instance had ample grounds for awarding indemnity costs in the circumstances. The applicant's application was one which was extraneous to the existing proceedings. It required a huge amount of effort from the respondent in terms of liaison, checking and legal consideration. The respondent had been fully entitled to resist the application in the public interest. These factors took the case outside the norm. An order for costs on the indemnity basis was justified.[36]

Litigants in person

7–08 Prior to 1975, litigants in person who were successful in proceedings could recover only their out of pocket expenses.[37] The Litigants in Person Fees and Expenses Act 1975 and the Rules of Court made subsequently, enable litigants in person to recover some payment for the time which they expend in conducting litigation. Rule 46.5 is so worded that it is possible for a litigant in person to recover payment for legal advice as well as payment for time spent in conducting the litigation. There is an absolute cap on the amount recoverable by the litigant in person, namely two-thirds of the amount which would have been allowed if he had been legally represented, plus disbursements reasonably expended. The Court of Appeal has decided that in principle a litigant in person is entitled to his time for researching his case at the rate fixed by statute, subject to a cap of two thirds of what he would have recovered if he had been legally represented.[38]

In certain specified proceedings, where any costs of a litigant in person are ordered to be paid by another party to the proceedings or in any other way, there may be allowed on the assessment or other determination of the costs sums in respect of any work done and any expenses and losses incurred by the

[34] *Siegel v Pummell* [2015] EWHC 195, Wilkie J.
[35] *Igloo Regeneration (General Partner) Ltd v Powell Williams Partnership (Costs)* [2013] EWHC 1859 (TCC), Akenhead J.
[36] *Tchenguiz v Serious Fraud Office* [2014] EWCA Civ 1471.
[37] *Buckland v Watts* [1970] 1 QB 27 CA.
[38] *R v Legal Services Commission Ex p. Wulfshon* [2002] EWCA Civ.

litigant in or in connection with the proceedings to which the order relates.[39] This provision applies to civil proceedings as follows:

(a) in the County Court, in the Senior Courts or in the Supreme Court on appeal from the High Court or the Court of Appeal;
(b) before the Lands Tribunal for Northern Ireland;
(ba) before the First-tier Tribunal or the Upper Tribunal; or
(c) in or before any other Court or tribunal specified in an order made under s.1 of the Litigants in Person (Costs and Expenses) Act 1975 by the Lord Chancellor.[40]

A litigant in person who does not fall within the provisions of the 1975 Act **7–09** may claim only out of pocket expenses, although these may include fees and expenses charged by a solicitor to a litigant to equip him to argue a case in person.[41] There is no provision for the costs of litigants in person in criminal proceedings. Proceedings before the VAT Tribunal are also excluded. The Court of Appeal has held that the power to award costs for tribunal hearings is confined to sums recoverable at common law.[42]

The official receiver, acting without a solicitor in disqualification proceedings, is a litigant in person, and is not limited to disbursements merely because he is salaried. Where costs over and above disbursements have been incurred these are pecuniary in nature and amount to pecuniary loss. The costs will be assessed in accordance with r.46.5.[43]

The court has no power to award costs to a litigant in person in respect of assistance given by a non-legally qualified acquaintance. "Legal services" refer to services that are legal and provided by or under the supervision of a lawyer. Any payment made by the litigant to the assistant is not recoverable because it is not a disbursement which would have been made by a legal representative. The assistance being given was not expert assistance within r.46.5(3)(c).[44]

Tugendhat J commented in *Mole v. Hunter*[45], that reform of the Rules was unnecessary to deal with the effect that litigants in person were increasingly having on the Courts. In his view, reform was unnecessary because the Court already had sufficient power to manage cases effectively where one or more parties were litigants in person. In this way it could, to a certain extent, ameliorate the procedural problems that litigants experienced. Notwithstanding this

---

[39] Litigants in Person (Costs and Expenses) Act 1975 s.1(1).

[40] The scope of the Act has been extended to the Employment Appeal Tribunal by the Litigants in Person (Costs and Expenses) Order 1980 (SI 1980/1159) and to Magistrates' Courts in England and Wales in relation to civil proceedings before these Courts by the Litigants in Person (Magistrates' Courts) Order 2001 (SI 2001/3438).

[41] *Buckland v Watts* [1970] 1 Q.B. 27; [1969] 3 W.L.R. 92; (1969) 113 S.J. 384; *Malloch v Aberdeen Corp* [1973] 1 W.L.R. 71; [1973] 1 All E.R. 304; 1973 S.L.T. (Notes) 5. See also *Commissioners of Customs and Excise v Ross* [1992] All E.R. 65; [1990] S.T.C. 353.

[42] *Nader (t/a Tryus) v Customs and Excise Commissioners* [1998] S.T.C. 806, CA, and see *Customs and Excise Commissioners v Ross* (1990) 2 All E.R. 65; [1990] S.T.C. 353, Simon Brown J.

[43] *Re Minotaur Data Systems Ltd* [1999] 1 W.L.R. 1129; [1999] 3 All E.R. 122; [1999] B.C.C. 571, CA. (Magistrates' Courts) Order 2001 (SI 2001/3438).

[44] *Uhbi (t/a United Building and Plumbing Contractors) v Kajla* [2002] All E.R. (D) 265, CA.

[45] [2014] EWHC 658 (QB).

view, a new r.3.1A has been introduced which imposes a positive obligation on the Court to take certain steps where at least one party is unrepresented. These include: adopting a formal procedure appropriate to furthering the Overriding Objective; and, where necessary, questioning witnesses. The new rule, in making explicit the Court's power to adapt its procedure to deal with a case justly and at proportionate cost for litigants in person, provides useful clarity.

The Court of Appeal refused to entertain an application under r.52.9A (Orders to limit the recoverable costs of an appeal), as the application had not been made as soon as practicable, as was required under r.52.9A(4). The fact that the defendant applicant was a litigant in person, and was ignorant of his rights, did not mean it was not practicable for him to make the application. There were not, nor ought there to be, special rules for litigants in person. The applicant's original claim should never have been brought, nor ought he to have appealed the Employment Tribunal's rejection of it. The fact that the other party had appealed the decision of the EAT would not have come as a surprise to the applicant. It would be unjust not to make an order for costs of the appeal against the applicant.[46] The status of this decision is not clear in the light of the rule amendment (r.3.1A) mentioned above.

McKenzie Friends

7–10 On 12 July, 2010 the Master of the Rolls and President of the Family Division handed down a Practice Note,[47] which applies to civil and family proceedings in the Court of Appeal (Civil Division), the High Court, County Courts and the Family Proceedings Court in the Magistrates' Courts. The Note is issued as guidance, not as a Practice Direction, and sets out to remind courts and litigants of the principles set out in the authorities.

Litigants have the right to have reasonable assistance from a lay person (McKenzie Friends), but McKenzie Friends have no independent right to provide assistance. They have no right to act as advocates or to carry out the conduct of litigation.

McKenzie Friends may: (i) provide moral support for litigants; (ii) take notes; (iii) help with case papers; and (iv) quietly give advice on any aspect of the conduct of the case. A McKenzie Friend may not: (a) act as a litigant's agent in relation to the proceedings; (b) manage litigants' cases outside court, for example by signing court documents; or (c) address the court, make oral submissions or examine witnesses. The Practice Note points out that while litigants ordinarily have a right to receive reasonable assistance from McKenzie Friends, the court retains the power to refuse to permit such assistance. It may do so where it is satisfied that, in that case, the interests of justice and fairness do not require the litigant to receive such assistance.

---

[46] *JJ Food Service Ltd v Zulhayr* [2013] EWCA Civ 1304.

[47] Practice Note (Sen Cts: McKenzie Friends: Civil and Family Courts) [2010] 1 W.L.R. 1881; [2010] 4 All E.R. 272; [2010] 2 F.L.R. 962.

The following factors should not be taken to justify the court refusing to permit a litigant receiving such assistance: (i) the case or application is simple or straightforward, or is for instance a directions or case management hearing; (ii) the litigant appears capable of conducting the case without assistance; (iii) the litigant is unrepresented through choice; (iv) the other party is not represented; (v) the proposed McKenzie Friend belongs to an organisation that promotes a particular cause; and (vi) the proceedings are confidential and the court papers contain sensitive information relating to a family's affairs.

A litigant may be denied assistance of a McKenzie Friend because its provision might undermine or has undermined the efficient administration of justice. Such circumstances might include: (i) the assistance is being provided for an improper purpose; (ii) the assistance is unreasonable in nature or degree; (iii) the McKenzie Friend is subject to a civil proceedings orders or a civil restraint order; (iv) the McKenzie Friend is using the litigant as a puppet; (v) the McKenzie Friend is directly or indirectly conducting the litigation; and (vi) the court is not satisfied that the McKenzie Friend fully understands the duty of confidentiality. **7–11**

The Note points out that McKenzie Friends do not have a right of audience or a right to conduct litigation, and it is a criminal offence to exercise rights of audience or to conduct litigation unless properly qualified and authorised to do so. The court may grant such rights to a McKenzie Friend on a case by case basis, but the courts should be slow to grant any application from a litigant for a right of audience or a right to conduct litigation to any lay person, including a McKenzie Friend. The court should only be prepared to grant such rights where there is good reason to do so, taking into account all the circumstances of the case. Such grants should not be extended to lay persons automatically or without due consideration. They should not be granted for mere convenience.

Litigants may enter into lawful agreements to pay fees to McKenzie Friends for the provision of reasonable assistance in court, or out of court by, e.g. carrying out clerical or mechanical activities such as photocopying documents, preparing bundles, delivering documents to opposing parties or the court, or the provision of legal advice in connection with court proceedings. Such fees cannot lawfully be recovered from the opposing party. Even where the court has granted a McKenzie Friend the right to conduct litigation, fees said to be incurred by a McKenzie Friend are, in principle, recoverable from the litigant for whom the work was carried out, but cannot lawfully be recovered from the opposing party. Where a McKenzie Friend is granted a right of audience, the fees incurred by the McKenzie Friend are, in principle, recoverable from the litigant on whose behalf the right is exercised, and are also recoverable, in principle, from the opposing party as a recoverable disbursement.

Questions and answers

Fixed Costs

Q1. What indications are there about fixed costs for the future? Are there any arguments for fixed fees?

7–12 Sir Rupert recommended (and still recommends) that there should be a fixed costs regime for the whole of the fast-track and at the lower end of the multi-track. Professor Paul Fenn carried out a great deal of work during the course of the Jackson Review and produced a matrix for fixed costs across the fast track based on a considerable amount of data which had been made available to him by the ABI and others. The matrix was published in the final report having been accepted both by Jackson LJ and his assessors. The fixed costs in relation to Low Value Personal Injury Claims in Road Traffic Accidents ("the RTA protocol") or for Low Value Personal Injury (Employers' Liability and Public Liability) Claims ("the EL/PL protocol") have been reduced significantly below the earlier figures which had been the result of industry-wide agreement. The new figures appear to have been arrived at following the prohibition of referral fees by reducing the previous figures by the perceived amount of referral fees. This has done nothing to reduce arguments about hourly rates since solicitors now argue that instead of paying referral fees, they have to pay the same or larger amounts in marketing costs.

The Government is clearly keen to address the question of fixed costs on the fast track and in clinical negligence cases[48]. The NHS Litigation Authority ('NHSLA') has drafted proposals for a fixed costs pilot scheme for clinical negligence cases. The proposals are still under consideration. The minutes of the July 2015 Civil Procedure Rules Committee meeting suggest that it has already been asked to draft rules prior to the public consultation. The Government envisaged that fixed fees would be introduced in October 2016, subject to a consultation opening towards the end of 2015.The Government, however, announced in November 2015:

> *"The consultation documentation, including the impact assessment, will be published in early 2016 subject to relevant committee clearances. We are working upon the assumption that there is nothing about fixed recoverable costs regime which will alter the percentage of unmeritorious claims.*
> *Any scheme proposed will include consideration of the right incentives to support a fairer and quicker process that provides the improvements to the system whilst maintaining access to justice."*

It is not clear whether the fixed fees will apply to cases up to £100,000 or £250,000.

[48] See the remarks of Lord Faulks in Chapter 1.

Q2. What guidance can be given about retainer arrangements to emphasise the importance of the advice to a client about these and ensuring that retainer arrangements are still clear and enforceable where a legal representative is asked to represent a client in litigation which will inevitably involve the application of fixed costs?

The situation must be clearly explained to the client. A solicitor may agree 7–13
that any charges will be limited to the amount recoverable from a paying party (i.e. the limit of fixed costs). If the legal representative intends to charge the client an amount which is likely to exceed the fixed recoverable costs, this must be explained to the client in clear terms. In respect of client care, r.2 of the 2007 Code of Conduct set out a detailed and prescriptive list of the type of information that solicitors were required to give to clients. Chapter 1 of the SRA Code of Conduct which came into effect on 6 October, 2011 sets out the general outcomes including that clients are in a position to make informed decisions about their matter. "Indicative behaviour" sets out how solicitors might go about this by, for example, agreeing an appropriate level of service with the client. The Solicitors Regulation Authority states that the new code allows greater flexibility according to the needs of the client and the type of work that the solicitor undertakes, but there is also greater emphasis on the needs of the individual client, particularly those who are vulnerable.

Chapter 1 of the Code does not specify the information that must be given to clients or the form it should take. This is because solicitors are required to focus on the principles and achieving the right outcomes for clients. The SRA Handbook points out:

> *"Providing clear information at the outset and as the matter progresses is a benefit not only to clients but also to [the solicitor's firm]. Some of the most common causes of complaints are lack of clear information about costs, failure to follow instructions, delay and failure to keep clients informed. It is important to monitor complaints to [the solicitor's firm] as these can indicate failure to provide good client care as well as other problems within the firm."*

Solicitors should only enter into fee agreements with their clients that are legal and which the solicitor considers are suitable for the client's needs and take account of the client's best interest. Clients must receive the best possible information both at the time of engagement and, when appropriate, as their matter progresses about the likely overall cost of their matter and must be informed of their right to challenge or complain about a bill and the circumstances in which they may be likely to pay interest on an unpaid bill.

Retainer is the name given to the contract which exists between a solicitor and the client. Where there is no retainer the relationship of solicitor and client does not exist and the solicitor is not entitled to render a bill. The contract between the solicitor and the client may be on any terms which are mutually agreeable provided that the terms do not infringe the restrictions laid down in Part III of the Solicitors Act 1974 or the statutory requirements relating to conditional fee agreements or damages-based agreements.

Q3. In proceedings in the Intellectual Property Enterprise Court where costs are awarded against a party for unreasonable behaviour does the stage costs cap in Part 45 apply?

7–14 A claimant had behaved unreasonably in the course of an interim application and costs were awarded under r.63.26(2). The court decided that those costs were themselves subject to the stage costs cap. Furthermore where there was more than one receiving party the stage costs had to be shared between them and did not apply to them individually.[49]

Q4. Following the decision in Chaplair v Kumari, it is clear that a landlord can recover costs of proceedings under a leasehold indemnity in its favour irrespective of whether the claim would fall within the fixed costs regimes of the small and fast tracks. What is the position in relation to residential possession claims under CPR Part 55, to which the fixed costs regime under CPR Part 45 applies?

7–15 The position in *Chaplair v Kumari* was as follows: A claim brought by a landlord for recovery of unpaid rent and service charges was allocated, by consent, to the small claims track. The claim was successful. In the lease there was a contractual right to recover the costs of proceedings. At first instance the District Judge awarded costs to the landlord but held that there was no power to award costs other than r.27.14 fixed costs. On appeal to the Circuit Judge, the appeal was successful and the defendant appealed to the Court of Appeal. The Court refused to grant permission on that particular issue as the law on the point was well established: where there was a contractual right to costs, the court should normally exercise its costs discretion to reflect those rights; r.27.14 should be read as being subject to r.44.5 which gives effect to the general principle set out above and which was not excluded from Part 27 by r.27.2. The rule-making power cannot, in any event, set aside or overrule a contractual entitlement which would be necessary for r.27.14 to have an exclusionary effect.[50]

So far as possession claims under Part 55 are concerned the White Book states (at 55.7.8):

> *"Fixed costs apply to certain types of possession claims—unless the court orders otherwise. CPR r.45.1 provides that fixed costs apply where—*
>
> - *The defendant gives up possession and pays the amount claimed (if any) and the fixed commencement costs;*
> - *One of the grounds for possession is arrears of rent, the court gave a fixed date for hearing, a possession order is made (whether suspended or not) and the defendant has either failed to deliver a defence or the defence is limited to specifying proposals for payment of arrears; and*
> - *The claim is brought under the accelerated procedure (Pt 55 Section 2) against*

[49] *Akhtar v Bhopal Productions (UK) Ltd* [2015] EWHC 154 (IPEC), HHJ Hacon.
[50] *Chaplair Limited v. Kumari* [2015] EWCA Civ. 798.

an assured shorthold tenant, a possession order is made and the defendant has neither delivered a defence nor otherwise denied liability

- *The claim is a demotion claim or a demotion claim is made in the same claim form in which a possession claim is made and the demotion claim is successful.*

The amounts of fixed costs are set out in CPR r.45.5, Table 3, and CPR r.45.6."

It is certainly arguable that, provided the "indemnity" costs provision in the Landlord and Tenant agreement is properly drafted, r.44.5 should apply. It might in fact be easier to persuade the Court to "order otherwise" rather than get into a discussion about whether the contractual terms should take precedence.

Costs on the Indemnity Basis

Q5. Is the indemnity basis applicable in cases where there is an abuse of process or where a party has been guilty of unreasonable conduct?

The Companies Court, in applying the decision in *Excelsior Commercial and Industrial Holdings Ltd*[51] ordered the claimant to pay the costs of an unfair prejudice petition on the indemnity basis where the petition had been an abuse of process and should never have been brought, and where the claimant had no basis for defending the company's claim for breach of duty as a director and employee. The costs of both actions had been increased significantly by virtue of the claimant's highly aggressive tactics in the conduct of the litigation. Overall the case constituted a departure from the norm, which made it just to order costs to be paid on the indemnity basis.[52] 7–16

A different Court ordered an unsuccessful claimant to pay costs on the indemnity basis and to pay interest on the costs from one year before the commencement date of the trial because of the claimants' unreasonable conduct in that the case had changed constantly throughout the course of the proceedings and the claimant had produced wholly unacceptable volumes of documentation.[53]

In another example, where claimants had sued their former financial advisor, the defendant, before serving its defence, applied for summary judgment. Four months later the application was withdrawn. The Court had to decide the question of costs. There was nothing sufficiently unusual about the case to justify departing from the general rule that the unsuccessful party should be ordered to pay the successful party's costs. The Court went on to make an order on the indemnity basis because the defendant was not justified in seeking summary judgment before filing the defence. The application constituted conduct which was sufficiently 'out of the norm' within the meaning in *Excelsior* and other authorities.[54]

---

[51] *Excelsior Commercial & Industrial Holdings Ltd v Salisbury Hammer Aspden & Johnson* [2002] EWCA Civ 879; [2002] C.P. Rep. 67.

[52] *Re Flex Associates Ltd* [2010] EWHC 3690 (Ch) David Donaldson QC.

[53] *ABCI (formerly Arab Business Consortium International Finance & Investment Co) v Banque Franco-Tunisienne (Costs)* [2002] EWHC 567 (Comm) HH Judge Chambers QC.

[54] *The Libyan Investment Authority v Goldman Sachs International* [2014] EWHC 3364 (Ch) Rose J.

Q6. What is the position of litigation funders in relation to orders for costs, particularly orders for costs on the indemnity basis?

7–17 Where claimants funded by third party litigation funders lost the claim, the litigation funders were ordered to pay the costs of the defendant on the indemnity basis up to the limit of their investment. Christopher Clarke LJ stated:

> *"Justice requires that when the case fails so comprehensively, not merely on the facts but because it was wholly bad in law, the funder should, subject to the Arkin cap, bear the costs order to be paid by the person whom or which he has unsuccessfully supported, assessed on the scale which the Court thinks it just for that person to pay in the light of all the circumstances, including but not limited to that person's behaviour and that of those whom that person engaged."*

The Judge stated that the funder should, absent special circumstances, follow the fortunes of those from whom he himself hoped to derive a small fortune. To do otherwise would be unfair to the defendants and their personnel. To make an order for indemnity costs would not be to penalise but to recompense. Christopher Clarke LJ further stated:

> *"If it serves to cause funders and their advisors to take rigorous steps short of champerty, i.e. behaviour likely to interfere with the due administration of justice—particularly in the form of rigorous analysis of law, facts and witnesses, consideration of proportionality and review at appropriate intervals—to reduce the occurrence of the sort of circumstances that cause me to order indemnity costs in this case, that is an advantage and in the public interest".*[55]

Q7. The rules suggest that costs management does not affect indemnity costs. However there is now a confusion about this since Coulson J's decision in Elvanite Full Circle Ltd v Amec Earth and Environmental UK Ltd[56] suggests otherwise.

7–18 On the facts of the case the Judge decided not to make an order on the indemnity basis but went on to consider whether, if the defendant had been entitled to indemnity costs, the costs management order was irrelevant and whether it was possible for the defendant to recover more than the sums in the costs management order. Having acknowledged that a costs management order is expressed to be relevant only to an assessment of costs on the standard basis, he continued:

> *"However as a matter of logical analysis, it seems to me that the costs management order should also be the starting point of an assessment of costs on an indemnity basis even if the 'good reasons' to depart from it are likely to be more numerous and extensive if the indemnity basis is applied . . .*
> *If [the budget] is an accurate estimate of all the costs that will be incurred then it*

[55] *Excalibur Ventures LLC v Texas Keystone Inc (Defendants and Costs Claimants) and Psari Holdings Ltd (Costs Defendants)* [2014] EWHC 3436 (Comm) Christopher Clarke LJ.

[56] *Elvanite Full Circle Ltd v Amec Earth and Environmental UK Ltd* [2013] EWHC 1643 (TCC).

seems to me that it should be the relevant starting point for an assessment of costs on an indemnity basis as well as for an assessment on the standard basis . . . There is concern that, if an order for indemnity costs allows the receiving party to ignore the costs management order, then that will encourage successful parties to argue for indemnity costs every time . . .A paying party will have fought the trial assuming that, even if it loses, its opponent will be unlikely to recover more than the amount recorded in the costs management order, unless there is good reason for any departure. That is the certainty that the new regime provides. Even if the paying party has to pay costs on an indemnity basis that does not seem to me automatically to justify an abandonment of that certainty and the encouragement of a costs free for all . . . .

In any given case it might be said that an award of indemnity costs—which does not require any assessment of proportionality—might be a 'good reason' to depart from the costs budget approved by the Court . . . I can well see that, in particular factual circumstances, an award of indemnity costs might be a good reason to permit such a departure. But that would be fact specific and it would not detract from the principle of at least starting the costs assessment by reference to the approved budget."[57]

It is probable that the Court of Appeal in *Denton* has overtaken this decision which was a decision under a pilot scheme which did not require the Form H to assert that it was in any way an attempt at proportionate costs. (See **Chapter 4** at para **4–20** and Qs **48** and **49** for further consideration of this topic)

Q8. In a County Court decision by a district judge, the Court ordered a claimant who had exaggerated his claim to pay costs on the indemnity basis. The Court found that the claim would have been resolved by the end of June 2012 had the claimant not exaggerated his claim.

Accordingly, the usual costs consequences of previous r.36.10(5) (now r.36. 13(5)),[58] did not apply. The claimant was awarded costs on the standard basis up to the 30 June 2012 but was ordered to pay the defendant's costs thereafter on the indemnity basis. The claimant was also ordered to meet the entire costs of gathering the surveillance evidence and the costs of the application.[59] 7–19

Litigants in Person

Q9.What is the position of a solicitor or barrister acting on his or her own behalf?

It is a question of fact whether a solicitor in sole practice is acting for himself as a true litigant in person or, is, instead, represented by himself in the firm name. It was relevant that the underlying litigation concerned a claim for 7–20

[57] paras 28–31.
[58] The wording has altered slightly.
[59] *Worthington v. 03918424 Limited* [2015] 16 June unreported.

professional fees with allegations of negligence and breach of duty since those were matters arising out of the solicitor's practice as a solicitor and not out of the course of his private life.[60]

In proceedings where the claimant was a solicitor who had, at the same time, practised as a costs draftsman until July 1999, the court had to decide whether or not she was a litigant in person before 26 April, 1999 and also whether she was a litigant in person after that date under the CPR. The question depended upon the criteria used to define the term "practising solicitor". Prior to 26 April, 1999, the Court found that the claimant was undoubtedly a practising solicitor from a regulatory point of view under the Solicitors Act and the Rules of Practice, but she was not a practising solicitor who was able to charge for her time for the purposes of RSC Ord.62 r.18(6) and the rule in *London Scottish Benefits Society v Chorley*.[61] The court therefore held that she was only entitled to recover costs for that period as a litigant in person. With regard to the period after 26 April, 1999, it was accepted by the claimant that if a Court found that she was not a practising solicitor for the purposes of RSC Ord.62 r.18 then she was unable to take advantage of PD 46, para.3.2. The court held that this provision was designed to do no more than preserve the rule in *London Scottish Benefits Society*. The criteria remained the same.[62]

Where the Bar Standards Board brought proceedings against a non-practising barrister before the Disciplinary Tribunal of the Council of the Inns of Court, the barrister successfully defended the proceedings in person. The Administrative Court expressed the view that the principle in *London Scottish Benefit Society* that a solicitor litigant acting in person was entitled to costs incurred in the expenditure of his own professional skill had been overturned by r.46.5(6) (formerly r.48.6(6)). Neither a solicitor nor a barrister acting in person could include in his proof of financial loss under r.46.5(4)(a) the cost of the provision of his own professional skill. Since a barrister was not a solicitor coming within the exception in PD 46(3) there was no means by which a barrister could avoid that conclusion and claim costs unless she employed someone else on her behalf. The Civil Procedure Rules did not apply however and were not even persuasive authority. If the Bar Standards Board wished to avoid having to pay the costs of a barrister's time and that barrister had successfully defended proceedings it was open to it to provide in its rules that the CPR should apply but it had not done so. The correct basis of assessing the cost was in accordance with the Board's own rules, namely to award such costs as the Tribunal thought fit. There was no basis for saying that the expenditure of a barrister's own time and skills should not be compensated where that barrister was successful.[63]

---

[60] *Hatton v Kendrick* [2002] EWCA Civ 1783; [2003] C.P. Rep. 32, CA.
[61] *London Scottish Benefits Society v Chorley* [1884] 13 Q.B.D. 872.
[62] *Joseph v Boyd & Hutchinson* [2003] EWHC 413 (Ch); [2003] 3 Costs L.R. 358, Patten J.
[63] *R (Bar Standards Board) v Disciplinary Tribunal of the Council of the Inns of Court and Sivanandan (Interested Party)* [2014] EWHC 1570 (Admin).

Q10. If a litigant in person instructs a barrister under the Direct Access scheme can the litigant recover any costs?

The Direct Access Scheme is a useful device for reducing costs, particularly in cases of a technical nature where a solicitor would otherwise be no more than a conduit between, e.g. a specialist tax practitioner and a specialist tax barrister. The scheme has however produced a difficulty in that a tax payer being advised by members of the Institute of Taxation and by counsel under the Direct Access Scheme appealed from a decision of the Commissioners and thence to the Court of Appeal where the tax payer was successful. Although it was conceded that the tax payer was entitled to his costs, there was considerable argument as to the extent of those costs. The Court of Appeal found that the tax payer had been acting as a litigant in person (although he had in fact taken no active part in the proceedings), that counsel's fee was recoverable since it was a disbursement which would have been made had solicitors been instructed but that the fees of the tax advisers were not recoverable save to the extent that they may have been acting in an expert capacity.[64] 7–21

From 6 January 2014 The Public Access Rules are Rules C119–C131 of the Code of Conduct in the Bar Standards Board Handbook. The Handbook contains rules and guidance on the conduct of barristers. The revised Code now forms Part two of the new BSB 'Handbook', which brings together all the BSB's regulations and guidance for barristers into one publication. For Public Access barristers, one of the key changes is that self-employed barristers are allowed to apply for an extension to their practising certificate in order to be able to conduct litigation. This means that, as long as Public Access barristers have the correct authorisation, their clients no longer have to act as a self-representing litigant or instruct a solicitor, should the case go to court.[65]

Q11. Is it possible for the Court to make an order for costs on the indemnity basis against a litigant in person?

Section 51 of the Senior Courts Act 1981 gives the Court full power to determine by whom and to what extent the costs are to be paid. In appropriate circumstances therefore, it is entirely open to the Court to make an order for costs on the indemnity basis against a litigant in person. In family proceedings, the father made committal applications against two CAFCASS officers and the mother's solicitor. The judge found the application to be fundamentally flawed with no real prospect of success. The mother's solicitor had written to the father at an early stage on an open basis setting out the grounds of the defence all of which had succeeded. The Court found that the father's very serious allegations had no evidential basis and the application having fatal procedural defects and no real prospect of success ought therefore to be 7–22

[64] *Agassi v Robinson (Inspector of Taxes)* [2005] EWCA Civ 1507; [2006] 1 W.L.R. 2126; [2006] 1 All E.R. 900; [2006] S.T.C. 580, CA.

[65] See: *www.barstandardsboard.org.uk/regulatory-requirements/for-barristers/public-access/*

regarded as an abuse of process. The mother's solicitor had incurred significant costs and the father was ordered to pay those costs on the indemnity basis.[66]

Q12. Is it possible for a firm of solicitors which is an LLP to be regarded as a litigant in person for the purpose of a costs assessment?

7–23 Rule 46.5(6) states:

> *"For the purposes of this rule, a litigant in person includes:-*
> *(a) A company or other corporation which is acting without a legal representative; and any of the following who acts in person (except where any such person is represented by a firm in which that person is a partner):*
> (i) *A barrister*
> (ii) *A solicitor*
> (iii) *A solicitor's employee*
> (iv) *A manager of a body recognised under section 9 of the Administration of Justice Act 1985; or*
> (v) *A person who for the purposes of the 2007 Act is an authorised person in relation to an activity which constitutes the conduct of litigation (within the meaning of that Act)."*

A defendant solicitor was ordered to pay the claimant's costs following his unsuccessful application for summary judgment. The claimant was a limited liability partnership of practising solicitors. They had represented themselves and instructed counsel (the Court did not deal with the significance of the instruction of counsel). At first instance, the defendant asserted that the claimant partnership was a litigant in person and that the costs should accordingly be limited. The Costs Judge did not accept that argument and the defendant appealed. The judge held that as the claimant was *"a company or other corporation"* which was acting with a legal representative, it was not a litigant in person under r.46.5(6)(a). The defendant argued that the claimant was a litigant in person under r.46.5(6)(b)(v). The Judge held that the rule had no sensible foundation if *"person"* included a corporation. The Judge queried why the rule should exclude from the definition of litigant in person an ordinary solicitors' partnership acting by one of its own solicitors (which was the effect of the rule) while including an LLP also acting by one of its own solicitors. Companies and corporations were dealt with comprehensively in r.46.5(6)(a) whereas r.46.5(6)(b) dealt with several categories all of whom were natural persons. The Judge further pointed out that in the rules individuals were described as acting in person but a company was described as acting *"without a legal representative"*[67].

Q13. To what extent will the Court grant some leeway to a litigant in person who fails to comply with a rule practice direction or Court order?

[66] *H v. Dent and McKay and Harman* [2015] EWHC 2228 (Fam.), Roberts J.
[67] *EMW Law LLP v. Halborg* [2015] EWHC 2005 (Ch), HHJ Purle QC.

This question was raised before the coming into force of r.3.1A (Case Management – Unrepresented Parties). Under that Rule, the Court must, when exercising any powers of case management, have regard to the fact that at least one party is unrepresented and is required to "adopt such procedure at any hearing as it considers appropriate to further the overriding objective". 7–24

The answer to the question will always be fact sensitive and the cases below give examples of the different approaches the Court may take. Where a defendant litigant in person failed to file an appeal bundle in breach of an unless order as a result of which her appeal was struck out, the Court refused an application for relief from sanctions under Rule 3.9, holding, in applying the *Denton* test, that the failure to file an appeal bundle was a significant breach. The process of registering a foreign judgment (which was the subject matter of the appeal) was meant to be swift and seamless but the process had been awkward and delayed. The Court was bound to treat the default as serious and significant. In giving judgment, the Court emphasised that not all litigants in person should be treated the same. The Court could take into account the needs of a litigant in person who was impecunious or unable to speak the language. In the instant case, the defendant was a sophisticated person with sufficient access to resources to protect her interest. There was no good reason for her breach. Although the Court would not usually take into account the underlying merits of the claim when making case management decisions in considering all the circumstances under r.3.9, the Court found that it was entitled to take into account the merits of the underlying proceedings and to conclude that the defendant had no right to delay registration of the foreign judgments further.[68]

In a case where proceedings had been brought against four defendants, one of the defendants owned and controlled another defendant. Judgment was entered against all four defendants. The litigant in person did not attend as a result of ill health. She appealed, arguing that she and her company should never have been parties to the proceedings and that her application to strike out the claims had not been dealt with by the Court at first instance. Two days before the appeal was due to be heard, the litigant in person realised she only had permission to appeal the judgment and costs order made against her in her personal capacity and not against the company. She applied for permission to file an appeal notice on behalf of the company at the appeal hearing itself. The Court of Appeal applied the three stage test in *Denton v. White* and found that the delay was serious and significant. The explanation was that the litigant in person did not realise that she also needed to appeal separately on behalf of the company. The Court held that the circumstances were "truly exceptional" and it was just to extend the time. A judgment against the company could, at least in theory, result in proceedings against the litigant in person under the Disqualification of Directors' legislation. The facts relating to the company were exactly the same as those relating to the litigant

[68] *Akcine Bendore Bankas Snoras (in Bankruptcy) v. Yampolskaya* [2015] EWHC 2136 (QB), Green J.

personally and the claimant was fully aware that both were, for the purposes of the litigation, to be regarded as one and the same.[69]

A litigant in person sought an adjournment of her trial for two weeks because she was dissatisfied with the specific disclosure provided by the Defendant, and wished to argue that this affected her ability to prepare for trial, and that, as a litigant in person, she needed more time to consider the newly disclosed material and to amend her skeleton argument. The Court refused her application holding that if it became apparent during the trial that further information was required this could be dealt with by the trial judge. An adjournment of the trial would have a very considerable impact. The defendant had already incurred substantial costs which would be lost or duplicated if the trial were adjourned and the adjournment would not be for two weeks but for several months, and given that the proceedings had commenced in 2007, it was in the interests of both parties that the issues be determined. The documents which had been disclosed were "*relatively peripheral*" to the case. The date of trial was put back by four days to give the litigant some further time in which to consider the new material and finalise their skeleton argument.[70]

In a case where only quantum was in dispute, the Court directed that there should be a meeting of experts on a specified date. The meeting did not take place because the claimant litigant in person fell out with his expert and had not paid his fees. The defendant applied to extend the time for the meeting and obtained an order that unless the experts met by the new date, the claimant's expert evidence should be struck out. The claimant's application to set aside the order and vacate the trial date and for new directions on expert evidence was dismissed. The judge held that the claimant was responsible for the expert ceasing to act, given his criticism of the expert's opinion and the non-payment of his fees. Also, it was not appropriate for the claimant to indicate that he would look to the expert for any shortfall in the sums he sought to recover. The judge considered the *Denton* principles and decided that the non-compliance with the relevant order was serious and significant and was the claimant's fault. It was not fair, just or reasonable in all the circumstances for relief to be granted.[71]

Where a litigant in person made eleven applications, all of which were wholly without merit, the Court granted an application for an extended civil restraint order against the litigant in person. The defendant complained that the Courts had never looked at the merits of her case and that she was a litigant in person who did not understand the procedure. In giving judgment the judge stated:

> "*if it is otherwise appropriate to make a civil restraint order, the fact that the litigant is a litigant in person who does not understand procedures and gets things*

[69] *Kishenin and Another v. Bleach and Others* [2015] EWCA Civ. 1184.

[70] *El-Demellawy v. European Bank for Reconstruction and Development* [2015] EWHC 3291 (QB), Hickinbottom J.

[71] *Sargeant v. UK Insurance Limited and Another* [2015] EWHC 3304 (QB), Picken J. See also *Brand and Goldsmith v. Berki* [2015] EWHC 3373 (QB), Jay J.

wrong is precisely supportive of making a civil restraint order rather than not making one. [The litigant in person] needs to understand that by making a civil restraint order. . . .she does not lose any rights at all. If she has an application or an appeal or a claim that has any merit the judge who hears or deals with an application for permission to launch such an application, appeal or claim will make an order permitting her to proceed. The civil restraint order is only a filter to preclude the making of unmeritorious applications".[72]

Q14. Is it possible for a company to be represented by a McKenzie friend?

Hildyard J found that a company may be represented by a McKenzie friend under rights of audience granted in exceptional circumstances. Although there was no direct authority on the point, the Court could rely on its power to regulate its own proceedings and in circumstances where otherwise the body corporate would have no-one capable of speaking for it, to prevent a failure of the administration of justice. The judge relied on Sch.3 of the Legal Services Act 2007 and on the Courts and Legal Services Act 1990 both of which assumed and recognised that the Courts had such jurisdiction even if it was not conferred expressly. The litigation concerned the attempt by the claimant bank to wrest a large group of companies in the Russian Federation from the control and ownership of the defendants. An application for disclosure by the defendants had been admirably argued on their behalf by their McKenzie friend. 7–25

The company referred to Rule 39.6 (Representation at Trial of Companies or Other Corporations) which provides:

"A company or other corporation may be represented at trial by an employee if:

(a) The employee has been authorised by the company or corporation to appear at trial on its behalf; and

(b) *The Court gives permission."*

The Judge stated in relation to a helpful note on the applicable framework for a McKenzie friend provided by counsel for the claimants:

"It suggests the conclusion that, given that CPR 39.6 does now allow an employee of a body corporate, duly authorised to do so by it, to appear at trial on its behalf with the permission of the Court, the Court does have the jurisdiction to allow a body corporate the assistance of a McKenzie friend, and in appropriate (and exceptional) circumstances to allow that McKenzie friend the right of audience on an ad hoc basis."[73]

Q15. Will the Court order interim payments to enable litigants in person to obtain Legal representation?

Defendant litigants in person who had left Russia and were in France (for their 7–26

[72] *KL Communications Limited v. Wenfei Fu* [2015] EWHC 2026 (IPEC), Warren J.

[73] *Bank St. Petersburg PJSC and Another v. Arkhangelsky and Others* [2015] EWHC 2997 (Ch), Hildyard J.

own safety) issued a counterclaim for $80 million. The eight week trial had already been adjourned twice.

The Defendants argued that without legal representation a fair trial was not possible and would not be ECHR Art. 6 compliant. They sought a further adjournment and an interim payment to enable them to instruct representatives.

The court found that it had to be satisfied that there were good case management reasons For making an interim payment and that if the matter went to trial the defendants would Obtain judgment for a substantial sum.[74] In ordinary circumstances the notion that an Interim payment should be made to fund a party's legal costs was fanciful, but there was The extraordinary factor in the instant case of the allegation that there would otherwise be an unfair trial. The counterclaim was complex and would require expert evidence. The prospect of identifying a separate issue with sufficient cohesion to be safely heard within five days, and deciding before then that the defendants would obtain judgment, was remote in the extreme. It would not be consistent with the court's judicial obligations, nor would it be fair to the bank, to order an interim payment.

The jurisdiction to award costs before the determination of an issue was normally confined To cases where there was a "common fund", such as in trust, company or matrimonial proceedings. The court was unlikely to exercise it outside of those circumstances to make one party fund another in a substantial amount going beyond disbursements reasonably required for the trial, and the application for costs was refused.

A definition of a fair trial was impossible and unwise. It was not impossible to afford the defendants proper access to the legal process and proper adjudication of claims. It was relevant that the defendants had voluntarily chosen England as a jurisdiction when they must have known of their travel difficulties, and that they had always encouraged the court's expectation that they would attend the trial, either themselves via video link or through their McKenzie friend. (**See the question above**).[75]

[74] See *Revenue and Customs Commissioners v GKN Group* [2012] EWCA Civ 57, [2012] 1 W.L.R. 2375.

[75] *Bank St. Petersburg PJSC and Another v. Arkhangelsky and Others* [2015] EWHC (Ch) 27 November, Hildyard J.

CHAPTER 8

Assessments of Costs and Payments on Account of Costs

Introduction

8–01 The overall intentions of the 2013 reforms in respect of the process for determination of 'between the parties' costs are to reduce the issues and lessen the time, and therefore the cost, expended upon this stage of a claim, recognising that in many cases the 'costs of the costs' had become unreasonable and disproportionate. This aim is achieved by a combination of changes—some introducing entirely new concepts and procedures and some being simply variations of what already existed. They are:

- Costs management designed, in part, to reduce the costs in dispute at the conclusion of a claim and reduce for the need for/the scope of assessments. This has been considered in **Chapter 4**.
- The introduction of the further fixed costs schemes considered in **Chapter 7**, removing any need for assessments.
- Improvements to the summary assessment regime.
- A more efficient detailed assessment hearing process.
- The introduction of provisional assessments.
- A change of approach to payments on account of costs.

It is the last four of these upon which we shall concentrate in this chapter.

Summary assessment

8–02 One of the options outlined by Jackson LJ in his preliminary report[1] was to abolish summary assessments altogether. He rejected this, describing the procedure as:

> *"a valuable tool which has made a substantial contribution to civil procedure, not least by deterring frivolous applications and reducing the need for detailed assessment proceedings."*

Instead, the process has been altered, but only slightly, and the emphasis on proportionality is likely to lead to more summary assessments in place of detailed assessments. The procedure for assessing costs by summary assessment is now found at CPR 44.6 and 44 PD 9. It remains familiar.

The court is charged with considering a summary assessment whenever it makes an order about costs that does not provide for fixed costs. The general

[1] Review of Civil Litigation Costs: Preliminary Report, May 2009.

rule is that a court will undertake a summary assessment at the end of a fast track trial and at the conclusion of any other hearing which has lasted not more than a day, unless there is good reason not to do so. There is a further steer to a summary assessment when appropriate at the end of a multi track trial in CPR 29 PD 10.5. There is an issue about whether or not only the judge who has conducted the trial/hearing and made the relevant award of costs order may undertake the summary assessment. In *Transformers and Rectifiers Limited v Needs Limited*[2] the court concluded:

> *"I consider that, in appropriate circumstances, another judge may be able summarily to assess the costs arising out of a hearing conducted (or an order made) by another judge. I do not consider that there is any binding authority under the current version of the CPR to the contrary."*

In fact CPR 44.1, to which no reference was made, does provide that a summary assessment 'means the procedure whereby costs are assessed by the judge who has heard the case or application'. Despite the comment above, in *Transformers and Rectifiers Limited* the court was only expressly considering the position in a more limited context, namely after a disposal of an application 'on the papers'. This is considered in more detail In the question and answer section of this chapter below (see **Q6** below).

The parties must file and serve statements of costs not less than two days before a fast track trial and 24 hours before the time fixed for any other hearing.

The slight changes to the process are:

i) there is a new N260—statement of costs (updated again in June 2015 and still in need of either further amendment or clear guidance in the CPR that where the proportionality transitional arrangements apply (CPR 44.3(7)) there must be two Forms N260 -one for each proportionality period); and
ii) the requirement to serve a statement of costs in advance now applies to Detailed Assessment hearings and the summary assessment of the costs of those proceedings.

i. The new N260—statement of costs

8–03 One of the major criticisms of the previous version of the N260, particularly where the summary assessment was of the entire costs of a claim, as distinct from a discrete application, was the lack of information that it contained. The new N260 ensures that the assessing judge has more detail by introducing a breakdown of the time spent on documents. CPR 44 PD 9.5(3) is no more prescriptive than its predecessor and only requires that "the statement of costs should follow as closely as possible Form N260". However, given the increased emphasis on enforcing practice direction compliance in the overriding objective at CPR 1.2(f), it will be a bold practitioner who uses a 'homemade' variation,

[2] *Transformers and Rectifiers Limited v Needs Limited [2015] EWHC 1687 (TCC).*

as there is likely to be little sympathy, rather the prospect of some sanction, if the form used does not provide the information necessary in clear terms.

ii. The requirement to serve a statement of costs in advance of detailed assessment hearings

Rule changes made by omission of previous provisions are often overlooked as they are harder to spot. The provision previously found at s.45.3 of the Costs Practice Direction is no more. Parties seeking the costs of a detailed assessment must comply with the provisions of CPR 44 PD 9.5(4) and file and serve an N260 24 hours before the assessment. **8–04**

The change of emphasis

A decision as to whether to undertake a summary assessment or to order a detailed assessment is a case management decision. The amended overriding objective applies to all case management decisions and requires the court to consider the proportionality of its decision. Notwithstanding the 'costs cap' in the provisional assessment regime (see below), there can be little argument that a summary assessment requires significantly less resource, both in costs and in court time, than a detailed assessment. Accordingly, there should be an increased number of summary assessments. The likelihood of this is enhanced by the fact that many of the multi track cases that might previously have gone to a detailed assessment will have been subject to costs management orders and, absent 'good reason', the court will only be troubled by the non budgeted costs—reducing the scope of, and the time needed for, a summary assessment. **8–05**

Parties wishing to seek summary assessment at the end of trials/hearing that exceed one day should ensure that Forms N260 are available to the court and have been served so that this is a realistic option for the court if time permits (even if summary assessment does not take place, the N260 can, in appropriate cases then be referred to as the basis for a payment on account). Whilst there is sometimes resistance to a summary assessment where the costs are substantial, it is interesting that para.F14.2 of the Admiralty and Commercial Courts Guide envisages summary assessments of the costs of interim applications where the statement of costs of the receiving party is no more than £100,000, but requires parties to be prepared for the court to undertake such an assessment even where the costs exceed this sum. This increased emphasis on the court to undertake summary assessments is illustrated by the provision at CPR 51 PDN 2.59, that, save in exceptional circumstances, the court will undertake such an assessment at the conclusion of cases proceeding under the Shorter Trial Pilot (which means summary assessment of cases where there has been up to a four day trial).

Detailed assessment hearing process

In chapter 45 of his Final Report, Jackson LJ set out a number of recommendations designed to produce a more efficient and proportionate detailed **8–06** assessment process. One, provisional assessment, is considered separately below. The others were:

- A new format of user-friendly bill that is inexpensive to prepare and ultimately can be linked to the same time capturing system that can prepare client costs estimates and Forms H for costs budgeting.
- Shorter and more focused Points of Dispute and Replies.
- Compulsory offers.
- The cross application of CPR 36 to detailed assessment proceedings generally and the requirement upon the paying party to make an open offer.
- Clarity on the date from which time runs to appeal decisions made in the detailed assessment.
- Paper assessments when only disbursements are in issue.

Save in respect of the first of these recommendations, in respect of which a voluntary pilot has been operating in the SCCO since 1 October 2015 (see CPR 51 PDL) with the intention that this becomes a formal pilot at some stage in 2016 (it was originally to be April, but has been deferred to an unspecified date, with the voluntary pilot being extended until 20 September 2016), the remainder were introduced in April 2013 by the following provisions:

- CPR 47 PD 8.2 requires Points of Dispute to be 'short and to the point'. If a Reply is served (and it remains optional) it must be limited to points of principle and concessions (CPR 47 PD 12.1).
- Under CPR 47 PD 8.3 the paying party must make an open offer to accompany the Points of Dispute.
- CPR 47.20 expressly applies the provisions of CPR 36 to detailed assessment proceedings (it is worth noting that any CPR 47.20 offer does not need to be the same as the open offer).
- CPR 47.14(7) makes it plain that where the assessment takes place at more than one hearing, the time for appealing does not run until the conclusion of the final hearing (presumably this also means that where there is only one hearing, but over many days, the time for appealing any decision, regardless of which day it was made upon, does not run until the conclusion of the assessment).
- CPR 47 PD 5.7 contains provisions for limited bills and paper assessments where the only dispute between the parties concerns disbursements.

Apart from the implementation of the recommendations above, the introduction of provisional assessment and the requirement to file and serve a Form N260 24 hours before the assessment hearing (see above), the procedure for detailed assessments largely remains as it was prior to April 2013. However, there have been two subsequent significant procedural amendments to detailed assessment proceedings – one to address the difficulties posed on an assessment of costs in a case subject to a costs management order pending the introduction of a new form of bill to facilitate comparison between any budgeted sum and the sum claimed on assessment for a particular phase and to identify those costs outside CPR 3.18 which remain for assessment on the basis of reasonableness and proportionality and the other to provide certainty as to the correct proportionality test to apply where the transitional proportionality provisions apply under CPR 44.3(7) – see Chapter 3 and in particular Question 5 for more detailed consideration of these arrangements. The specific provisions apply from 6 April 2016 and are as follows:

- CPR 47.6 and CPR 47 PD 5.8(8) provide that where a costs management order has been made and the costs are to be assessed on the standard basis (so CPR 3.18 applies see Chapter 4), the bill must be divided into separate parts so as to distinguish between the costs claimed for each phase of the last approved or agreed budget, and within each such part the bill must distinguish between the costs shown as incurred in the last agreed or approved budget and the costs shown as estimated. To make the comparison even easier CPR 47.6(1)(c) requires the bill to be accompanied by a breakdown of the costs claimed for each phase of the proceedings. An amendment from October 2015 introducing CPR 47 PD 5.2(f) and 13.2(m) already required the paying party to serve and file a breakdown of the costs claimed for each phase of the proceedings. CPR 47 PD 5.1A refers to the new Precedent Q in the Schedule of Costs Precedents to CPR 47 PD as a model form of such a breakdown.
- CPR 47 PD 5.8(7) provides that in any cases commenced on or after 1 April 2013, where the bill is to be assessed on the standard basis and covers costs for work done both before and after that date, the bill must be divided into parts so as to distinguish between costs shown as incurred for work done before 1 April 2013 and costs shown as incurred for work done on or after 1 April 2013.

Provisional assessment

In his final report, Jackson LJ recommended the introduction of provisional assessment under a pilot scheme. The pilot took place in certain courts in respect of bills for £25,000 and under. In the April 2013 amendments, the scheme was extended to all courts and applies to any 'between the parties' bill where the costs claimed are £75,000 or less. 8–07

A provisional assessment is one undertaken by the court on the basis of papers filed, without an oral hearing and any attendance by the parties. There is a limited opt-out provision found at CPR 47.15(6), under which the court may at any time consider the bill unsuitable for provisional assessment and may list for hearing with the procedure for a detailed assessment hearing then applying.

The procedure is set out at CPR 47.15 and 47 PD 14. It can be divided into four stages as follows:

i) Pre-assessment.
ii) The assessment.
iii) After the assessment excluding an oral hearing.
iv) Oral hearings.

i) Pre-assessment

8–08 The title given to CPR 47 relates exclusively to detailed assessment. There can be no doubt that a provisional assessment is a form of detailed assessment. As such it is not surprising that many of the procedural provisions relating to the request for an assessment borrow heavily from those for detailed assessment hearings. However, at the pre-assessment stage there is a fundamental difference in respect of documents required. Other than the documents that must be filed with the request itself under CPR 47 PD.13.2 and 14.3(b)–(e) there is no requirement to file further documents in support of the bill between 14 and 7 days before the assessment—although the Senior Court Costs Office ("SCCO") Guide 2013 makes provision for a specific order to comply with the CPR 47 PD 13.2 filing obligation if the request has not been accompanied by these documents. Significantly, CPR 47 PD 13.11 does not apply to provisional assessments, but the court retains the power to direct the filing of any further documents which the court considers that it needs to reach a decision. At the moment there appear to be conflicting practices around the country with some courts requiring all documents in support as if this were a normal detailed assessment hearing, some simply making requests for specific documents when needed and some requesting no documents at all. This is entirely a matter of judicial discretion. Note that unlike the position for detailed assessment hearings, the receiving party must file any CPR 36 offers (in a sealed envelope marked "Part 36 or similar offers", but which does not reveal which party/ies have made the offers). The rationale is obvious—parties are not present to draw the attention of the court to any relevant offers as they would be at the end of a detailed assessment.

ii) The assessment

8–09 Strictly there is no requirement either for the court to fix a date for a provisional assessment or to give notice of it as CPR 47 PD 13.4 and 13.6 do not apply and the parties are not permitted to attend the assessment. The only obligation on the court is to use its best endeavours to undertake the assessment within six weeks of receipt of the request. In practice in the SCCO and the County Court, non attended hearing dates are being allocated—in other words the judge has time specifically allocated in the list to deal with a provisional assessment even though no parties attend. Some come with a further order that should the court be able to undertake the assessment at an earlier date it will do so without notice to the parties. The rationale behind these orders is understandable. The Costs Judges and the District Bench simply cannot accommodate these assessments in addition to other work requirements and so discrete time is made available within lists. However, should lists go short and there not be other work, then the further order enables the court to undertake these assessments earlier than listed.

CPR 47.15(4) is clear that the assessment is based on the information in the bill, the supporting papers and the contentions in Form G (the Points of Dispute and any Reply to it). Documents filed beyond those required by the rules or by specific requests from the court may be ignored by the assessing judge and met with a request to arrange collection of them from the court staff. The rules are clear as to what documents must be considered and there is no obligation on the assessing judge to look at further documents filed unbidden (particularly when the time set aside for the assessment will not have been based on consideration of unrequested paperwork).

iii) After the assessment

After the assessment the court will return the Form G (and the bill or any other documents, if decisions have been recorded on these). Whilst CPR 47 PD 14.4(2) suggests that the court's decisions will be on the Form G, the decisions may be on that, may be on the bill or on a separate document—for example where the court is giving a written judgment on a substantive point and there is insufficient room to do this on the bill or Form G. On this point parties would be well advised to allow sufficient space for the judicial decision—too often a lengthy Point and Reply are followed by an utterly inadequate box for the reasoned determination. **8–10**

The parties must agree the amount at which the court has assessed the bill within 14 days and any party wishing to challenge any aspect of the provisional assessment must file and serve a written request for an oral hearing within 21 days. If no request for an oral hearing is filed and served within that period then, save in exceptional circumstances, the provisional assessment is binding.

Practice varies on how costs of the provisional assessment itself are assessed where there is no challenge to the assessment. Some courts make costs orders when conducting the provisional assessment on alternative bases depending on whether or not any offers prove to be relevant. This becomes more complicated when the bill, or part of it, is subject to the proportionality cross check under CPR 44.3(2)(a) after the court has determined what is the reasonably incurred and reasonable in amount sum. (see **Q.21** below).

The costs of the assessment are subject to the provisions of CPR 47.20 and the general rule is that the receiving party is entitled to the costs. CPR 47.15(5) caps the maximum costs the court will award to either party (other than the costs of drafting the bill and excluding court fees and VAT) at £1,500.

iv) Oral hearings

Any written request for an oral hearing must identify the item(s) challenged and provide a time estimate for the hearing of the challenge(s). On receipt of the notice the court will then fix a date for the hearing, giving at least 14 days notice to the parties. **8–11**

The party requesting the oral hearing will pay the costs of that hearing unless it achieves an adjustment in its favour of 20 per cent or more of the sum provisionally assessed or the court orders otherwise. This potential costs penalty clearly is designed to preclude minor challenges. On a bill where the costs are limited to £75,000 anything other than a challenge to an item of substance is unlikely to result in a 20 per cent adjustment. There is limited guidance in CPR 47 PD 14.5 as to when the court may order otherwise, indicating that conduct and offers will be taken into account. As yet no authorities have emerged to supplement this guidance.

It is worth reiterating that a request for an oral hearing, as opposed to an application for permission to appeal, is the correct procedure to challenge any decision made on a provisional assessment.

A final word

8–12 Those keen to ensure that they comply with all relevant rules in the light of the more robust compliance regime now in place may find it a relief that CPR 47 PD 14.2(2) does not require compliance with CPR 47 PD 13.9 as this provision does not seem to exist.

Payment on account

8–13 Prior to April 2013 where the court made an order that a party was to pay costs it could order a payment on account of those costs pending an assessment. There was no presumption that it would do so, as was made clear in *Blackmore v Cummins*.[3] The April 2013 reforms reversed this by the introduction of CPR 44.2(8), which provides that where the court makes a costs order and provides for a detailed assessment of those costs, then it will order a reasonable sum on account of those costs, unless there is good reason not to do so. This provision has also changed, seeming to make a temporal link between the order for costs to be assessed and the payment on account. Many courts interpret this to mean that there can only be one payment on account, with this being ordered at the time of the costs order and that any further interim sums can only be obtained under the procedure for an interim costs certificate *after* the receiving party has filed a request for a detailed assessment hearing.

In pursuit of proportionality the court is likely to adopt a robust procedure when determining the amount of any payment on account. In *Kazakhstan Kagazy PLC & ors v Zhunus & ors*[4] Leggatt J was asked to list a 1/2 day hearing to determine the amount of any payment. In dealing with the matter without a hearing he concluded:

> *"The third request made in the claimants' letter is that, if the court intends to make an order for a payment on account of costs, a half day hearing should be fixed for this purpose for which the claimants would wish to instruct a specialist costs counsel. Not only is this request contrary to the terms of the order agreed by*

[3] *Blackmore v Cummins* [2009] EWCA Civ 1276.

[4] *Kazakhstan Kagazy PLC & ors v Zhunus & ors [2015] EWHC 404 (Comm).*

the claimants for the matter to be dealt with on paper, but to incur the costs of a half day hearing to argue about the amount of a payment on account of the costs of a two day hearing would be utterly disproportionate and wasteful."

Questions and answers

Summary and detailed assessment

Q1. What is the position when form N260 is either served/filed late or not at all?

CPR 44 PD.9.6 maintains the previous position—namely that a failure to file and serve form N260 without reasonable excuse will be taken into account when the court determines what order to make about costs of the claim or hearing (as appropriate) and about the costs of any further hearings/assessments which the failure may necessitate (so the failure is relevant both to the award, as well as the amount, of assessed costs). **8–14**

The leading pre-April 2013 authority on this provision is *MacDonald v Taree Holdings Ltd.*[5] The appellate court held that despite the use of the word 'must', the provision is not mandatory and the judge had been wrong to refuse the successful party's application for summary assessment of his costs on the grounds that he had not served a statement of costs upon the respondent 24 hours in advance. The court made a distinction between cases where there had and had not been factors aggravating the failure to serve a statement. If there were no aggravating features then a party should not be deprived of all his costs. The court should take the matter into account but its reaction should be proportionate. In these cases the court was presented with three options as follows:

- Whether it would be appropriate to have a brief adjournment for the paying party to consider the statement and then to proceed to a summary assessment of the costs. In such a case the 'sanction' was that the judge should err in favour of awarding a lighter figure.
- Whether the matter should be stood over for a detailed assessment.
- Whether the matter should be adjourned for summary assessment at a later date or for summary assessment to be dealt with in writing.

Does this approach survive the April 2013 reforms? In *Webb v E-Serv,*[6] albeit in an entirely different context of considering the time period to renew a request for permission to appeal, Turner J held that the word 'must' did convey a mandatory requirement. If this applied to a failure to comply with the provisions of CPR 44 PD 9.5 a party otherwise entitled to a costs order may not secure it as that provision makes the preparation, lodging and serving of a statement of costs a condition precedent to applying for costs (CPR 44 PD 9.5 **8–15**

[5] *MacDonald v Taree Holdings Ltd* [2001] C.P.L.R.439; [2001] 1 Costs L.R.147, Neuberger J.

[6] *Webb v E-Serv* [2014] EWHC 49 (QB) Turner J.

refers to the fact that a party intending to seek costs must prepare a written statement and CPR 44 PD 9.5(4) states that this must be filed and served the prescribed amount of time before the hearing).

However, the outcome of two cases, one where no statement of costs had been filed or served and the other where the statement had been filed and served late, suggests that the court is still resisting complete disallowance of costs.

In *Wheeler v The Chief Constable of Gloucestershire Constabulary*,[7] neither party had filed a statement of costs in advance of an appeal. The upshot for the successful party was an order for costs to be the subject of a detailed assessment, but with the receiving party to pay the costs of those proceedings.

In contrast, in *Kingsley v Orban*,[8] where the successful party had filed and served a statement late and the first instance court had pressed on and assessed those costs without any concession to the late service, the appellate court looked at whether there were aggravating factors, determined there were not, but that the first instance court ought to have adjourned for a short period to allow the paying party time to consider the statement before proceeding to assess, and allowed the paying party to raise further points on appeal (all of which failed). However, it is worth mentioning that the judgment makes no reference to the decision in *Wheeler*, instead determining that there was no reason not to apply *MacDonald*

8–16 A halfway house was adopted by Akenhead J in *Group M UK Ltd v Cabinet Office*,[9] where a statement of costs was served only three hours before the handing down of a judgment when costs would be considered and, even then, that N260 did not contain the breakdown of time spent on documents. Akenhead J applied the *Denton v T H White*[10] three stage test to the breaches, concluding that the breaches were serious, that there was good reason for them and that it would be wholly disproportionate to allow no costs and, instead, imposed a 'delay discount' of £2,240 as a sanction for what he described as a breach "at the lower end of serious".

Inevitably decisions will be case-specific. For example, whilst it may be appropriate to adjourn some cases for a detailed assessment where there is failure to file and serve a statement, if this failure were to occur in respect of a discrete application where the costs would be minimal, the court may take the view that an adjournment for a subsequent summary or detailed assessment in such a case would, applying the overriding objective, be disproportionate (even if the receiving party had to pay the costs of the assessment, as court time would have to be allocated to this). In such a case the court may determine that the successful party forfeits the right to a costs order on the application.

Avoid the uncertainty and the risk—comply!

[7] *Wheeler v The Chief Constable of Gloucestershire Constabulary* [2013] EWCA Civ 1791.
[8] *Kingsley v Orban* [2014] EWHC 2991 (Ch) Nugee J.
[9] *Group M UK Ltd v Cabinet Office* [2014] EWHC 3863 (TCC) Akenhead J.
[10] *Denton v T H White* [2014] EWCA Civ 906.

Q2. Does the introduction of the breakdown of time spent on documents on the Form N260 mean that the court will deal with challenges to this on an item by item basis or will the court make one overall assessment of time spent on documents?

Notwithstanding the additional information provided in the documents schedule to the costs statement, the process remains a summary assessment. 8–17
As such it would be inappropriate to expect the court to resort to micro management. The schedule was not introduced to turn summary assessments into quasi detailed assessments. Indeed, in his Final Report Jackson LJ indicated that he thought the 'old' N260 was adequate in respect of interim applications. His concern was that:

> *"in respect of summary assessments at the end of a trial or appeal, I consider that Form N260 provides insufficient information. The court is assessing not only costs related to the trial or appeal, but also the costs of the whole pre-trial process. In the short term, I recommend that a revised and more informative version of Form N260 be prepared for use in connection with summary assessments at the end of trial".*

Whilst we would expect the court to entertain submissions that the document time is unreasonable by reference to some examples from the schedule, the court is extremely unlikely to determine disputes over individual items in the schedule—rather it will use the schedule to inform the decision over the total document time that is reasonable or the total time for a particular task, e.g. drafting statements.

Q3. How does the proportionality cross check at CPR 44.3(2) work in the summary assessment process that is already one undertaken with a broad brush?

In *Morgan v Spirit Group Ltd*,[11] when overturning the decision of a recorder, the 8–18
Court of Appeal made the obvious point that the court must undertake either a summary or detailed assessment of the costs. The recorder had not done so. Instead, in a paragraph, the recorder had simply determined a proportionate figure and added something to that to allow for the existence of what he had, erroneously, described as 'a contingent fee agreement'. Summary though the assessment is intended to be, the court concluded that what had taken place here was not a summary assessment. So, summary though the procedure may be, it must still recognisably be an assessment.

These comments resonate loudly under the new regime, where the court is required to undertake an assessment of what is reasonably incurred and reasonable in amount for those items reasonably incurred and then step back and apply the proportionality cross check under CPR 44.3(2)(a). If the summary assessment is too summary, then the court will struggle to draw a distinction between the determination of what is reasonable and the determination

[11] *Morgan v Spirit Group Ltd* [2011] EWCA Civ 6.

of what is proportionate. The court must undertake the determinations of reasonableness and proportionality separately as to do otherwise makes the flawed assumption that the conclusions always elide. They do not. Whilst they will in some cases, there will be cases where the reasonable costs fall within what is proportionate (in which case the court need do no more than articulate that, having considered the factors at CPR 44.3(5), the reasonably assessed costs are also proportionate), there will also be cases where the reasonable costs are not proportionate (in which case the court then determines the figure that is proportionate and assesses the recoverable costs in that sum—see **Chapter 3** on proportionality for more detail as to how the court will undertake this exercise).

Q4. How can the court use the costs budgets at assessment of the costs of the claim when neither the N260 nor the bill is divided into the same phases as the Form H to enable easy comparison?

8–19 It is certainly the case that the N260 does not match the budget phases, making ready comparison impossible. In his Final Report, Jackson LJ looked forward to the day when time capture recording systems would lead to "a new software system should be developed, which will be capable of generating bills of costs at different levels of generality". That day has become closer in the light of CPR 47.6(1)(c), 47 PD 5.8(8) and the voluntary pilot under CPR 51 PDL in the SCCO and the introduction of CPR 47.6(1)(c), 47 PD 5.8(8) and Precedent Q as a temporary fix in all other detailed assessments (see **8–06** above). In the meantime, the 'broad brush' of summary assessment will make it difficult to challenge the sums budgeted for phases that the court has costs managed. As a practical exercise, the budgeted sums will have to be deducted from the total sum claimed in the N260 to calculate what sum must relate to the non budgeted costs and only that sum is, unless there is a 'good reason' to depart from the budget for a specific phase/phases, 'live' at the assessment.

If there is a successful argument that there is a 'good reason' under CPR 3.18 to depart from the budgeted sum for a phase, then the court will have to assess the sum for that phase, deduct the budgeted sum for that phase from the overall budgeted sum and add back what it has assessed.

A more challenging exercise, in a summary assessment where there is no requirement for a breakdown in Precedent Q, or similar, format, will be to argue that the receiving party has overspent on a particular budgeted phase (and compensated for this by an equivalent under spend on another budgeted phase), where the overall sum in the N260 does not exceed the budgeted sums and the costs set out as incurred in the Precedent H at the time of the budget. Of course there is no reason why a party should not produce a breakdown of the budgeted costs on a summary assessment. Whilst this may involve a larger time and costs investment in producing the N260, there is certainly a compelling argument to assist recovery of this namely that this makes it easier for the court to undertake a summary assessment and a summary assessment is more proportionate than deferring to a detailed assessment.

However, even when/if both a new form of bill/N260 are compulsory that enable direct comparison between sums budgeted and spent per phase challenging issues will remain in any claim that has settled and it is found or accepted that not all budgeted work under a particular phase has been completed at the time of settlement (and this is surely a 'good reason' to depart from the budget), it will be difficult to determine what deduction should be made to the bill. This is because the phase budget has rightly been set by reference to what is a reasonable and proportionate sum for that phase and not 7.10 and by an assessment of hourly rate multiplied by time (see CPR 3 PD E.7.3, 7.10 and see **Chapter 4** on case and costs management above). Accordingly, as the budget figure has not been set by overall time multiplied by hourly rates, it is inappropriate simply to work out what work has been done on that phase by reference to such a calculation and to deduct it from the total for that phase. Instead, the court may have to adopt a broad brush and determine what is reasonable and proportionate as a lump sum for the work done on the phase up to settlement and deduct that from the total phase figure.

The preceding paragraphs have concentrated on problems linking budgets to the documents required for assessments and on calculating partial expenditure on phases in settled claims. It would be wrong not to balance the scales by pointing to a couple of positives. One is considered below under payments on account. The other is the simplicity of the assessment where there is no 'good reason' to depart from the budget. A useful illustration of this is the case of *Slick Seating Systems v Adams*.[12] In this case the trial judge had also case and costs managed the case throughout. In fact he concluded that an award of indemnity costs was appropriate (and duly assessed those summarily), but his approach amply illustrates the benefits of costs management as he was able to avoid a detailed assessment (as would probably have been the outcome prior to the costs management regime) and undertake the simplest of summary assessments as follows: **8–20**

> *"By running this case with a costs budget, I approved a budget of a grand total of £359,710.35 pence for doing this case through to trial. In my judgment that budget was proportionate to what was at stake: the £4.4million sum that I have just awarded. The claimants have laudably kept within that budget and have exercised due control over their activities and expenditure in an exemplary fashion. The statement of costs on 13.5.13 (which is today) is favourably compared with the costs estimate of 22.5.12. The form is signed by the partner of the solicitors and a member of the client company as well, Mr Beasley; the grand total is £351,267.35 pence. In my judgment that is a sum which is, looking at each of the phases, within the budget that was set and the claimants are to be commended with controlling the budget throughout this particular period.*
>
> *That will be the sum that I would award to be paid within 14 days without the need for detailed assessment, detailed assessment becoming otiose . . ."*

[12] *Slick Seating Systems v Adams* [2013] EWHC 1642 (QB); [2013] 4 Costs LR 576, HH Judge Simon Brown QC.

Q5. Albeit in a family context, does not the case of SB v MB (Costs)[13] suggest that summary assessment is confined to fast track trials and other hearings lasting a day or less?

8–21 In *SB v MB (Costs)* Hayden J declined to undertake a summary assessment as to do so was "likely to fall foul" of what was para.13.2 of the Costs Practice Direction. In fact, the relevant provisions he identified of what was 13.2 (namely that this was not a fast track trial and that the hearing had exceeded one day) are in the same terms as what now appears at CPR 44 PD 9.2(a) and (b)). However, it is clear that the possibility of 'falling foul' of the Practice Direction was not determinative. Hayden J had already identified that there were elements of costs which would require consideration beyond the time and information available to the court that day. As such there was no need for the court to consider the application of the 'general rule' at what is CPR 44 PD 9.1 and was Costs PD 13.1 and the other steers referred to above illustrating that CPR 44 PD 9.2 is not an inflexible strait jacket (e.g. CPR 29 PD 10.5).

Q6. Does the decision in Transformers and Rectifiers Limited v Needs Limited[14] mean that summary assessments of the costs a) of applications, whether disposed of either at a hearing or on the papers and, b) after trials, may be conducted by a judge other than the one who dealt with the application/trial?

8–22 As set out at paragraph 8–02 above, CPR 44.1 seems clear that if there is to be a summary assessment after a hearing or a trial, this can only be undertaken by the judge who conducted the hearing or trial. Strictly this definition does not seem to apply where an application is disposed of on the papers, as was, in fact the case in *Transformers and Rectifiers Limited,* This is because CPR 23.8 makes it clear that the court may 'deal' with an application without a hearing. In this situation the less prescriptive provisions of CPR 44 PD 9.7 apply. Applying these the court reached its conclusion by noting the substitution of the word *'may'* in the current version instead of the word *'must'* in the previous versions in the phrase *'may give directions as to a further hearing before the same judge'* and interpreted this as permissive of a summary assessment by another judge, stating that:

> *'"The provision at paragraph 9.7 of the PD is permissive: if time does not permit the summary assessment then and there, it may be heard later by the same judge. Equally, therefore, it may be heard by another judge"*

If this interpretation is correct and any judge may deal with the summary assessment at a further hearing, then what purpose do the words *'by the same judge'* serve in CPR 44 PD 9.7? The alternative construction, and one that makes use of the words *'by the same judge'* purposeful, is that where a summary assessment is appropriate, but not possible immediately upon disposal of

[13] *SB v MB (Costs)* [2014] EWHC 3721 (Fam).
[14] *Transformers and Rectifiers Limited v Needs Limited [2015] EWHC 1687 (TCC).*

an application, the word *'may'* is permissive of a choice, between either a summary assessment at a later date before the same judge or of a detailed assessment.

Q7. In the light of the voluntary 'new bill' pilot introduced in the SCCO what, if anything, should practitioners be doing in anticipation of the new bill format becoming compulsory?

In essence this question is not only about the format of the 'new bill' in the form of Precedent AA,, but also about the way in which solicitors' time is recorded and the adoption of J-codes. One reason that the 'compulsory pilot scheme' in the SCCO has been put back reflects concern that it is premature because insufficient numbers of practitioners have been recording time adopting the J-codes, or in some other fashion which enables similar information to be produced as easily, to enable production of bills in the new format by the proposed start of that pilot. Given that: **8–23**

- A primary purpose of the new bill is to enable ready comparison between costs claimed and costs budgeted (see page 12 of Precedent AA).
- Pending the compulsory introduction of a new bill, CPR 47 PD 5.2(f) requires a breakdown of the costs claimed for each phase of the proceedings in claims in which a costs management order has been made.
- Costs management appears here to stay (see **Chapter 4**).
- CPR 47.6(1)(c) and CPR 47 PD5.8(8) require a paying party to be able to divide the costs claimed between phases and, within phases, between incurred and budgeted sums (see **8-06** above).

the sooner that solicitors time is recorded using a system that readily provides the information that permits easy comparison between overall costs claimed and non-budgeted (incurred costs at the time of the costs management hearing) and budgeted sums (costs subject to a costs management order) by phases, the better. This should not be something new. In any claim subject to a costs management order since the inception of the regime almost three years ago, solicitors ought to have been recording time in a way that enables them to monitor expenditure against budget for those phases budgeted.

Another obvious advantage of time recording in such a specific manner means that the entire time recording process becomes a more transparent one in the event of any dispute over fees between solicitor and client.

Q8. Who is responsible for the costs of providing the breakdown required in a model form like Precedent Q?

As production of this information is now a requirement in cases where a costs management order has been made and the bill must be divided into parts matching the budgeted phases, then this forms part of the bill preparation item. As such, subject to the receiving party being awarded the costs of the assessment, then it should recover the reasonable and proportionate costs **8–24** of preparation of the form. However, certainly to begin with, if time has not been recorded in a fashion that leads to easy allocation to a particular phase, what is reasonable and proportionate may be the source of some argument—(the same point applies to bill preparation time).

Q9. Does qualified one-way costs shifting ("QOCS") apply to the detailed assessment procedure?

8–25 To date there has been very little authority on QOCS. The question of what constituted proceedings for the purpose of CPR 44.13 was considered in *Wagenaar v Weekend Travel Ltd (T/A Ski Weekend and Nawelle Serradj*.[15] There was no doubt that the claim between claimant and defendant was a personal injury claim, but the court construed "proceedings which include a claim for damages for personal injuries narrowly" and determined that an additional claim by the defendant for an indemnity from the third party was not 'proceedings' for the purpose of CPR 44.13. However, the court was clear that where there is a single claim against one or more defendants which includes a claim specified in CPR 44.13(1) (even if there are other components to the claim such as property damage), QOCS applies to the entire claim.

Applying *Wagenaar*, it might seem that if the detailed assessment is in respect of costs in a single claim against one or more defendants for one of the types of claim specified in CPR 44.13(1), then QOCS protection applies to the costs of the assessment process. However, *Wagenaar* was not considering this situation and the judgment is confined to consideration of the substantive litigation between the parties. The wording of CPR 44.14(2) appears to support the alternative view:

> *"44.14(2) Orders for costs made against a claimant may only be enforced after the proceedings have been concluded and the costs have been assessed or agreed."*

The use of the word 'and' suggests that the process of assessment or agreement of costs is in addition to the proceedings, which conclude at the end of the substantive dispute involving one of the types of claim in CPR 44.13(1). On that basis we lean to the conclusion that QOCS protection does not apply to the costs of the detailed assessment process. This conclusion gains further support from CPR 47.20(7) which, albeit in the context of consideration of CPR Part 36, expressly provides that detailed assessment proceedings "are to be regarded as an independent claim".

This may be a moot point where it matters not by what route the claimant has to pay any costs of the detailed assessment (namely where the damages are such that QOCS protection would not prevent off-setting in full anyway against damages and it is only the route by which the court reaches this outcome that turns on the construction of 'proceedings'), but, where there is insufficient to off-set, this argument is pertinent. A definition

[15] *Wagenaar v Weekend Travel Ltd (T/A Ski Weekend and Nawelle Serradj* [2014] EWCA Civ 110.

of 'proceedings' for the purpose of CPR 44.13–44.17 would provide welcome certainty.

See **Chapter 6** for a detailed consideration of QOCS.

Q10. Is there any sanction if a paying party fails to make an open offer under CPR 47 PD 8.3?

On the face of it no sanction applies to this provision. However, the Court of Appeal expressly considered provisions of the CPR which contain mandatory language, but where no sanction is provided for any failure to comply in *Altomart v Salford Estates (No.2) Ltd.*[16] The court accepted the proposition that there might be implied sanctions which were capable of engaging CPR 3.9 and equally there might be cases not analogous with CPR 3.9 and where it was a matter for the court to determine the consequence of non compliance. 8–26

Accordingly, it seems that if a paying party wishes to rely on an open offer made after the service of the Points of Dispute, where no such offer accompanied that document, then, by implication the court should approach this as analogous to an application for relief from sanction. The outcome of any applications made by 'receiving parties' for some sort of sanction are far less predictable. It is clear that the open offer does not form part of the Points of Dispute (it merely accompanies that document) and therefore it is difficult to see how any argument suggesting that the Points of Dispute should be struck out will find favour (indeed there is a risk it will be seen as an attempt to turn the rules into 'tripwires' and invoke possible costs sanctions). Perhaps a more measured approach is to identify the failure to comply to the paying party promptly, suggesting a short period for rectification, and, in default of compliance reserve the position to the question of costs of the assessment, if relevant, under 'conduct' within CPR 47.20(3)(a).

Provisional Assessment

Q11. Does the £75,000 limit for provisional assessment include or exclude VAT?

This is a purely procedural point. CPR 47.15 and its PD provisions describe the limit of £75,000 as being in respect of costs. The definition of 'costs' in CPR 44.1 does not include a reference to VAT (albeit that this is not an exhaustive list)—in fact, VAT is defined separately in the same rule. Accordingly, it seems that the £75,000 limit does not include VAT and refers to the total profit costs and disbursement sum. There is also a clear logic to this. Why should one bill fall within the scheme and one not where the difference is the VAT and one party is VAT registered and the other is not where the non VAT sums claimed are equal? Notwithstanding this, many practitioners are not completing the provisional assessment part of form 8–27

[16] *Altomart v Salford Estates (No.2) Ltd* [2014] EWCA Civ 1408.

N258 and are requesting detailed assessment hearings where the total sum only exceeds £75,000 because of the VAT.

Q12. Does the £75,000 limit for provisional assessment include 'additional liabilities' (where the transitional provisions still permit recovery of these between the parties)?

8–28 Yes. The limit of £75,000 makes no reference to 'base' costs, referring instead simply to 'costs'. The definition of 'costs' under the previous regime at what was CPR 43.2(1)(a) included 'additional liabilities.

Q13. There seems to be a feeling that a paying party who does not serve Replies to the Points of Dispute is at a disadvantage at a provisional assessment. Should receiving parties serve Replies in this situation as a matter of course?

8–29 CPR 47.13, which makes Replies optional, and CPR 47 PD 12, which requires Replies to be limited to points of principle and concessions, both apply to provisional assessment by virtue of the provisions of CPR 47 PD 14.2. Accordingly, the court ought not to be penalising a party who complies with these provisions. Indeed the reverse is true and the court ought to be astute not to entertain Replies that contain 'general denials, specific denials or standard form responses'. Replies should not be filed as a matter of routine and there should be no disadvantage to the receiving party as a result.

By the same token, paying parties should not serve 'extended' Points of Dispute in an attempt to make up for the fact that there will be no opportunity for oral submissions. CPR 47 PD 8.2 is unambiguous—Points of Dispute must be 'short and to the point'.

Q14. Does the costs cap include or exclude success fees (where the transitional provisions still permit recovery of success fees between the parties)?

8–30 The costs cap may include both base costs and success fees. The qualification is that combined they cannot exceed £1,500. So, by way of examples:

- If the base costs are assessed at £750 and the success uplift is allowed at 100 per cent, then both base costs and success fees are recoverable in full, as together they do not exceed the cap.
- If the base costs are assessed at £1,000 and the success uplift is allowed at 100 per cent, then the base costs are recoverable in full, but only £500 of the success fee is recoverable.
- If the base costs are assessed at £1,500 and the success uplift is allowed at 100 per cent, then the base costs are recoverable in full, but none of the success fee is recoverable.

Q15. Can the court make an award of indemnity costs under CPR 36.17(4)(b) in provisional assessment proceedings and, if so, what, if any effect does this have on the costs cap of £1,500.

The starting point is that CPR 36.17(4) is relevant in provisional assessments by virtue of CPR 47 PD14.2, which applies CPR 47.20 to these proceedings. However, whilst CPR 36.17(4)(b) applies, an entitlement to costs on the indemnity basis does not mean that the cap may be exceeded. Instead, it simply means that the court approaches the determination of costs up to the cap of £1,500 on the basis of allowing reasonably incurred and reasonable in amount costs, with the benefit of any doubt going to the receiving party. 8–31

Whilst the decision in *Broadhurst v Tan*[17] provides that an award of indemnity costs to a claimant under CPR 36.17(4)(b) in a fixed costs regime case under CPR 45 permits escape from that regime, as is clear from what is set out in the paragraph above, such an award does not have the same effect in the provisional assessment regime. This is because although CPR 36 applies to detailed assessment proceedings (CPR 47.20(4)), and provisional assessments are a form of detailed assessment proceeding (CPR 47.15(1)), an indemnity costs order for the claimant under CPR 36.17(4)(b) in provisional assessment proceedings does not alter the fact that the maximum recovery in such proceedings is £1500. This is because CPR 47.15(5) is a specific rule and, as such, trumps any more general provisions of CPR 47, including 47.20 and, therefore, by cross reference CPR 36.Whilst CPR 47 PD 14.2(1) applies CPR 47.20 to provisional assessments, there is nothing in either the rule or the practice direction which provides that the £1,500 cap does not apply when there is an award of indemnity costs under CPR 36.17(4). Accordingly, the effect of an indemnity costs order does not remove the claimant from the restraints of CPR 47.15(5). Instead it means that when determining the claimant's recoverable costs the court does so applying the indemnity basis test at CPR 44.4(1)(b), but with a maximum award of £1,500. 8–31A

Q16. Does the costs cap include the additional amount under CPR 36.17(4)(d) as applied by CPR 47.20?

The 'additional amount' under CPR 36.17(4)(d) is not defined in CPR 36.17, CPR 47.20 or elsewhere in the rules. Perhaps of more significance is that the phrase does not appear in the definition of costs in CPR 44.1. In these circumstances it is certainly arguable that it is a sum outside the cap. This interpretation would make sense of the word 'additional' and also give effect to the purpose of CPR 47.20, namely to encourage settlement by the threat to the paying party of a heightened liability if a reasonable proposal is not accepted. This view is supported by the decision in *OOO Abbott v Design and Display Ltd*,[18] where it was argued that the 'additional amount' counted towards the £500,000 cap in the Intellectual Property Enterprise Court. HHJ Hacon held that the 'additional amount' had nothing to do with compensation, but was solely to do with a procedure to serve as an incentive to encourage claimants 8–32

[17] *Broadhurst v Tan* [2016] EWCA Civ 94

[18] *OOO Abbott v Design and Display Ltd* [2014] EWHC 3234 (IPEC) HHJ Hacon.

to make appropriate offers. In other words 'additional amount' is not defined because it is simply that, an additional amount.

Q17. How does the £1,500 cap operate in respect of cases that are dealt with under the provisional assessment provisions, but where there are interim applications, e.g. to set aside a default costs certificate, for an interim costs certificate or for relief from sanction?

8–33 It is important to stress that the costs cap of £1,500 at CPR 47.15(5) is the maximum amount that the court will award to any party as the costs of the assessment.

If there is an application to set aside a default costs certificate, then it seems that cannot be an application made within the assessment, as by definition, at that time, there is a default costs certificate with the costs of the assessment proceedings dealt with under CPR 47.11. As such, any application to set aside a default costs certificate appears to be a free standing application and the costs under any award of costs fall to be assessed (one would expect summarily) there and then as costs of that discrete application.

Similarly, an application for relief from sanction—presumably in connection with the late service of a Reply to the Points of Dispute—seems to be a free standing application. It is not part of the assessment process set out in CPR 47. As such it follows that any costs awarded on such an application would not be costs of the assessment and would be entirely separate from the cap. Indeed, in both this scenario and that relating to default costs certificates, it is conceivable that the costs of these applications will be awarded to a different party than the one which is awarded the costs of the assessment.

It is arguable that there is no jurisdiction for the court to issue an interim costs certificate in a provisional assessment. This is because CPR 47.16(1), which enables the court to issue such a certificate, relates to cases where the receiving party has filed a request for a detailed assessment hearing. The very nature of the provisional assessment regime dispenses with hearings save where the court determines that the matter is unsuitable for the regime and lists a hearing or, after the assessment on paper, when a party requests an oral hearing. Having said this, CPR 47 PD 14.2 applies CPR 47.14(1) to the provisional assessment regime and the wording of that provision refers to a 'request for a detailed assessment hearing'. In reality, the point is unlikely to arise as CPR 47 PD 14.4(1) provides that the court will use its best endeavours to undertake the provisional assessment within six weeks of receipt of the request. This is reinforced in para.10.2(e) of the SCCO Guide 2013, which states that any application for an interim costs certificate in a case proceeding to a provisional assessment will not be listed for hearing before the date fixed for the provisional assessment unless there is some good reason for an early listing.

Q18. Is the amount of the bill or the sum in which it is assessed in a provisional assessment likely to inform how much of the capped fee is

awarded, e.g. does a bill of £70,000 justify an award of a higher proportion of the £1,500 than a bill of £20,000?

There is no straightforward answer to this. The cap is not set as a sliding scale. It will depend entirely upon what the court determines is the reasonable and proportionate sum in any given case. Value alone does not determine this. There may be complex points of principle raised for determination within the assessment of a £20,000 bill that do not arise in a bill of £70,000. This links to the factors defining proportionality at CPR 44.3(5) and factors relevant to the assessment of costs at CPR 44.4(3). 8–34

Q19. Can the court make more than one award of costs for the provisional assessment and, if so, is the total amount apportioned between the parties limited to £1,500 or may there be separate awards to each party, each with a cap of £1,500?

CPR Pt 47.20 applies to the principle of the award of costs of the assessment proceedings. As such there is a general rule (47.20(1)(a)) that the receiving party will recover the costs of the assessment. However, this is immediately qualified to permit the court to make some other order in respect of all or part of the costs of the assessment (47.20(1)(b)). CPR 47.20(3) then lists specific considerations, amongst all the circumstances, that the court must take into account and CPR 47.20(4) applies CPR 36. It is clear from this that the court may decide to make more than one costs award in the assessment (perhaps taking into account when a CPR 36 offer was made). However, when considering this the court must consider the terms of CPR 44.2(6) and (7). This may lead to two awards of costs for separate and specific periods or one award, but of a specified percentage only. 8–35

If the court does make awards of costs to more than one party to the assessment, the wording of CPR 47.15(5) seems clear—the maximum it will award to 'any party' is £1,500. So, if there are two parties who both receive costs awards for certain specified periods of the assessment, it appears that each may recover up to £1,500. However, given the amount of work required in the provisional assessment process, it seems unlikely that a reasonable and proportionate amount would see the combined costs exceed £1,500 by much (save if it was a case where there is still a success fee recoverable between the parties).

Q20. Does the £1,500 cap on costs under CPR 47.14 include costs incurred in 'Costs Only Proceedings' under CPR 46.14?

It would seem not. The argument that the costs of the CPR 46.14 process are not costs of the substantive claim and so, by definition, must be costs of the provisional assessment (relying on the judgment of Brooke LJ in *Crosbie v Munroe*[19]) and included within the £1,500 limit, was dealt a fatal blow by the Court of Appeal in *Tasleem v Beverley: Bartkauskaute v BartKauskiene*.[20] As Sharp LJ concluded: 8–36

[19] *Crosbie v Munroe* [2003] EWCA Civ 350.

[20] *Tasleem v Beverley: Bartkauskaute v BartKauskiene* [2013] EWCA Civ 1805.

> *"The bringing of Part 8 costs-only proceedings is not the commencement of, or part of, the detailed assessment proceedings, albeit it is a necessary preliminary to that process if there are no underlying proceedings in existence. This is because detailed assessment proceedings are distinct from the proceedings whether under Part 7 or Part 8 which have given rise to the costs order (see CPR rule 47.6(1))."*[21]

Accordingly, any costs awarded under CPR 46.14 are entirely separate from the costs cap in CPR 47.14. Of course, the outcome of the provisional assessment may inform what award of costs the court makes on the CPR 46.14 proceedings—for example, the paying party may have made an offer before those proceedings in a sum that exceeds the receiving party's subsequent recovery on the assessment. For this reason it may be inappropriate for the court to decide who is entitled to the costs of the CPR 46.14 proceedings until after the assessment of the costs of the substantive proceedings has taken place. An appropriate order may defer the award of costs until the conclusion of the detailed assessment (whether by provisional assessment or not) and, if that is by settlement, give liberty to either party to restore for this purpose. The court will then deal with the award and any consequent summary assessment.

8–37 This may seem an obvious conclusion as the simple fact is that Pt.47.15 states that it only applies to certain "detailed assessment proceedings" and Pt.46.14 proceedings are not detailed assessment proceedings (as is clearly apparent from the title 'Costs only Proceedings'). If further support was needed, it can be found in CPR 44.1 where 'detailed assessment' is defined as a procedure for determining the amount of costs under Pt 47. 'Costs only Proceedings' may enable a party to start detailed assessment proceedings, but they do not determine the amount of costs—obvious until one remembers that in *Crosbie*, Brooke LJ had concluded that:

> *". . . assessment proceedings cover the whole period of negotiations about the amount of costs payable through the Part 8 proceedings to the ultimate disposal of those proceedings, whether by agreement or court order."*[22]

However, the Court of Appeal in *Tasleem* specifically considered *Crosbie* and took the view that it served only to support its conclusions.

Q21. How does the court deal with the proportionality cross check after a provisional assessment where the assessed bill is returned to the parties to do the arithmetic?

8–38 As time passes and cases fall within the new proportionality provisions of CPR 44.3(2)(a) rather than the old '*Lownds*' provisions (see **Chapter 3—Proportionality**), this will become a pertinent issue. It is unlikely that the court will calculate the total of the bill immediately after assessing what is reasonably incurred and reasonable in amount (not only because CPR 47 PD

[21] para.18.
[22] para.34.

14.4(2) places the responsibility for agreeing the total sum at the door of the parties, but also because of the time it may take to do this and in case it makes an arithmetical mistake).

As some cases with the new proportionality test have already started to work their way through the provisional assessment process, it seems clear that there are already two schools of thought. They are that:

i) The court returns the bill, the Form G and any separate rulings to the parties to do the arithmetic, but adds an order as follows (or in similar terms):

"The proportionate sum pursuant to CPR 44.3(5) factors is £x. If the reasonably incurred and reasonable in amount costs exceed £x when the bill is recalculated then anything over £x is disproportionate and the bill is provisionally assessed at £x. If the reasonably incurred and reasonable in amount costs are less than £x when the bill is recalculated then those costs are proportionate and the bill is provisionally assessed in the recalculated sum."

This completes the provisional assessment and time for requesting an oral hearing is triggered by this order.

ii) The court requires the parties to confirm the recalculated sum after assessing what is reasonably incurred and reasonable in amount, together with any submissions on proportionality, and this is then referred back to the assessing judge to determine proportionality. Having done so the bill is then returned to the parties provisionally assessed in the recalculated sum, if it was proportionate, or, provisionally assessed in a lower figure (being the sum determined proportionate) if the recalculated sum was disproportionate. The provisional assessment is only completed for the purpose of the time for requesting an oral hearing at this stage.

There are attractions to both procedures. The advantages of the former are that it concludes the provisional assessment earlier, leads to quicker payment and involves less time and costs commitment by the parties and the court. It is also prevents problems if the assessment was undertaken by a part-time member of the judiciary who may not be available to do the subsequent proportionality element of the assessment if it is deferred. 8–39

The advantages of the latter approach are that the parties have the yardstick of the reasonably incurred and reasonable in amount sum when considering and making submissions on proportionality and the assessing judge has the same yardstick when assessing proportionality.

As the assessment of proportionality under CPR 44.3(5) is an entirely free standing one, the time, costs and judicial continuity arguments seem the more compelling at first blush. However, this approach seems to overlook the wording of CPR 44.3(2)(a), which only refers to the fact that the court *may* disallow or reduce reasonably incurred costs if they are disproportionate. Surely until the costs reasonably incurred and reasonable in amount have been calculated the parties are not in a position to make specific submissions and, therefore, the court is not in a position to reach a decision? An illustration of this is where the receiving party wishes to rely upon CPR 44.3(5)(d) to argue that the conduct of the paying party generated specific additional work. Until it is clear what the court has allowed in respect of the reasonably incurred and reasonable in amount costs for that additional work, it is impossible to determine whether the argument is purposeful—for if the court allowed none of that work anyway, then it cannot sound in the proportionality argument.

Q22. Is there a sanction if the receiving party fails to file the required documents with the request for provisional assessment and can this be rectified? If so how?

8–40 It is necessary to start by setting out what documents must be filed at a provisional assessment. A list of these is set out at CPR 47 PD 14.3 (which in turn refers back to CPR 47 PD 8.3 and 13.2). In addition, as it applies to provisional assessments by virtue of CPR 47 PD 14.2(2), CPR 47 PD 13.13 permits the court to require the receiving party to produce any documents it requires to reach its decision, but the court may put that party to its *Pamplin*[23] election in respect of reliance.

8–41 What is the position if a receiving party fails to file the documents required by the rules or by specific order? This was precisely the position that confronted the court in *Mehmi v Pincher*[24]. The Points of Dispute raised a dispute about the receiving party's liability to pay costs to his solicitor. In breach of CPR 47 PD 13.2(i) the receiving party failed to file the requisite documentation in respect of his retainer agreement. The assessing judge provisionally assessed the costs at nil. The claimant requested an oral hearing and applied for relief from sanction under CPR 3.9. These were listed together and the relief application was taken first. The court concluded that the decision was a sanction and so CPR 3.9 applied, dismissed the application for relief and upheld the nil assessment as a result. On appeal the court concluded that the PD itself did not prescribe an explicit sanction for non compliance and nor could one be implied. Instead, as part of the assessment of costs, the court had simply concluded that on the available evidence there was a breach of the indemnity principle and so assessed the costs at nil, rather than imposing that assessment outcome as a sanction for non compliance. The appeal was allowed and the matter was remitted for the oral hearing, with an indication that CPR 47 PD 13.13 could be used by the court to afford the receiving party another opportunity to file the missing documentation.

8–42 In addition the court highlighted in the judgment a standard order in use in that court to address routine non compliance with CPR 47 PD 13.2(i). That order provided for:

[23] *Pamplin v Express Newspapers Ltd (Costs) [1985] 1 W.L.R. 689.*

[24] *Mehmi v Pincher County Court at Liverpool hearing 20.7.15 unreported HHJ Wood QC.*

- an adjournment of the provisional assessment to a later date;
- the use of CPR 47 PD 13.13 to make an 'unless order' requiring compliance, with default resulting in an assessment at nil and an adverse costs order; and,
- a prospective reduction of 50 per cent of any costs of the provisional assessment to which the receiving party might subsequently become entitled if there was compliance with the 'unless order', presumably in recognition of, and as a sanction for, the original non compliance with CPR 47 PD13.2.

This decision raises three interesting procedural issues, as follows: **8–43**

(1) Does the reference to *'any document'* in CPR 47 PD 13.13 include documents that the receiving party ought to have filed anyway under the mandatory requirement at 13.2? In strict terms there can be no doubt that where there is a dispute about retainer, the actual retainer documents are understandably necessary to enable the court to reach its decision on this issue—falling within the wording of the provision. Similarly the rule refers to *'any'* and not *'any further'* document. However, it seems illogical that one element of a specific procedural provision makes the filing of identified documents mandatory, whilst another element affords an unfettered opportunity for the court to disregard this without any involvement of either party.

(2) CPR 47 PD13.2 is mandatory—it uses the word 'must'. There is a body of post March 2013 authority in different contexts e.g. time for renewing a request for permission to appeal at an oral hearing (CPR 52.3(5))[25] and applying promptly to set aside judgment in default (CPR 13.3(2))[26], suggesting that even though no sanction is prescribed, the word 'must' means that when considering any extension of the time permitted for compliance with CPR 47 PD 13.2(i), the court should still consider the three stages set out in *Denton v T H White Ltd*[27]. Accordingly, either if the court of its own volition engages 47 PD13.13 to remedy a breach of the requirements of 13.2 (ignoring the question posed in (1) above and assuming that it can do so), or whether it requires the receiving party to apply retrospectively to extend the time period for compliance with 13.2, the ultimate decision requires a reasoned judgment

(3) Is it proportionate to adjourn the provisional assessment to permit late compliance with the filing obligation? The court will have lost the time already set aside and will have to allocate a further provisional assessment listing. The alternative is that the court proceeds with the assessment and is likely to conclude that the retainer is not proved and assess the costs

25 *Webb Resolutions Ltd v E-Surv Ltd [2014] EWHC 49 (QB).*
26 *Mid East Sales Ltd v United Engineering & Trading Company (PVT) Ltd [2014] EWHC 1457 (Comm).*
27 *Denton v T H White Ltd [2014] EWCA Civ 906.*

at nil and leaves it to the receiving party to decide whether to apply for an oral hearing and an extension of time within which to comply with CPR 47.PD 13.2(i) —a route that may (as opposed to definitely will) lead to further court time being expended. It is right to record that the court in *Mehmi* did implicitly consider this in the broader context of managing a large court where the issue had been occupying significant resources and explicitly felt an adjournment preferable to the *'more cumbersome process of the inevitable oral review'*.

One unarguable certainty is that compliance with the documentary filing requirements avoids 'interesting procedural issues'.

Q23. What happens in respect of the costs where at an oral hearing a party does not achieve an adjustment in its favour of 20 per cent or more, but the adjustment made does make a CPR 47.20 offer relevant?

8–44 This question is best answered by reference to a specific example. In the example the paying party makes a Part 36 offer to pay the receiving party £10,000. The bill is provisionally assessed at £10,500. The paying party seeks an oral hearing at which the bill is reduced to £9,900. On the face of it the receiving party has not obtained an outcome (under CPR 47.20(4)(e)) more advantageous than the Part 36 offer. However, the oral hearing has only seen an adjustment in favour of the paying party of 5.7 per cent (£600 divided by £10,500).

It is important to note that the question raises the costs of the provisional assessment generally and not just the costs of the oral hearing. They raise separate issues and need to be considered individually.

The costs of the oral hearing

8–45 CPR 47.15(10) provides a general rule that the party requesting the oral hearing pays the costs of and incidental to that hearing. There are two qualifications to this general rule. The first is that the party requesting the oral hearing sees an adjustment in its favour of 20 per cent or more. In our example that has not been achieved. The second is if the court orders otherwise.

Which CPR provision prevails—47.15 or 47.20 (and by implication 36.17))? The simple answer seems to be that a specific rule trumps a general rule (see for example *Solomon v Cromwell Group Plc*[28] in support of this proposition) and as CPR 47.15 relates specifically to oral hearings as part of the provisional assessment process, that provision prevails. So, in our example, the starting point is that the paying party still pays the costs of the oral hearing. However, as stated this is the 'starting point' as the second qualification to the general rule in CPR 47.15(10) permits the court to order otherwise. There is some guidance as to when it might do otherwise in CPR 47 PD 14.5. This requires the court to take into account the conduct of the parties and any offers made when considering whether to depart from the general rule. Whilst it is a matter of

[28] *Solomon v Cromwell Group Plc* [2011] EWCA Civ 1584.

discretion, this suggests that the CPR Part 36 offer will still be relevant to the oral hearing, but not as a CPR Part 36 offer, with the consequences attached to that, but simply as an offer under CPR 47 PD 14.5. The court must then determine what, if any, departure from the general rule in CPR 47.15(10) is appropriate.

The costs of the provisional assessment (excluding the oral hearing)

CPR 47.15(10) relates only to the costs of the oral hearing. Accordingly, **8–46** CPR 47.20 applies and when determining the costs of the provisional assessment (excluding the costs of the oral hearing) the court looks at the end result. In our example the receiving party has failed to obtain an outcome more advantageous than the paying party's CPR Part 36 offer and so, by cross application, CPR 36.17(3)) applies.

A final word

Suppose in our example it had been the receiving party who had made the **8–47** relevant CPR Part 36 offer, which it had not exceeded under the initial assessment, but which it had after the oral hearing (although again not achieving an adjustment of 20 per cent or more at the oral hearing). If, after considering whether to depart from the general rule, the court had determined that the receiving party should be awarded the costs of the oral hearing, would the additional sum under CPR 36.17(4)(d) be payable on that sum? There is certainly a compelling argument (based on the specific rule trumping the general rule) that it would not be payable, as costs relating to the oral hearing have been awarded under CPR 47.15(10)(b) and not under CPR 47.20 and by application CPR 36.17(4)). However, as explained in **Q15** above, CPR 47 PD 14 applies to proceedings under CPR 47.15 and as such there may be no tension between CPR 47.15(10) and 47.20(4) where a claimant does better than a claimant's Part 36 offer and achieves a favourable adjustment of 20 per cent or more at an oral hearing. This is because the starting point at CPR 47.15(10) awards the claimant the costs of the oral hearing and there is no conflict between this and the application then of CPR 36.17(4)(d), which permits the court to order those costs on the indemnity basis. Accordingly there is no need for any determination as to which is a specific rule and which a general rule in this situation. If this is correct, then there is no reason why CPR 36.17(4) should not apply in full in respect of the oral hearing in this discrete situation (subject to this issue raised at **Q24** below as to whether the claimant can recover an additional sum on both the costs of the provisional assessment and the costs of an oral hearing given the qualifying words at the outset of CPR 36.17(4)(d)). Of course, in any event, for those costs excluding the oral hearing, the additional sum would be payable as those costs would be awarded under CPR 47.20 specifically applying CPR 36.17(4).

Q24. Under CPR 36.17(4)(d) can a party recover the additional sum on a detailed assessment by operation of CPR 47.20 if it has already

received an additional amount in respect of the substantive award in the claim?

8–48 This question raises a semantic issue that arises when considering the subtle qualification that appears at the beginning of CPR 36.17(4)(d) with the words *'Provided that the case has been finally decided and there has not been a previous order under this sub-paragraph'* and the wording of CPR 47.20(7) which provides that:

> *"For the purposes of rule 36.17, detailed assessment proceedings are to be regarded as an independent claim"*

Is a case finally decided before the costs of that case have been resolved and, is 'a claim' the same thing as 'a case'? The plot thickens when CPR 47.1 is considered. At first blush this seems to suggest that detailed assessment comes after a final decision. However, this rule talks of a final decision in *'the proceedings'*. Are proceedings the same as 'a claim' and/or 'a case'? None of these three descriptive terms are defined in CPR 2 or in the Glossary at the end of the CPR. However, as the only purpose of CPR 47.20(7) seems to be to distinguish detailed assessment proceedings from the substantive litigation, the scales appear to weigh in favour of answering 'yes' to the question posed. This interpretation and conclusion is supported by the fact that CPR 47 PD 1.1 clearly identifies a final decision as being of all the substantive issues other than costs. This does raise the interesting question of whether the claimant is able to recover an additional amount on both the costs of the provisional assessment and the costs of any oral hearing see **Q23** above. The logical conclusion is that as both the provisional assessment and an oral hearing following it are both component parts of one set of detailed assessment proceedings, then only one CPR 36.17(4)(b) award may be made. However, they are clearly separate components (CPR 47.15(7) refers to an oral hearing 'when a provisional assessment has been carried out' and there are clearly different starting points for the award of costs for each (47.20(1) and 47.15(10)). As such it seems that the costs of each must be dealt with separately which would suggest that only one may attract the additional amount.

Q25. Is the determination of disbursements under the procedure set out at CPR 47 PD 5.7 a provisional assessment?

8–49 No. This procedure is not included within either CPR 47.15 or CPR 47 PD 14. It is a free standing detailed assessment procedure. Its origins can be found in Jackson LJ's Review of Civil Litigation Costs: Final Report, December 2009[29]. Although in the report the procedure was discussed in terms of disbursement only disputes in fast track cases where the profit costs are subject to a fixed fee regime, CPR 47 PD 5.7 contains no such restriction and the procedure is, therefore, available in appropriate multi track cases as well.

As the procedure is not akin to a provisional assessment and a paper disposal

[29] Review of Civil Litigation Costs: Final Report, December 2009 Chapter 45 para 5.2

is expressly provided for, it seems that any challenge to the outcome must be by appeal in the usual way.

One practical difficulty is the assessment of the costs of the assessment itself. Logically (and for reasons of proportionality) one would expect this also to be undertaken as a paper exercise with the parties filing statements of costs for summary assessment and offers in sealed envelopes. As the exercise is not a provisional assessment the fee cap in CPR 47.15(5) does not apply, although it is difficult to imagine a situation where the court would allow more than that cap where the disputed disbursements do not exceed the provisional assessment costs limit of £75,000.

Payments on account

Q26. Is there any rule of thumb as to what proportion of the costs claimed the court will order as a reasonable sum by way of payment on account?

There never has been any genuine 'rule of thumb'. *Mars UK Ltd v Teknowledge Ltd (Costs)*[30] is often cited as authority for the proposition that two-thirds of the sum claimed is an appropriate amount. In fact, the route by which the payment on account was reached in that case is far from straightforward and does not endorse any specific percentage as a general rule. 8–50

The decision is fact specific in each case. This is a point reiterated by Clarke LJ in *Excalibur Ventures LLC v Texas Keystone INC. & ors*[31] when ordering 80 per cent of the sum claimed on account stating:

> *"What is a reasonable amount will depend on the circumstances, the chief of which is that there will, by definition, have been no detailed assessment and thus an element of uncertainty, the extent of which may differ widely from case to case as to what will be allowed on detailed assessment"*

He went on to tender this approach to payments on account, which reinforces the case specific nature of the determination of amount:

> *"A reasonable sum would often be one that was an estimate of the likely level of recovery subject, as the costs claimants (sic) accept, to an appropriate margin to allow for error in the estimation. This can be done by taking the lowest figure in a likely range or making a deduction from a single estimated figure or perhaps from the lowest figure in the range if the range itself is not very broad"*

In *Rallison v North West London Hospitals NHS*[32], a clinical negligence claim settled for £450,000 (where a much larger sum had been sought) and where the claimant sought a payment on account of costs of £574,000 and the defendant was offering £250,000, the court stressed that determination of the likely level of recovery at assessment necessarily involved consideration of

[30] *Mars UK Ltd v Teknowledge Ltd (Costs)* [1999] 2 Costs L.R. 44 Jacob J.
[31] *Excalibur Ventures LLC v Texas Keystone INC. & ors [2015 EWHC 566(Comm).*
[32] *Rallison v North West London Hospitals NHS [2015] EWHC 3255 (QB).*

proportionality of the costs claimed (other than, of course, in cases where the award of costs is on the indemnity basis as proportionality does not arise). The court awarded a payment of £306,763 on account.

However, the advent of costs budgets may assist and simplify the process by creating greater certainty over likely recovery on any subsequent assessment because part of the costs are budgeted as reasonable and proportionate already and absent 'good reason' under CPR 3.18 will be the sums recovered on assessment for that part of the costs. In *Elvanite Full Circle Ltd v AMEC Earth & Environmental (UK) Ltd,*[33] Coulson J used the budget set as the basis for a determination of the reasonable sum to be paid on account stating, "the costs management order is likely to be the benchmark for the costs to be recovered", and based the payment on account on the conclusion that the receiving party's costs were unlikely to be much under the budgeted sum. Of course, the budgeted sums cannot include costs that had been incurred at the time the budget was set, although in *SARPD Oil Ltd v Addax Energy SA & anor*[34] the court did take account of both when considering the 'amount' of any security for costs that might be ordered in a costs managed case, the court appears not to have been taken to CPR 3.15(1) and the phrase 'costs to be incurred' (this case is considered in more detail in **Chapter 4 Q27**). Accordingly, it may be that in the absence of an indication that the budget is to be subject to some fundamental challenge under 'good reason to depart from the budget' under CPR 3.18, a starting point will be the budgeted sum. Indeed, in *Thomas Pink Limited v Victoria's Secret UK Limited,*[35] Birss J concluded that the advent of costs budgets had altered the position. The budget was £678,000. The claimant sought £644,000 as a payment on account and the defendant proposed £350,000 (which the court accepted was 'the sort of figure one would have expected to have awarded'). However, having posed the question whether the costs budgeting rules have a significant impact on orders for payments on account, Birss J concluded that:

> *"The sum sought by the claimants is essentially the budgeted sum at the time they asked for it. It seems to me that the impact of costs budgeting on the determination of a sum for a payment on account of costs is very significant although I am not persuaded that it is so significant that I should simply award the budgeted sum. Bearing in mind that unless there is good reason to depart from the budget, the budget will not be departed from, but also taking into account the vagaries of litigation and things that might occur and the fact that it is, at least, possible that the assessed costs will be less, although no good reason why that is so has been advanced before me, I will make an award of 90% of the sum in the claimant's budget (£644,829.10) rounded up to the nearest thousand."*[36]

[33] *Elvanite Full Circle Ltd v AMEC Earth & Environmental (UK) Ltd* [2013] EWHC 1643 (TCC) Coulson J.
[34] *SARP Oil Ltd v Addax Energy SA & anor [2015] EWHC 2426 (Comm).*
[35] *Thomas Pink Limited v Victoria's Secret UK Limited* [2014] EWHC 3258(Ch) Birss J.
[36] para.60.

Q27. Must a party have filed a Form N260 (or equivalent statement of costs) if it wishes to seek a payment on account of costs?

In Astonleigh Residential v Goldfarb[37] the court concluded that the CPR contained no requirement that a party seeking a payment on account had to have produced a statement of costs to inform the court's decision. Of course, in most CPR 7 multi track claims the court will have the better detail of a costs management order to inform its decision (**see Q26 above**). It seems inevitable that in the absence of either a budget or a statement of costs, the court is likely to be conservative in determining the amount of any payment on account. 8–51

Q28. When may a departure from the general rule at CPR 44.2(8) be justified?

There may be facts particular to a case that render a payment on account inappropriate. As an example, in Rawlinson & Hunter Trustees SA v ITG Ltd & ors[38] *the court was asked either to order an immediate detailed assessment of an interim costs order or, if it was not prepared to do so, to order a payment on account of costs. In fact it declined to do either for the same reasons—namely that the claimant might later secure a costs order against the defendant, may have difficulties in enforcing that and, if it had already paid costs would have lost the chance to set off what if owed against what it was due.* 8–52

[37] *Astonleigh Residential v Goldfarb [2014] EWHC 4100 (Ch).*
[38] *Rawlinson & Hunter Trustees SA v ITG Ltd & ors.*

CHAPTER 9

The Effect of the Jackson Civil Justice Reforms on Solicitor–Client Costs

Introduction

The Legal Aid, Sentencing & Punishment of Offenders Act 2012 and associated secondary legislation, together with the reforms to the Civil Procedure Rules introduced in April 2013, have had a significant effect on the conduct of litigation and on the scope of costs recovery between the parties. 9–01

Apart from the imposition of a number of statutory caps on the levels of success fees (in personal injury claims) and on the levels of the 'payments' under Damages Based Agreements, and some relatively minor procedural amendments aside, those changes do not directly address the question of solicitor–client costs.

It is important to note that the fundamental legal principles underpinning the ability of a solicitor to charge a client and the ability of a client to dispute those charges are unaffected. The law in this regard emanates from a combination of statutory provision (primarily ss.56–75 of the Solicitors Act 1974) and common law and it is doubtful that amendments to the CPR alone would have the standing to alter those principles.

However, a number of the key changes undoubtedly have an indirect impact on the question of costs as between the solicitor and the client, and the solicitor therefore needs to be alert to this in order to avoid negative consequences. In some areas of reform, such as costs budgeting, it appears that the attempt to control solicitors charging by the back door was intentional. In others, for example in relation to proportionality, the effect was perhaps less intentional, and the precise impact less obvious to see at this stage.

Those key changes will be considered in turn. It is beyond the scope of this section to consider in detail the established legal principles relating to assessment of solicitor client costs, beyond by way of brief overview and consideration of how those principles have been, or may be, affected by those changes. Risk management and law firm management are also outside the scope of this book. However, by pointing out where issues arise as a result of the Jackson reforms, this chapter aims to give readers a clear steer that they should consider carefully and, if appropriate, seek further guidance. It is also a plea for detailed guidance to be given by those who can.

One of the inadvertent consequences of the reforms is that they have shone a bright spotlight on issues surrounding changes in funding, for example concerning the reasonableness of a switch from public funding to a case being funded with a Conditional Fee Agreement. A combination of anecdotal evidence and a number of first instance decisions[1] indicate that in the run up to 1 April 2013 there may have been a substantial number of cases where such changes took place. In such cases, where the claimant is awarded costs, opponents may have an incentive to challenge the circumstances of such changes in order to try and avoid payment of any additional liabilities or even to identify some technical defect which might allow it to avoid paying costs altogether. Whilst the basic test for the reasonableness of such a change appears to have been set as long ago as 2002[2], the particular combination of circumstances following the reforms is likely to lead to the parameters of those principles being closely examined and tested. In many such cases, one of the key issues in dispute will be the quality of the advice provided to the client about the change in funding and the between the parties cases may well have a marked effect on and implications for more general issues about the quality of the advice to be given to clients about costs and funding options generally[3]. A number of first instance decisions are likely to come to appeal in 2016 and may reach the Court of Appeal or higher in late 2016 or into 2017.

A brief overview

9–02 There is a fundamental distinction between costs on a solicitor–client basis and costs between the parties. The latter are payable as a result of any costs order or agreement between the parties and are subject to the very broad discretion conferred on the court by s.51 of the Senior Courts Act 1981 and any rules of procedure made thereunder.

However, costs on a solicitor–client basis are payable as a result of the contract between the solicitor and the client. Subject to specific statutory and procedural restrictions, the key determining factor therefore is the terms of the contract between the solicitor and client.

As with any other form of costs payable under a contract where the liability is a contractual one, the costs are payable on the indemnity basis, unless the contract otherwise provides (see CPR 44.5 for the position in relation to costs payable under contracts generally).[4]

Accordingly, the starting point is that a solicitor–client costs dispute is a contractual dispute and is subject to any limitations within that contract.

However, as noted, there are numerous statutory, common law and procedural restrictions imposed which fundamentally change the character of the claim as between solicitor and client. These exist primarily as a combination of a recognition of the peculiar position of solicitors and the court's

[1] See for example *Hyde v Milton Keynes NHS Trust* [2015] EWHC B1 (Costs) – (appellate judgment [2016] EWHC 72 (QB) and *Surrey v Barnet & Chase Farm Hospitals* [2015] EWHC B16 (Costs), due to be heard on appeal in May 2016, as well as *AMH v The Scout Association*, SCCO, Case No HQ 13X05225, *Proctor v Raleys Solicitors (A Firm)* [2015] EWCA Civ 400 and *McDaniel & Co* (a firm) [2014] EWHC 3826.

[2] See *Sarwar v Alam* [2002] 1 WLR 125.

[3] Including the question of whether and if so to what extent concepts of 'informed consent' akin to those seen in the Supreme Court's decision in *Montgomery v Lanarkshire Health* Board [2015] UKSC 11 are relevant in a solicitor–client context.

[4] The introduction of the concept of indemnity basis assessment of costs between the parties only came much later, with the introduction of the concepts of 'standard' and 'indemnity' basis in 1986.

supervisory jurisdiction over them and a form of what would, in modern parlance, be termed 'consumer protection'.

These provisions may be analysed in three main categories.

Retainers

Firstly, provisions which govern the nature of the contract that a solicitor may enter into with a client are primarily restrictive—that is to say they limit the nature of the arrangements beyond what would be permitted in an ordinary commercial context. **9–03**

These arrangements, in turn, fall primarily into two main categories, namely those relating to what is termed 'non-contentious business' and those relating to contentious business. As to what is and is not contentious business, there is a very circuitous definition of both at s.87 of the Solicitors Act 1974, whereby contentious business is defined as business done "in or for the purposes of proceedings begun before a court or before an arbitrator . . . not being business which falls within the definition of non-contentious business" and non-contentious business is defined as "any business done by a solicitor which is not contentious business". The key point to note is that work which would have been classed as non-contentious business will be classed as contentious business provided that that work was done with a view to proceedings being begun and proceedings were in fact begun.[5]

If further guidance on this issue is required, the most comprehensive recent consideration of the issues is to be found in Chief Master Hurst's judgment in *Tel-Ka Talk Ltd*.[6]

The primary statutory provisions in this regard are s.57 of the Solicitors Act 1974, which, at s.57(2) sets out the very broad nature of the arrangements that a solicitor may lawfully enter into with their clients in relation to non-contentious business ("Non-Contentious Business Agreements", of 'NCBA's), including what might be described as contingency, or outcome based arrangements, and specified the requirements for such arrangements, and s.59 which sets out the ability of solicitors to enter into Contentious Business Agreements (CBA's) with clients.

It is important to note that both Contentious and Non-Contentious Business Agreements with clients are merely optional and that it is not necessary for a solicitor–client retainer in respect of contentious business, for example, to take the form of a CBA.

In contrast to s.57, s.59 expressly provides that nothing in that section shall give validity to (inter alia) any agreement by which the solicitor retained stipulates for payment only in the event of success (a "conditional" fee), or by way of a percentage of recovery (a "contingent" fee).

This reflects the proposition that s.59 does not prohibit such arrangements

[5] See *Re Simpkin Marshall Ltd* [1959] Ch 229.
[6] *Tel-Ka Talk Ltd v HMRC* [2010] EWHC 90175 (Costs).

but equally is not to be taken to permit them, in contrast to s.57 which does expressly permit, for example, payment by way of a percentage for non-contentious business.

9–04 The restriction on such arrangements comes not from the Solicitors Act 1974 therefore but from the common law prohibition on champertous arrangements, which could have been overridden by the statutory provision at s.59 of the 1974 Act, but expressly was not. That common law prohibition has, however, been relaxed by express statutory provisions in s.58 of the Courts & Legal Services Act 1990 (permitting Conditional Fee Agreements that comply with the requirements of ss.58 and 58A) and then more recently s.58AA of the same Act permitting Damages Based Agreements that comply with the requirements of that section.

It has been recognised judicially that such relaxation of the ability of solicitors to enter into such arrangements is a matter to be decided upon by Parliament and not a matter for incremental judicial expansion.[7]

Any conditional or contingency fee agreement relating to contentious business which does not comply with those requirements is unenforceable, either by operation of the express provisions of those sections or the common law.

Both s.58 and s.58AA contain provisions (s.58(5) and s.58AA(9) making clear that the statute does not limit the right to enter into a conditional or contingency fee agreement for non-contentious business—save in respect of employment matters). Accordingly, the position remains that as between solicitor and client the nature of arrangements that may be lawfully entered into, and the formality requirements that must be complied with in relation to those arrangements, are substantially more restrictive where the subject matter of the retainer relates to what may be classed as contentious business rather than non-contentious business.

If a solicitor enters into an unlawful and unenforceable retainer with his client, the likely effect is that the solicitor will not be entitled to payment of any fees for the work done, even if the solicitor's work was not done as the conducting solicitor, but is still seen as the provision of litigation services (see, for example, *Rees v Gateley Wareing (a firm)*[8]).[9]

A number of issues relating to the ability of solicitors to 'transfer' retainers, whether by assignment or otherwise, have arisen following the reforms. These commonly arise in a between the parties context, though since they are based on an attempt by opponents to take advantage of the indemnity principle at their heart is a contention that the retainer between one or other of the firms of solicitors involved and their client has 'failed' in some way. This issue is addressed is some detail in the Chapter on Funding and is not separately addressed here.

---

[7] See Lord Neuberger MR (as he then was) in *Sibthorpe & Morris v LB Southwark* [2011] EWCA Civ 25; [2011] 1 WLR 2111 at 40–41.

[8] *Rees v Gateley Wareing (a firm)* [2014] EWCA Civ 1351.

[9] ss.57 & 61 respectively.

Entitlement to payment

The second category of provision relating to a solicitor's entitlement to payment from their client concerns the way in which a solicitor should bill that client in order to be able validly to claim fees from the client. 9–05

Again, the primary provisions are to be found in the Solicitors Act 1974 and again, the primary consequence is to impose a series of obligations and restrictions which differentiate the position from that of a normal contractual dispute.

Firstly, in relation to CBAs and NCBAs, the broad effect is that they determine the client's liability without right on the client's part to a full assessment. However, they are subject to an ability on the court's part to set aside the agreements if they are considered to be unfair or unreasonable. Where such agreements provide for remuneration by hourly rate, the time spent on the case is capable of assessment.

The Act also provides the basic requirements for the form of a solicitor's bill of costs for both contentious and non-contentious business (s.69). A bill complying with s.69 (known as a 'statute' bill) is a fundamental requirement before a solicitor can bring an action to recover his costs. Errors in the form of a bill are not infrequently a flaw in such actions. The statutory requirements have been amplified in case law such that it is now well established that a statute bill must be reasonably complete, must have a sufficient narrative[10] (though what is sufficient may be fact dependent) and should contain a satisfactory breakdown of the fees claimed.

An exception to the latter exists in relation to contentious business where a solicitor may deliver a 'gross sum' statute bill (s.64), though if this option is chosen certain additional rights to request further detail and/or challenge the bill are conferred on the client. 9–06

The rendering of a statute bill, whether on an interim or final basis, is important because it is the delivery of the bill that triggers the client's right to assessment of the costs claimed in the bill. There are strict time limits which apply, whereby the client's right to such an assessment reduces from an absolute right (s.70(1)), to a discretion on the court's part, which may be subject of conditions (s.70(2)), to a situation where either the client may have to show 'special circumstances' to obtain an assessment or the court's power to order an assessment may be removed completely (s.70(3)).

However, it is important to note that where the fees are unpaid and the solicitor sues the client for the unpaid fees the client is likely to have a common law right to dispute the quantum of the claimed fees, and therefore obtain an effective assessment, regardless of the time limits in s.70.[11]

---

[10] See *Garry v Gwillim* [2002] EWCA Civ 1500 at 59–60.

[11] See *Turner & Co v O Palomo SA* [2000] 1 WLR 37. However, it is important to note in this context that a common law assessment is not precisely the same thing as an assessment pursuant to s.70 Solicitors Act 1974 and, in particular, that s.70(9) of the Act—which applies a robust presumption that the client will be awarded the costs of the assessment if the bill is reduced by 20 per cent or more—does not apply. See in particular *Ahmud & Co v Macpherson* [2015] EWHC 2240(QB). In such a case, the client should rather follow the approach in more conventional litigation of seeking to make Part 36 offers in order to achieve a measure of adverse costs protection.

The necessary form of a statute bill aside, perhaps the key issue which arises in solicitor client disputes is that in order to be able to render a statute bill on anything other than a final basis (that is to say other than when the work has been fully completed) there either must be an express or implied agreement allowing the solicitor to render 'interim' statute bills,[12] or the court must be able to identify a 'natural break'[13] in the matter at which it was appropriate to render a statute bill. If neither of these apply, then any interim bill will be merely an 'on account' bill, at best and will neither give the solicitor a right to sue for payment, nor trigger the time limits for the client's rights to assessment.

Solicitor–client assessment and disputes

9–07 The third set of provisions relate to the procedure for resolving solicitor–client disputes. As already noted, s.70 of the Solicitors Act 1974 sets out a set of time limits which apply to a client's right to assessment, such time limits generally being triggered by the delivery of a statute bill.

The basic principle is that a client may apply (usually by way of Part 8 claim or by defence to a claim by the solicitor) for an assessment of any bill or series of bills within these time limits and to satisfy any applicable test (such as special circumstances), though a solicitor is entitled to apply for an order for assessment of his own bill.

Where such an assessment is ordered, as a matter of discretion or right, prior to April 2013, CPR 48.8 applied. Until April 2013, CPR 48.8 confirmed that any assessment was to be on the indemnity basis. However, it also went further. In addition to the two key general indemnity basis principles (that is to say: (i) the fact that a test of proportionality does not apply; and (ii) that where a doubt persists as to whether an item was reasonably incurred or reasonably in amount the benefit of the doubt will be given to the receiving party[14]), CPR 48.8 confirmed:

(i) that where the costs were incurred with the express or implied approval of the client they shall be presumed to be reasonably incurred;
(ii) that where the amount of the costs was expressly or impliedly approved by the client, the amount shall be presumed to be reasonable; but that
(iii) where they are of an unusual nature or amount and the solicitor did not tell the client that as a result they might not be recovered in full between the parties, they are presumed to have been unreasonably incurred.

This latter point (CPR 48.8(2)) is an important point and may have a particular impact in the context of 'unusual' disbursements. It is a significant gloss on the general application of the indemnity basis.

---

[12] There is substantial case law in this area. See *Re Romer & Haslam* [1893] 2 QB at 293 for the fundamental principle.
[13] For example, see *Re Hall & Barker* (1878) 9 Ch D 538.
[14] See now, CPR 44.4(2) and (3).

Although CPR 48.8 did not strictly apply on a 'common law' assessment, the general practice of the courts appears to be to treat such an assessment in a similar fashion to a statutory assessment and in particular to approach the assessment on an indemnity basis. 9–08

CPR 48.10 (there was no CPR 48.9) and CPR 48 PD 54.1 provided a set of more practical guidance as to the mechanics of the conduct of a solicitor–client assessment (these provisions survived the reforms largely unchanged and the April 2013 amendments are considered below).

The key remaining statutory provision to note at this point is s.70(9) of the Solicitors Act 1974. This applies a very specific provision for determining liability for costs of the solicitor–client assessment, known as the '20 per cent rule'. Where the bill (or that part of the bill which has been referred for assessment—see s.70(5)) is reduced by one-fifth (20 per cent) or more, the solicitor pays the costs of the assessment.[15] Otherwise, the client pays the costs.

This is subject to the court being able to make a different order where it considers there are 'special circumstances', a situation which appears to have been open to greater argument in recent years, particularly where one or other party has made an effective offer.[16] The Court of Appeal has recently confirmed that where part or all of a bill is disallowed because of some problem with the solicitor's retainer with the client—rather, for example, than the more common reason that the costs claimed in that part were unreasonable—the 20 per cent rule still applies to the whole bill. Accordingly, provided the client reduced the bill by more than 20 per cent, whether that was because of the retainer problem or because the costs were unreasonable, the client would benefit from the presumption of being awarded his costs unless there were special circumstances which warranted another order[17].

Accordingly, it can be seen that both in terms of the nature of the retainer, the ability of the solicitor to bill the client and sue for its costs and the mechanism that is used to determine any such dispute, the position as between solicitor and client is, and has long been, heavily modified from that which generally applies as between 'trader' and 'customer'.

In conclusion in this section, the availability of alternative remedies through the Legal Ombudsman should not be ignored. The ability of the Ombudsman to provide enforceable rulings in relation to fee disputes which are binding

[15] Save where the assessment was requested by the solicitor and the paying party did not attend the assessment.

[16] See for example *Angel Airlines v Dean & Dean* [2008] EWHC 1513 (QB).

[17] *Wilsons Solicitors LLP v Bentine* [2015] EWCA Civ 1168. One issue left open by this case is whether the court should consider the 20 per cent 'rule' by reference to each individual statute bill which has been assessed or whether it can and/or should consider the totality of the bills. In both the case dealt with in *Bentine*, the latter approach was adopted, though this seems to have been without demur by and/or at the request of the parties. This will often be eminently sensible where a number of statute bills are assessed as a result of a single application. The position is not helped by the fact that s.70(9) appears to have been drafted in anticipation of a single assessment in respect of a single bill – perhaps a historical legacy reflecting times when the idea of interim statute bills, rather than a single statute bill at the conclusion of the work, was far less common. Although the point is open to argument, it would seem difficult in principle to the court making a single costs order in respect of the assessment of a number of statute bills where those bills were the subject of a combined application. The 'costs of the assessment' would relate to the assessment of all of the bills. However, in light of the wording of the statute, there would seem to be a strong argument that any such order would have to properly reflect the outcome in respect of each individual bill and whether the solicitor or client was the 'winner' by reference to s.70(9).

on the solicitor, provided the client agrees to the ruling,[18] in circumstances where the Ombudsman will take into account, but is not bound by the decisions a court might make in similar circumstances,[19] and to order the payment of compensation in addition where appropriate,[20] in what is usually a no costs environment,[21] and where the client's complaint, though subject to some basic time limits,[22] is subject to less complicated restrictions than under the Solicitors Act 1974, arguably provides a far more flexible and effective and, from a solicitor's perspective, potentially more dangerous source of redress for a client.

Effect of the Jackson reforms

9–09 This will be considered under a number of headings. Many of these headings relate to issues which have been considered in detail elsewhere and only their effect on the solicitor–client position will be considered here.

Changes to the procedural rules in relation to solicitor–client assessments

9–10 CPR 48.8 and 48.10 no longer exist, but have been repeated in substantially identical terms in CPR 46.9 and 46.10, including the important provision, now at CPR 46.9(3)(c) relating to the presumed unreasonableness of costs where they are of an unusual nature or amount and the client was not warned that they may not be recovered from the other party to litigation as a result.

For reasons which are not entirely clear, there has been a slight amendment to the wording such that where the rule used to provide that they were presumed to be unreasonable if the client was not warned that he might not recover 'all of them', the rule now merely provides that they are presumed unreasonable if the client was not warned that the costs 'might not be recovered'. This would appear to be merely a tidying up of the wording and is not thought to have been intended to introduce any substantive change.

Costs budgeting

9–11 Costs budgeting is addressed elsewhere.[23] From a solicitor–client perspective, the most significant impact is likely to be that, where a costs management order is made reflecting either agreement between the parties or approval by the court after making revisions, there exists a clear restriction from that point onwards on the costs that the client is likely to be able to recover from the opponent if the litigation succeeds.

It is important that the client is made aware of that restriction and its effect. In particular, where, as will commonly, though not always, be the case, the retainer between solicitor and client provides that the client's liability is not limited to costs recovered between the parties, it will be extremely important,

[18] Scheme Rules 5.49.
[19] Scheme Rules 5.37(a).
[20] Scheme Rules 5.38(b).
[21] Scheme Rules 5.39.
[22] Scheme Rules 4.4 and 4.5.
[23] See Ch.4.

though perhaps difficult to achieve in practice, that the client is made aware of the likely shortfall in costs and is provided with an opportunity to provide an informed agreement to costs which fall outside the approved budget being incurred.

The practical approach to this is likely to differ from case to case (or at least type of case to type of case). However, as a minimum, it should be expected that at the outset the client will be told in clear, written, terms of the risk of a shortfall of costs even if the claim succeeds and costs are awarded, and of particular types of costs which will not or might not be recovered. The obvious example, post April 2013, is a success fee. Save for a limited class of cases, it is inexcusable not to tell the client, in clear terms, that where a success fee will be charged that success fee will not, in any circumstances, be recoverable from the opponent, even if costs are otherwise awarded and will be payable by the client alone. The same point applies to the costs of setting up a particular form of funding, or of considering After The Event insurance. More fact dependent examples might include the possibility of instruction of a QC, or of particular experts, or of particular types of costs being incurred (perhaps if an unusually large disclosure exercise is being contemplated).

Equally, the common warning in the past, that as a rule of thumb a between the parties recovery of two thirds (or 70 per cent) was likely is probably now both inaccurate and insufficient. What the client needs to be made aware of is the risk of a substantial shortfall generally, of particular items of costs that might be incurred and that those costs in particular might not be recovered, and that the client has a choice, which he should be given reasonable information in order to make, as to whether such costs are to be incurred (whilst, where appropriate, being informed whether, and if so why, the solicitor considers that those costs are appropriate, desirable or necessary).

Reference has already been made to the presumptions which apply under **9–12**
what is now CPR 46.9. A failure to make it clear to the client that a cost to be incurred is one which falls outside the budget (because, for example, it is not a recoverable cost or it is a cost not included on approval of the budget) may well result in that cost being seen as falling within CPR 46.9(3) and/or (b) or, in any event, may lead to the court being satisfied that it is unreasonable for the client to be held liable to pay that cost. By the same token, obtaining the client's express approval to the cost being incurred despite the probability of it being irrecoverable between the parties, because it is outside the approved budget, will give the solicitor the benefit of the s.46.(3)(a) and/or (b) presumptions.

It is, of course, in any event good practice (and possible essential) to provide the client with clear and accurate costs estimates, see for example Solicitors Code of Conduct 2011, IB 1.14–1.19.

Despite initial suggestions to the contrary (see, for example, HH Judge Simon Brown QC[24]), when CPR 3 Pt II was introduced, there was no requirement to

[24] HH Judge Simon Brown QC, "Costs control Costs management & docketed judges: are you ready for the big bang next year?" (2012) 6 April & 13 NLJ 498–499.

obtain the client's signature or to record in any other way the client's approval or agreement that the costs in the Precedent H budget submitted to the court were reasonable or proportionate or in any other way were an appropriate sum to expend on the case. In addition, oddly, there is also no requirement that the terms of any costs management order are served on the client. The provision on the pilot scheme in the Commercial Courts under CPR 51 PD 51G para.6, which provided that the client should be notified with seven days of the budgeting hearing of the budget set by the court was also not carried through to the wider reforms.

However, it was clearly an intention of the costs budgeting reforms that effective between the parties costs management, whilst not fixing the price between the solicitor and client,[25] would be in the interests of the clients.[26] In the absence of express provision in the rules on costs management, it seems that in practice this might be achieved by the courts, on any subsequent solicitor–client assessment, placing a high burden on solicitors who charge clients sums above the costs budget to show that the client received proper information in this regard and was given an informed choice as to whether to incur such costs, or at the very least was made aware when such costs were being incurred that they were unlikely to be recoverable between the parties.

9–13 Both caution and good practice suggest that where the costs budget which is prepared shows costs potentially claimable between the parties which are materially less than those the client is liable to pay, the client should be given clear prior information and explanation in relation to this. The party/party costs budget filed under CPR 3.13 is the client's costs budget, not the solicitor's, and if the budget indicates any 'limitation' on the costs which might be claimed, let alone recovered or allowed, between the parties then the client should be informed of this.

One way to address this might be by producing a modified budget for the client, showing the additional sums the client may be liable to pay.

It is important to remember that between the parties costs are not generally intended to be a full indemnity for the client. There will almost invariably be an element of costs incurred which simply are not and never would be recoverable between the parties (a classic modern example being the costs of arranging or considering various forms of funding[27]). In addition, it will be rare that the costs awarded on a between the parties basis cover the full costs which might have been reasonably incurred on the clients instructions. The fact that the indemnity basis is the default basis for solicitor–client assessments expressly recognises this.

Equally, and perhaps even more importantly in light of the 'new' proportionality test, no test of proportionality applies on a solicitor client basis.

It is, therefore, unrealistic to expect that costs budgets, subject to rigorous

[25] See *Judiciary: Lord Justice Jackson's paper for the Civil Justice Council conference* (21 March, 2014), paras. 5.2 and 5.7.
[26] See Final Report, p.415, para.7.3 for example.
[27] See *Motto v Trafigura* [2011] EWCA Civ 1150; [2012] 1 WLR 657.

review on the standard between the parties basis, applying a test of proportionality, should be expected also to set the proper level of costs on a solicitor–client basis, or that such budgets should simply be used by solicitors as their costs estimates on a solicitor–client basis unless those solicitors wish to restrict unduly the costs they might reasonably charge their clients.

What the budgeting provisions do emphasise, however, is the fundamental importance of solicitors providing clients with clear and regular costs information both as to costs they may have to pay to their solicitor and costs they may recover from the other side if they are successful in their litigation (and which they may have to pay the other side if they lose) and, in particular, of explaining in clear terms how and why the costs the client may be liable to pay may differ from the costs to be allowed between the parties. A simple statement that 'if you are awarded costs against your opponent, the costs awarded are unlikely to cover our full costs' is no longer sufficient. A great deal more detail is now required—explanation of the test(s) of proportionality, of what costs budgeting means, of the various tests on assessment, the meaning of the retainer and so on. The standard retainer letter wording is unlikely to be enough. This needs to be tailored to the individual client and repeated at various intervals. With regard to the effect of costs budgeting, if the client is closely involved in the process and there is a process set up for what happens if the court does not allow costs, it may make for less argument later.

Proportionality

This has been touched on above. The new test of proportionality, introduced **9–14**
by CPR 44.3(5), was expressly intended to reverse the unsatisfactory test as clarified in *Lownds*[28] with a view to reducing the costs of litigation, at least where the assessment of costs is being carried out on a standard basis.

The precise effect of this new test is addressed elsewhere in this supplement. However, it seems clear that the new test, reinforced by the amendment to the overriding objective and in conjunction with the wider use of costs budgeting and of summary assessment, is a robust tool in the judicial armoury[29].

If 'new proportionality' is to serve its intended purpose, the ultimate outcome seems to be that there will be a reduction in between the parties costs[30]. Further, that this will, by the very nature of the test and its intended use as a 'backstop' following the initial consideration of whether the costs are reasonable, be a somewhat arbitrary test, the precise effect of which will be difficult to predict in any given case.

Its impact seems likely to be greater in cases of relatively modest value, though again this remains to be seen.

All of this means that there is likely to be a greater shortfall between the costs recovered between the parties and those for which the client is prima

[28] *Lownds v Home Office* [2002] 1 WLR 2450.

[29] See, for example, *Hobbs v Guy's And St Thomas' NHS Foundation Trust* [2015] EWHC B20 (Costs).

[30] See the notes in the Chapter on Proportionality as to how this new approach is taking effect in practice.

facie liable on a solicitor–client basis and that this shortfall will potentially be proportionately all the greater in the very cases where the successful client's damages are lower. However, because of the uncertainty surrounding proportionality, the actual amount of reduction is hard to specify.

This serves to emphasise further the points in the preceding section as to the increased need for clear and regularly updated guidance to clients as to any potential shortfall. Even if this is just in broad terms and all that can be said is that there is likely to be a shortfall and no one can say for certain in what amount.

Whilst no test of proportionality applies on a solicitor–client assessment, a solicitor is obliged to discuss with a client, in a clear and accessible form, whether the potential outcome of a case is likely to justify the expense involved. Where a solicitor fails to provide clear information in this regard both at the start and during the case, and where the solicitor fails to warn the client, particularly in a low value claim, that there may be a substantial shortfall, it may reasonably be anticipated that the courts will take an increasingly hard line towards solicitor–client assessments of the shortfall costs.

The wider effect of 'Jackson'

9–15 The costs management reforms were intended to be part of a coherent package of reforms aimed at not merely reducing the cost of litigation, but improving the process.

It is the express purpose of costs management that the court should manage not merely the costs to be 'incurred by the parties' (note, not merely 'recovered by' or 'allowed to' the parties), but also the steps to be taken.

In this regard, the reforms extend beyond the introduction of costs management and seek to give the courts more robust powers in relation to case management generally. These include explicit powers to restrict expert evidence by reference to specific issues (CPR 35.4), to limit the issues to be addressed by witnesses and the length and format of statements (CPR 32.2) and to take a more focused, and where appropriate, restricted approach to disclosure (CPR 31.5).

Although these matters do not necessarily directly impact on solicitor–client costs, they can arguably control spend. It is clearly an issue of vital importance that clients are made aware that, to the extent that there was before, there is no longer any guarantee of a system whereby the client can simply engage in 'chequebook' litigation. Clearly a client must be informed on occasions that, although it is open to the client to take a Rolls Royce approach to an aspect of litigation, the cost of doing so is unlikely to be recovered between the parties (for example, the instruction of a QC where the court considers it disproportionate).

Equally, there will increasingly be occasions where the client must be told that, however much it is prepared to spend, the cost will be to no benefit. This is not a question of recoverability but of restrictions on the client's options because of case management decisions There is little point in the client engaging a number of costly experts if it is likely that the court will direct evidence from a single expert on limited issues only and the client must be warned of this increased risk before the cost in incurred.

Case and costs management is looked at in more detail in **Chapter 4**.

Fixed costs claims

An element of fixed costs, whether in relation to certain aspects of the costs (such as trial costs in Fast Track claims) or the whole of the profit costs (for example in low value RTA claims) is an increasing part of the CPR and is a feature which is likely to expand in future, perhaps particularly to lower value clinical negligence claims. **9–16**

In principle, the ability of a solicitor to charge a client for work done is unaffected by the fact that the costs are fixed in whole or part on a between the parties basis. However, it is a clear and obvious point that, where the solicitor's retainer does not limit the costs payable by the client to those recovered between the parties, the client must be told in clear terms that the costs of the claim are, or might be, fixed and that, even if successful, there is likely to be a significant difference between the costs payable by the client and those recovered from the opponent. A failure to do so is likely to lead to an inability to recover any shortfall between the two.

It is important to remember that any arrangement whereby the costs to be charged to the client are limited to sums recovered between the parties is a species of Conditional Fee Agreement (a CFA 'lite'), on the basis that it is "an agreement . . . which provided for fees and expenses, or any part of them, to be payable only in specified circumstances",[31] even where it does not provide for a success fee, and therefore such an agreement must comply with s.58 of the Courts & Legal Services Act 1990 if it is to be enforceable.

Conversely, it should be remembered that between the parties cost are an entitlement of the client and are recovered in the client's name. In a fixed costs claim (and assuming that the indemnity principle is effectively disapplied),[32] where the costs recovered between the parties exceed the sums the client is liable to pay under the retainer, the balance belongs to the client, not the solicitor. Accordingly, where fixed costs are likely to apply, the retainer should usually provide that if fixed costs apply, the sum charged shall (as a minimum, whether or not also as a maximum) be set at the level of the applicable fixed costs.

Further details in relation to Fixed Costs generally may be found in Chapter 7.

Additional liabilities

Further details in relation to additional liabilities and funding options may be found in **Chapter 2**. **9–17**

[31] Courts & Legal Services Act 1990 s.58(2).

[32] See *Butt v Nizami* [2006] EWHC 159 (QB); [2006] 1 WLR 3307, as approved in *Kilby v Gawith* [2008] EWCA Civ 812; [2009] 1 WLR 853.

Save in limited circumstances addressed in other chapters, additional liabilities are no longer recoverable on a between the parties basis in relation to funding arrangements entered into on or after 1 April, 2013.

In practice, particularly in the context of lower value personal injury litigation, prior to April 2013 it was rare for a client to be charged a success fee where that success fee was not recovered on a between the parties basis, save possibly where a small additional percentage was charged in respect of the delay in payment, as opposed to the risk of the claim winning or losing.

Whilst the charging of an unrecovered success fee to the client was more common in higher value and commercial litigation, it nevertheless remained relatively rare that such success fees ever became subject of a solicitor–client assessment.

The removal of between the parties recoverability is likely to see such success fees being challenged increasingly on a solicitor–client basis.

CPR 46.9 expressly includes a provision (CPR 46.9(4)) stating that in such circumstances the success fee is to be assessed by reference to all the relevant factors as they reasonably appeared to the solicitor (or counsel) at the time the CFA was entered into or varied (i.e. the same test that applies on a between the parties assessment) though, as noted, on a solicitor–client assessment, the benefit of any residual doubt goes to the benefit of the solicitor.

Accordingly, it will be at least as important as before that the solicitor keeps an accurate risk assessment in order to support any claimed success fee. Indeed, arguably the importance is increased since it is to be reasonably anticipated that the courts may take a harsher line towards the charging of success fees, particularly in lower value claims, where the success fee is being paid by a client or from a client's damages rather than by an opponent.

9–18 Of course, in personal injury claims, success fees are subject to maximum limits by reference to percentages of certain types of damages (essentially general damages and past loss) recovered. Nevertheless, it should not be assumed that this 'cap' on the maximum success fee chargeable will necessarily mean that the success fee cannot be challenged as long as it does not exceed that cap.

For example, if the permitted classes of damages were £20,000 and the success fee, set at 100 per cent, amounted to £5,000 (which is precisely 25 per cent of the prescribed damages, and therefore the 'capped' maximum), it would still be open to the client to argue that the 100 per cent success fee was too high and should be reduced on assessment.

It will therefore be important to ensure that the success fee is set at a reasonable level, that the reasons for doing so are properly recorded, and that the client is made fully aware that the success fee will not be recoverable between the parties but will fall to be paid by the client.

A specific issue in this regard arose in relation to low value personal injury claims involving children (and possibly protected parties), where, pursuant to CPR 46.4, the general rule is that the court must order a detailed assessment of the costs payable by or out of any money belonging to a child or protected party.

In a number of cases it had been held on such assessments that it is 'unreasonable' to charge the child a success fee and to seek to deduct the same from the child's damages. The precise reasoning for this appears to be legally flawed—CFAs with success fees are a legitimate means of access to justice and the loss of recoverability between the parties was part of a package of reforms, including an increase in general damages, intended to offset (in part at least) the effect of lost recoverability.

This was a repetition of an early problem following the original introduction of CFAs in 1995, when success fees were not recoverable, which was cured by a specific provision when the CPR was introduced in 1999 (CPR 48.9(5)), but which was removed in due course because it was thought unnecessary following the introduction of between the parties recoverability of success fees. The short point is that the court should be able to reduce the success fee because it was set at an unreasonable level, but otherwise should not disallow such fees. **9–19**

The position was addressed by virtue of the amendment to CPR 21.12 with effect from 1 April, 2015. Rather than the more simplified approach taken under the original 1999 regime, the amendment to CPR 21.12 imposes limitations on the sums a Litigation Friend is entitled to out of any money recovered on behalf of a protected person.

A different approach is adopted depending on whether or not the damages awarded or agreed exceed £25,000. If they do not, the Litigation Friend's ability to recover costs will be limited to the (reasonable) success fee or sum payable under a Damages Based Agreement. If the sum awarded or agreed exceeds £25,000, a new CPR 21.12(7) will limit the Litigation Friend's ability to recover costs to a sum not exceeding 25 per cent of general damages and past pecuniary loss. Whether such restrictions are necessary given the ability of the court to scrutinize the reasonableness of costs and expenses and whether these restrictions will have an inhibiting effect on the willingness of individuals to act as Litigation Friends, or solicitors to act for protected persons, remains to be seen.

The decisions of Regional Costs Judge Lumb in the cases of *A&M v Royal Mail Group*[33] may be seen as the courts seeking to explore the proper working of these new arrangements, both in terms of the new procedure and of how to approach the previously rarely asked question of how to assess the reasonableness of success fees which are to be paid out of the damages of child claimants. Two points to note emerge. The first is that the procedure provided for under CPR 21 and the accompanying Practice Direction—including the provision of proper evidence of why the claimed success fee is said to be reasonable—is there to be followed and a failure to follow it may lead to losing the ability to claim the success fee. The second is that the courts cannot be expected to simply 'sign off' on claims for success fees at a high percentage, particularly in low value claims, or to allow a practice whereby a high percentage success

[33] Unreported, Birmingham County Court, 27 August 2015 and 1 October 2015.

fee is routinely applied simply because the client will then be 'protected' by the 25 per cent LASPO 'cap'. The correctness or otherwise of the particular decision in A&M is less important than the message that claims for success fees on a solicitor–client basis, particularly from child or other protected party claimants, will require careful preparation and delicate handling.

The introduction of Damages Based Agreements will bring a relatively new aspect to solicitor–client assessments. Although such arrangements have always been possible in non-contentious business, they have been rarely used and whilst a relatively limited number of DBAs appear to have been entered into since April 2013, there is no reported decision yet of a solicitor–client costs dispute in relation to such an agreement[34].

In contrast with the position in employment cases, there are no specific regulatory requirements for advice to the client prior to the entering into of a DBA and accordingly, given the nature of DBAs, there is substantial scope for argument at the conclusion of the case as to whether the fee claimed was 'reasonable'. Cases will be heavily fact dependent, but where a DBA is used there is a clear requirement for very clear information to be given to the client as to the basis on which any DBA fee is set, for clear records to be kept of cogent reasons for setting the fee at the level chosen and, perhaps above all, for clear written information to be given to the client about the difference between the DBA payment being charged and the basis on which fees might be recovered between the parties if the case is won.

Reference has already been made to the Legal Ombudsman, which has already expressed its critical view as to the lack of clarity of CFAs and its concerns as to the risks of the same with DBAs.[35] Solicitors should not underestimate the need to make the key facts in relation to CFAs and DBAs clear in plain and, if necessary, repeated terms. The present reluctance to use DBAs in light of the poor drafting of the DBA Regulations 2013 should not obscure the fundamental need to ensure a consumer focused approach to the drafting of such agreements and related documentation where they are used.

The introduction of DBAs, the changes to CFAs and the loss of recoverability between the parties of After The Event insurance premiums, together with the likely changes in between the parties costs recovery, mean that the range of funding options available to a client and the permutations in any given case are greater than ever. Whilst the risks have always been present, they are greater than ever and the obligation to give a client proper advice in order to allow the client to make an informed choice as to the appropriate funding option should not be ignored.[36]

---

[34] DBAS, the regulations surrounding them and the reasons why they have been little used to date are considered in depth in the Funding Chapter, along with the Civil Justice Council Working Committee's Report and some of the possible future amendments to the rules and regulations surrounding DBAs.

[35] See 'Complaints in focus: 'No win, no fee' agreements: *http://www.legalombudsman.org.uk/publications/no-win-no-fee/* [Accessed 29 January, 2015].

[36] See *Truex v Kitchin* [2007] EWCA Civ 618 (solicitor's claims for costs disallowed for failure to advise as to the availability of legal aid) and *McDaniel & Co v Clarke* [2014] EWHC 3826 (QB) (solicitor's claim disallowed for failure to advice of availability of trade union funding) for two examples of the dangers.

Questions and answers

Q1. Have the 'Jackson' reforms changed the basis on which I, as a solicitor, can charge my client?

No, save that in theory the scope of lawful arrangements has widened to include DBAs. That apart, the ways in which you can agree with your client to pay you remain the same, though the Jackson reforms have had a material effect on whether certain major elements of those costs, primarily the success fee, can be recovered from an opponent. 9–20

In personal injury claims, that loss of between the parties recoverability has resulted in a limit being imposed on the maximum amount of the success fee you can charge your client.

Those matters apart, it was beyond the scope of the reforms, for example, to change the indemnity basis for assessment of solicitor client costs and that was neither their intention, nor is it their effect. The basic principle that such costs are to be assessed on the indemnity basis remains, and the core CPR provisions in relation to such an assessment, now at CPR 46.9, remain unchanged.

However, the anticipated reduction in between the parties costs, combined with the changes in funding methods, including the loss of recoverability of success fees, means that there is likely to be a greater number of cases, in particular in low value claims, where the solicitor seeks to charge a 'shortfall' to the client where, in the past, such a shortfall might not have been charged.

This is likely to bring a more regular and greater scrutiny to such claims, either by the courts or by the Legal Ombudsman.

Accordingly, whilst the basis on which you can charge your client remains largely the same and whist the basis on which such costs will be assessed has not changed, the practical effect is that, particularly in personal injury claims, it is likely to be far more common that the client will be asked to meet some of the costs out of their damages and both as a result of this and other changes it seems probable that claims for 'shortfall' costs will be more regularly disputed than before.

Q2. Can you advise the client of the full range of funding options but then say but we as a firm do not offer X, or Y or only offer X or Y on this basis?

Yes. This was a common situation with publicly funded cases (when public funding was more widely available). 9–21

A solicitor's duty is to consider, at the outset (i.e. at the time the client first seeks to instruct the firm) what forms of funding are reasonably available to the client and to advise the client accordingly. This includes advising the client that there may be other forms of funding available which the firm does not provide. This may include public funding or may, in certain circumstances, include other forms of funding such as CFAs or DBAs which the firm may not offer.

Section IB(1.16) of the Solicitors' Code of Conduct 2011 indicates that the solicitor should discuss with the client how the client will pay, including whether public funding may be available, whether the client has insurance that might cover the fees and whether the fees may be paid by someone else, such as a trade union. This should not be treated as an exhaustive list, nor indeed as a list that applies full in every case. It is an indication only and, as with many examples in this context, is particularly suited to personal injury claims.

The ultimate requirement is to treat the client fairly and to ensure that the solicitor complies with the duty to act in their best interests, even if that might mean advising them of a form of funding which the firm does not offer which means that the client chooses to instruct a different firm.

Provided this is done, it is entirely proper to indicate that if the client wishes to instruct the firm the only terms which the firm is prepared to offer are the X or Y referred to.

Q3. My case is subject to costs management. Am I required to seek my client's approval to the budget and does the budget, if agreed or approved, limit the costs I can charge my client?

9–22 In answer to the first part of the question, no. There was some discussion of a requirement for the client to sign the budget, or the solicitor to confirm the client's agreement to the budget, but this did not make it into the final rules.

However, as a matter of practice, it is important that the client is aware of the likely costs of the claim and of how the costs which might be recovered from the opponent relate to the cost that the solicitor is likely to charge the client. It is also important that the client is made aware of how the likely costs of the claim might impact on the conduct of his claim. For example, if, as a result of the costs being seen to be disproportionate on a between the parties basis, the scope or extent of witness or expert evidence is likely to be restricted, the client needs to be made aware of the reasons for this and the options available to address it.

The client should be receiving regular costs estimates and updates on a solicitor–client basis anyway and differences between these and the between the parties budget should be highlighted so that the client has an informed choice as to whether or not to incur the additional costs.

As to the second part of the question, again the answer is 'no', unless the solicitor–client retainer is such that the costs chargeable to the client are limited to sums recovered between the parties. Even then, the final effect will not be known until the end of the case, when it is known whether the client has won, what costs order has been made, whether indemnity costs are awarded (CPR 3.18) and whether, if the budget applies, the budget is to be departed from for any 'good reason' (CPR 3.18). In any event, the budget only 'bites' on costs from the date of the budget (CPR 3 PD 3 E para.7.4).

Q4. Do the revised rules on Part 36 apply in a solicitor–client assessment?

9–23 There is a lack of clarity in this regard. There is a primary statutory provision dealing with the incidence of costs at the conclusion of a statutory assessment of solicitor–client costs, namely s.70(9) of the Solicitors Act 1974.

This provision cannot be, and has not been, displaced by CPR Pt 36 and continues to apply. However, that provision is subject to s.70(1), whereby the court can depart from the otherwise mandated outcome if there are 'special circumstances' (as to which, see *Wilsons Solicitors LLP v Bentine*, supra). It seems to be increasingly accepted that the making of effective offers by the parties to the assessment is capable in principle, dependent upon the particular facts, of amounting to a special circumstances, and this would appear to fit with the ethos of both the CPR generally and the Jackson reforms in encouraging the making of offers to compromise disputes at an early and less costly stage.[37]

Accordingly, the making of a Part 36 offer may, on the facts of a case, be capable of amounting to a special circumstance, but the automatic provisions of CPR 36.10 and CPR 36.14 do not appear to apply because they conflict with s.70(9).

Whether a successful Part 36 offer therefore attracts any greater benefit than a Calderbank offer is open to argument. Given that the full rubric of Part 36 cannot apply, and Part 36 is intended to be a complete and self-contained code, it seems more likely that a successful Part 36 offer should be treated as an admissible offer under the court's general discretion under CPR 44.2(4)(c), assuming that the automatic consequences under s.70(9) do not apply.

In 'common law' assessments (i.e. those which are based on a common law right to dispute the reasonableness of a claim for unpaid fees, rather than assessments under s.70 of the Solicitors Act 1974) Part 36 would appear to apply and to be an important aspect of any such claim—see *Ahmud v MacPherson* (supra).

Q5. Can I charge/recover for preparing the solicitor–client estimate?

It is assumed that this question refers to the costs of provision of costs information to the client rather than the costs of preparing a Precedent H for the purposes of between the parties costs management, which are limited by CPR 3 PD 3 E, para.7.2. **9–24**

The (reasonable) costs of preparing such a between the parties Precedent H will, of course, form part of the costs payable by the client.

Time reasonably spent advising the client in relation to their own costs, whether by way of costs estimates, funding arrangements or the like should ordinarily form a part of the charges payable by the client. However, there will be a limit on the extent to which such time is recoverable. It is to be expected that solicitors have systems in place which allow them to properly record, monitor and analyse time spent and the cost of these is an overhead. The court will not expect that, save in exceptional cases, the solicitor will have to

[37] As an aside, similar principles developed under the CPR, such as penalising a party in costs for failing to negotiate also seem to be capable of being 'special circumstances'—see *Allen v Colman Coyle LLP* [2007] EWHC 90075 (Costs).

spend substantial time providing an initial estimate or updating that in due course.

Q.6 It is still not clear how solicitors should go about doing estimates of costs for their clients and the extent to which Precedent H is sufficient/ useful for this purpose. Can you express a view?

9–25 A solicitor must provide a clear explanation to a client of the solicitor's fees and if and when they are likely to change (Solicitors Code of Conduct 2011 IB 1.14). This information must be given in a clear and accessible form which is appropriate to the client's circumstances and needs (IB 1.19). It is particularly important that they receive the best possible information, both at the time of the engagement and as their matter progresses, about the likely overall cost of their matter (O1.13).

Taking these requirements and indicative behaviours collectively, best practice would require the provision of an estimate and costs benefit analysis at the start of any retainer, together with regular updates and revisions of the estimate, particularly when there are any material changes which might affect the likely costs or the costs benefit analysis.

Precedent Forms H produced for the between the parties costs management process may be a useful tool in this process and it may well be that some solicitors develop a practice of using a Precedent H type model to provide costs estimates to their clients from the outset of cases, particularly following the introduction of J Codes. However, care must be taken to make the client aware of any differences between the amounts set out in the between the parties Precedent H and the sums that the client may be required to pay.

Where a budget is agreed or approved on a between the parties basis, the client should be made aware of any differences between the sums agreed or approved and those which were sought and as to the client's liability for such sums (if any).

Index

Abuse of process
fixed costs, 7–16
Additional claims
costs management, 4–36
Additional liability
provisional assessment, 8–28
solicitor and client costs, 9–17–9–19
Adjudication
settlement, 5–35
After the event insurance
clinical negligence proceedings, 2–11
generally, 2–10–2–11
questions and answers, 2–24–2–25, 2–37, 2–38, 2–39, 2–40
Allocation hearings
costs management, 4–07
Alternative dispute resolution
settlement, 5–26–5–27, 5–63
Appeals
Part 36 offers, 5–05
Arbitration
settlement, 5–36, 5–69
Assignment
conditional fee arrangements, 2–41
Assumptions
costs management, 4–38
Barristers
acting on own behalf
fixed costs, 7–20
Before the event insurance
qualified one-way costs shifting, 6–18
Calderbank letters
settlement, 5–28, 5–62
Case management
costs management and, 4–22
proportionality
conduct of paying party, 3–13
generally, 3–03
Case management directions
costs management, 4–08, 4–48
Clinical negligence
after the event insurance, 2–11
costs budgets, 1–03
Co-defendants
Part 36 offers, 5–51
Compensation Recovery Unit
conditional fee agreements, 2–04
Compliance
costs management, 4–03–4–05
Conditional fee agreements
assignment, 2–41
backdating, 2–22
generally, 2–02
group claims, 2–31
implementation issues, 2–08–2–09
insolvency proceedings, 2–32, 2–38
notice of funding, 2–34, 2–36
notification requirements, 2–07
personal injury claims, 2–04–2–06
pre-1 April 2013 agreements, 2–35
qualified one-way costs shifting, 6–23–6–24, 6–27
questions and answers
assignment, 2–41
backdating, 2–22
group claims, 2–31
insolvency proceedings, 2–32, 2–38
notice of funding, 2–34, 2–36
pre-1 April 2013 agreements, 2–35
success fees, 2–19–2–21, 2–23, 2–28–2–31
success fees
calculation, 2–28
capping, 2–30
counsel, 2–29
group claims, 2–31
recoverability, 2–19–2–21, 2–23
transitional provisions, 2–03
Conduct
proportionality
assessment stage, 3–14
case management stage, 3–13
generally, 3–12
Consent orders
Part 36 offers, 5–47
Costs assessments
detailed assessment
assessment, 8–09
compliance, 8–12
generally, 8–06
oral hearings, 8–11
post-assessment, 8–10

pre-assessment, 8–08
questions and answers, 8–14–8–26
introduction, 8–01
payments on account
generally, 8–13
questions and answers, 8–50–8–52
proportionality, 3–03
provisional assessment
additional liabilities, 8–28
additional sums, 8–48
cost cap, 8–32–8–37
disbursements, 8–49
generally, 8–07
indemnity basis, 8–31
oral hearings, 8–44–8–47
proportionality cross check, 8–38–8–39
replies to the points in dispute, 8–29
sanctions for failure to file documents, 8–40–8–43
success fees, 8–30
VAT, 8–27
questions and answers
costs budgets, 8–19–8–20
family law, 8–21
item-by-item challenges, 8–17
late filing of N260, 8–14–8–16
'new bill' format, 8–23
post-hearing summary assessments, 8–22
Precedent Q, 8–24
proportionality cross check, 8–18
provisional assessment, 8–27–8–49
qualified one-way costs shifting and, 8–25
sanctions for failure to make open offer, 8–26
summary assessment
change of emphasis, 8–05
generally, 8–02
questions and answers, 8–14–8–26
statements of costs, 8–03–8–04

Costs budgets
benefits of, 1–02
Bill of Costs, 1–10–1–11
clinical negligence, 1–03
"Confronting Costs Management", 1–02–1–05
detailed assessment and, 8–19–8–20
German model, 1–08–1–09
insolvency proceedings, 1–07
issues with, 1–02
J-Codes, 1–12
Jackson reforms, 1–01–1–14
Mustill Lecture, 1–06
Part 36 offers, 5–50
proportionality, 3–03
proposed amendments, 1–13
qualified one-way costs shifting, 6–17
solicitor and client costs, 9–11–9–13, 9–22
summary assessment and, 8–19–8–20

Costs capping orders
costs management, 4–91

Costs estimates
over-estimating, 4–34

Costs management
case management and, 4–22
cases subject to, 4–15
changes to existing CPR provisions
compliance, 4–03–4–05
directions questionnaires, 4–06
disclosure, 4–09
discretion in track allocation, 4–07
expert evidence, 4–11
generally, 4–02
introduction of costs management, 4–14
oral evidence of experts, 4–12
settlement proposals, 4–13
standardised directions, 4–08
witness statements, 4–10
court powers, 4–18
effect of order on subsequent assessment, 4–20–4–21
fixed costs, 7–18
introduction, 4–01
procedural requirements, 4–16–4–17
questions and answers
absurdly low budgets, 4–35
additional claims, 4–36
appeal against decision on interim application, 4–86
application to claims under Part 8, 4–27
application to disposal stage, 4–26
assumptions in budgets, 4–38
breakdown between disbursements and fees, 4–64
budgeted sum exceeding retainer sum, 4–77
case management directions, 4–48
contingencies, 4–43
contractual right to indemnity costs, 4–29
cost capping, 4–91

costs management conferences, 4–44, 4–45, 4–49
costs sanction, 4–70, 4–74
departures from budget, 4–69, 4–73, 4–74
detailed assessments, 4–76, 4–85
disproportionate budgets, 4–63
failure to file costs budget, 4–46
fast track re-allocated to multi track, 4–78
hourly rates, 4–56–4–60
incurred costs, 4–50–4–55, 4–61
indemnity basis, 4–71–4–72
J-Codes, 4–42
litigants in person, 4–79, 4–90
monitoring budgets, 4–68
opting out of costs management, 4–25
over-estimating costs, 4–34
percentages to be applied, 4–65
pre-trial checklists, 4–80
Precedent H, 4–30–4–31, 4–33, 4–37, 4–39, 4–40, 4–42, 4–43
prescriptiveness of wording, 4–23–4–24
proportionality, 4–89
provisional allocation to multi track, 4–28
re-filing budgets after CCMC, 4–66
relief from sanction, 4–87, 4–88
Shorter Trial Pilot Scheme, 4–32
standard basis, 4–71
statement of truth, 4–75
summary assessment, 4–83–4–85
surveillance costs, 4–41
variation of budgets, 4–67, 4–81, 4–82
without prejudice, 4–47, 4–62
variation of budgets, 4–19, 4–67, 4–81, 4–82
Costs management conferences
costs management, 4–44, 4–45, 4–49
Counterclaims
Part 36 offers, 5–40, 5–49
Damages-based agreements
between the parties costs recovery, 2–16
CFA 'lite' and, 2–17
employment proceedings, 2–14
future amendments, 2–18
generally, 2–13–2–15
hybrid DBAs, 2–17, 2–33
notice of funding, 2–27
personal injury claims, 2–15
problem areas, 2–17
questions and answers
enforceability, 2–45
hybrid DBAs, 2–33
indemnity costs, 2–46
notice of funding, 2–27
termination, 2–17
'ultimately recovered', 2–17
Defamation
funding arrangements, 2–43
Detailed assessment
see also **Costs assessments**
assessment, 8–09
compliance, 8–12
costs management, 4–76, 4–85
generally, 8–06
oral hearings, 8–11
Part 36 offers, 5–55
post-assessment, 8–10
pre-assessment, 8–08
questions and answers
costs budgets, 8–19–8–20
item-by-item challenges, 8–17
late filing of N260, 8–14–8–16
'new bill' format, 8–23
Precedent Q, 8–24
qualified one-way costs shifting and, 8–25
sanctions for failure to make open offer, 8–26
Direct Access Scheme
fixed costs, 7–21
Directions questionnaires
costs management, 4–06
Disbursements
provisional assessment, 8–49
Disclosure
costs management, 4–09
Discontinuance
qualified one-way costs shifting, 6–22
Dishonesty
qualified one-way costs shifting, 6–08, 6–10–6–11, 6–22
settlement, 5–29
Disposal hearings
costs management, 4–26
Dispute resolution
solicitor and client costs, 9–07–9–08
Early neutral evaluation
settlement, 5–33
Employers' liability claims
fixed costs, 7–03–7–05
Part 36 offers, 5–22–5–25
Employment proceedings
funding arrangements, 2–14

Estimates
solicitor and client costs, 9–24, 9–25
Expert evidence
costs management, 4–11, 4–12
Family law
costs assessments, 8–21
Fatal accident claims
qualified one-way costs shifting, 6–04, 6–08
Fixed costs
abuse of process
unreasonable conduct, 7–16
background, 7–01
barrister acting on own behalf, 7–20
costs management, 7–18
Direct Access Scheme, 7–21
employers' liability claims, 7–03–7–05
exaggerated claims, 7–19
indemnity basis
basis of assessment, 7–06
circumstances justifying, 7–07
litigants in person, 7–22
intellectual property claims
unreasonable conduct, 7–14
litigants in person
Direct Access scheme, 7–21
failure to comply with rules, practice direction or court orders, 7–24
generally, 7–08–7–09
indemnity costs, 7–22
interim payments for legal representation, 7–26
limited liability partnerships, 7–23
McKenzie friends, 7–10–7–11, 7–25
solicitors and barristers acting on own behalf, 7–20
litigation funders, 7–17
low value personal injury claims
EL/PL Protocol, 7–03–7–05
RTA Protocol, 7–02
McKenzie friends
companies represented by, 7–25
generally, 7–10–7–11
possession claims, 7–15
public liability claims, 7–03–7–05
questions and answers
abuse of process, 7–16
barrister acting on own behalf, 7–20
costs management, 7–18
Direct Access Scheme, 7–21
exaggerated claims, 7–19
future of, 7–12
litigants in person, 7–20–7–26
litigation funders, 7–17
possession claims, 7–15
retainer arrangements, 7–13
solicitor acting on own behalf, 7–20
unreasonable conduct cases, 7–14, 7–16
retainers, 7–13
RTA Protocol, 7–02
solicitor acting on own behalf, 7–20
solicitor and client costs, 9–16
unreasonable conduct
abuse of process, 7–16
intellectual property claims, 7–14
Fraud
settlement, 5–29
Funding arrangements
after the event insurance
clinical negligence proceedings, 2–11
generally, 2–10–2–11
questions and answers, 2–24–2–25, 2–37, 2–38, 2–39, 2–40
clinical negligence proceedings, 2–11
conditional fee agreements
generally, 2–02
implementation issues, 2–08–2–09
notification requirements, 2–07
personal injury claims, 2–04–2–06
questions and answers, 2–19–2–23, 2–28–2–32, 2–34–2–36, 2–38, 2–41
transitional provisions, 2–03
Coventry v Lawrence, 2–12
damages-based agreements
between the parties costs recovery, 2–16
CFA 'lite' and, 2–17
employment proceedings, 2–14
future amendments, 2–18
generally, 2–13–2–15
hybrid DBAs, 2–17, 2–33
notice of funding, 2–27
personal injury claims, 2–15
problem areas, 2–17
questions and answers, 2–27, 2–33, 2–45, 2–46
termination, 2–17
'ultimately recovered', 2–17
defamation cases, 2–43
employment proceedings, 2–14
fixed costs, 7–17
insolvency proceedings
conditional fee agreements, 2–32, 2–38
generally, 2–42

introduction, 2–01
long stop date for issue of proceedings, 2–26
personal injury claims
conditional fee agreements 2–04–2–06
damages-based agreements, 2–15
qualified one-way costs shifting, 2–01
questions and answers
after the event insurance, 2–24–2–25, 2–37, 2–38, 2–39, 2–40
arbitration, 2–44
conditional fee agreements, 2–19–2–23, 2–28–2–32, 2–34–2–36, 2–38, 2–41
damages-based agreements, 2–27, 2–33, 2–45, 2–46
defamation cases, 2–43
insolvency proceedings, 2–42
pre-LASPO 2012 arrangements, 2–26
Group litigation
conditional fee agreements, 2–31
Indemnity basis
costs management, 4–29, 4–71–4–72
fixed costs
basis of assessment, 7–06
circumstances justifying, 7–07
litigants in person, 7–22
Part 36 offers, 5–52
proportionality, 3–15, 3–17
provisional assessment, 8–31
Insolvency proceedings
funding arrangements
conditional fee agreements, 2–32, 2–38
generally, 2–42
Jackson reforms, 1–07
Intellectual property claims
fixed costs
unreasonable conduct, 7–14
Interest
Part 36 offers, 5–41
Interim payments
litigants in person, 7–26
"Jackson reforms"
generally, 1–01–1–14
solicitor and client costs
assessment procedure, 9–10
costs budgeting, 9–11–9–13
introduction, 9–09
overview, 9–15
proportionality, 9–14
Judicial decision-making
proportionality, 3–07
Limited liability partnerships
fixed costs, 7–23
Litigants in person
costs management, 4–79, 4–90
fixed costs
Direct Access scheme, 7–21
failure to comply with rules, practice direction or court orders, 7–24
generally, 7–08–7–09
indemnity costs, 7–22
interim payments for legal representation, 7–26
limited liability partnerships, 7–23
McKenzie friends, 7–10–7–11, 7–25
solicitors and barristers acting on own behalf, 7–20
Litigation funding
see **Funding arrangements**
Low value personal injury claims
fixed costs
EL/PL Protocol, 7–03–7–05
RTA Protocol, 7–02
McKenzie friends
fixed costs
companies represented by, 7–25
generally, 7–10–7–11
Mediation
settlement, 5–31–5–32, 5–64–5–65
Multiple defendants
see **Co-defendants**
Negotiation
settlement, 5–30
Notices
funding arrangements
conditional fee agreements, 2–34, 2–36
damages-based agreements, 2–27
Offers
see **Part 36 offers**
Open offers
Part 36 offers and, 5–61
Oral hearings
detailed assessment, 8–11
provisional assessment, 8–44–8–47
Part 8 claims
costs management, 4–27
Part 36 offers
acceptance, 5–09–5–13
appeal proceedings, 5–05
background, 5–01
challenging offers, 5–67
change of terms, 5–07–5–08
EL/PL Protocol, 5–22–5–25

form and content, 5–06
post-5 April 2015, 5–04
questions and answers
cap on damages, 5–56
clarification, 5–48
consent orders, 5–47
costs budget not filed on time, 5–50
counterclaims, 5–40, 5–49
detailed assessments, 5–55
full liability plus costs, 5–57
generally, 5–37–5–39
indemnity basis, 5–52
interest, 5–41
lower additional amount, 5–53
multiple defendants, 5–51
open offers and, 5–61
pre-action costs, 5–46
pre-action offers accepted before service, 5–42
preliminary issues, 5–45
recovery of costs following, 5–58
small claims, 5–60
split trials, 5–45
without prejudice communications, 5–59
reforms, 5–02
solicitor and client costs, 9–23
transitional provisions, 5–03
unaccepted offers, 5–14–5–20
withdrawal, 5–07–5–08
Payments on account
generally, 8–13
questions and answers, 8–50–8–52
Personal injury claims
funding arrangements
conditional fee agreements 2–04–2–06
damages-based agreements, 2–15
Personal injury claims
qualified one-way costs shifting, 6–04
Possession claims
fixed costs, 7–15
Pre-action costs
Part 36 offers, 5–46
Pre-action disclosure
qualified one-way costs shifting, 6–04
Pre-action offers
Part 36 offers, 5–42
Preliminary issues
Part 36 offers, 5–45
Proportionality
case management, 3–03
conduct of paying party
assessment stage, 3–14
case management stage, 3–13
generally, 3–12
costs assessments
generally, 3–03, 8–18
provisional assessments, 8–38–8–39
costs budgets, 3–03
costs management, 4–63, 4–89
criteria for determining, 3–03–3–04
effect on litigation, 3–05
general concept, 3–02
introduction, 3–01
meaning, 3–03
questions and answers
application of 'cross check', 3–09
benchmarks, 3–19
claims affected, 3–16
conduct of paying party, 3–12–3–14
costs exceeding sums in dispute, 3–18
'fixed sum' throughout life of claim, 3–08
'good reason' to depart from budget, 3–09
indemnity costs orders, 3–17
indemnity principle, 3–15
judicial discretion, 3–07
less than necessary costs, 3–20
purpose of assessment, 3–15
reasonableness and, 3–06
'sums in issue in the proceedings', 3–11
transitional provisions, 3–10
relief from sanctions, 3–03
solicitor and client costs, 9–14
Provisional assessment
see also **Costs assessments**
additional liabilities, 8–28
additional sums, 8–48
cost cap, 8–32–8–37
disbursements, 8–49
proportionality cross check, 8–38–8–39
replies to the points in dispute, 8–29
sanctions for failure to file documents, 8–40–8–43
success fees, 8–30
VAT, 8–27
"Public liability claims"
fixed costs, 7–03–7–05
Part 36 offers, 5–22–5–25
Qualified one-way costs shifting
adverse costs orders, 6–01, 6–02, 6–07, 6–08, 6–12, 6–14
before the event insurance, 6–18
breach of contract, 6–25

clinical negligence claims, 6–26
conditional fee agreements, 6–23–6–24, 6–27
costs assessments and, 8–25
costs budgets, 6–17
defamation claims, 6–14
discontinuing proceedings, 6–22
dishonest claims, 6–08, 6–10–6–11, 6–22
fatal accident claims, 6–04, 6–08
funding arrangements, 2–01
introduction, 6–01–6–02
personal injury claims, 6–04
pre-action disclosure, 6–04
pre-commencement funding agreements and, 6–20
privacy claims, 6–14
questions and answers
before the event insurance, 6–18
breach of contract and, 6–25
clinical negligence claims, 6–26
conditional fee agreements and, 6–23–6–24, 6–27
costs budgets, 6–17
discontinuing proceedings, 6–22
extension to other areas, 6–16
mixed personal injury and non-personal injury claims, 6–15
pre-1 April 2013, 6–19
pre-commencement funding agreements and, 6–20
unnecessary costs, 6–21
rules
effect of, 6–07–6–13
introduction, 6–03
scope of, 6–04–6–06
set off, 6–08–6–09
striking out, 6–09, 6–21, 6–22
transitional provision, 6–05, 6–24, 6–27
unnecessary costs, 6–21
use of, 6–14
"Questions and answers"
alternative dispute resolution, 5–63
arbitration, 5–69
Calderbank offers, 5–62
conditional fee agreements
assignment, 2–41
backdating, 2–22
group claims, 2–31
insolvency proceedings, 2–32, 2–38
notice of funding, 2–34, 2–36
pre-1 April 2013 agreements, 2–35
success fees, 2–19–2–21, 2–23, 2–28–2–31
costs assessments
costs budgets, 8–19–8–20
family law, 8–21
item-by-item challenges, 8–17
late filing of N260, 8–14–8–16
'new bill' format, 8–23
post-hearing summary assessments, 8–22
Precedent Q, 8–24
proportionality cross check, 8–18
provisional assessment, 8–27–8–49
qualified one-way costs shifting and, 8–25
sanctions for failure to make open offer, 8–26
costs management
absurdly low budgets, 4–35
additional claims, 4–36
appeal against decision on interim application, 4–86
application to claims under Part 8, 4–27
application to disposal stage, 4–26
assumptions in budgets, 4–38
breakdown between disbursements and fees, 4–64
budgeted sum exceeding retainer sum, 4–77
case management directions, 4–48
contingencies, 4–43
contractual right to indemnity costs, 4–29
cost capping, 4–91
costs management conferences, 4–44, 4–45, 4–49
costs sanction, 4–70, 4–74
departures from budget, 4–69, 4–73, 4–74
detailed assessments, 4–76, 4–85
disproportionate budgets, 4–63
failure to file costs budget, 4–46
fast track re-allocated to multi track, 4–78
hourly rates, 4–56–4–60
incurred costs, 4–50–4–55, 4–61
indemnity basis, 4–71–4–72
J-Codes, 4–42
litigants in person, 4–79, 4–90
monitoring budgets, 4–68
opting out of costs management, 4–25
over-estimating costs, 4–34
percentages to be applied, 4–65
pre-trial checklists, 4–80

Precedent H, 4–30–4–31, 4–33, 4–37, 4–39, 4–40, 4–42, 4–43
prescriptiveness of wording, 4–23–4–24
proportionality, 4–89
provisional allocation to multi track, 4–28
re-filing budgets after CCMC, 4–66
relief from sanction, 4–87, 4–88
Shorter Trial Pilot Scheme, 4–32
standard basis, 4–71
statement of truth, 4–75
summary assessment, 4–83–4–85
surveillance costs, 4–41
variation of budgets, 4–67, 4–81, 4–82
without prejudice, 4–47, 4–62

damages-based agreements
enforceability, 2–45
hybrid DBAs, 2–33
indemnity costs, 2–46
notice of funding, 2–27

fixed costs
abuse of process, 7–16
barrister acting on own behalf, 7–20
costs management, 7–18
Direct Access Scheme, 7–21
exaggerated claims, 7–19
future of, 7–12
litigants in person, 7–20–7–26
litigation funders, 7–17
possession claims, 7–15
retainer arrangements, 7–13
solicitor acting on own behalf, 7–20
unreasonable conduct cases, 7–14, 7–16

funding arrangements
after the event insurance, 2–24–2–25, 2–37, 2–38, 2–39, 2–40
arbitration, 2–44
conditional fee agreements, 2–19–2–23, 2–28–2–32, 2–34–2–36, 2–38, 2–41
damages-based agreements, 2–27, 2–33, 2–45, 2–46
defamation cases, 2–43
insolvency proceedings, 2–42
pre-LASPO 2012 arrangements, 2–26

mediation, 5–64–5–65

open offers, 5–61

Part 36 offers
cap on damages, 5–56
clarification, 5–48
consent orders, 5–47
costs budget not filed on time, 5–50
counterclaims, 5–40, 5–49
detailed assessments, 5–55
full liability plus costs, 5–57
generally, 5–37–5–39
indemnity basis, 5–52
interest, 5–41
lower additional amount, 5–53
multiple defendants, 5–51
open offers and, 5–61
pre-action costs, 5–46
pre-action offers accepted before service, 5–42
preliminary issues, 5–45
recovery of costs following, 5–58
small claims, 5–60
split trials, 5–45
without prejudice communications, 5–59

payments on account, 8–50–8–52

proportionality
application of 'cross check', 3–09
benchmarks, 3–19
claims affected, 3–16
conduct of paying party, 3–12–3–14
costs exceeding sums in dispute, 3–18
'fixed sum' throughout life of claim, 3–08
'good reason' to depart from budget, 3–09
indemnity costs orders, 3–17
indemnity principle, 3–15
judicial discretion, 3–07
less than necessary costs, 3–20
purpose of assessment, 3–15
reasonableness and, 3–06
'sums in issue in the proceedings', 3–11
transitional provisions, 3–10

provisional assessment
additional liabilities, 8–28
additional sums, 8–48
cost cap, 8–32–8–37
disbursements, 8–49
proportionality cross check, 8–38–8–39
replies to the points in dispute, 8–29
sanctions for failure to file documents, 8–40–8–43
success fees, 8–30
VAT, 8–27

qualified one-way costs shifting
before the event insurance, 6–18

breach of contract and, 6–25
clinical negligence claims, 6–26
conditional fee agreements and, 6–23–6–24, 6–27
costs budgets, 6–17
discontinuing proceedings, 6–22
extension to other areas, 6–16
mixed personal injury and non-personal injury claims, 6–15
pre-1 April 2013, 6–19
pre-commencement funding agreements and, 6–20
unnecessary costs, 6–21

settlement
alternative dispute resolution, 5–63
arbitration, 5–69
Calderbank offers, 5–62
mediation, 5–64–5–65
open offers, 5–61
options available, 5–66
Part 36 offers, 5–37–5–61
small claims track, 5–68

small claims track, 5–60, 5–68

solicitor and client costs
agreement of client to costs budget, 9–22
effect of reforms on charging, 9–20
estimates, 9–25
notifying client of options available, 9–21
Part 36 offers, 9–23
preparation of solicitor/client estimate, 9–24

success fees
calculation, 2–28
capping, 2–30
counsel, 2–29
group claims, 2–31
recoverability, 2–19–2–21, 2–23

Reasonableness
proportionality and, 3–06

Relief from sanctions
costs management, 4–87, 4–88
proportionality, 3–03

Retainers
fixed costs, 7–13
solicitor and client costs, 9–03–9–04

Road traffic accidents
fixed costs
RTA Protocol, 7–02

Sanctions
costs management, 4–70, 4–74

Set-off
qualified one-way costs shifting, 6–08–6–09

Settlement
adjudication, 5–35
alternative dispute resolution, 5–26–5–27, 5–63
arbitration, 5–36, 5–69
Calderbank offers, 5–28, 5–62
costs management, 4–13
dishonesty, 5–29
early neutral evaluation, 5–33
expert evaluation, 5–34
fraud, 5–29
mediation, 5–31–5–32, 5–64–5–65
negotiation, 5–30
open offers, 5–61
options available, 5–66

Part 36 offers
acceptance, 5–09–5–13
appeal proceedings, 5–05
background, 5–01
cap on damages, 5–56
challenging offers, 5–67
change of terms, 5–07–5–08
clarification, 5–48
consent orders, 5–47
costs budget not filed on time, 5–50
counterclaims, 5–40, 5–49
detailed assessments, 5–55
EL/PL Protocol, 5–22–5–25
form and content, 5–06
full liability plus costs, 5–57
indemnity basis, 5–52
interest, 5–41
lower additional amount, 5–53
multiple defendants, 5–51
open offers and, 5–61
post-5 April 2015, 5–04
pre-action costs, 5–46
pre-action offers accepted before service, 5–42
preliminary issues, 5–45
questions and answers, 5–37–5–61
recovery of costs following, 5–58
reforms, 5–02
small claims, 5–60
split trials, 5–45
transitional provisions, 5–03
unaccepted offers, 5–14–5–20
withdrawal, 5–07–5–08
without prejudice communications, 5–59

questions and answers

alternative dispute resolution, 5–63
arbitration, 5–69
Calderbank offers, 5–62
mediation, 5–64–5–65
open offers, 5–61
options available, 5–66
Part 36 offers, 5–37–5–61
small claims track, 5–68

Small claims
Part 36 offers, 5–60

Small claims track
settlement, 5–60, 5–68

Solicitor and client costs
additional liabilities, 9–17–9–19
dispute resolution, 9–07–9–08
effect of Jackson reforms
assessment procedure, 9–10
costs budgeting, 9–11–9–13
introduction, 9–09
overview, 9–15
proportionality, 9–14
entitlement to payment, 9–05–9–06
fixed costs, 9–16
introduction, 9–01
overview, 9–02
questions and answers
agreement of client to costs budget, 9–22
effect of reforms on charging, 9–20
estimates, 9–25
notifying client of options available, 9–21
Part 36 offers, 9–23
preparation of solicitor/client estimate, 9–24
retainers, 9–03–9–04

Solicitors
acting on own behalf
fixed costs, 7–20

Split trials
Part 36 offers, 5–45

Standard basis
costs management, 4–71

Statements of truth
costs management, 4–75

Striking out
qualified one-way costs shifting, 6–09, 6–21, 6–22

Success fees
conditional fee agreements
calculation, 2–28
capping, 2–30
counsel, 2–29
group claims, 2–31
recoverability, 2–19–2–21, 2–23
provisional assessment, 8–30

Summary assessment
change of emphasis, 8–05
costs management, 4–83–4–85
generally, 8–02
questions and answers
costs budgets, 8–19–8–20
family law, 8–21
item-by-item challenges, 8–17
late filing of N260, 8–14–8–16
'new bill' format, 8–23
post-hearing assessments, 8–22
Precedent Q, 8–24
proportionality cross check, 8–18
sanctions for failure to make open offer, 8–26
statements of costs
generally, 8–03
service, 8–04

Surveillance
costs management, 4–41

Unreasonable conduct
fixed costs
abuse of process, 7–16
intellectual property claims, 7–14

Variation
costs management, 4–19, 4–67, 4–81, 4–82

VAT
provisional assessment, 8–27

Without prejudice communications
costs management, 4–47, 4–62
Part 36 offers, 5–59

Witness statements
costs management, 4–10